Pc

Popular Culture in Canada

Edited by

Lynne Van Luven
University of Victoria

Priscilla L. Walton
Carleton University

Prentice Hall Allyn and Bacon Canada
Scarborough, Ontario

Canadian Cataloguing in Publication Data

Van Luven, Marlene A. D. Lynne, 1947–
  Pop Can : popular culture in Canada

Includes index.
ISBN 0-13-680067-X

1. Popular culture—Canada.   I. Walton, Priscilla L.   II. Title.

FC95.4.V36 1999   306'.0971   C99-930183-7
F1021.2.V36 1999

Prentice-Hall, Inc., Upper Saddle River, New Jersey
Prentice-Hall International (UK) Limited, London
Prentice-Hall of Australia, Pty. Limited, Sydney
Prentice-Hall Hispanoamericana, S.A., Mexico City
Prentice-Hall of India Private Limited, New Delhi
Prentice-Hall of Japan, Inc., Tokyo
Simon & Schuster Southeast Asia Private Limited, Singapore
Editora Prentice-Hall do Brasil, Ltda., Rio de Janeiro

ISBN 0-13-680067-X

Vice President, Editorial Director: Laura Pearson
Acquisitions Editor: Nicole Lukach
Marketing Manager: Kathleen McGill
Developmental Editor: Jean Ferrier
Production Editor: Andrew Winton
Copy Editor: Judith Turnbull
Production Coordinator: Peggy Brown
Art Director: Mary Opper
Cover Design: Julia Hall
Cover Illustration: Stephanie Power

1 2 3 4 5 03 02 01 00 99

Printed and bound in Canada.

Visit the Prentice Hall Canada Web site! Send us your comments, browse our catalogues, and more at
www.phcanada.com. Or reach us through e-mail at **phabinfo_pubcanada@prenhall.com**.

Contents

Preface

Popular culture is all around us. It is a diffuse ambience which by its very prevalence is sometimes invisible. It can be taken for granted and is frequently discounted because of its accessibility. Because it is seen on the streets, on billboards, and on playing fields, it has until recently been perceived as unworthy of serious critical attention. Despite popular culture's growing vitality in this country, many Canadians assume that it originates only in the United States or that it must be imported from abroad, from "elsewhere." They often refer to American films, magazines, or rock music — all consumed with gusto in Canada — and assume there is no Canadian popular-culture equivalent.

Such cultural consumers overlook the Canadian directors, actors, writers, athletes, musicians, and singers working in this country. Or, worse yet, they may note them and dismiss them because, "if they were any good at all, they'd be pursuing their fortunes in the U.S." This sort of thinking is wrong-headed. Just how wrong-headed was proven in 1996 with the publication of *Mondo Canuck: A Canadian Pop Culture Odyssey,* edited by Geoff Pevere and Greig Dymond. The authors argued that, "there is more Canadian popular culture now than ever, but it's also more *popular* than it ever was." The book was both irreverent and informative in presenting the wide range of lively and appealing mass entertainment produced in Canada. *Mondo Canuck* showed that such entertainment runs the gamut from Don Cherry to Alanis Morissette, and from Stompin' Tom Connors to Leonard Cohen.

Pop Can attempts to take its readers one step further: the essays in this volume show critics, writers, journalists, and academics in the process of consuming, reacting to, and analysing Canadian popular culture as it is demonstrated in a variety of forms, ranging from Anne of Green Gables to basketball to Web sites. The articles spring from only one given: that a vital popular culture exists in Canada and that close study of it can teach us new understandings of ourselves as citizens and as consumers.

As co-editors of this anthology, Priscilla Walton and I approach popular culture from different political and generational viewpoints, a divergence we hope adds depth and variety to this text. We do agree heartily upon one thing: Canadian popular culture is multifarious and dynamic. Furthermore, it is growing even more exciting as Canada's population becomes increasingly diverse and the "publics" consuming popular culture continue to fragment. It is safe to say that the term "popular culture" draws strength from the many "sub-cultures" that exist within its boundaries, and that are always pressing these boundaries outwards in unexpected ways.

In reading the essays in this collection, one might conclude that the process that William Gibson termed "cultural mongrelization" and Marshall McLuhan likened to "multiple borderlines" is an integral reality of today's popular cultures (yes, note the plural) in Canada. In many respects, Canadian popular culture is marked by its powerful impetus towards fusion; it is illustrated by forms of music, film, recreation, and communication that draw upon the past even as they comment upon the present by predicting a future. Attempting to erect walls around any sort of creative expression has always been counter-productive, and never has it been a less fruitful task than among today's artists.

In *The Presumption of Culture,* Ottawa fiction writer and critic Tom Henighan notes that the vitality of a society's culture is as important to society as its "health, education and welfare in making life worth living for all citizens." Many politicians — at the municipal, provincial, and federal levels — appear to disagree with that statement when they vote to cut cultural support and funding. Such civic leaders seem to regard culture as a "frill," although they are prepared to spend billions bailing out dysfunctional businesses or beefing up international trade delegations. And they would be unlikely to make distinctions between different forms or levels of cultural expression.

Pop Can's contributors stand firmly in another camp, whatever their political analysis, because they believe that cultural expressions of all forms are the lifeblood of any healthy society. Furthermore, they'd concur that the forms and levels culture assumes should be determined only by the energy, vision, and imagination of the creators, and that popular culture represents one of the most "happening" sites of expression, witty play, and commentary in Canada.

Lynne Van Luven

Introduction

In the summer of 1996, a Labatt's advertisement circulated across Canada's broadcast airwaves. The commercial featured a Canadian vacationer (identifiable by the seemingly requisite "eh?") touting the superiority of the Canadian product. Sipping an implicitly American beer, the vacationer discards it because it "tastes like water"; then, reaching for a Labatt's, he sips, nods, and says, "Now, that's beer!" The ad concludes with the vacationer winking at the camera and confiding, "And our Falls are better." This "message" from Labatt's provides a springboard from which to investigate Canadian popular culture, since its covert message (some things in Canada are better than their American counterparts) foregrounds both anxiety over the inferiority/superiority of Canadian culture as well as a site — Niagara Falls — that performs as a matrix of cultural clash.

Indeed, as the 1995 CBC drama series *Taking the Falls* illustrates, Niagara Falls comprises a peculiar mélange of the sublime and the ridiculous. In its first episode, *Taking the Falls* utilizes the cultural blend its setting offers, and begins with one of the protagonists, played by Cynthia Dale, attempting to cross the border from Niagara Falls, Ontario, to Niagara Falls, New York. Because she smart-mouths a border official, her car is searched, and a dead body is discovered in the trunk. She contacts her lawyer cousin, and the two hold their initial interview in the "House of Frankenstein" waxworks museum. Later, gazing out over the Falls, the protagonist sighs and exclaims, "Yup, it's one of the wonders of the world," and then goes on to explain why she chooses to live there: "Where else can you go when you run out of souvenirs in the middle of the night?" The episode concludes with the discovery that dead bodies have been serving as conduits for drug smuggling between the two countries.

While *Taking the Falls* did not attract sufficient audience attention to last beyond its first season (perhaps because it stopped using its locale to full advantage), it does spotlight the curious conglomeration of cultures that Niagara Falls presents. In many ways, Niagara Falls operates as a testament to the diversity of Canadian culture and the anxieties that surround its physical manifestations. Since the American Falls, while beautiful, are nowhere near as theatrically awesome as the Horseshoe Falls, the continuing thrill many Canadians feel at the sight of "our Falls" affirms a pride in "our" superior natural vista. In turn, Niagara Falls, Ontario, embodies a space of spectacular, even "sublime," beauty (the Falls) that is crisscrossed with popular culture (that curious amalgam on Clifton Hill of burger joints, souvenir shops, and "museums," such as Louis Tussaud's Waxworks, Ripley's Believe It or Not!, the Criminals [sic] Hall of Fame, the Guinness World of Records, and so on). In more ways than one, then, Niagara Falls is a site where trash, in all forms, commingles — be it the popular culture on Clifton Hill or the infamous toxic seepage from the Love Canal, just across the border in Niagara Falls, N.Y. Moreover, as a nexus of daredevils (the first person to go over the falls successfully was a woman, Annie Taylor — her barrel is on display at the "Daredevil Hall of Fame" in the Niagara Falls Museum, "the oldest in North America"), honeymoon retreats (Niagara Falls was the most popular spot for post-marital journeys in the early twentieth century), and power in its most basic form (the electricity generated by the plants at Niagara Falls lights up a goodly portion of northeastern North America), Niagara

Falls and its conglomeration of "sex, death, and power" evoke headlines the envy of many a tabloid editor (and if the *Globe* were still situated in Montreal, this might well be the case). Alternatively, in the immortal words of Marilyn Monroe, "The falls produce a lot of electricity, but the honeymooners don't use very much of it at night."

On another level, Niagara Falls occupies an important historic location. Its neighbouring sister-town, Niagara-on-the-Lake, witnessed a session of the first parliament of Upper Canada, in 1793. Two miles away along the Niagara Gorge, Queenston Heights is the burial ground of Sir Isaac Brock, the birthplace of Laura Secord (of chocolate-box fame), and the setting of numerous War of 1812 skirmishes. Earlier, Niagara Falls served as one of the mouths of the Underground Railway, offering many African Americans a gateway from slavery to "freedom." But, as Rinaldo Walcott has suggested, the railroad goes both ways, and I would like to extrapolate from his observation here. In the larger schema, Canadian preoccupation tends to be with the east–west axis of the railroad in general, celebrated as a focal point of nationalism in such works as Pierre Berton's *The Last Spike*; but that railroad also runs north–south. In so doing, it provides a major access, in more ways than one, to our American neighbours. Still comprising one of the most frequently crossed border points between the two countries, this axis of intersection is perhaps best memorialized by Marilyn Monroe's stroll along the border in *Niagara*. Marilyn's walk made cinematic history (she was described as the first actor who "walked away" to stardom), and it additionally testifies to the cultural coupling between the two countries. Like it or not, Canada and the United States share more than the "world's longest undefended border."

Yet, to acknowledge the north–south movement of culture is also to accept how influence circulates between Canada and the U.S., and this is an acknowledgment that not all Canadians wish to proclaim. With the advent of Canadian nationalism in the 1970s and its efforts to hallmark Canadian culture, a definition of what is "Canadian" solidified. And, while such a delineation manifested an important step for Canadians at the time, it has also come to mean that a great deal of Canadian culture was, and is, written-off owing to its incompatibility with the commonly accepted categorizations. Overlooked, then, are cultural forms that define themselves in a north–south context, as opposed to the more acceptable east–west formulations: black Canadian culture (see Walcott's essay), lesbian and gay culture (see Pottie's), and so on.

Indeed, the "popular" in Canada, as it has taken shape in institutionally legitimized forms, is more regional, recreating early stages of Canadiana — from eastern jigs, to western rodeos, to CBC reproductions (usually shot in Toronto, but bespeaking peculiar efforts at "regionality," such as dialects that can only be rooted somewhere east of Newfoundland and west of Vulcan). The importance of regional art forms is not to be contested; however, to showcase Tommy Hunter as a king of popular culture, as did the CBC for many years, is to ignore media, both within the mainstream and without, that have also contributed to the Canadian multicultural popular mosaic.

Unfortunately, what has resulted from institutionalized nationalist efforts is a form of cultural policing, implemented by the Canadian Radio-television and Telecommunications Commission (CRTC) and other bureaucratic agencies in conjunction with their academic and intellectual counterparts, over the definition of Canadian as well as the Canadianicity of particular artifacts. The recent refusal to qualify Bryan Adams's music as "Can Con" is an example of this, since the singer's recording label was deemed to outrank his Canadian citizenship and disqualified him from the approved list of "Canadian" performers. What then is to happen to Alanis Morissette, Sarah McLachlan, Jann Arden, and Céline Dion? Will their American successes also generate their erasure from the lists of accepted Canadian content? Such a state of affairs leads to a curious conundrum, for, on occasion, Canadian successes in the U.S. work to convince us that our talent is "better" (witness the cases of Anne Murray and Gordon Lightfoot), while others get lost in the "American" heap. And although government agencies like the CRTC have ensured that some forms of Canadian culture are preserved, this preservation has taken place on the backs of other cultural artifacts. While I have discussed, above, the elision of minority forms in the nationalist construction, other popular figurations are likewise unacknowledged. I am reminded of a TVOntario interview, which aired around the time of the publication of Geoff Pevere and Greig Dymond's book on Canadian popular culture, *Mondo Canuck*. The interviewer asked, with apparent horror, if Pevere was suggesting that "we" should devise our own versions of *Baywatch* and call them culture? Pevere shied away from the question, but it seemed to escape both interviewer and interviewee that *Baywatch* star Pamela Anderson is a Canadian.

Certainly, many Canadians have "made it" south of the border, including "America's sweetheart," Mary Pickford, and Ottawa's own Paul Anka, yet their achievements in the U.S. seem paradoxically to deflate their significance in Canada (although Ottawa does boast a "Paul Anka Drive"). Satirized documentaries like "The Canadian Conspiracy" serve to educate audiences about the Canadian comedians who dominate American programming, but those successes in an "American" context engender their contiguous deletion from the Canadian schema. Conversely, when American programs are set in Canada, the public is delighted — when David Duchovny succeeded in moving *The X-Files* from its home in Vancouver to Los Angeles, there was a national outcry. Yet, when pictures of Margaret Atwood are featured on American Barnes and Noble shopping bags, many Canadians scream "cultural appropriation" rather than see this as a recognition of Canadian talent south of the border.

Curiously, then, it would appear that if the railroad moves north, bringing Americans to Canada, Canadians are (secretly) pleased. But if it runs south, carrying Canadians to the United States, it leads to ostracism. Still showing traces of a colonial mentality, Canadian producers are often quite willing to exploit their own and to accept Americans as "better." In the first years of the broadcast network WTN (the Women's Television Network), Canadian talent donated time and energy to help program the new network, but as WTN grew more successful, Canadians stopped contributing because they discovered that their American counterparts were being paid more for the labour they devoted to the network's offerings (see Off's essay). Alternatively, when the American book chain Borders wished to open Canadian branches, it was refused entry on the grounds of threatening Canadian culture. But, when Chapters, a Canadian chain, opened and featured the American firm Starbucks in its cafes as opposed to the Canadian Second Cup, no outburst occurred over the Americanization of Canadian taste buds.

The collection gathered here sets out to "write-in" some of the artifacts that have been written-off as Canadiana, and in so doing to expand definitions of "Canadian." It is not our intention to define the terms of Canadian popular culture, for the futility of such a project is clearly apparent in the potential further marginalizations such an effort to categorize would engender; rather, we are trying to generate recognition for the Canadian talent in mainstream media in addition to regional success stories. Indeed, this introduction is itself guilty of "regionalism" given its focus on southern Ontario, but *Pop Can*, as a whole, attempts to bring together various strands of Canadian popular art forms, from east to west as well as from north to south. Notably absent from this collection is the popular culture of Quebec, a lack caused by the language barrier, but a lack that points to how *Pop Can* is already guilty of cultural ostracism. Concomitantly, what *is* present here is a commemoration of those aspects of Canadian culture that have not been accorded "official" recognition as legitimate cultural expressions — from sports to movies, from music to murder. And yes, some of these expressions have signified on American forms, but it is time to look more closely at those cultural couplings. The construction of Stan Mikita's doughnut shop in *Wayne's World* (a parodic play on Tim Horton's, and a play that I would venture to suggest most Canadians "got" and most Americans missed) or the many Canadian jokes interspersed throughout American prime-time television programs (probably due to the Canadian screenwriters who work south of the border) are just as representative of Canada as National Film Board documentaries. In short, *Pop Can* attempts to open the door to further explorations of Canadian popular forms, but it is just that: an opening of the door. There is much work yet to do, and thus, to conclude with the words of a popular American comedian (who happens to be Canadian), this collection is authoritative — not.

Priscilla L. Walton

THE POPULAR
ARTS

INTRODUCTION

The 1997 Oscar ceremonies offered a particularly intriguing scenario for Canadian viewers. James Cameron's film *Titanic* was a favoured candidate for Best Director and Best Picture, Atom Egoyan's *The Sweet Hereafter* had also earned him a nomination for Best Director, and the *Titanic*'s theme song, as interpreted by Céline Dion, was a contender for Best Song. Of course, Egoyan lost out to Cameron, whose film earned 11 awards, but this only demonstrated why this particular Oscar night was heralded as a battle between and for Canadians. Most newspaper and television coverage, overlooking how much of the talent in Hollywood has always derived from Canada, signalled the 1997 ceremony as a moment of national pride. Cameron's success re-bestowed upon him the Canadian citizenship he had seemed to ignore for so long, and his new status as Canada's "fair-haired boy" brought him honorary awards from a number of universities, as well as invitations to various film festivals.

Some cynics derided the open-arms reception Cameron received from his birth-country, wondering what might have happened if the director had lost: Would he still have received all the honours? Would he have been heralded as a successful "Canadian" nonetheless? Perhaps, perhaps not. Whether he had won or lost, his film still provides a rich example of the complexity inherent in American/Canadian popular cinema. Cameron had moved "south of the border" from his native Ontario, and while one can only speculate, presumably the money available in Hollywood was an element in his "defection." This might lead one to denigrate Cameron in favour of the more "loyal" Egoyan, but before doing so, one should note the ways in which *Titanic* showcased Canada and Canadian talent. Québécoise singer Céline Dion, as mentioned, was chosen to deliver the film's theme song, "My Heart Will Go On."

The movie itself continues to bring waves of tourists to Nova Scotia to view the site of the graves of many *Titanic* survivors. Is the American-made *Titanic*, then, American or Canadian? This question, needless to say, is impossible to answer, but the film does demonstrate how hard it is to draw lines between the borders of countries and their cultural products.

Atom Egoyan's work illustrates some of the challenges of remaining "at home." Although his first low-budget efforts generated critical acclaim, it was not until the 1994 *Exotica* that Egoyan managed the segue from art house to Cineplex. In other words, where only a few had seen Egoyan's early features, a much wider audience could see *Exotica* and *The Sweet Hereafter*. The filmmaker's Oscar nomination for *The Sweet Hereafter* would seem to have confirmed Egoyan's place on a larger stage as a contemporary writer-director of import (yet it is not insignificant that it took American acclaim to help establish Egoyan's reputation).

In this section of the book, Eleanor Ty analyses *Exotica* as a paradigm of Canadian multiculturalism. Exploring the ways in which Egoyan shapes and fragments identities, Ty argues that the film stands as a testament to a particularly Canadian search for identity. Leslie Sanders's critique of the Toronto production of *Show Boat* demonstrates some of the complications involved in determining such an identity; her chapter examines the turmoil that the theatrical production generated during its Toronto run.

While Canada has earned an international reputation for the Stratford and Shaw Festivals, it has not achieved similar acclaim for its home-grown productions. The Great Canadian Theatre Company in Ottawa continues to showcase Canadian plays and actors, as do many other theatre companies throughout the country, but these productions lack the prestige of a Shakespeare play or the "blockbuster" glitz of more mainstream productions, such as the musicals of the British Andrew Lloyd Weber or the American Bob Fosse. Canadian promoter and former head of Cineplex Garth Drabinsky decided that Toronto would provide a perfect jumping-off point for Broadway, and *Show Boat* was one of his first efforts to establish Toronto as this pre-Broadway stop. In revitalizing the 1930s musical, Drabinsky adapted the American script for a Canadian audience — with extremely contentious results. As Sanders outlines, different histories and different times generate different audience reactions, and while *Show Boat* went on to win a Tony for its Broadway production, the controversy it generated remains a divisive cultural issue in metropolitan Toronto.

Unlike film or theatre, music is an area where Canadians have excelled internationally for years. From Guy Lombardo in the 1940s, to Gordon Lightfoot in the 1960s, to the current wave of Canadian musicians like Alanis Morissette, Sarah McLachlan, Jann Arden, and Tragically Hip, Canadian artists have succeeded on the airwaves. Rather that focusing on such well-known performers, the two essays collected here turn to musical forms that tend to be overlooked in the annals of Canadian music. Rinaldo Walcott explores rap and its relationship to Canada's black culture, while Ajay Heble outlines the impact of jazz on a small Ontario community.

Canadian popular literature, like film and theatre, has tended to be ignored as a viable art form. Many of its practitioners (for example, Alistair McLean in the 1960s) sought fame in the United States, and these writers, needless to say, do not usually figure in courses on Canadian literature. Even so, Canadian popular writing has been a significant force, particularly in the realm of genre fiction (fiction that falls into a specific category — mysteries, romances, thrillers, etc.). Priscilla L. Walton and Manina Jones appraise detective fiction as a literary form that has had major input from Canadian authors. Science fiction is another genre in which Canadians have made their mark. William Gibson's "cyberpunk" novels, for example, revolutionized 1980s science fiction and fantasy works. As Derek Foster notes in his essay, Gibson's innovations might well be due to the author's play upon the non-fictional reflections of Canadian media theorist Marshall McLuhan.

Although the following section does not contain an essay on romance novels, it is important to note that Harlequin, one of the major publishers of that genre (and one of the most successful global publishing houses), was for a long time located just outside Toronto.

The following essays, then, discuss popular film, literature, music, and theatre, and at the same time offer diverse critiques of these art forms. Here, various critics turn to the popular arts and provide alternative means of analysing their effects. Indeed, just as there are different "types" of films or literature, so there are different ways of "reading" them. You may find that you don't agree with these authors, but such disagreement is just another aspect of the intellectual debate: these chapters are intended to provoke thought, not to enlist disciples. If they make you think and re-evaluate, then they have achieved an important goal.

SPECTACULAR PLEASURES

Labyrinthine Mirrors in

Atom Egoyan's *Exotica*

Eleanor Ty

I am very conscious of belonging to a tradition. As an English-speaking Canadian, for a long time, I believed in being able to forge a link between the critically acclaimed film and Hollywood. More and more I've come to realize, with Exotica *in particular, that it is impossible, that I come from a tradition other than the classical American film. This realization has liberated me.[1]*

Atom Egoyan

Director Atom Egoyan, whose seventh feature film, *The Sweet Hereafter*, won the Grand Prix in 1997, the highest award ever given to a Canadian film at the Cannes Film Festival, has been a longtime favourite with festival-goers and critics. But it was not until his sixth feature film, *Exotica*, in 1994, that his name became known to the public at large. Despite his assertion that he comes from a different tradition than American filmmakers, Egoyan has created what a Toronto newspaper has called an "art-house hit" with *Exotica*. The *Globe and Mail* reported that, during its first weekend on seven U.S. screens, the movie grossed $100 654 (U.S.). Moreover, it is "the first Canadian film in more than a decade to receive wide theatrical release in the United States."[2]

In *Exotica* as in his other films, Egoyan plays with images and representation. Film critic Tobin writes: "The theme of voyeurism, which forms an integral part of the universe of Atom Egoyan, is pushed to its limits ... it is a film about mirrors, about the image of oneself that others reflect back."[3] For his part, Egoyan says: "In my films, the images can transport you, but only in as much as you are aware of it. The audience ought to know that he enters this territory in order to discover a form of identification."[4]

In this essay, I'll begin by highlighting this aspect of representation in *Exotica*, showing how the film manipulates our awareness of the way media and different technologies influence and even construct our version of reality. In the movie, we become spectators who watch the voyeuristic tendencies of others. Egoyan reinterprets the common belief that the practice of observation through media intermediaries is a negative, passive, or innocent act. He notes, "Everyone gives voyeurism a bad rap, but in fact, so much of our personality and character in this society is based on how we *watch* things."[5] In *Exotica*, he plunges us into a mysterious, sinister, but sumptuous world to show how watching and being watched are part of our everyday experience.

Secondly, this essay will show that, in contrast to his other films, *Exotica* became a hit because Egoyan uses a hybridization of familiar genres from popular literature — the police story, the tabloid, fantasy, and melodrama — to construct a phantasmagoric mirror of our society. Even if *Exotica* cannot be classified strictly as a Hollywood film, it reflects a world populated by the heroes and villains of television drama who already live and work in our neighbourhood. The element of the exotic, of otherness, of fantasy, closely linked to the erotic and the forbidden, is also explored and shown to be part of ordinary existence.

Finally, my essay studies the way *Exotica* becomes an emblem of the cinematographic expression of English Canada. This tradition, which has only recently come into its own, has its own distinct features; it is neither European, nor American, nor Québécois. *Exotica* is an excellent example for analysis, as it raises many of the concerns of our contemporary society and reveals the cultural attitudes that are particularly characteristic of English Canada in the late 1990s. Through its structure, which is based on the mirror and on parallelism, *Exotica* succeeds in crossing a number of boundaries — between high and low culture, between heterosexual and homosexual preferences, and between differences created by racial origins.

MEDIA CULTURE AND REPRESENTATION

A dominant theme in the oeuvre of Atom Egoyan is the powerful influence of media culture in our lives. In films such as *Next of Kin* (1984), *Family Viewing* (1987), *Speaking Parts* (1989), and *The Adjuster* (1991), the protagonists are obsessed with images on the screen, whether homemade videos, shows on television, or the movies. In *Next of Kin*, for example, the life of a young man of 23 is radically changed when he decides to adopt an Armenian family after seeing them on a video at his therapist's office. In the same way, in *Family Viewing*, the breakdown of a marriage and the restoration of a family are shown and documented through a collection of video images — television clips and pornographic and home movies. Critic Geoff Pevere remarks: "In Egoyan's films, media become environment. Since he sees experience as something circumscribed entirely by mediated message systems, his films are about people whose very existence depends on the media that make experience possible."[6] For Egoyan, the fascination with media is more than a game. The *mise en scène* is an important element in the appreciation of his films. He says:

> What fascinates me about the fact of telling stories which effectively uses one of the ways of recording (photography, film, video, etc.), is that the spectator has the possibility of being witness to the actual impulses and the decisions of the principal characters at the moment when they engage in the process in which the director himself is implicated. In this way, the

public can have access to all the realms, extremely complex, which unfurl between the objective and soul of a character. While the spectator watches the images projected from the film, he also sees the images which show him how the characters who are in the process of watching project these same images around them, and what they reveal of themselves in the process.[7]

The author's insistence on the process of recording contributes to the complexity and opacity of his first films. A critic has remarked, for example, that Egoyan's early films are "cerebral puzzles that seem to be missing an affective piece — the catalyst that makes us feel, that allows any real achievement in art … to operate simultaneously on an intellectual and visceral plane."[8]

With *Exotica*, this problem is resolved somewhat. Here, the role of televisual media is less pronounced than before. But Egoyan remains fascinated by images, spectacles, and productions that use sounds, music, costumes, and representation — all those things related to film and television. At the cabaret called Exotica, despite the fact that there are no cameras, everyone is constantly being "surveilled." At one level, the female strippers dancing before their clients are surveilled by Eric, the master of ceremonies, and by Zoé, the owner of the club. At another, the clients on the balcony are watching all those below. At a third level, there is the movie audience, the ultimate voyeurs. In *Exotica*, the video and camera equipment is almost invisible but always present. It is no longer necessary to thematize the ubiquity of media culture, as that culture is omnipresent and visible everywhere. As Egoyan says, "in *Exotica*, everyone is already on show…. Each, in a theatrical way, searches for his own identity."[9] Because the boundary between fantasy and reality does not exist, it is difficult to distinguish between the actors and the spectators. In other words, everyone is playing a role in his or her own imaginary film. For Francis, the civil servant who has lost his family, the dancer Christina functions as an object of his desire and as a substitute for his murdered daughter. For Christina, Francis is the caring and proud father she never had in her childhood. Another girl, Tracey, permits Francis to indulge in the fantasy of being the father by playing the role of the baby-sitter, even when there is no baby to sit.

Other characters, like Zoé and Thomas, search for happiness by abandoning themselves to their own fantasies. Both are owners of exotic locales — hot houses where rare life is cultivated. Zoé, at the cabaret Exotica, directs a bevy of almost nude dancers against a background of tropical palms, an artificial waterfall, and Oriental music. Thomas manages an animal boutique that specializes in fish and fowl from strange lands. Zoé wishes to create a place where the ambience is special, just as her mother had done, and at the same time, she wants to become a mother. We know that she is conscious of life as a spectacle, as an image, and as entertainment when she says, "We are here to amuse, not to heal." Her appearance changes every day; she wears extravagant outfits and wigs of different colours. Her counterpart, Thomas, is not at all concerned with his appearance, but he, too, leads a life surrounded by media culture. When the film begins, Thomas, retrieving his bags at the airport, is being watched by customs officers through a one-way mirror. For him, spectacles and media events — ballets, operas, and concerts — are not only things to savour, but also pretexts for sexual encounters with strangers. Behind his glasses and his respectable appearance, Thomas is a smuggler, a tax fraud, and an adventurer. In contrast to Egoyan characters who watch films over and over again, Thomas already inhabits a gangster culture and adventure films. Through the eggs that he hatches, through his artificial sanctuary, and through his night excursions to the opera, he, in his own way, indulges in psychodramatic rituals as intensely as Francis and Christina.

PLAYING WITH POPULAR NARRATIVES

Critics are in agreement that *Exotica* is one of Egoyan's most ambitious, chic, and seductive movies. Much of the charm comes from the way stories are told. Tobin remarks that "the scenario is constructed like a puzzle in which the pieces are apparent, but which the director assembles progressively: the memory of an atrocious murder is the principal piece, while the smuggling of exotic animals is another."[10] Another critic, Noreen Golfman, like Egoyan himself, compares the structure of *Exotica* to a "slow strip-tease, exoticizing our passive spectator experience into a darkened display of desire and need."[11] Rick Groen notes that "the narrative is structured like a mystery, complete with an ongoing series of carefully planted clues, and nicely organic imagery. To be sure, it's no simple whodunnit."[12] In my view, *Exotica* borrows from a mixture of genres from popular culture — the murder mystery, newspapers, melodrama, and erotica — but is not limited by them. Egoyan is not content simply to use these genres, but attempts to question their powers to entertain and divert. He installs the conventions from pop lit in order to test them. The result is that what one discovers is often the opposite of what one expects.

First, Francis's story is a murder mystery without the final chapter. Francis remembers a murder, but the movie concludes without ever giving a satisfactory resolution to the whodunit. We never find out who actually committed the crime. The identity of the murderer, so central to the dénouement of a mystery, simply becomes one of the red herrings of the film. Instead, we have a father, laden with sorrow, who is intimately linked to two very young girls. Francis is a victim, but he is also a blackmailer and a killer *manqué.* Here Egoyan seems to be manipulating the conventional expectations of a murder mystery. He does not focus on the intentions and the actions of the murderer before the crime as is done in mysteries, but on the intentions and the actions of the father of the victim after the crime. A Hollywood film with this much tension and violence would probably end with a shoot-out scene rather than a scene of embrace and understanding between two men who are suspicious of each other. In *Exotica* then, unlike in Disney films, the heroes and the villains are barely distinguishable. Because the drama takes place as much in the psychic interior as it does in the exterior, the action of the film consists of emotional, intellectual, and psychological interactions rather than physical encounters.

Nevertheless, the familiar world of the murder mystery is ever present within *Exotica.* Francis uses the investigative methods and practices of police detectives. He convinces Thomas to act as his secret agent in order to find out what Christina thinks of him after his transgression. As in a spy film or police story, Francis listens to the conversation of Thomas and Christina in his car through a tape recorder affixed to Thomas's body. In addition to this amateur detective work, there are many mysterious scenes in the movie. Alain Masson notices that "for about half an hour, the viewer does not understand anything. The rifts multiply in order to prevent him from finding the unity of action."[13] From the beginning, we are plunged into a world of discord and confusion, where it becomes necessary to act as a detective or as a spectator of a mystery. Egoyan shows one bizarre scene after another — a pregnant woman in a strip club, a group of young people walking in a field — and leaves it to his audience to find the links between these characters and scenes. Ultimately, it is up to us to assemble the pieces of the puzzle.

Another form of popular literature that Egoyan uses is melodrama, the kind one finds in serial novels, in soap operas, or in tabloid newspapers. The plot of *Exotica* consists of a number of sensational or exaggerated events. As Thomas Bourguignon has noted, "The story is based on an unspeakable trauma: the life of a tax inspector reverts continually to the past, to when his daughter is murdered and when his wife dies in a car accident (after he learns of her affair with his brother)."[14] This plot risks being a cliché, of course, but it is through the presentation and structure that Egoyan avoids banality. In contrast to blockbuster films, this film does not show the murders, nor does the camera linger on the adultery. All the melodramatic elements are contained in brief flashbacks. These retrospectives appear without logic or sequence, and they are distanced for us by the constant reminder of the intervention of the media in these events. At times, as in Francis's memories of his daughter and wife, the flashbacks are presented like home videos of poor quality. Bourguignon remarks: "It is through silent images, or those which do not deal with the essential, that we reach scraps of the past: video images endlessly repeated of the daughter and the baby-sitter at the piano; a recurring mental and mysterious image of nature, where the disc jockey and the stripper meet for the first time and end up by discovering the cadaver of the daughter."[15] By highlighting how the past is captured by photographic and video images, Egoyan shows us not only the importance of media culture in our lives, but also how our experiences can be relived. Video and other media technologies are more than simply tools that allow us to remember the past; they are also the stuff and essence of our fluid past. For Francis, the past is nothing but images on bits and pieces of film that resemble scenes of bad melodrama.

This vision of Egoyan's — that of a past constructed entirely by media technology — became a reality for millions of North Americans the year after *Exotica* was released. In 1995, what North American television audiences followed daily for an extended period of time was not the plot of a soap or a riveting news story, but news as serial television. With the trial of O.J. Simpson, we saw how it was possible to create the past, manipulate the emotions of the spectators, and have great TV ratings. Significantly, the plots and intrigues of O.J. and *Exotica* are similar: they consist of reconstructing the story of a murder through the memories of traumatized people, with the aid of media technology. In both cases, the truth is less important than the spectacle. The televised trial of O.J. and the film *Exotica* satisfied the compulsive need for repetition and detail in people whose lives in the late twentieth century are full of fast changes. The elements of the O.J. case that fascinated consumers of tabloids and popular dailies — violence, nudity, sexy women, an atmosphere of mystery, and melodrama — are precisely the elements that Atom Egoyan uses in his film, repeating them in a ritualized manner. It is not so much that the film anticipated the O.J. trial, but that Egoyan was astute enough to discern the potential of the combination of media and popular culture and to use them quite successfully in his film.

Finally, *Exotica*, as the name suggests, is a film of fantasy. From the beginning, we are transported to an exotic, quasi-Oriental world with the help of Indian music, tropical animals and plants, the foreign accent and the strange costumes of Zoé, and the unreal quality of the strip club. Egoyan creates a rich and utopian place where the rules of the quotidian world do not apply. To enter into the world of *Exotica* is to enter into the realm of imagination and image. Though the action of the film takes place in Toronto, it is a Toronto that even Torontonians do not recognize. Mary Corliss comments that before she knew of Egoyan's films, she did not know that Canada was like this — "this hotbed of erotic metaphor."[16] Craig MacInnis notes that cinematographer Paul Sarossy uses "greens and golds that speak of nature and splendor but seem corrupted by a hidden hand. The place is ludicrously rococo — archways, gondolas, Edwardian furnishings."[17] For me, the effect is more like the paintings of Henri Rousseau, where there are elements that neither quite go together nor suit the setting. What Egoyan seems to be aiming at is a quasi-fantastic universe.

The choice of a strip club as a location for a study of the human condition is doubtless reflective of a macho dream. In an interview, Egoyan said he was fascinated by what is called "table dancing" in Toronto — by paying five dollars or more, one can watch a woman dance almost nude in front of one's table. For Egoyan, the fantasy element is not simply on the man's part. He says, "A dancer's not going to tell you who they are and you're probably not going to tell them who you are, but you create a fantasy of yourself as they create a fantasy of themselves."[18] For him, *Exotica* is an attempt to "work out the charade of sexuality and the possibility of creating a sexual environment in which the relationships were quite platonic."[19] For her part, his wife, Arsinée Khanjian, an actress who has appeared in several Egoyan films, states that she has never "felt uncomfortable with Atom's portrayal of sexuality." She says, "It probably fulfils my own hidden fantasies, God knows."[20] In the film, the desire for sexual liberty is cherished as much by women as by men. In addition, Zoé believes that she can have the freedom of reproduction through the contract she has signed with Eric, whose baby she is carrying. If the fantasy for men in the strip club Exotica is a visual fantasy, for Zoé and for the other women it is rather a fantasy of power, of being supreme author. She says that she admires her mother for her sense of liberty and tries to have the same. Having a child by a pre-arranged agreement rather than by marriage ensures that she will remain the sole parent of her child and thus in control of her domestic life. In her work life, her office in Exotica is a Panopticon tower of observation, like the ones in the prisons described by Michel Foucault.[21] From there, she is able to control and survey her dancers and their clients.

EXOTICA AS A MIRROR OF ENGLISH CANADIAN CULTURE

If the strip club Exotica suggests a place of liberty and fantasy, it is ironically a typical Canadian utopia, particularly an English Canadian one. One could say that to enter into Exotica is to enter into the world of transgression and of ritualized spectacles, but it is a site of pleasure very much controlled and authorized by officials, like the carnivals described by Mikhail Bakhtin. What Bakhtin writes of the medieval feast applies to Egoyan's strip bar: "The feast was a temporary suspension of the entire official system with all its prohibitions and hierarchic barriers. For a short time life came out of its usual, legalized and consecrated furrows and entered the sphere of utopian freedom. The very brevity of this freedom increased its fantastic nature and utopian radicalism, born in the festive atmosphere of images."[22] Because the club opens nightly, the limitation is not the brevity of the carnival, but the fact that one can enjoy this freedom only at certain hours of the night and only if one has the money to pay for drinks. This contemporary version of the Bakhtinian carnival has much less laughter than there must have been at medieval fairs, but the other elements of the carnival described by Bakhtin are all there — the rituals, the flesh and bodily images, the mask. The strippers each have a particular piece of music, a character type with a corresponding costume or mask, and an act that is repeated for customers regularly. This act has many common elements with the mask as noted by Bakhtin: "The mask is related to transition, metamorphosis, the violation of natural boundaries, to mockery and familiar nicknames. It contains the playful element of life; it is based on a peculiar interrelation of reality and image, characteristic of the most ancient rituals and spectacles."[23]

According to this definition, the dancers and customers in Exotica are all participating in a mask. While Francis knows very well who Christina is, she metamorphoses into the coquettish and enticing schoolgirl for him during the whole of the Leonard Cohen song

"Everybody Knows" and every time she dances privately for him. The emotional and psychological power of their relationship is contained somewhat by the club rules and the playful element of the ritualized dance. Landscape and locale, then, not only create the experience of the exotic and erotic, but at the same time are the means by which the exotic and erotic are kept at bay.

The club Exotica exists as a realm of fantasy, but it can function as such only with rules and taboos. In the club, one can observe women dancing, but one also has to observe the prohibition of touch.[24] The club attracts men who want to abandon themselves to passion and excitement, yet without incurring any danger. It is a clean, proper, and polite world, very much like Toronto the Good, the city in which the film was made. Egoyan shows us a society where ordinary people search for the exotic in their somewhat banal lives. In his films, his characters often have prosaic jobs — tax auditors, insurance adjusters, censors. It is not necessary to glorify or sanitize their world, as there is a tendency to do in American films; we see the way their lives can be just as painful, brutal, and violent as the worlds depicted in gangster films or in French *nouvelle vague* films. The difference is that, in Egoyan's world, there is a veneer of respectability and order emblematic of the culture of English Canada. Characters do not drive around town in fast cars or carry guns, but they are seething with the same kind of emotional anger and disturbance as those who do. The club Exotica functions as a cathartic experience for them, where their feelings can be assuaged, where they can repeatedly live the danger and thrill missing in their monotonous day jobs.

If *Exotica* filmically reflects the condition and spirit of anglophone Canada, what the film reveals is that this state is one of in-betweenness. Egoyan is conscious of not belonging to *one* tradition, but to many. In the same way, in all his films there is a strong sense of dislocation and alienation. One of his favourite settings is the airport. For example, in *Next of Kin* the camera focuses on a luggage carousel at the start, while in *Exotica* the film begins with Thomas going through customs. Noreen Golfman notes that Egoyan's films lead us on cinematic journeys "through that psychic space we call the divided (Canadian) self."[25] For Egoyan, a Canadian of Armenian origins who was born in Egypt, to be Canadian is to be always in the process of going or coming. Many of his films deal with this anguish of non-identity or have to do with a crisis of identity. In *Exotica,* even the motifs and structure of the film indicate this state of dislocation. The characters are displaced, like the exotic eggs that Thomas, the pet store owner, smuggles into Canada by strapping them around his waist. In addition, as Alain Masson notes, the "refrain" of the film is one character giving money to another: that is to say, "all the relationships tend to be a form of contractual giving."[26] Egoyan shows how money becomes the only stable entity in a society of constant change and movement. As well, the repetition of scenes of departure — the young girls getting out of cars, the family that has disappeared — shows the weakness of traditional familial and sexual relationships. I am not suggesting that the themes prevalent in Egoyan's films reveal that Canada is more dislocated, more liberal, or more materialistic than the United States, but that the films produced in English Canada are generally more self-conscious of these issues and tend to take a more critical stance on contemporary culture than those movies made in Hollywood.

However, what results from the dislocation of the individual and the disintegration of the nuclear family — the cultural problems that repeatedly surface in Egoyan films — is not altogether negative. With Egoyan, there is always a vibrant sense of the heterogeneity of Canadian culture. If this society is without roots, it is also rich in diversity. Structurally, Egoyan juxtaposes a series of opposing elements that contribute to the sense of multiplicity and fullness. The point of view never stays with one character or with one location; rather, it changes frequently. What links two scenes or two characters is the comment of the narrator or the music that continues like a thread running through them. For example, Cohen's song is played when Christina does her stage show and continues through to the next scene as Thomas goes to the opera. The music links these two scenes, which rely on staging, representation, and masquerade. In another example, Egoyan links two scenes that both take place on balconies: a scene showing Thomas and the customs officer attending the ballet is juxtaposed with a scene of Christina dancing for Francis at the balcony level of Exotica. The scenes mix respectable people with those who are decadent or somewhat seedy. They highlight the position of in-betweenness of the film and of the culture — the high-brow culture of the opera and ballet is just as important as the pop song and the popular culture of night clubs. Music, dance, spectacle, and rituals are the means by which one fills the emptiness of one's life no matter where on the social ladder one finds oneself. It is as if the longing for the exotic cuts through cultural, social, racial, and sexual boundaries.

Finally, the production and casting of *Exotica* reflect and reinforce the aspect of heterogeneity in the world of Egoyan that I have been discussing. What is simply noted as "a man" in the script is played by a black homosexual in the film — that is, not by a heterosexual WASP, as one would expect. For Egoyan, it is not unusual to encounter people of different racial origins and of diverse sexual orientations. In contrast to what might be expected on Disney television, one does not need to make a big deal of one's homosexuality on prime-time TV. In Egoyan's films, the banal can become exotic, while the controversial — questions of race and sexuality — is treated without much ado. Egoyan plays with the expectations of the spectators just as he plays with the rules of the genres he uses. For this reason, it is not easy to find the moral of his films. Everything depends upon images; thus, everything lurks in the realm of the ambiguous. What Egoyan demands of us is our awareness and acceptance of the full spectrum of life and our appreciation of those people who engage with life in all its facets. He says:

> That's what I really admire about my characters. That's why I like to depict these people. These are people who are doing things I would like to do sometimes. Sometimes for dark reasons I'd prefer to avoid, but they're all directors. They're all engineering other people to do something, and the passion and conviction with which they do that is something I find really striking.[27]

ENDNOTES

1. Michel Ciment et Philippe Rouyer, "Entretien avec Atom Egoyan," *Positif* (Décembre 1994): 83 [my translation].

2. Christopher Harris, "Arts Link," *Globe and Mail* (8 March 1995), C1, and "Arts Link," *Globe and Mail* (23 March 1995), C1.

3. YT. [Tobin], *"Exotica," Positif,* n° 401–402 (juillet-aout 1994): 67 [my translation].

4. Ciment et Rouyer, "Entretien avec Atom Egoyan," 81 [my translation].

5. "The Exotic Side of Atom Egoyan," *Vancouver Sun* (14 October 1994), C5.

6. Geoff Pevere, "No Place Like Home: The Films of Atom Egoyan," in *Exotica* (Toronto: Coach House Press, 1995), 17.

7. Atom Egoyan, "Calendar," *Positif* (décembre 1994): 94 [my translation].

8.   Rick Groen, "Stripping away the layers," *Globe and Mail* (23 September 1994), C1.

9.   Ciment et Rouyer, "Entretien avec Atom Egoyan," 81 [my translation].

10. YT. [Tobin], *"Exotica,"* *Positif,* n° 401–402 (juillet-aout 1994): 67 [my translation].

11. Noreen Golfman, "Reach and (Don't) Touch Someone: From Luggage Carousel to Strip Club with Atom Egoyan," *Canadian Forum* 73, no. 836 (January-February 1995): 28. See also John Griffin, "Egoyan's *Exotica* is Psychosexual Riddle," *Montreal Gazette* (8 October 1994), D7.

12. Groen, "Stripping away the layers," C1.

13. Alain Masson, *"Exotica*: La monnaie vivante," *Positif,* n° 406 (décembre 1994): 76.

14. Thomas Bourguignon, *"Exotica*: L'homme-perroquet," *Positif,* n° 406 (décembre 1994): 78.

15. Bourguignon, *"Exotica,"* 78.

16. Mary Corliss, "Cannes '94: The Cowboy and the Lady," *Film Comment* 304 (July-August 1994): 6.

17. Craig MacInnis, *"Exotica*/Erotica," *Toronto Star* (23 September 1994), C8.

18. Geoff Pevere, "Difficult to Say: An Interview with Atom Egoyan," in *Exotica* (Toronto: Coach House Press, 1995), 49.

19. Pevere, "Difficult to Say," 48.

20. Brian Johnson, "Exotic Atom," *Maclean's* (3 October 1994): 47.

21. See Michel Foucault, *Discipline and Punish* (New York: Vintage, 1979).

22. Mikhail Bakhtin, *Rabelais and His World,* trans. Helene Iswolsky (Cambridge, Mass.: MIT Press, 1968), 89.

23. Bakhtin, *Rabelais and His World*, 39–40.

24. *Exotica* was filmed when club patrons were not allowed to come into any contact with dancers. Subsequently, in Ontario a number of clubs allowed body contact; these acts were called "lap dancing" as opposed to "table dancing."

25   Golfman, "Reach Out and (Don't) Touch Someone," 27.

26. Masson, *"Exotica*: La monnaie vivante," *Positif,* 76.

27. Pevere, "Difficult to Say," 55.

AMERICAN SCRIPTS, CANADIAN REALITIES

Toronto's *Show Boat*

Leslie Sanders

The *coup de grâce* is announced in the Toronto *Globe and Mail* for October 22, 1994:

SHOW BOAT WOWS U.S. BLACK MEDIA

After enduring accusations of racism in Toronto, the Canadian production of *Show Boat* has won raves on Broadway from Afro-American newspapers.

New York's *Amsterdam News,* which bills itself as "The New Black View," singles out director Harold Prince for developing the musical's black characters.

The *Washington Afro-American* praises Prince's production team for erasing the "negative image of shiftless black Americans that Hollywood once thought was entertaining."

Some black groups protested at the 1993 Toronto opening, saying that the show revived outdated caricatures of southern blacks.

The *Show Boat* controversy which transfixed Toronto for almost a year, from February 1993 until the opening of the North York Performing Arts Centre production of the play eight months later, comprises a complex playing out of the effects of American infiltration of Canadian culture. It raises a variety of questions in many areas, only two of which will concern me in this essay. What happens when a local script is read in an transnational context? And what do we mean when we say a text is racist? The questions are interconnected, of course, because both culture and context influence how any work is received and understood. In the course of dealing with these questions, I hope to account for the poverty of the discourse around the *Show Boat* controversy, and to point out some of the ironies that arose during the debate.

Briefly, the idea for opening the North York Performing Arts Centre — a forty-eight million dollar public venture, later to include a school for the performing arts — with that icon of American musical theatre history, *Show Boat*, began with a request from director Harold Prince, to his friend producer Garth Drabinsky, owner of Live Entertainment (Livent). Prince saw the new centre as a promising venue for preparing a production for Broadway.

Originally published by University of Toronto Press in *Diaspora* 5, no. 1: 99–117. Reprinted by permission of University of Toronto Press.

Drabinsky, a close associate of Mel Lastman, Mayor of the City of North York, had already contributed resources to the construction of the NYPAC (recently re-named the Ford Centre for the Performing Arts) in return for free tenancy, with only maintenance costs. Drabinsky agreed. The book for this new production was to be based on the original text, but include material from various stage and film productions; original lyrics were to be featured ("Centre of attention"; Drabinsky).[1] Announcements of the venture produced an immediate, negative reaction from the black community, who were uneasy with the portrayal of black characters in the work, and felt they had a right to express their concern because of the publicly funded nature of the venue. Their concerns became more focused, and also somewhat muddied, when, in her protest against the planned production, North York School Trustee Stephanie Payne questioned why all those involved in *Show Boat*, from Edna Ferber, author of the novel, to Oscar Hammerstein, Jr., lyricist, and Garth Drabinsky, producer of the planned production, were Jewish, an attack for which she later apologised.[2]

The controversy over *Show Boat* raged for eight months, culminating in a boycott of the production organized by a Coalition Against *Show Boat*, a group composed largely of people from the black community. The boycott ultimately failed to produce adequate support. *Show Boat* opened, was widely praised — even by such prominent American publications as *Newsweek* and the *New Yorker*, which uncharacteristically journeyed to Canada to see what the fuss was about. It continued to play to packed houses until it closed in May 1995, its local following swelled by a large number of theatre tours from south of the border.[3]

The press almost univocally sided with Drabinsky and against the black community, although some journalists intensely objected to opening a new Canadian theatre with an American production. However, the protest was not without effect. In May 1993, Livent contracted Henry Louis Gates, Jr. to produce "educational materials for schools" — a response to the fear that boycotts by school boards would lose revenues for the production. Moreover, the plan to use the original script was scrapped, and a modified script was prepared. However, demands by representatives of the black community, whose preferred outcome was abandonment of the production and/or to see the script prior to its being adopted, were denied. Gates was also invited to Toronto to speak on black-Jewish relations.

The most illuminating commentary on the *Show Boat* controversy came from the African Canadian writer M. Nourbese Philip, who published *Showing Grit: Showboating North of the 44th Parallel*, a history and analysis of *Show Boat*, both the novel and the play, and an extended commentary on the social and political issues surrounding productions of both the past and the present. Many aspects of Philip's analysis are germane here, but one in particular is the point of departure for my paper. Philip points out that the story of *Show Boat* depends entirely on the disappearance of its principal black character. Julie, the star of the *Cotton Blossom* entertainment, is driven out of the show because she is "passing" and because she is married to a white man. The scene in which her husband pricks her finger and drinks her blood so that he can honestly refute the charge of miscegenation is the core of the play's protest against racist legislation. It is, however, as Philip notes, unmarked by song or musical theme of any kind. Julie gone, Magnolia, imbued with the black music she learned from Julie, completely displaces her, first in the show, and later as purveyor of her music. Julie later re-appears, briefly, when the abandoned Magnolia is seeking employment as a singer in the Trocadero, a Chicago nightclub. The club's vocalist is none other than Julie, who overhears Magnolia auditioning with a song Julie taught her. Julie slips away, telling the owner to hire her. As a result of this break, Magnolia eventually becomes a star.

Philip employs Toni Morrison's analysis, in *Playing in the Dark*, of the interdependence of black and white in American literature, and the representation of the black character in particular, but she is also interested in the appropriation of black voice and music as central to *Show Boat*'s meaning. It is this theme I wish to examine more fully.

It is well known that Jerome Kern's achievement lies, in great measure, in how fully aspects of black music pervade his score. In fact, novel, book and music enact and are virtually about the appropriation of black culture, music in particular, and for good reason. Written and produced in 1927, *Show Boat* represents the culmination of the Twenties' absorption of African American musical forms and, indeed, particular representations of the African American character, as intrinsic to the dominant culture's self-understanding and expression. Three aspects of the period's cultural history are particularly germane: the appropriation of jazz by white musicians and composers, the arrival on the white stage of a range of black characters, and the African American debate over their contributions to the dominant culture.

In 1924, the aptly named musician Paul Whiteman presented a jazz concert at Aeolian Hall, "the stronghold of academic music. There had been other concerts where jazz of sorts had been played," writes jazz historian Marshall Stearns, " but this was the first jazz concert that captured the imagination of an influential part of the American public" (Stearns, 120).

Of course, at its purest, most innovative and best, jazz lived in Harlem, to whose nightclubs whites flocked for entertainment; and at those dives and rent parties, black musicians cultivated and expanded the still comparatively new musical idiom. In 1927, Duke Ellington played at the opening of the Cotton Club. Elsewhere in town one might encounter: James P. Johnson, Fats Waller, Willie "The Lion" Smith on piano; and the bands of Fletcher Henderson, Sam Wooding, Cecil Scott, Chick Webb and Don Redman. Or, one might hear Bessie Smith, Ethel Waters, Butterbeans and Susie, Snake Hips Tuck and Louis Armstrong (Stearns, 131–33).

Principally, during this period, white jazz comprised dance music flavoured with jazz traces. It rarely, and then only for brief moments in a performance, was considered "hot." Nonetheless, jazz during this period attracted some white musical and popular attention. George Gershwin's *Rhapsody in Blue* was premiered in 1924; "symphonic jazz" attracted the efforts of Paul Whiteman and George Gershwin, and also black musicians Scott Joplin and James P. Johnson. African American composers, as well as their European counterparts, sought to wed black music to European modalities.

Generally in the Twenties, as Langston Hughes remarked in his autobiography *The Big Sea*, "the Negro was in vogue." The period which marked the Harlem (or Black) Renaissance also brought changes in how African Americans were depicted on the American stage. We need recall this history, in particular, to place *Show Boat* in its historical context. In the same year as the first production of *Show Boat*, Ethel Barrymore in black-face starred in DuBose Heywood's *Porgy*, and Paul Green's compelling, if deeply flawed, condemnation of black oppression, *In Abraham's Bosom,* won the Pulitzer Prize. Plays which contained serious depictions of black life, in which black characters were portrayed as other than buffoons and their concerns were sympathetically represented, were relatively new to American theatre. However, their arrival was less a result of the desire to express social protest through art and more a consequence of the influence of the nascent American folk theatre, as well as an expression of the search for the American folk from which, as German romanticism would have it, authentic culture springs. "Plays of Negro Life" — the term is the title of Alain Locke's and Montgomery Gregory's 1927 anthology — by white writers typically naturalized black suffering and white oppression, even while sympathetic to the former and condemning of the latter. With the possible exception of Eugene O'Neill's *All God's Chillun*, no play in the Twenties by white writers depicted the urban black sympathetically, or analysed the condition of the newly arrived migrants. Philip's observation that in *Show Boat* African Americans are connected to the Mississippi, their essence, mysterious like that of the River, and their fate inevitable, aptly summarizes the tenor of the American folk play's handling of black life.

In contrast, black musical theatre flourished on Broadway in the Twenties, and *Show Boat* bears this influence. The years 1921 to 1923 saw nine shows written by and starring black performers, and black shows continued to be plentiful throughout the decade. The white impresario Lew Leslie's black revues provided the bulk of the black entertainment on Broadway after 1924; nonetheless, so abundant was the black presence that a newspaper review proposed, in 1928, that the "Great White Way" be re-named the "Great Black Way."[4] Two shows, early in the decade, *Shuffle Along* (1921) and *Runnin' Wild* (1923), deserve special mention. *Shuffle Along*, Flornoy Miller and Aubrey Lyles, libretto, and Noble Sissle and Eubie Blake, music and lyrics, ushered in a period during which black musicals and revues were at the height of popularity; *Runnin' Wild* is important because it introduced the dance that immediately became all the rage: the Charleston.

Show Boat, then, draws on many developments during the decade. Conventionally regarded as the "first true American musical drama," it was initially reviewed as light opera or operetta (Alpert, 99). It was ground breaking in its score, its scope and in its attention to serious issues; that is, to race. More important for my argument, it also was immensely topical.

Coincidentally, also in 1927, James Weldon Johnson, who had had his own career in musical theatre, republished his 1912 novel, *Autobiography of an Ex-Colored Man*, with a foreword by Carl Van Vechten. This novel is the story of a musically talented young man who finally decides to "voice all the joys and sorrows, the hopes and ambitions, of the American Negro, in classic musical form" (Johnson, 474). In the course of his research, however, he witnesses a lynching. Light enough to pass, he abandons his plans, his music and his race. The passing motif is frequent in American literature. Either threat or tragedy in the hands of white writers, in the hands of black writers it interrogates the meaning of "twoness, — an American, a Negro" of which W.E.B. DuBois spoke so eloquently in *The Souls of Black Folk*.

In *Show Boat*, miscegenation law, not passing, is condemned. However, the threat of violence should Julie remain, and her expulsion from the *Cotton Blossom*, are portrayed as inevitable; neither is judged. Early in the decade, the Dyer anti-lynching bill had been passed in the House of Representatives, but defeated in the Senate. It was during the Twenties that the NAACP began concerted legal attacks on discriminatory laws and practices; nevertheless, the relation of law to segregation and other racist practice was ambiguous in the American popular mind, both black and white. In *Show Boat,* Parthy's fear that her daughter Magnolia has been contaminated by her relationship with Julie, as well as the threat of violence, require Julie's dismissal. The handling of the black characters in *Show Boat*, then, in the context of the Twenties, is utterly conventional — even if new in musical theatre. Black characters are part of the landscape of the South; they suffer uncomplainingly, serve their "white folk" devotedly, comment on life's misery, and humbly accept exclusion from life's triumphs. To do otherwise is to meet the fate of Abe McCranie in *In Abraham's Bosom*, death at the hands of a lynch mob.

It is telling that a new advertisement appeared on the radio in Toronto in August of 1994: *Show Boat* had become, in the hands of its publicity agents, a play about the birth of jazz. It is so, however, only in respect of its time span and its implied reference to the massive northern migration of blacks, which began during World War I. By including black dancers in all its Chicago scenes, *Show Boat* alludes to this migration, but not in an accurate time frame. In fact, the 1921 scene in front of the Palmer House, in which first black dancers and then white dancers perform the Charleston, is anachronistic, two years premature for the introduction of that dance. Nevertheless, both thematically and musically, *Show Boat* literally is about the impact and appropriation of African American culture by white America.

Its conclusions, in some respects, are a not inappropriate but quite perverse response to debates then current within the African American community. Included in that manifesto of the Twenties, *The New Negro* (1925), is an article by Albert C. Barnes, who writes:

> Through the compelling powers of his poetry and music the American Negro is revealing to the rest of the world the essential oneness of all human beings.
>
> The cultured white race owes to the soul-expressions of its black brother too many moments of happiness not to acknowledge ungrudgingly the significant fact that what the Negro has achieved is of tremendous civilizing value.... The unlettered black singers have taught us to live music that rakes our souls and gives us moments of exquisite joy. The later Negro has made us feel the majesty of Nature.... He has shown us that the events of our every-day American life contain for him a poetry, rhythm and charm which we ourselves have never discovered.... His insight into realities has been given to us in vivid images loaded with poignancy and passion. His message has been lyrical, rhythmic, colorful. In short, the elements of beauty he has controlled to the ends of art. (Barnes, 23–24)

Over a decade before Langston Hughes bemoaned: "They've taken my blues and gone ...," Alain Locke wrote, in the introduction to the 1927 *Plays of Negro Life*, concerning the plays by white writers included in the volume:

> Indeed for the present, the white dramatist is [the black playwright's] advantaged rival, by virtue of his more natural objectivity toward this special material of the race life and his more intimate schooling in the theatre. But if the mastery which is within sight, but not yet achieved, is to come at all, it must arise not from objective study merely, but from deep spiritual penetration into the heart and spirit of Negro life.... But to this body freedom [sic] of the Negro drama must also come inner freedom which only the Negro dramatist and the enlightened audience of the future can bring.... With all due allowance for a possible mirage of special hope and interest on our part, it is to be hoped that the reader will see in reality at the horizon the great American tragedy and comedy at which we must in time arrive. (Locke, n.p.)

Of jazz, J.A. Rogers notes, in his contribution to *The New Negro*, that it is difficult to say whether "jazz is more characteristic of the Negro or of contemporary America ... it is of Negro origin plus the influence of the American environment. It is Negro-American." Insistent that only African Americans genuinely are capable of creating real jazz, he nevertheless welcomes the interest of white musicians (for example, he quotes conductor Leopold Stokowski and mentions such modernists as Auric, Sate and Milhaud) and concludes:

> [W]here at present it vulgarizes, with more wholesome growth in the future, it may on the contrary truly democratize. At all events, jazz is rejuvenation, a recharging of the batteries of civilization with primitive new vigor. It has come to stay, and they are wise, who instead of protesting against it, try to lift and divert it into nobler channels. (Rogers, 219, 223–24)

Many intellectuals and artists of the Harlem Renaissance, Locke primary among them, believed cultural contributions would effect social and political change. Thus African

American cultural contributions signified the real place of African Americans within America — as soul and substance, warp and woof of the American cultural fabric. The 1926 debate about how the "Negro Was To Be Portrayed" (a seven part symposium in the NAACP organ, the *Crisis*) was less interested in who did the portrayal than in the resulting portrait. *Show Boat*'s response is perverse not because its music is imbued with jazz and other forms of black musical expression, but because it does away with Julie and relegates all the other black characters to the margins and the chorus. In his article in *The New Negro*, "The Drama of Negro Life," Montgomery Gregory writes:

> President-Emeritus Charles William Eliot of Harvard University recently expressed the inspiring thought that America should not be a "melting-pot" for the diverse races gathered on her soil but that each race should maintain its essential integrity and contribute its own special and peculiar gift to our composite civilization: not a "melting-pot" but a symphony where each instrument contributes its particular quality of music to an ensemble of harmonious sounds. Whatever else the Negro may offer as his part there is already the general recognition that his folk-music, born of the pangs and sorrows of slavery, has made America and the world his eternal debtor. (153)

If Julie's fate is taken as the response, the debt is not acknowledged.

I intend, by the above, to explain why *Show Boat* looms so large in the American imagination. This is not to imply that African American response to the play has been without resistance. Paul Robeson's insistence on altering the lyrics of "Ol' Man River" is well known, although it occurred in the 1930s, and not during the earlier productions. Speaking of the 1928 London production, in which Robeson took London by storm in spite of mixed reviews for the show, J.A. Rogers, at the time the European correspondent for the New York *Amsterdam News,* reported that he had talked to "fully some thirty Negroes of intelligence and self-respect" who expressed "their disapprobation of the play," and he had "also heard many harsh things said against Robeson for lending his talent and popularity toward making it a success." "If anyone were to call him a 'nigger,'" Rogers quoted one informant as saying, "he'd be the first to get offended, and there he is singing 'nigger, nigger' before all those white people." Rogers also objected to the character of Joe's being simply another instance of the "lazy, good-natured, lolling darkey" stereotype "that exists more in white men's fancy than in reality." The obvious solution, he wrote, was for blacks to write their own plays and books, but because he recognized that "it will be a long time before this is done," Rogers felt he could not "join in the indignation against those actors and writers who sell their service to the whites," much as he did regret that *Show Boat* represented a "deliberate attempt on the part of the White American to carry his anti-Negro propaganda into Europe" (216–24).

In London, even a few whites objected to the show in the press. In the United States, the black press had been so critical that the *New York Times* had risen to the play's defence against "negro newspaper editors." The defence was "artistic detachment" and the argument that individuals such as Robeson, and Jules Bledsoe in the New York production, acted as "leavening agents" (Duberman, 114–15).

Nonetheless, *Show Boat* has become a staple of the American musical theatre, at both the professional and community level. I would argue that the revision of this icon is what so pleased the African American community, whose historical relationship with white America, no matter how vexed and painful, is also intimate. *Show Boat* is truly an American classic, an extremely familiar mapping of the iconography of race relations, a mapping whose changes, then, are carefully charted, and noted with satisfaction. *Show Boat*'s argument is also part of a long cultural debate to which, by now, there has been forthright African American cultural response. African American artists, writers and playwrights in particular have a presence in the United States that was a long time coming, but now is vibrant and undeniable.

So what is wrong with African Canadians, whose protest Drabinsky arrogantly termed an embarrassment to the city and an "intellectual travesty" ("New Vancouver theatre to open with Show Boat")?

Many factors affected the Toronto black community's reaction to *Show Boat*, and I cannot treat all of them here. Extremely tense relations between the community and the police, frustration over unemployment, the backlash against immigration and any equity gains made under the NDP government, increasing fear of crime which is blamed on the black community; these, among others, were brought to bear upon the struggle over culture. This was the second time in the last few years that the representation of blacks and African culture had been the centre of controversy, and in both cases, public institutions (the Royal Ontario Museum regarding the "In the Heart of Africa" exhibit, and *Show Boat* in a public venue) met the concerns of the community with lack of understanding, or contempt. Many of these issues are well explored in *Showing Grit*.

What interests me for purposes of this paper begins with the fact that the black community in Toronto — numbering 250,000 — is overwhelmingly from the Caribbean. Its history is not the same as that of African Americans; moreover, white culture, for this community, is British first and now also Canadian — as well as American in the sense that American culture has become, since the end of World War II, transnational. Largely an immigrant population, it includes people from many areas of the former British empire, and so the community understands, and shares, a variety of concerns that have been termed postcolonial, including a tradition of ambivalence, if not resistance, to metropolitan culture, a culture rendered even more problematic, of course, for reasons of race. It is important to note here that the 1928 black audience, whose resistance to *Show Boat* in London was reported by J.A. Rogers, was likely of Caribbean extraction as well. One might say that Rogers' anger over the exporting to Europe of American racial paradigms presages the Toronto debate.

Show Boat may be a familiar script for African Americans; it is not for people of African descent from the Caribbean, whose slave experience, while equally horrific, differed in various respects. For example, slaves were not systematically dispersed so as to avoid tribal groupings; owners were most likely absentee and typically owned large numbers of slaves. As well, slavery is a generation more remote in the Caribbean, and Africans of Caribbean descent have not attempted to recollect and recuperate their slave past in the concerted way that Americans have, literally, since Emancipation.

The majority population in most Caribbean countries are primarily of African descent and Caribbean culture has many more obvious African traces in, for example, the Jamaican language, Anansi stories, and many cultural practices. Moreover, its burgeoning literature and other forms of cultural production have had a very different relation to a culturally dominant, if distant, white audience. Metropolitan acknowledgement of modern cultural production is a product of the 1950s rather than, in the United States, of the 1920s, if not earlier. Finally their expectations, as an immigrant group, are resistant to being relegated in Canada to the margins and the chorus.

Moreover, the community reads the implications of *Show Boat*, rightly I would argue, as a Canadian adoption of the American racial script. *Show Boat*'s blacks are not happy, but they are quiescent and accepting of their place. They are the context for the show's main story; as Toni Morrison suggests, whiteness is defined in relation to its "other." Canada's narrative of its historical relation to its black community is, in itself, slight. It includes being the terminus of the Underground Railroad, but it barely acknowledges the existence of slavery within its borders, and subsumes people of African descent into its policy of multiculturalism, although its black citizens are as diverse as the African diaspora. Blacks are not only racially "other," when acknowledged at all; they are "immigrants," in the tricky rhetoric of multiculturalism, people not quite Canadian because they retain loyalties to elsewhere.

Constantly pouring over the border, however, as around the world, is the American racial script, which is adopted selectively, and not well understood. African American history, it is implied, is the history of all Africans in the New World; there is room for no other. Yet African American resistance is represented as necessary there, given American racial realities, but unnecessary in Canada. In Canadian schools, children read *The Adventures of Huckleberry Finn*, but no African American writers before, perhaps, Alice Walker; by and large, they learn of no African American historical personages between Harriet Tubman and Martin Luther King, Jr., and perhaps, recently, Malcolm X. Moreover, to a large extent, for this community, black figures in American cultural texts are simply metonymic for American racial oppression.[5] *Show Boat* is part of a complex cultural fabric, only shreds of which migrate.

The irony is that in the debate over *Show Boat,* both white and black Canadians read the play out of context. Defenders of the play, on the whole, suggested that the black community could not or would not appreciate great art, canonizing *Show Boat* as self-evidently of such artistic merit as to render it above criticism. For its defenders, *Show Boat*'s avowed perfection is in its magnificent music and its spectacle (it certainly isn't in its story, for its story is purely sentimental, and often nonsensical). It dazzles. "Ol' Man River," in this view, becomes an adequate representation of three hundred years of unmitigated oppression.

The black community also reads the play out of context, and does not like what it reads. From the perspective of a black audience, the representation of blacks is far from satisfactory. It may or may not know the songs that have endured: "Ol' Man River," "Make Believe," "Can't Help Lovin' Dat Man" and "Bill." But they will naturally be sensitive to the way *Show Boat* purports to be a play about them, and they will not recognize themselves. For in *Show Boat*, as in virtually all work by white writers that is about black and white characters, blacks are generalized in ways that whites are not. This isn't a play about "whites" and "blacks"; it is a play about some people who are white and about "blacks."

Regional art that travels is necessarily read out of context, except by those who know enough to supply its regional setting. What was mystified in the debate over *Show Boat* was its specificity. The very columnists who scolded the black community for its failure to appreciate the play would be quick to point out American and Canadian differences, in other contexts. The legacy of modernist views of art as self-contained also confused the debate utterly. The public debates valorized *Show Boat* as great art, by implication suggesting it possesses formal qualities and inherent meaning of transcendental significance. Hostile critics became, at best, Philistines — an odd designation in a debate about popular culture.

Paradoxically, another aspect of the debate was concerned with reception. Some columnists and reviewers, notably Bronwen Drainie, H. J. Kirchhoff and Michael Valpy in the Toronto *Globe and Mail*, and Michele Lansberg and Richard Gwyn in the *Toronto Star,* acknowledged that black audiences might find the play offensive. By and large, however, the spectre of "political correctness" and of "censorship" haunted the reception debate. In this vein, the enthusiastic reviews of the production were used to criticize the community's discomfort. The reception in the U.S. by the African American community — at least as represented by the New York *Amsterdam News* and the *Washington Afro-American* — became final evidence that the Toronto black community was wrong in its assessment. But what was being assessed?

Here the question becomes more difficult. Certainly a director of Hal Prince's experience and seven million dollars must produce a work with high theatrical values; the money bought him a top line (almost entirely American) cast, magnificent sets, excellent musicians and dancers, and as the great middle-brow director, he knows what will move an audience. What was being assessed was whether or not the play is racist, not whether or not it is a gratifying spectacle.

This issue is also a large one, so I will confine my discussion, for purposes of this essay, to how the charges of racism were understood by Drabinsky and Prince, as reflected in the changes they made. In short, I would argue that in 1927, in New York, *Show Boat* constituted a significant departure from the conventional stage representation of the black in musical theatre, and in its handling of contemporary social and cultural debates was not racist in intention. It is a white play, and its creators used existing conventions to represent their story. In the period depicted, as well as the period in which the play was written, southern settings always implied a black context, and so black life is the necessary context for the play, although it is not the subject of the plot. Black characters in this theatrical context have no autonomy; their individual lives are not the subject to be explored. The interjection of the theme of black oppression within this southern setting was a first; not, as is often said, a particularly daring one, but a first, nonetheless.

Aside from acknowledging that the original lyrics of "Ol' Man River" were insulting, and that the African number at the Chicago Exhibition was beyond the pale (and also made the play even longer), Prince and Drabinsky chose to modernize the black characters by developing performances as far from stereotype as possible, and by having blacks and whites mingle and interact unself-consciously in crowd or dance scenes. That is, they accepted and interpreted the criticism as meaning that what constitutes the racism of the text is the representation of blacks as subservient.

However, Toronto's *Show Boat* was, it seems to me, racist in ways that are more troubling than the original version. It was especially problematic when viewed in the context of the historical claims so widely disseminated through all the publicity around the production, program notes, souvenir literature, as well as the discourse in the press and, purportedly, the material prepared by Henry Louis Gates, Jr. for schools.[6]

Show Boat's primary claims to historical accuracy refer to two facets of the play: the existence of showboats and the depiction of racism against and the oppression of African Americans. The former, of course, is the play's principal setting and ostensible subject; the latter is expressed through plot and the presence of African Americans in the play. Historically, in the period depicted, African Americans did "tote barges and lift bales," providing menial labour both in fields and in towns. Moreover, in literary terms, what Toni Morrison calls "the Africanist presence" signals the southern setting; it is commonplace knowledge that *Show Boat* marks the introduction of social issues in a social fashion to the American musical stage, but the nature of the statement is hard to reconstruct meaningfully.[7]

History cannot be learned at *Show Boat* because the relations between white and black in the play are utterly mystified, even more so in this production because the camaraderie between whites and blacks, particularly in crowd/dance scenes, but elsewhere as well, is most improbable. For example, at the end of the play, in the long final dance number, at one point two black male dancers dance for Magnolia's blond and blue-eyed celebrity daughter Kim in a way that would have resulted in a lynching in Natchez of 1927 — and in protest in a New York theatre of the same period. What is conceded to black characters in this production is also immediately truncated; for example, in one of the lengthy Chicago street dance sequences, two black male dancers are given the spotlight for about one minute, the only black dance duet in the scene and one of very few spotlighted black numbers in dances by the entire company. Later a group of black dancers, showing the passage of time, do the Charleston; their initial introduction of the dance, however, is soon displaced by a larger white version stage centre.

Also in attempting to create a definitive, yet modernized, text, paradoxically, the production retains things that seem simply insulting to the black performers. Aside from the first part of the initial rendition of "Ol' Man River," every time Joe appears to sing a reprise, the scenery begins to change, the "rolling, rolling, rolling" of the scenery (for it is audible) literalizing the rolling river of which he sings. In *Show Boat: The Story of an American Classic*, Miles Kreuger relates that short scenes served as distractions for scene changes, especially necessary before the emergence of certain technology in the 1940s. Particularly noticeable in this production is the fact that Joe only once, in the early moments of the play, has the stage to himself. Moreover Joe wanders on stage twice in the Chicago portion of the play to sing a reprise of "Ol' Man River," thus insisting upon the universality, rather than the specificity, of life's burdens and the wisdom of endurance. Elsewhere, the mixed cast of children who populate scenes on the levee and join various dance numbers mix unselfconsciously, as they might in a contemporary elementary school. At one point in a company dance, Magnolia joins hands and dances with a black child in an unlikely fashion.

However, the entire play depends on the separation of white and black, the marginality and subservience of the black characters. This production attempts to deflect criticism by having the black actors discard the stereotypes on which the play depends, in subtle ways to increase the black presence — particularly through Joe's refrains, and restoring Queenie's "Mis'ry's Comin' Aroun'"; but the impact is to intensify the racism inherent in the play. If the black characters move so unself-consciously among the whites, and have such an apparently equal relationship, then why do they act as they do in other respects? The incongruity is particularly noticeable when Queenie encourages the reluctant black hangers-on to fill the segregated gallery of the Cotton Blossom's theatre, when both Joe and Queenie observe Julie's banishment without comment, and when Julie relinquishes her job in favour of Magnolia. The impact of the rectified script, therefore, is to suggest that blacks accepted their roles, not by suggesting, however, as could easily have been done, that, in Paul Laurence Dunbar's words, "[they] wear the mask." Drabinsky and Prince sought a cosmetic remedy when they could have truly modernized *Show Boat* by playing up its datedness, for example, by having the black characters send up or distance themselves from the roles the script demands of them. One recalls that Hal Prince is, indeed, a producer of mass entertainment for white audiences, and not interested in a *Show Boat* that might comment on its 1994 context.

The question of when is a text racist is complex, and extremely difficult to answer. Certain texts, for example, Thomas Dixon's *The Clansman* and the film made from it, *Birth of a Nation*, are obviously so, in that their avowed purpose is to depict a certain group of people, African Americans, as racially inferior and dangerous, and to advocate repression. The question of whether *The Adventures of Huckleberry Finn*, for example, is racist is more complex. For purposes of this discussion, it is important to note that Twain despised racism, that he intended the text, not as a delightful story for school children, but as a moral fable for adults, and that irony comprises the workings of its anti-racist message. Nevertheless, the text's portrait of Jim and his subservience to two young boys, is, understandably, unpalatable to black readers, and the manner in which it serves an anti-racist cause is difficult to recuperate a century later. In schools it is read "straight" as a triumph of the American vernacular and a manifesto of a variety of American values, racial attitudes ambiguously situated among them. Thus its impact has utterly changed, and those who see it as racist, although they may not be "reading" it historically, are not misguided. In fact, in a contemporary context, it can easily be read to uphold those very attitudes which, a century ago, it was understood to attack.

Contemporary theories of reading, whether deconstruction or reader-response, both of which, in some fashion, place text at the mercy of its reader, would seem to support reception, broadly understood, as in the eyes of the beholder, and thus obviate the accusation that one set of views "has it right and the other wrong." If that is so, then it is the political and emotional need of the majority to be acknowledged as right as well as powerful that is at stake, and not the excellence of a particular text, when "resisting readers and viewers" are disparaged, as they were during the *Show Boat* controversy.

Put differently, is racism inherent in a text, or is it contextual (or *also* contextual)? In posing the question this way, I am indebted to the work of Michele Wallace, particularly to the final section of *Invisibility Blues,* and to Walter Benjamin's remarkable essay in *Illuminations*, "Theses on the Philosophy of History," to which she refers. Wallace is always interested in the workings of cultural hegemony, and in "how cultural production represents a complex process that is not fundamentally altered by any single cultural event" (Wallace, 248) — or, I might add, any single product.

In his essay, Benjamin delivers to "historical materialists" a meditation on the underlying dynamics of history:

> To the historians who wish to relive an era, Fustel de Colanges recommends that they blot out everything they know about the later course of history. There is no better way of characterizing the method with which historical materialism has broken.... [A]ll rulers are the heirs of those who conquered before them. Hence, empathy with the victor invariably benefits the rulers. Historical materialists know what that means. Whoever has emerged victorious participates to this day in the triumphal procession in which the present rulers step over those who are lying prostrate. According to traditional practice, the spoils are carried along in the procession. They are called cultural treasures, and a historical materialist views them with cautious detachment. For without exception the cultural treasures he surveys have an origin which he cannot contemplate without horror. They owe their existence not only to the efforts of great minds and talents who have created them, but also to the anonymous toil of their contemporaries. There is no document of civilization which is not at the same time a document of barbarism. And just as such a document is not free of barbarism, barbarism taints also the manner in which it was transmitted from one owner to another. A historical materialist therefore dissociates himself from it as far as possible. He regards it as his task to brush history against the grain.
>
> The tradition of the oppressed teaches us that the "state of emergency" in which we live is not the exception but the rule. We must attain to a conception of history that is in keeping with this insight.... One reason why Fascism has a chance is that in the name of progress its opponents treat it as a historical norm. The current amazement that the things we are experiencing are "still" possible in the twentieth century is *not* philosophical. This amazement is not the beginning of knowledge — unless it is the knowledge that the view of history which gives rise to it is untenable. (Benjamin, 256–57)

If, as Benjamin suggests, barbarism is necessarily a component of all works of civilization, this two-sidedness is particularly evident (if not read that way) in works depicting American race relations. Noticing becomes a form of resistance, and so threatening in itself. Resistance is also, I would argue, a local phenomenon; that is, it takes place at particular points in time in specific situations or against specific regimes. In the case of Toronto's *Show Boat*, the resistance is against a text divorced of its context; the context is absent not because of the ignorance of those resisting (or those applauding, for that matter) but because it is *Show Boat*-in-Canada, and so, as it were, a free floating signifier which, when valorized as "great culture," became attached to Canadian soil and, by implication, expressive of Canadian realities. Yet what Canadian realities does it express? Given Canada's struggles with its own forms of racism, what meaning can be accorded the representation of blacks in this work? The question is a fair one.

Those who protested the production would have preferred that *Show Boat* had never docked on Canadian shores at all, of course. However, the *Show Boat* that African American audiences applauded had, in fact, been shaped by the Toronto protest, for changes were made to the book and the performances modified in response to pre-production pressures by the black community. Thus the use of the positive African American reaction to rebuke that community for its protest is deeply ironic.

My argument begs the question of whether a work is inherently racist, in favour of a position that suggests that yes, a work may be so, but judgments regarding racism must take into account the complexity inherent in all cultural production. Certainly the black community's resistance to *Show Boat* was far from "intellectual travesty." It has everything to teach us about what happens when America's racial script travels.

ENDNOTES

1. As the many listeners of CBC AM Metro Morning show learned when an early announcement of the controversy opened with a rendition of the original lyrics for "Ol' Man River": "Niggers all work on the Mississippi...." In his autobiography, which was excerpted in the *Toronto Star*, March 19, 1995, Drabinsky relates that he had staged a reading of Prince's script in October 1991 and that:

    > [i]n revising Oscar Hammerstein's book, Hal gathered material from the first 1927 production, the London script, the 1936 film, and the 1946 Broadway revival. He consulted John McGlinn's 1988 EMI-Angel recording of the complete *Show Boat*, consisting of the 1927 production and all the musical material written for it over the years, as well as Miles Kreuger's superb historical chronicle, *Show Boat: The Story of a Classic American Musical.*

    Revisions to Prince's October 1991 book occurred after the controversy began.

2. Payne's remarks did give rise to a vexed and prolonged exchange between members of the two communities. Howard Adelman argues that it was the anti-Semitic discourse that caused the failure of the protest, although members of the Jewish community were on both sides of the *Show Boat* controversy. It is not irrelevant to my argument that this unfortunate venture into anti-Semitism was immediately linked, in the press, to the troubled state of African American–Jewish relations. However Adelman argues, rightly I believe, that the relations between the two communities is not at all like that in the United States; they have none of the shared history of alliance or antagonism.

3. The advertising campaign for *Show Boat* provides a visual narrative of the conflict. Early advertising featured prominent portraits of white characters, with black characters in the background. In smaller ads, the white characters alone were featured. Later *Show Boat* advertisements featured Joe and Queenie alone, often under the caption "A Southern Romance." However, adver-

tisements (in bus shelters) seen by this writer in Vancouver, October 1995, prior to *Show Boat*'s opening in that city, had nary a black character in sight.

4. Woll argues that the period between 1910 and 1921, during which virtually no black plays appeared on Broadway, was a period of intense musical theatrical development *within* the black community, and that *Shuffle Along* is a result of that fertile period.

5. The relation of African Canadians to African American culture is complex. In "Black Like Them," African Canadian writer André Alexis argues that Canadian blackness is distinctive and mystified by the popularity of contemporary theorists — he cites African American writers bell hooks and Cornel West in particular — and certain African American styles among, at least, the younger members of the community. Rinaldo Walcott reads Canadian blackness through Paul Gilroy's notion of the "Black Atlantic," yet he, too, proposes (in conversation) that the articulated terms of African American resistance do not adequately define and illuminate Canadian contexts. Neither, however, concern themselves with the representation of blacks in white American culture. In some respect, in so far as African American cultural production signifies on that of white America, reading it abroad (for Canada is "abroad") produces a different reading from that which takes in what is being signified upon.

6. The video advertising *Show Boat*'s schools program announced the existence of materials prepared by Henry Louis Gates, Jr.; however, they could only be obtained by school groups who actually purchased the "school package," which consisted of classroom materials and a pre-performance program at the theatre during which a video on the history of *Show Boat* was shown and students were taken backstage to meet performers and tour the theatre. All my attempts to obtain the materials for review were rebuffed by Livent; Gates' office informed me they had no copies of the material, which they had sold to Livent, and various school officials in possession of the materials would not lend them. Moreover, none of the various "anti-racist education" consultants at the school boards in the greater metropolitan Toronto area were able to obtain copies of the material, presumably lest they critique it in any way. I later discovered, in conversation with Henry Louis Gates, Jr., that he had never prepared any such materials, nor had he been contacted to do so (December 29, 1996).

7. Black musical comedies had broached the fact and impact of oppression, albeit obliquely and through humour, since the beginning of the century.

REFERENCES

Adelman, Howard. "Blacks and Jews: Racism, Anti-semitism, and *Show Boat.*" In *Multiculturalism, Jews and Identitites in Canada,* ed. Howard Adelman and John Simpson, 128–78. Jerusalem: Magnes Press, 1996.

Alexis, André. "Borrowed Blackness." *This Magazine* 28, no. 8 (May 1995): 14–20.

Alpert, Hollis. *Broadway!: 125 Years of Musical Theatre.* New York: Arcade, 1991.

Barnes, Albert C. "Negro Art and America." In *The New Negro,* ed. Alain Locke, 19–28. 1925; New York: Atheneum, 1992.

Benjamin, Walter. "Theses on the Philosophy of History." In *Illuminations*, trans. Harry Zohn. New York: Schocken, 1969.

"Centre of Attention," *Globe and Mail* [Toronto], 16 October 1994: C1, C8.

Drabinsky, Garth. "Behind the scenes at the *Show Boat* showdown," *Toronto Star*, 19 March 1995: E1, E4.

Duberman, Martin. *Paul Robeson.* New York: Knopf, 1988.

Gregory, Montgomery. "The Drama of Negro Life." In *The New Negro*, ed. Alain Locke, 153–60. 1925; New York: Atheneum, 1992.

Hughes, Langston. *The Big Sea*. 1940; New York: Hill and Wang, 1963.

Johnson, James Weldon. *Autobiography of an Ex-Colored Man*. 1927. In *Three Negro Classics*. New York: Avon, 1965.

Kreuger, Miles. *Show Boat: The Story of a Classic American Musical*. 1977; New York: A Da Capo, 1990.

Locke, Alain. "Introduction." In *Plays of Negro Life: A Source-book of Native American Drama*, ed. Alain Locke and Montgomery Gregory. New York: Harper, 1927.

———, ed. *The New Negro*. 1925; New York: Atheneum, 1992.

Morrison, Toni. *Playing in the Dark: Whiteness and the Literary Imagination*. New York: Vintage, 1990.

"New Vancouver theatre to open with Show Boat," *Globe and Mail* [Toronto], 25 October 1994: C2.

Philip, M. Nourbese. *Showing Grit: Showboating North of the 44th Parallel*. Toronto: Poui Publications, 1993.

Rogers, J.A. "Jazz at Home." In *The New Negro*, ed. Alain Locke, 216–24. 1925; New York: Atheneum, 1992.

"*Show Boat* Wows U.S. Black Media," *Globe and Mail* [Toronto], 22 October 1994: C9.

Stearns, Marshall. *The Story of Jazz*. New York: Mentor, 1958.

Walcott, Rinaldo. "Voyage through the Multiverse: Contested Canadian Identities." *Border/Lines* 36 (1995): 48–52.

Wallace, Michele. *Invisibility Blues: From Pop to Theory*. New York: Verso, 1990.

Woll, Allen. *Black Musical Theatre: From Coontown to Dreamgirls*. Baton Rouge: Louisiana State University Press, 1989.

"KEEP ON MOVIN"

Rap, Black Atlantic

Identities and the Problem

of Nation

Rinaldo Walcott

History is always written from the sedentary point of view and in the name of a unitary State apparatus, at least a possible one, even when the topic is nomads. What is lacking is a Nomadology, the opposite of a history.

Deleuze and Guattari[1]

COLLECTING DISPERSALS

Soul II Soul's signature song, "Keep on Movin," asks its listeners to "keep on movin' don't stop." It's an injunction on stasis and an invitation to accept the fluidity of identity and cultural practices as an ever-present and upfront part of how we might understand the self and the world. The album, in both its idea and its organization, is representative of this fluidity. Jazzie B, the musical arranger, vocalist, rapper and founder of the ensemble Soul II Soul, for example, acts as the only reoccurring member. Jazzie B, or the "Funky Dread," is himself a hybrid of a British roots culture, characterized by its syncretic mixture of Jamaican Rastafarian stylings and African-American popular cultural practices — all of which are elements refashioned and shaped to fit the specificities of black Britain's music and dance scenes. Soul II Soul's music is a journey through contemporary forms of diasporic black music (popular culture) and so Soul II Soul symbolically and actually represents the fluidity of black diasporic relations and cultural expressions and exchanges.

Originally published by Insomniac Press in *Black Like Who? Writing Black Canada.*

The emergence of the ensemble on the international music scene in 1989 signalled what might be characterized as the undeniable cultural exchanges and expressions that exist between diasporic black cultures. The announcement of those relations was made in both song/sound and image. The cultural references, while positioned in the specific and local of black Britain, referenced and cited the "deeper structures" of diasporic black cultures. Soul II Soul released three more albums, all of them international successes: these releases blend a number of black musical genres — rap, dance music, rhythm and blues, soul, reggae and jazz. As well, the creative founder of Soul II Soul, Jazzie B, has become involved with the Jamaican music industry and collaborated with a number of other artists.

In this sense, Jazzie B aided in contemporary refigurations of the Middle Passage, a site which continues to represent one of the primary psychic spaces that black people (both dispersed and continental) need to continually address. The trauma of the Middle Passage is a cultural silence that only now is slowly being recognized as a constituent part of black diasporic memory. Langston Hughes lovingly reimagined Africa for "new world" blacks with negroes dreaming of the Nile; Zora Neal Hurston, in *Moses Man of the Mountain*, rewrote the Exodus story, opening a space for discussions of leadership and community to take centre stage in relation to remembrance and possible futures; and the desire to reconnect with Africa has been expressed by works like Frantz Fanon's *Wretched of the Earth* and *Towards the African Revolution*, M. Nourbese Philip's *Looking for Livingstone*, Toni Morrison's *Beloved*, Charles Johnson's *Middle Passage* and Edward Kamau Brathwaite's *Middle Passages* — all of which attempt to make the "unspeakable spoken" and thus place the "discredited" and "subjugated" knowledges of the "dark diaspora" on the agenda of contemporary politics by reconfiguring the history/memory of the Middle Passage for black Atlantic people.[2] These "literatures of reconnection"[3] represent a significant change in how we might understand both the social and cultural formation of black diasporic communities and what those communities might share beyond phenotype.

What I want to do is look at the ways in which the citational and referential practices of rap music disrupt the notion of the modernist nation-state. The referencing and citing of other songs/sounds or musicians in rap is not the only gesture towards a larger community. That rap musicians persist in making links between practices and events in their localities to practices and events beyond the boundaries of their locale is important in terms of demonstrating how various state authorities are understood as seeking to control blackness both locally and extralocally. For example, narratives concerning relations with police exist in numerous rap songs from various places. The practices of citing and referencing across borders, when coupled with the movement of actual black bodies across state lines, prove disruptive, in profound and disturbing ways, to the romantic, fictive narratives of the unified nation-state. This is particularly true when the songs seem to suggest that similar practices (for example, the regulatory and disciplinary practices of police and immigration officers) are used to control blackness in different locales. The transmigration of the racial metaphor that "black equals criminal" seems to work across space and time, and suggests that while locality is important, some practices spill their borders. It is this spillage that is recouped as a moment of diasporic black identification.

Evidence of the collapse of the unified nation-state is everywhere today. Glaring examples exist in the former Yugoslavia, the conflicts in Somalia and Rwanda, and the resolution of conflicts in Ethiopia and Eritrea. Even the recent peace treaties between Israel, Jordan and the Palestinians seem to suggest the emergence of a new Palestine — though it's not necessarily a "nation" in the modernist sense. In fact, the creation of an Israeli nation-state in 1947 could be read as a signal of the collapse of the modernist nation-state, even before the fall of the Berlin Wall. Israeli citizenship, for example, was not dependent upon the "usual" criteria of birth and so forth. "Jewishness" — which is much more malleable than birth right or language — was more important to the organization of the "new" Jewish/Israeli nation-state. What constitutes Jewishness, however, has been questioned. Some felt that the Ethiopian Falashas, for example, might only be tangentially Jewish, and that their religious practices might be too anachronistic. Russian émigrés, who often have only one Jewish parent, have also posed problems. Recent reports of a group of people from the Indian subcontinent claiming Jewishness and seeking membership in the nation-state of Israel have also pushed the limits of Israel and called into question the very notion that the nation-state is founded on sameness.[4]

The histories, memories and experiences of dispersed peoples always act as a transgression of nation-state principles. If we look at the history of Canada, with its ethnic mix of English, French, Ukrainians, Italians, Jews, Germans, Poles, Portuguese and other Europeans, as well as Japanese, Caribbean, Chinese, South Asian, continental African, black Canadian and Native peoples, what we get is a complex picture of who and what the Canadian might be. All of these groups (except for the Natives) migrated at different points in time, and have found themselves placed differently in the narratives of the nation, in ways which complicate the fiction that the modern nation-state is constituted from a "natural" sameness. While it is clear that many of the European groups have been able, through the mechanisms of white supremacy, to become Canadian in ways that those who are not white have not been able to achieve, it is also clear that each successive migrant group represented a rupture in the myth of the nation as constituted from sameness. What the European groups demonstrate, as well, is that sameness is constituted in the process of forgetfulness, coercion and various forms of privilege and subordination.

It is, however, the migration of non-whites that has continually disrupted the fictions of the nation-state because they show up attempts to both conceal and deny otherness within the nation and to produce racial sameness as the basis of the nation-state. Canadian fictions of sameness seek to make acceptable the massacre and continued disenfranchisement of Native groups and the continued oppression and resistance of formerly colonized people who have migrated to the "satellite" nations (Canada, America, Australia, New Zealand, etc.) of former colonial powers. It is these Others who have most clearly challenged the fictions of nation-state sameness as a racialized code that produces Canada as a "white nation." Consequently, the Somali refugee community in Canada has also aided in the continued transgression of nation-state fictions of unity and oneness. The emerging Somali community might represent the newest black migration to Canada, but as a whole they are quickly having to become "black" in ways that other black Canadians can identify with. What does rap music have to do with Somali refugees, and the construction of the Canadian nation-state? It is this question that has provoked what follows.

THEORIZING THE NATION-STATE

Theorists of the nation-state have continually debated the terms that make the state intelligible to those who identify as members or citizens. Benedict Anderson[5] pinpoints "print-capitalism" and its unification of language patterns and use as constituting the ways in which the nation-state became imaginable for large groups of people who shared a common language. Anderson locates three reasons for how the nation became an imagined community based upon print-capitalism. First, the printed languages became "unified fields" which allowed the literate to communicate exclusively with each other and thereby create an imagined community of readers. Second, the printed language gave the vernacular languages a new fixity that produced codes and usages that only those who read could relate with. Third, these new standard languages created enclaves of power that benefited those who knew the codes and could thus decipher and trade in discussions concerning important questions of the day.

Anderson's schema is important for understanding how a nation might imagine itself in the moments of early state formation, and it's particularly salient for European nation-state formation. But his schema becomes much more murky when applied to nation-states founded after colonial encounters. For these places the politics of language use and its relation to state formation is often played out between the twin forces of internal strife and, more importantly, local class antagonism and neo-colonial or imperialistic practices (for example, countries where the official language is English but the everyday language is different: in Malta, English is the language of business but Maltese is the language of everyday use). Post-colonial nation-states raise a number of important questions and necessitate reconsiderations of Anderson's theory, and perhaps most important among them is the need to refigure the role that language plays in a national consciousness. On the other hand, Anderson's[6] theory does help us to understand the ways in which the "Janus-faced" nature of the nation is achieved (Bhabha).[7]

The Janus-faced nature of the nation is its often two-sided, contradictory, conflictual and unclear articulation of what it means to be a citizen. Official multicultural policy in Canada plays such a role. The policy textually inscribes those who are not French or English as Canadians, and yet at the same time it works to textually render a continued understanding of those people as from elsewhere and thus as tangential to the nation-state. It also characterizes those others as people whose static cultural practices are located both in a past and elsewhere. Bhabha's Janus-face metaphor alerts us to the fact that the nation-state is always about more than at first seems apparent. Conceiving the nation in this way helps us to understand the textual practices of the nation-state as they work both to subordinate and produce inside/outside binaries, and also suggest other possible positions for cultural subjectivity.

In a more recent elaboration and contemplation on the theory and politics of the nation-state, Partha Chatterjee has both supported Benedict Anderson and critiqued him.[8] What is important about Chatterjee's argument is his insistence on the need to develop a language of nation-state theory and politics that can seriously account for community. Using India as his case study he argues that the models for nationalism were so determined by Euro-American notions of the state that the possibilities for post-coloniality were severely limited. Chatterjee suggests that such limitations have led to a separation of public/private notions of community which results in a normalization of the state as an ostensibly public entity. Chatterjee writes:

> The result is that autonomous forms of imagination of the community were, and continue to be, overwhelmed and swamped by the history of the postcolonial state. Here lies the root of our postcolonial misery: not in our inability to think out new forms of the modern community but in our surrender to the old forms of the modern state. If the nation is an imagined community and if nations must also take the form of states, then our theoretical language must allow us to talk about community and state at the same time. I do not think our present theoretical language allows this. (11)

Chatterjee poses a fundamental question, one that forces us to confront whether building a community is possible. In the context of Canada, the nation as imagined community is organized around the idea that it's innately based upon phenotype and language. Thus the Canadian nation-state has no way of making sense of communities founded across and upon difference. Official multicultural policy in Canada actually works to produce a definition of community that's about one's relationship to another nation-state. Because community is understood as the public qualities of language, "culture," and ethnicity, official multicultural policies at both the federal and provincial level support this idea through a discourse of heritage — in Canada "heritage" always means *having hailed from somewhere else*. What follows will demonstrate, through a number of readings of black Atlantic cultural practices, that an understanding of how community might be constituted outside the discourses of the modernist nation-state can be derived from diasporic cultures.

NARRATING THE MULTICULTURAL NATION

The "textual accomplishment"[9] of Canadian multicultural policy has been the main focus for addressing the ways in which the Other is imagined or not imagined in the Canadian nation-state. The multicultural narrative is constituted through a positioning of white Anglophone and Francophone Canadians as the founding peoples of the nation, with a "special" reference to Native Canadians.[10] All Others exist and constitute the Canadian ethnic mix or multicultural character. Thus the colonizing English and French are textually left intact as "real" Canadians while legislation is needed to imagine other folks as Canadian.

In everyday and common-sense usage, *multicultural* means that all those who are not white (i.e., of European descent) represent the ethnic mix. The debates concerning Neil Bissoondath's *Selling Illusions*[11] are an indication of this. His arguments are mainly constructed around dismissing the claims that people of colour make concerning various forms of domination in Canada. And all of the debates and discussions which took place in the mainstream media about his book were centred around the cultural practices of those who are not phenotypically white. The use of multicultural as a category of naming and administration, however, closes down as many possibilities as it opens up because it can also be used to reference the "white ethnics" (Italian, Portuguese, Polish, Yugoslavian, etc.) who are often invoked on "special" occasions to demonstrate the economic promise Canada offers new immigrants. (One recent example occurred on a news segment called "On The Street"; it showcased the "success" of a former Yugoslavian who now owns his own Pizza Pizza franchise after only fourteen years in Canada, [*CBC Evening News with Bill Cameron*, 1994]). Primarily though, multicultural, as a category, is reserved for those who need to be imagined as adjunct to the nation. And they are usually people who are not "white."

The other important issue that needs to be identified here is the way in which Canadian state multiculturalism locates specific cultural practices in an elsewhere that appears to be static. The various arts funding bodies — the Canada Council, Ontario Arts Council, Toronto Arts Council — not to mention theatre groups, artist-run spaces, museums, and galleries, all continually produce the fiction of Canada as a place of whiteness.[12] Thus the key word "heritage" organizes the approach that the state takes towards the culture of the other. Some might like to argue that it is multiculturalism that is the main narrative structure of the intelligibility of the Canadian nation-state, but often such arguments do not take into account the important ways in which popular notions of multiculturalism as meaning "non-white" are replayed in state narratives. So while the specific narrative of federal policy does not define multicultural as "non-white," discussions of the questions of immigration and education, for example, often tend to engage in the popular notion of multiculturalism as referring to "non-whites." These appropriations of the term are rife with the recurring myth of Canada as a benevolent, caring and tolerant country that adapts to "strangers" so that strangers do not have to adapt to it.

Canadian rap artists and dub poets (who are now being referred to as "spoken word artists") have continually challenged both the notion of benevolence and belonging and how these notions are constructed by and through the dominant discourses of the administrative categories of the nation-state. They have referenced and alluded to official forms of multiculturalism as textual attempts to hide the inequities of Canadian society. As well, they are at the forefront of challenging the various fictions of what Canada is, and their work is an attempt to produce new fictions of what Canada might be.

THE LEAKY CATEGORY OF BLACK

Clifton Joseph[13] is one of Canada's leading dub poets. In his poem/song "Pimps" he ridicules not only state sponsored multiculturalism, but in a double-voicing, signifying[14] mode, he also locates those who are named by the media and government officials as community leaders as "pimps." They are the people who, he says, pedal-push the discourse and language of race relations "to get some money position or their kicks." What Joseph attempts to address in his poem/song is the relative complicity that those who are willing to be marked and marketed as representatives of "ethnic" communities find themselves in. Those inside/outside positions allow for proscribed access to the practices and discourses of dominant authorities. For Joseph these individuals are "multicultural pimps." On the album that features "Pimps" the relations of "diasporic identifications" are made clear and evident.

The hybrid jazz-funk of his song/poem "Chant for Monk 3" remembers Thelonius Monk through chant and song. Using his voice as both instrument and instrumentation for the lyrics, Joseph brings Monk back to life in what can be identified as repetitions of black cultural practices which continually reproduce the circularity of black cultural expression.[15] It is Joseph's repetitions that signal his disruption of the Canadian nation-state as we know it — for by not only chanting for Monk, but by engaging in the uncanny and intangible practices of black diasporic cultures, Joseph locates his sense of self beyond the boundaries of the nation-state. It is those musical transgressions that continually recur to disrupt the romance of the unified nation-state. Joseph's work unravels and makes it necessary to (re)contain blackness or attempt to render blackness absent from the nation. However, as Morrison[16] has argued about the American situation, blackness remains an absented/presence in the imagined community and landscape of Canada, and continues to work as a foil to whiteness. Blackness represents what Canada is not, and thus Joseph's identification with other black people, across space and time, resists the notion of the specificity of the nation-state as offering a unique experience or history. At the same time, his identification with other blacks insists on more from the Canadian nation-state.

Like Joseph, Lillian Allen has also positioned an "elsewhere"[17] that is both a reference to and a citation of the history of black diasporic experiences in her poems/songs. These histories often diverge from the concepts and the practices of the modern nation-state. Allen[18] sings/reads on the track "I Fight Back":

ITT ALCAN KASIER
Canadian Imperial Bank of Commerce
these are privilege names in my country
but I am illegal here

...

I came to Canada
found the doors of opportunity
well guarded

...

And constantly they ask
"Oh beautiful tropical beach
with coconut tree and rum
why did you leave there
why on earth did you come"

AND I SAY:
For the same reasons
your mothers came[.]

Allen dismantles the notion that the nation-state is familial and protective. But even more important for my purposes is her construction of the nation-state as "something" that must be fled. Clearly, Allen (rather the poem's narrator) had to leave an "elsewhere" to find herself in Canada. The migratory practices of the dispersed are plainly charted, and both colonialism and neo-colonialism are invoked in the process. From Allen's perspective post-coloniality simply does not deliver all the goods. Also just as important (for my purpose here as well) are the ways in which she deconstructs, or at least makes available the resources needed to deconstruct, the myth of Canada as a benevolent, caring and tolerant nation. She is "illegal here," and those who imagine themselves "Canadian" position her as an outsider when they ask "why on earth did you come?" Allen's deconstruction is not some mere acquiescence to "outsiderism," however: she "fights back," calling up the history of European colonial expansion and even more recent European migratory crossings ("For the same reasons / your mothers came"). Her poem, in fact, might be read as a reinvention of universality from the underside.

What Allen, Joseph, Dionne Brand, and rappers like Devon, Maestro Fresh-Wes and the Dream Warriors (whose work I will discuss later) suggest about black migratory politics/histories and experiences is a continual (re)negotiation and (re)articulation of what nation, home and family mean. All these artists produce work that can only be accurately described as ambivalent and ambiguous in its relation to the nation-state. They at once want to hold on to it (nation), as both something that is Canadian and a product of "elsewhere," and to reconstruct it as something much greater than the western modernist project of nation-building suggests.[19] Such practices often leave them embracing what can only be characterized as a diasporic understanding of "nation," one that's constituted through history, experience, and positionality. The more problematic versions of this are expressed as a romantic, pastoral, pre-colonial Africa of kings and queens and overdetermined notions of gender equality. Such versions are founded on what Wole Soyinka refers to as a "saline consciousness"[20] because of the geographic centredness of the narrative. In a world where black diasporic experiences seem to converge and diverge in important ways, these artists force us to continually rethink and reassess what we mean by nation, home, and community.

Devon, who is the best and clearest link between dub poetry and rap music in Canada, and who toured with Lillian Allen and Clifton Joseph before moving more firmly into popular music, is also much more symbolically fluid in his work. It is evident that a "nomadic aesthetic" informs the work he has produced to date. I want to focus on one of his songs that continually engages in the citational and referential practices that I have suggested organize black diasporic cultural practices because it gives texture to the arguments that I am making here. On his first album, *It's My Nature*,[21] Devon, like Soul II Soul, works with a large body of black musical genres — though rap and funk are central. The track "Mr. Metro" illustrates the ways in which black diasporic identifications work. The song was first released as a single in 1989, and it served as an emotional call for an end to police violence against young blacks. It is the police and/or those who enforce "law and order" (i.e., Immigration officers, security guards, teachers, etc.) that continually recur as the principal "administrators" through which we might continue to speak of diasporic political identifications that exceed the boundaries of the local. What those narratives often reference is how similar "actors" seem to be involved in the regulation and discipline of black bodies — even across national boundaries.

Police relations tend to be one of the most pressing issues for many diasporic black communities. Whether we are talking about the Rodney King incident, or police shootings in Canada, Jamaica, Barbados, or Britain, the police seem to be the agents through whom the dominant culture enforces its position. Devon, whose band is called (in signifying tones) the Metro Squad (a play on the Metropolitan Toronto Police force), in "Mr. Metro" raps that Metro's "number one problem" is that no one trusts them. He goes on to rap that if you pick up a copy of the *Toronto Sun* or the *Toronto Star*, you would see the headline "Metro Gets Another One." The song suggests that alleged police misconduct is responsible when "another one bites the dust".

His lyrics locate one of the many policing practices which situate blackness outside the nation as criminal, deviant other. At the same time, these policies also work to contain blackness within the nation; because, the argument follows, black bodies must be managed, policed and controlled.

Arguments and policies that position black youth as pathologically criminal, that say strict action is needed to curtail deviant behaviour — for example, the Scarborough school board's "Zero Tolerance" initiative against school violence — evoke long-held beliefs about black people as criminals. Those policies suggest that black people need to be managed with a firm and strict hand. Zero Tolerance policies draw on historical practices of slavery that position the black body as uncivil: the social integration of the black body is possible only if it's firmly managed, policed, and, from time to time, not-so gently reminded of who exactly is in charge. Devon's music aims to resist and rework narratives that, across time and space, seek to subjugate black bodies. His contribution to an album from which proceeds supported voter registration and education in the recent South African elections is just another example of diasporic ethics at work: community is clearly built across the boundaries between nations.

FOR THE LOVE OF "NOMADICISM"

It is the subjugation of black bodies that is most evident in the ongoing debate around community and thus nation that is occurring around the situation of 3,000 Somalis living in one of Canada's condominium complexes. Dixon Road, in Etobicoke, Ontario, is home to about 3,000 of Canada's 70,000 Somali refugee claimants.[22] The district is also a conservative, white, middle-age, middle-class suburban neighbourhood, built in the 1970s when suburbia offered an escape from what was perceived as the too-quickly-growing city infused with its flux of immigrant workers and increasing crime. The area around Dixon Road was promoted as a place to raise a family on a stable middle-class salary and instill what could now be called good family values. This was the case until the 1980s, when the Somalis arrived.

By the summer of 1993, the "problem" had firmly announced itself with a "mini-riot" in the parking lot of the Dixon Road condominium complex. One of the "riots" was sparked when security guards issued a parking ticket to a Somali resident on July 30, 1993. Since then, the area has been a hotbed of controversy, singling out all those who Lillian Allen[23] names in her poem/song as: "Immigrant, law-breaker, illegal, minimum wager/refugee." The white residents attempt to argue that the problems come from an "elsewhere," and this defines the Somali community as outside what is allowably and imaginably Canadian.

In 1992 the then Conservative Minister for Immigration refused to increase the quotas for Somali claimants wanting to come to Canada. He argued that they were "nomadic" and would not settle down. He was not using the term critically like Deleuze and Guattari[24] but as an anthropologic putdown rife with ethnocentric clutter. Because of this prejudice, he could see no sense in increasing the number of Somali entry visas. They would only stay for a short period before they would roam off somewhere else. Following the federal immigration minister's comments, the provincial Liberal Party made it its policy to "expose" Somalis who were either "unfairly" collecting social assistance or engaged in some practice that might be construed as contravening their refugee status.[25] Reports concerning everything from social assistance cheques being used to fund the war in Somalia, to illegal herbal practices, to genital mutilation or female circumcision (naming is important here depending upon one's stance on the issue) made headlines in the Canadian press. Folks somewhere were working overtime to make sure that Somalis never became a part of the imagined community and landscape of Canada.

While the reports attempted to place Somalis outside the Canadian imagination, at the same time they were also concerned with how to manage blackness. Describing the Somalis as nomadic was an attempt to make them culturally unintelligible just as they were being forced into the North American black criminal paradigm. The desire to regulate and discipline blackness was exposed when condominium owners hired security guards to patrol and contain *The Somalis* (blackness). The "nomadicism" of blackness has caused a great amount of concern for the keepers of Canadian national identity — a Canadian identity that can hardly come to terms with its slave holding past, let alone deal with the contemporary existence of black bodies in its midst.

The first few Somalis arrived in Etobicoke in 1989 — the year Soul II Soul emerged internationally, commanding us to "keep on movin' don't stop," and the year that Devon released "Mr. Metro," his plea to police to "ease up, Don't shoot the youth." They chose Dixon Road because it was near the airport, never imagining that such a choice would be used to position them as outsiders. Theirs was not a choice of privilege but one of pragmatic necessity. Living on Dixon Road made it easy to meet migrating relatives and friends at little expense (taxi fares); as well, the area provided relatively cheap housing. This is how the decisions of the world's migratory peoples are made: the need for cheap housing is the primary reason behind the "blackening"[26] of the Somali population in Ontario.

By blackening I mean to signal two important but related ideas. First, that nation-state administrators try to force what it means to be black on people through various mechanisms of domination and subordination. They are, in effect, telling you that you have very little, if any, relation to the nation. This process often involves arguing that black people are primitive, backwards, and not worthy of citizenship. Contemporary modifications of these myths are much more complex, and they're constantly shifting in late capitalist North America, where blackness is also a commodity (i.e., like hip-hop cultural artifacts, music and clothing). On the other hand, blackening also signals the various inscriptions that black people mark their bodies with (T-shirts, jewellery, etc.) and the discourses and articulations that both contest and resist subordination and domination. The articulations of lifestyles that do not continually respond to a reflex of domination are important to this process. Blackening as a performance, then, is how, at any given point in time, any particular person marked as black might act out a discourse of blackness from the multiple positions that are possible. This acting out, whether as subordination, resistance, or something else, can often be forced. It depends upon the situation one finds oneself in. However, blackness is also a way of being and becoming in the world. Blackening, then, is the continual fluidity of the process.

To white condominium owners, the everyday practices of the Somali community (especially their food odours and gatherings) were an affront to "Canadian ways of living." As Homi Bhabha writes: "The scraps, patches, and rags of daily life must be repeatedly turned into the signs of a national culture, while the very act of the narrative performance interpolates a growing circle of national subjects."[27] It is these everyday differences, that refuse the subordinating discourses of the nation, which have led to what can only be characterized as the fascist imposition of condominium statutes of exact and minute detail upon the Dixon Road housing complex. Complaints about food odours, and cultural differences that some residents just cannot understand, not to mention ludicrous accusations about everything from feces in elevators to apartment overcrowding, have surfaced in attempts to position Somali residents as unsuitable. For Somalis the "scraps, patches, and rags of daily life" are not being recouped as a sign of national belonging and culture; instead, they are being used to position them as outsiders. The absentee landlords that the Somalis rent from have been virtually silent about the alleged abuses that the condo owners have enforced with hired mock police (security guards). They simply collect the rent to pay their mortgages and/or make profits. So how does the Somali community under siege in Etobicoke relate to rap music and black Atlantic cultures?

The condominium statutes are being enforced to the letter by a security guard service patrolling the complex. What the guards actually do is police the Somali community. They've in effect been hired to enforce statutes designed to address accusations of Somali parking violations, vandalism and so on. Thus the guard service is representative of the macro-political practice of policing black bodies at the micro-level. On the regional and national, or macro-level, the various metropolitan police forces manage "blackness," while on the micro-level security guards with dogs do the trick.[28] Ultimately, it's the stringent policing of the Somali community that has led to the two specific incidents that the local press has labelled the Dixon Road "riots." Policing practices have clearly conditioned and fostered the recurring debates about the place/space of blackness in the Canadian imagination.

When Devon raps in pleading tones with police forces across North America (such as the Royal Canadian Mounted Police, the Los Angeles Police Department, and the Ontario Provincial Police) to "ease up don't shoot the youth" he is signalling that the management of black bodies by various police forces organizes a transnational blackness. While Devon's song is located in the specific and the particular of various Canadian localities, his metahistorical commentary suggests that approaches to blackness are somehow related across time and space. Thus Devon's invocations of Orange County and the LAPD are not mere examples of naming but of naming with a point in mind, one that demonstrates the articulation of a border-crossing sensibility. His is a practice that strikes at the epistemological foundations of how black bodies are perceived and treated within the confines of the nation-state. Furthermore, his practice is one that reconfigures the nation-state by making links which produce more rich and textured histories/memories of black positionalities across space, time and nation.

Devon's rapped plea of "Don't shoot the youth" resonates and reverberates loudly, especially when one considers that in the case of the Somalis it is the youth who have resisted and who are the ones being marked as trouble-makers in a "troubled community."[29] The processes of criminalization are underway. Trespass notices prevent youths from visiting friends in other buildings. Blackness has taken on a whole new meaning for Somalis, and this has led one community leader to remark that their troubles are "an education for their children, preparing them to lead the lives of *blacks* in a white land" (emphasis added).[30] The performativity of the category black here suggests that Somalis who probably did not expect to live with the North American discourse of race intervening in their daily existence, have to do so now — simply in order to survive.

"KEEP ON MOVIN"

In the summer of 1994, when Canada's financially successful rapper Maestro Fresh-Wes released his new album from New York, his "new home," his intentions were clear. The CD was titled *Naaah, Dis Kid Can't Be from Canada* with the "Can't" underlined for emphasis. Fresh-Wes makes a signifying move that opens up a number of ways that we might think about a trans-national or diasporic blackness. First, his insistence that the "kid can't be from Canada" is a disruption of the idea that the "dopest" rap songs can only be performed by African-Americans. Fresh-Wes takes a shot at ethnic absolutist notions which attempt to historicize rap as an African-American invention and thus write black Atlantic exchanges out of rap's historical narratives. As well, he made it clear that his relationship to Canada was at best ambivalent (and possibly non-existent) — he left the nation. On the other hand, "naaah this kid can't be from Canada" could be Fresh-Wes' response to the discourses of nation that continually position his black body outside of Canada. Geneva Smitherman[31] argues that the role of double negatives is important in black speech patterns as an indication of the affirmative, thus Fresh-Wes' "Naaah" and "Can't" represent an assertion of national identity: in this way he worries the category Canadian.

The location of his new home is also important. Because while it might represent his desire to be marketed by the forces of American capital that could expose him globally in ways that Canadian capital cannot, he's located in a city of nomads, and, in particular, black migrant peoples. His movement symbolically suggests that black allegiances to "nation" are contingent upon the ethical practices of state administrators and narratives of the nation. This is neither a nomadic politics of play nor an example of the anthropological, colonialist idea of the exotic nomad, wandering and wild; but rather a disruption, contemplatively so, of the modernist nation-state. "Home is not where the heart is": it's where the self might be differently desired, imagined, lived and experienced.

Fresh-Wes' flight south reconfigures yet another myth of Canada's racial past. Yes, slaves from the U.S. fled north to Canada, "land of the free." But Canada's racial forgetfulness *has* resulted in a Canadian articulation of blackness that can sometimes seek, and desire to work with, a form of racism that speaks its name differently in the south (the form of

American racism that does not mask itself as benevolent). Ironically the work of Canadian literary critic Frank Davey,[32] which announces the "post-national" state, still locates the discussion of nation within the confines of Canada's modernist growing pains — it's the kind of two solitudes analysis (the English/French dualities and tensions) that does not begin to get at the ways in which the work of Other Canadians, some of whom he reads, creates too much dissonance for talk of nation to be heard.

As I suggested earlier, diasporic cultures can teach us much about the demise (or at the least the troubling of the category) of the nation-state. Like Davey, Canada's well-known postmodern theorist Linda Hutcheon,[33] in an attempt to demonstrate how Other Canadians ironically split the image of what is Canadian, creates a number of readings that do not allow for the ways in which the Others of the Canadian imaginary find themselves both inside and outside the nation. Hutcheon reads the work of Dionne Brand, for instance, alongside Italian poets, positioning all of them as producers of homogenized ironic "immigrant" works that split the category Canadian. Yet one is left with no sense of how the histories of those who seem not to be able to live out or perform the discourses of whiteness are differently incorporated into the nation and thus possess divergent "immigrant" histories. Even progressive critics like Davey and Hutcheon, those who are willing to announce the collapse of the modernist nation as we know it, seem unable to read in complex and engaging ways the histories of those whom Gilroy[34] has termed the "counterculture of modernity," or who I call the "pre-postmodern postmodern voyagers."

The contemporary politics of race and nation in Canada, to echo M.G. Vasanji, represents "no new land." However, the promise remains: "the fighting back" of the Somalis and rap artists alike might reconfigure, remap and chart a notion of nation as a new land not concerned with narratives of geographic and textual boundaries but a nation that is constituted through the practices of justice, ethical politics and progressive race relations.

ENDNOTES

1. Deleuze and Guattari, *Capitalism and Schizophrenia*, 28.
2. Gilroy, "Cultural Studies and Ethnic Absolutism." Gilroy first used the term "black Atlantic" in this essay as a way of making sense of black cultural and political exchanges and resisting ethnic claims concerning black intellectual contributions. See Gilroy, *Black Atlantic*. The black Atlantic is developed conceptually and theoretically as an expansive space that traverses time, history, memory and the workings of black, and in particular black metropolitan, communities' cultural practices. I use the term after Gilroy to reference the importance of black diasporic cultures, practices of exchange, and dialogues, and how those patterns might structure local politics and trans-national politics. I do not use black Atlantic as a way to essentialize blackness across space and time.
3. Edward Kamau Brathwaite, "The African Presence in Caribbean Literature." Brathwaite argues and demonstrates through a reading of Paula Marshall's *Praisesong for the Widow* that African elements in Caribbean literature are important moments of not only acknowledgement of an African past but of a desire and a practice of what he calls reconnection. I think that Brathwaite's insight can be usefully extended to other syncretic, artistic "new world" black practices like film, fine art, dance and music.
4. Clearly, Palestinian claims to parts of the territory of Israel complicate the question of Israel as a nation-state. However, without denying that important history, I am attempting to gesture to the fluidity of the origins of the Israeli nation-state and to address some of the contemporary "problems" that have accompanied claims to the nation-state outside of Palestinian demands.

5. Anderson, *Imagined Communities.*

6. Ibid.

7. Bhabha, "Introduction: Narrating the Nation."

8. Chatterjee, *The Nation and Its Fragments.*

9. I borrow this term from Roxana Ng, "Multiculturalism as Ideology."

10. Canadian Multicultural Act; Federal Multicultural Policy.

11. Bissoondath, *Selling Illusions.* This is the Canadian equivalent to the American conservative cultural agenda. While Bissoondath's critique of multiculturalism is generally warranted, he too is tied to notions of Canada and thus nation as fundamentally dualistic. He can perceive of no way beyond the dichotomous bind other than to suggest taking on either the "culture" of Quebec or Anglo Canadians. He believes the former has a more secure sense of self and is thus exemplary. His approach harks back to the modernist nation-state narrative of one unified people when he argues that only Quebecers know their culture and thus they should be the model that is used to renew Canada as a viable nation-state. Such assertions seem to advocate a cultural imperialism of the worst kind, one which has been generally applauded by the mainstream media.

12. For an extensive discussion of these institutions see M. Nourbese Philip, "The 'Multicultural' Whitewash: Racism in Ontario's Art Funding System."

13. Joseph, *Oral/Trans/Missions.*

14. I use "signifying" here in the way that H.L. Gates Jr., in *The Signifying Monkey*, uses it: to denote the African-American practice of black diasporic practices of double-voicing, revision of dominant meanings, and other ways of inverting meaning so as to not only act as a form of resistance but to also pass on information that only those intimate with the culture or those who are subtle cultural readers might understand.

15. Snead, "Repetition as a Figure of Black Culture."

16. Morrison, *Playing in the Dark.*

17. Boyce-Davies, *Black Women, Writing and Identity.* Boyce-Davies engages in a theoretical discussion of the "elsewhereness" of diasporic sensibilities as important to black women's writing and black cultural politics in general.

18. Allen, *Revolutionary Tea Party* and *Women Do This Everyday: Selected Poems of Lillian Allen.* In the preface to her selected poems Allen writes of having to "finalize" poems for the page, poems she had never thought of as final. The process of finalization evokes the tensions between the oral and the written and the performativity of both in her work.

19. See Dionne Brand's numerous collections of poetry, in particular *No Language Is Neutral* and *Winter Epigrams & Epigrams to Ernesto Cardenal in Defence of Claudia.* On Maestro Fresh-Wes' most recent album, his hypercommentary on Canada, the track titled "Certs Wid Out Da Retsyn," might be read as Canada's attempt to deny colour at its centre; the Dream Warriors, on their first album *And Now the Legacy Begins*, have a track titled "Ludi" in which they name almost every Caribbean island as well as Canadian localities as an indication of who and what they are.

20. Soyinka, "The African World and the Ethnocultural Debate." I want to suggest that some articulations of Afrocentrism produce the pastoral romantic Africa or the Africa of kings and queens; some of the work that I am discussing is not immune from such discourses but I have focused on the fluid tracks as a way of demonstrating what I believe to be the undeniable relations of diasporic groups.

21. Capital Records-EMI of Canada.

22. Sharrif, "Highrise Divide" and "Somali dust-up with guards sparks riot." A television documentary on the Dixon Road controversy aired on *The Journal* on the CBC. Some of my information is based on that documentary.

24. Ibid.

25. Saenger, "Somalia's Welfare Warlords." The author of the article is at great pains to point out how widespread welfare fraud is among Somalis but is only able to offer evidence of two convictions. Saenger then proceeds to implicate Nigerian immigrants in past welfare fraud but produces no evidence. Much of the article is concerned with locating exactly where Somalis are living in Canada, almost as if to suggest that they need not be here at all.

26. I use "blackening" here to point to a process or practice of racialization. Important, however, are the ways in which that process might be performed by those who are at once named as black and at the same time use it as the basis of their counter-hegemonic discourse. J. Butler (*Bodies That Matter*) suggests that the way in which performativity works is that it puts a discourse into practice. Thus blackness/black as categories only become intelligible when the discourses that constitute them are acted out either as relations of subordination or as practices of (re)fashioning the self.

27. Bhabha, "DissemiNation: Time, Narrative and the Margins of the Modern Nation."

28. The epistemology of racism runs deep in the battle. The introduction of dogs into the picture draws heavily on racialized imagery of black people's supposed fear of dogs. Islamic practices concerning dogs, and in particular dog bites, can cause great trauma for any "good" practising Muslim, and this complicates things further. The owners insist on employing guards with dogs despite a task force report recommendation that suggested the guard force itself was unnecessary since no major crime problem exists. In fact, crime apparently decreased when the Somalis arrived. In the most recent battle, the underlying sexual stereotype of aggressive black males has surfaced: white neighbours claim that they cannot send their daughters for groceries because "youth" (read black males) are hanging around outside the store.

29. In the CBC documentary the camera idles for quite some time on the T-shirt of one outspoken youth. The significance of his T-shirt is that the words "Malcolm X" adorn the front.

30. Sharrif, "Highrise Divide."

31. Smitherman, *Talkin and Testifyin.*

32. Davey, *Post-national Arguments.*

33. Hutcheon, *Splitting Images.*

34. Ibid.

REFERENCES

Allen, L. *Revolutionary Tea Party.* Toronto: Verse to Vinyl Records, 1985.

———. *Women Do This Everyday: Selected Poems of Lillian Allen.* Toronto: Women's Press, 1993.

Anderson, B. *Imagined Communities: Reflections on the Origin and Spread of Nationalism.* London: Verso, 1983.

Bhabha, H. "Introduction: Narrating the Nation"; "DissemiNation: Time, Narrative and the Margins of the Modern Nation." In *Nation and Narrations,* ed. H. Bhabha. London: Routledge, 1990.

Bissoondath, N. *Selling Illusions: The Cult of Multiculturalism in Canada.* Toronto: Penguin Books, 1994.

Boyce-Davies, C. *Black Women, Writing and Identity: Migrations of the Subject.* New York: Routledge, 1994.

Brand, D. *No Language Is Neutral.* Toronto: Coach House Press, 1990.

Brathwaite, K. "The African Presence in Caribbean Literature." In *Roots.* Ann Arbor, Mich.: University of Michigan Press, 1993.

Butler, J. *Bodies That Matter: On the Discursive Limits of "Sex."* New York: Routledge, 1990.

Canadian Multicultural Act. House of Commons Canada, 1988.

Chatterjee, P. *The Nation and Its Fragments: Colonial and Postcolonial Histories.* Princeton, N.J.: Princeton University Press, 1993.

Davey, F. *Post-national Arguments: The Politics of the Anglophone-Canadian Novel Since 1967.* Toronto: University of Toronto Press, 1993.

Deleuze, G., and F. Guattari. *Capitalism and Schizophrenia: A Thousand Plateaus,* trans. B. Massumi. Minneapolis: University of Minnesota, 1987.

Dream Warriors. *And Now the Legacy Begins.* Scarborough, Ont.: Island Records, 1991.

Gates, H.L. *The Signifying Monkey: A Theory of African-American Criticism.* Cambridge: Oxford University Press, 1988.

Gilroy, P. "Cultural Studies and Ethnic Absolutism." In *Cultural Studies,* ed. Lawrence Grossberg et al. New York: Routledge, 1992.

———. *The Black Atlantic: Modernity and Double Consciousness.* Cambridge: Harvard University Press, 1993.

Hutcheon, L. *Splitting Images: Contemporary Canadian Ironies.* Toronto: Oxford University Press, 1991.

Joseph, C. "Pimps"; "A Chant for Monk 3." *Oral/Trans/Missions.* Toronto: Verse to Vinyl Records, 1989.

Maestro Fresh-Wes. *Naaah, Dis Kid <u>Can't</u> Be from Canada.* Toronto: Attic Records, 1994.

Morrison, T. *Playing in the Dark: Whiteness and the Literary Imagination.* Cambridge, Mass.: Harvard University Press, 1992.

Philip, M. Nourbese, "The 'Multicultural' Whitewash: Racism in Ontario's Art Funding System." In *Frontiers: Essays and Writings on Racism and Culture.* Stratford, Ont.: Mercury Press, 1992.

Saenger, E. "Somalia's Welfare Warlords." *Western Report,* 8 November 1993.

Sharrif, A. "Highrise Divide." *Now Magazine* (Toronto), 1993.

———. "Somali dust-up with guards sparks riot." *Now Magazine* (Toronto), 1994.

Smitherman, G. *Talkin and Testifyin: The Language of Black America.* Detroit: Wayne State University, 1977.

Snead, J. "Repetition as a Figure of Black Culture." In *Out There: Marginalization and Contemporary Cultures,* ed. R. Ferguson, M. Gever, T. Minh-ha, and C. West. New York: New Museum of Contemporary Art and MIT Press, 1990.

Soyinka, W. "The African World and the Ethnocultural Debate." In *African Culture: The Rhythms of Unity,* ed. M.K. Asante and K.W. Asante. Trenton, N.J.: Africa New World Press, 1990.

CAPITULATING TO BARBARISM

A Case Study of Jazz

and/as Popular Culture

Ajay Heble

"Anyone who allows the growing respectability of mass culture to seduce him into equating a popular song with modern art because of a few false notes squeaked by a clarinet, anyone who mistakes a triad studded with 'dirty notes' for atonality," says Theodor Adorno in his notorious denunciation of jazz, "has already capitulated to barbarism" (205). Adorno's attack on jazz, his insistence that "the much announced rebelliousness and originality of jazz is just a stylistic trick developed by the culture industry in order to sell more product" (Tester, 44), is, of course, part of his well-known critique of mass culture or, to use the phrase that Adorno and fellow Frankfurt School member Max Horkheimer would themselves come to prefer, of the culture industry. Concerned with what happens when art gets turned into a "species of commodity ... marketable and interchangeable like an industrial product" (Adorno and Horkheimer, 158), Adorno saw the industrialization of culture as the "means by which capitalism could erase any possibility of opposition and thus of social change" (Fiske, "Popular Culture," 324).

Marxists such as Adorno were not, of course, alone in their attacks on mass culture. Similar critiques of mass production and lookings-back to pre-industrial community-based arts initiatives can also be found in F.R. Leavis and Denys Thompson's traditionalist lament for organic communities in their 1933 book *Culture and Environment*. Interestingly, Canadian culture, during the heyday of nationalist consciousness in the sixties and seventies, would be contextualized in strikingly analogous terms, "represented readily," as one critic has put it, "as an organic 'lived tradition' facing extinction at the hands of a commercially-produced and technologically dominated American mass culture" (Gruneau, 15).

The publication in 1996 of Geoff Pevere and Greig Dymond's *Mondo Canuck: A Canadian Pop Culture Odyssey* may well mark a pivotal point in the development of popular culture analysis in Canada. Its main argument, that Canada is every bit as distinct in its approach to popular culture as it is to high art "and that the former may indeed reveal vastly more of a national distinction than the latter" (x), makes possible a significant recasting of our traditional understanding of some of the key theoretical, social, and political issues at stake in the study of popular culture in Canada. Indeed, if, as Naomi Klein suggests in her endorsement on the book's back cover, *Mondo Canuck* is the "first work to take Canadian culture seriously enough to trash some national treasures and dig the treasures out of the nation's trash," then the force of the book resides not only in its insistence that we attend to hitherto neglected cultural activity, but also in its attempt to move us beyond the kind of limiting analyses of the popular that have tended to dominate Canadian cultural criticism. While the nationalist arguments I mentioned earlier often assumed "that Canadian culture was not yet a capitalist mass culture" and thus that "it was necessary to defend local popular cultural forms and other indigenous cultural initiatives against the homogenizing commercial forces centred south of the 49th parallel" (Gruneau, 16), the emphases, as *Mondo Canuck* illustrates, have now shifted: "If one *does* begin," say Pevere and Dymond, "to think about Canada in terms of the pop culture it produces, both nationally and internationally, one not only begins to move away from the us-verses-them national-victimhood model of the past, one in fact starts to see something so different as to be strikingly so" (x).

Indeed, *Mondo Canuck*, at least in part, forces us to recognize the inadequacy of conceptual frameworks that theorize popular culture either, as was evident in some nationalist Canadian models, as a site of indigenist resistance to *someone else's* standardized and mass-produced culture or, as Adorno and the mass culture theorists would have it, as the very "culture of subordination that massifies or commodifies people into the victimized dupes of capitalism" (Fiske, *Reading the Popular,* 7). In an important essay introducing the volume *Popular Culture and Social Relations*, Tony Bennett, taking his lead from Antonio Gramsci, tells us that popular culture "consists not simply of an imposed mass culture that is coincident with dominant ideology, nor simply of spontaneously oppositional cultures, but is rather an arena of negotiation between the two within which — in different particular types of popular culture — dominant, subordinate and oppositional cultural and ideological values and elements are 'mixed' in different permutations" (xv–xvi). What I'd like to do in this essay, as the remarks from Adorno with which I began have perhaps already suggested, is to open up questions about the place of jazz in debates about popular culture.

Long touted as a resistant form whose nose-thumbing at bourgeois culture has inspired a wide range of oppositional artistic practices (think, for example, of Jack Kerouac and the Beat Movement or of John Coltrane's relationship to the Black Nationalist Movement), jazz, as even its fiercest admirers have recently been forced to concede, has been assimilated "within the logic of our culture's economy … with the emergence of new interest in its archives by the Sony Corporation, with the successful development of major journals such as *Jazz Times*, and mostly with the remarkable resurgence of jazz recordings by means of the compact disc revolution" (Merod, 4). Jacques Attali, in his book *Noise: The Political Economy of Music*, suggests that music became a commodity when a broad market for popular music was "produced by the colonization of black music by the American industrial apparatus" (103). Is jazz, then, as thoroughly standardized and commercialized as Adorno would have it? And how, precisely, ought we to theorize jazz in relation to the politics of the popular? Is jazz popular music or high art? Can an essay on jazz properly be said to belong in a volume on popular culture, especially a volume on *Canadian* popular culture? Or does the fraught nature of jazz's very relation to the popular itself unsettle our traditional assumptions about "proper" forms of cultural belonging?

In gesturing towards some, however provisional, attempts to address these questions, I want, by way of example, to look at a small-scale Canadian jazz festival that I (as artistic director) founded along with some friends and fellow jazz enthusiasts in the city of Guelph in 1994. Having recently completed its fourth year of operation, the Guelph Jazz Festival has, in the words of Mark Miller in the *Globe and Mail*, "already established a striking personality of its own" for its innovative programming ("Good beat"). While this is not the place to detail the history of the festival or even to document its substantial growth and evolving national and international reputation, I want to suggest that this small, localized Canadian example offers a highly resonant site not only for thinking through jazz's relation to the popular, but also, by way of revisiting some of the issues addressed by Adorno and Leavis, for raising pressing questions about the efficacy and the sustainability, not to mention the value, of small-scale, community-based, volunteer-run arts organizations.

The Guelph Jazz Festival, as Miller points out in his review of its 1996 season, has successfully managed to make a virtue of its smallness: "It's small and proud of it. In a field where bigger is generally held to be better, Guelph offers convincing evidence to the contrary" ("Good beat"). Heralded as "the best small jazz festival in Canada" by internationally acclaimed, award-winning saxophonist Jane Bunnett, the festival has, from its very inception, sought to present innovative and leading-edge performers of jazz and creative improvised music in the context of a small, community-based setting. Therein, precisely, lies the rub — innovative world-class music in a community setting — and, in the context of a consideration of jazz as a popular art form, the Guelph Jazz Festival, I want to argue, makes a fitting object for case study.

On the surface, there would appear to be very little of the popular in the festival's choice (indeed, *my* choice as artistic director) of programming. Artists such as Pauline Oliveros, Myra Melford, Amina Claudine Myers, Gerry Hemingway, Lee Pui Ming, David Mott, Ned Rothenberg, and Mark Feldman — all important innovators whose recordings and performances push the boundaries of the genre we traditionally call "jazz" — are certainly not household names; nor is their often-challenging music likely, at least in most contexts, to appeal to large numbers of an uninitiated public. What, then, is the festival's relation to the popular arts, and in what ways, if any, might the festival's activities be seen to participate in what Adorno saw as the commodification of increasingly large sectors of artistic culture?

Jazz itself, according to a number of critics, is the music of the people. Sidney Finkelstein, in his appropriately titled *Jazz: A People's Music*, suggests that jazz "reasserts the fact that music is something people do as well as listen to; that art is not to be limited to a specialized profession, but should be in the possession of everybody" (27). Eric Hobsbawm, one of the leading historians of our generation, says that jazz, "one of the most significant phenomena of twentieth-century world culture" (xxiv), "has become, in more or less diluted form, *the* basic language of modern dance and popular music in urban and industrial civilizations, in most places where it has been allowed to penetrate." He continues: "The social history of the twentieth century arts will contain only a footnote or two about Scottish Highland music or gypsy lore, but it will have to deal at some length with the vogue for jazz" (xliv). In Guelph, the vogue for jazz, as I hope to suggest in a moment, is peculiar indeed, reflecting the fact, perhaps, that, as Hobsbawm goes on to say, jazz "has developed not only into the basic idiom of popular music but also towards something like an elaborate and sophisticated art music, seeking both to merge with, and to rival, the established art music of the Western world" (xliv–xlv).

Jazz, then, may well be the musical genre *par excellence* that breaks down received distinctions between popular culture and high art: "Jazz, of course, is a minority music," write Stuart Hall and Paddy Whannel. "But it is popular," they say, concurring with Finkelstein, "in the sense of being of *the people*" (73). Like the blues, argue Hall and Whannel, jazz is a popular music "not because millions sang or knew [it], but because [it] grew out of a common experience, an experience central to the life of a whole people, which they transposed into art" (92). They also point out that "one of the great — perhaps tragic — characteristics of the modern age has been the progressive alienation of high art from popular art. Few art forms are able to hold both elements together: and popular art has developed a history and a topography of its own, separate from high and experimental art" (84). It is in this context that an analysis of the Guelph Jazz Festival might be instructive, for the festival has been highly successful in introducing innovative musicians — musicians who, in other contexts, might be seen not as popular artists but as proponents of an élitist high culture — to wider audiences and, as per its mandate, in enlarging the constituency traditionally defined as a jazz audience. When avant-bop percussionist Gerry Hemingway (well known in jazz circles for his work with Anthony Braxton's legendary quartet) performed a solo recital during the 1996 edition of the festival, he played to a sold-out and highly attentive audience that ranged in age from young children to seniors, an audience that, as one reviewer noted, "would have kept [Hemingway] there all night if they could have, judging from the enthusiastic response he generated" (Bali). The fact that such an innovative artist — indeed, Hemingway's was, perhaps, the most challenging concert we presented during the '96 festival — played to such a wide-ranging and appreciative audience — most of whose members had likely never heard of Hemingway before — tells us something about the festival's success in transgressing the traditional boundaries between high art and popular culture.

One way, therefore, in which the Guelph Jazz Festival has maintained its links with the popular is by participating in the dismantling of the time-honoured popular culture/high art divide. In fact, the festival's relation to the popular is perhaps best defined not so much in terms of the specific artists or their performances (artists who, again, would traditionally be categorized as practitioners of high art), but rather through the complex ways in which these artists and performances are presented to and received by a public. If, as popular culture theorist John Fiske writes, "popular culture is always in process … its meanings can never be identified in a text [or performance], for texts [including performances] are activated, or made meaningful, only in social relations and in intertextual relations" (*Reading the Popular,* 3), then an understanding of the festival's popularity needs to be predicated on a consideration of the social conditions under which performances take place and are received: what, for example, are the demographics of the audience, and in what ways might those demographics shape or determine our understanding of a performance's public relevance? Relevance, after all, says Fiske, "is central to popular culture, for it minimizes the difference between text and life, between the aesthetic and the everyday that is so central to a process- and practice-based culture (such as the popular) rather than a text- or performance-based one (such as the bourgeois highbrow one)" (*Reading the Popular,* 6). Material considerations such as ticket prices and the size and nature of the venue, factors such as the marketing strategies used to promote a performance, and decisions about how to signal corporate sponsorship and involvement — these are just some of the considerations that are likely to have an impact on how we construe the Guelph Jazz Festival's relation to the popular.

Also critical to our analysis of the festival as a manifestation of the popular arts is an understanding of the community-based nature of the event. One of the difficulties we, as organizers of the festival, have been facing has to do with how best to negotiate between, on the one hand, an artistic mandate that has as one of its key features the promotion of innovative forms of musical expression and, on the other, a strong commitment to remaining a community-based festival. How, that is, do we continue to present and promote what we see as being the most compelling forms of jazz and creative improvised music without, in our relatively small community, running the risk, say, of alienating audience members who might prefer more traditional forms of jazz? Indeed, there are always *some* audience members who are quite offended by the "more challenging" music. And, if the festival's popularity depends to a large extent on its continuing efforts to preserve links with the community, then what, specifically, ought to be the role of the local in determining the festival's activities?

Let me try to be more precise about why I think that the festival needs to be seen as a community-based event. From its very beginnings, the festival has insisted that its activities be affordable in ways that the activities, say, of the other two (more established) music festivals in the city (the Guelph Spring Festival and the Hillside Festival) have not always been. To this end, we have remained committed to presenting world-class artists at remarkably low ticket prices (Hemingway tickets, for example, were only five dollars) and to staging several free concerts throughout the festival, including a series of outdoor concerts in a centrally located public space in the downtown core. Indeed, our use, for the most part, of popular public spaces — outdoor squares, cinemas, churches, university campus courtyards — rather than traditional concert halls has much to do with the festival's rootedness in the community.

Another of the festival's key links to the community involves the jazz performed in many of the city's restaurants and clubs, and therein lies the tale of the local. In his essay "Local Jazz," James Lincoln Collier remarks that while "[j]azz criticism and jazz history have always concentrated on the big names, the stars, and the famous clubs and dance halls where they worked … in fact, perhaps ninety percent of the music has always been made by unknown players working in local bars and clubs for audiences drawn from the surrounding neighbourhood, town, and country" (997). Says Collier, "there are thousands of towns in which the appearance of a star jazz musician is a rare event, but that offer local jazz bands on a weekly basis" (999). The role that these local musicians play in helping to define jazz as a popular art form cannot be underestimated. As Collier notes, "Big city music clubs today charge customers as much as twenty-five dollars admission" (1004), while the local players, by contrast, work in places that, at least in the context of Guelph's festival, have either no coverage charge or a very modest one. Insofar as the local musicians perform at venues that are readily accessible to those whose financial constraints might prevent them from purchasing tickets to main-stage concerts, there might be said to be something genuinely oppositional at work here, something that, at least in terms of what Attali calls music's political economy, might, however modestly, contribute to an effort to resist dominant processes of commodification. In terms of the larger artistic design of the Guelph Jazz Festival, however, when seen, that is, in relation to the innovative main-stage artists, the local artists who perform in the clubs and restaurants might be said to embody — to adapt Stuart Hall and Paddy Whannel's formulation — "the *substructure* of the popular" (82) in the overall context of a festival of high seriousness.

Now, lest I be misunderstood, let me make it clear here that I am not wanting to reinforce any easy distinction between local artists as popular and main-stage artists as high art, largely, as I've been arguing, because the festival's attempts to intervene in the ways in which notions of the popular are negotiated and determined complicate any such binary distinction. Nevertheless, audiences attending the Guelph Jazz Festival in search of traditional forms of jazz are more likely to find what they are expecting in the clubs than at the main-stage concerts. In other words, if access to widespread public appeal needs to be seen as a criterion for measuring the festival's links to the popular, then the participation of the local artists ensures the festival's success even as it runs the risk of compromising the nature and scope of the festival's mandate to alter the forces that have traditionally governed the reception of innovative forms of musical expression.

I'd like, for a moment, to return to Adorno here. When Adorno attacks jazz, saying that "[w]hat enthusiastically stunted innocence sees as the jungle is actually factory-made through and through, even when ... spontaneity is publicized as a featured attraction" (202), he is responding in part to what he sees as the standardization of jazz. For him, this means "the strengthening of the lasting domination of the listening public and of their conditioned reflexes. They are expected to want only that to which they have become accustomed and to become enraged whenever their expectations are disappointed and fulfillment, which they regard as the customer's inalienable right, is denied" (202). Adorno's comments, I think, speak directly to the Guelph Jazz Festival's struggle to sustain a meaningful balance between innovation and tradition. If the wide-ranging and appreciative audience at our innovative main-stage events can be read as a measure of our success in being able to attract and cultivate listeners who think about, reflect on, are challenged by, and learn from what they have heard, rather than an audience that routinely accepts the music as a form of conventional entertainment, then the audiences who attend the more traditional events in the local clubs and restaurants are more likely to have their expectations, their desires to achieve standardized levels of musical coherence, fulfilled. What, then, is the festival's position vis-à-vis the debates that have evolved around the theories of popular culture? While, at one level, its attempt to present innovative music to new audiences has enabled the festival to participate in a dismantling of the received distinctions between popular culture and high art, at another level the very division of its events into a main-stage/local club structure forces it to fall back on the very distinctions it has worked to unsettle.

Mark Miller, this time in his *Globe and Mail* review of the 1997 edition of the festival, remarks astutely on what he sees as the gap between the main-stage events and the community-based nature of the festival. "In just four short years," he says, "the Guelph Jazz Festival has gone from a small, community event to something, rather, well, grander. The community aspect of the Festival is still apparent, what with performances by local musicians in several of the city's night spots and a free, outdoor concert ... in St. George's square downtown. At the same time," he continues, "the festival ... has mounted an increasingly impressive series of concerts by important international figures." The contrast between these two aspects of the festival interests Miller: "The result is almost a set of parallel festivals, one of mainstream jazz for passersby and the other of contemporary music for a more daring audience. The distinction between the two," he concludes, "can only grow as the festival continues to attract notice outside the immediate Guelph area with the venturesome side of its programming, inevitably drawing even more listeners for whom the rest of the music will hold little interest" ("Guelph features").

Indeed, the festival *has* attracted significant attention outside the community, both in terms of its growing international media profile and in terms, as Miller says, of the people who come from afar (British Columbia, Alberta, California) to attend its events, and who, as we continue to point out in our fundraising applications to the city, bring their dollars into our community. This attention has, I should add, certainly generated a buzz: the city's merchants do a booming business during the festival, and, indeed, a prominent downtown restaurant owner has told us that the jazz festival weekend in September is his busiest weekend of the year. Surely, then, this "buzz" says something about the festival's relation to the popular, its rootedness in the community. But Miller's point is that the gap between the innovative mainstage artists and the community-based (read: popular) local performers will only grow as the festival attracts wider notice, that in effect we are really running two festivals, one featuring high art for an international audience and the other featuring popular local artists for the immediate community. Am I misguided, then, in wanting to reinvigorate our understanding of the popular social function of an innovative music festival? Am I wrong to insist that, even with its progressive artistic mandate, the festival can stay rooted in the community?

I want to continue to think that the festival's activities, as well as the nature and scope of its overall structure, illustrate the problematic nature of the high-art/popular-culture model endorsed by Adorno and members of the Frankfurt School. The case of the local artists suggests, in fact, that popular culture is not, as Adorno would have had it, monolithic, that it can in some contexts be emancipatory even as it reinforces standardization and reasserts dominant models of knowledge production and consumption. I'd also like to point to the need to move beyond (while genuinely learning from) Adorno's model into modes of analysis that, as Pevere and Dymond's *Mondo Canuck* may tentatively begin to show us, can apply analogous and equally rigorous critical methods to a range of different cultural activities. The Guelph Jazz Festival, with its own range of events, offers a unique site for precisely this kind of critical work, not only because it confronts head-on questions about jazz as a popular art form, but also because its very structure as a volunteer-based organization is of interest. Attali is, of course, right when he tells us that music "has become a commodity, a means of producing money. It is sold and consumed" (37). And jazz, as many have pointed out, has perforce become part of that very process of commodification. Yet there is something about a small, volunteer-run jazz festival that attempts, even if in highly complex and overdetermined ways, to stay rooted in the community that makes it seem, if not preindustrial or, to use Leavis's favoured term, organic, then at least somehow to be resisting entry into the economy of labour. For its first four years, the festival has managed to operate on the basis of volunteer commitment and direct local organization, resisting, wherever possible, forms of corporatization. But as Stuart Hall and Paddy Whannel point out in their assessment of Leavis's nostalgia for organic communities, while it may be important "to resist unnecessary increases in scale and to re-establish local initiatives where we can ... if we wish to re-create a genuine popular culture we must seek out the points of growth within the society that now exists" (39). With evolving popularity, as the Guelph Jazz Festival has seen, come growing pains and increased budgets. The key question confronting festival organizers as I write seems to focus on the extent to which the sustainability of our grass-roots ideology may be in jeopardy when the festival ceases to be a volunteer-run organization, when it is forced, in short, to enter into an economy of labour.

REFERENCES

Adorno, Theodor. "Perennial Fashion — Jazz," trans. Samuel and Shierry Weber. In *Cultural Theory and Society: A Reader,* ed. Stephen Eric Bronner and Douglas MacKay Kellner, 199–209. New York: Routledge, 1989.

Adorno, Theodor, and Max Horkheimer. *Dialectic of Enlightenment,* trans. John Cumming. New York: Herder and Herder, 1972.

Attali, Jacques. *Noise: The Political Economy of Music,* trans. Brian Massumi. Minneapolis: University of Minnesota Press, 1985.

Bali, Paul. "Drums, drums, and more drums at this year's Guelph Jazz Festival." *Ontarion,* 10 September 1996: 20.

Bennett, Tony. "Introduction: Popular Culture and 'the turn to Gramsci." In *Popular Culture and Social Relations,* ed. Tony Bennett, Colin Mercer, and Janet Woollacott, xi–xix. Milton Keynes: Open University Press, 1986.

Collier, James Lincoln. "Local Jazz." In *Reading Jazz: A Gathering of Autobiography, Reportage, and Criticism from 1919 to Now,* ed. Robert Gottlieb, 997–1005. New York: Pantheon, 1996.

Finkelstein, Sidney. *Jazz: A People's Music.* New York: DeCapo, 1975.

Fiske, John. "Popular Culture." In *Critical Terms for Literary Study,* ed. Frank Lentricchia and Thomas McLaughlin, 321–35. 2nd ed. Chicago: University of Chicago Press, 1995.

———. *Reading the Popular.* London: Routledge, 1989.

Gruneau, Richard. "Introduction: Notes on Popular Cultures and Political Practices."In *Popular Cultures and Political Practices,* ed. Richard Gruneau, 11–32. Toronto: Garamond, 1988.

Hall, Stuart, and Paddy Whannel. *The Popular Arts.* New York: Pantheon, 1965.

Hobsbawm, Eric. *The Jazz Scene.* New York: Pantheon, 1993.

Leavis, F.R., and Denys Thompson. *Culture and Environment.* 1933; London: Chatto and Windus, 1960.

Merod, Jim. "Jazz as a Cultural Archive." *boundary 2* 22 (Summer 1995): 1–18.

Miller, Mark. "Good beat at tiny perfect festival." *Globe and Mail,* 9 September 1996: C4.

———. "Guelph features all that jazz." *Globe and Mail,* 8 September 1997: C4.

Pevere, Geoff, and Greig Dymond. *Mondo Canuck: A Canadian Pop Culture Odyssey.* Scarborough, Ont.: Prentice Hall, 1996.

Tester, Keith. *Media, Culture and Morality.* London: Routledge, 1994.

MURDER INK

Detective Fiction in Canada

Priscilla L. Walton

At a recent meeting of the Ottawa chapter of Sisters in Crime, one member (the co-owner and operator of Prime Crime, Ottawa's crime and mystery fiction bookstore) recalled how numerous customers enter her shop and inquire about the availability of Canadian crime fiction. Invariably, she watches the surprise cross their faces when she points them towards the shelves of Canadian detective novels. I begin with this story, not to illustrate the lack of publicity that Canadian mystery writers garner in this country (although that is a crucial issue), but to emphasize how Canadianicity is erased from histories of crime fiction, an erasure that results in a public largely unfamiliar with Canadian interventions into this genre. One need only flip through the 400 pages–plus of David Skene-Melvin's *Canadian Crime Fiction* to attest to the fact that — yes, Virginia — there is Canadian mystery writing, and there's lots of it. Nonetheless, as Rinaldo Walcott has suggested, a fact is not a fact until it is publicly acknowledged as such,[1] and the "fact" that Canadian crime writers exist and flourish seems not yet to have registered in the Canadian cultural consciousness.

Canadians have been writing detective fiction virtually since its inception. Indeed, another fact that often escapes public notice is the nationality of Ross MacDonald, a Canadian who was one of the progenitors of the "hard-boiled" school — that most American mode of mystery writing. Even more neglected is the fact that MacDonald took up mystery writing after his interest was sparked by the success of his partner, Margaret Millar (another Canadian), with the genre. This double-edged paradigm (i.e., the erasure of MacDonald's Canadian citizenship and the virtual eradication of Margaret Millar's name from the annals of the mystery genre) appears to influence and play out in later exemplars of the genre, for it is only recently that Canadians as *Canadians* have begun to make their mark in crime fiction. Perhaps because writers like MacDonald were perceived as American, contemporary writers tend to foreground Canadianicity in their texts. And, since many of these writers are women, Millar's fate may provide further impetus for the novelistic emphasis on gender, both the authors' own and that of their protagonists. Whatever the reason, much Canadian detective fiction focuses on explicitly Canadian inversions of known detective tropes, which are often further subverted by the highlighting of alternative gender roles.

Among the first Canadians to attract widespread attention were Eric Wright and Howard Engel. Wright's protagonist, Inspector Charlie Salter of the Toronto Police Department, frequently investigates crimes in academic settings. Engel's Benny Cooperman has captured the imagination of the international crime scene. Cooperman, a Jewish private investigator (PI) from a thinly disguised St. Catharines (called "Grantham" in the novels), effects an alternative to representations of the American private eye. Cooperman's signature food order — chopped egg on white bread, with a glass of milk — is, as Manina Jones has suggested, an apt metaphor for the counter-construction of the Canadian hard-boiled[2] (which, as Cooperman's metaphoric order implies, is not quite soft-boiled but rather "chopped"). Moreover, Cooperman walks the "genial" streets of a small town (in contrast to Raymond Chandler's construction of the "mean streets" of the urban city), and his operative strategies regularly perform as subversive inversions of American precedents.

While the American hard-boiled infuses its contents with a tough and macho edge, Cooperman's texts use their homegrown setting to different effect. In *Dead and Buried,* Benny and an informer are dragged off to Lake Ontario by Mafia thugs for what presumably will be an unpleasant death. Before his body is tossed into the lake, however, Benny is saved by the bell, or rather the voice of an old friend:

> I tried to see what there was out in the harbour that might still have life aboard this late in the season. I couldn't detect a thing. I should stick to tracing oil-company receipts.
>
> "Benny! What are you doing here?" It was a voice from behind us. A woman's nasal accusation. "We weren't expecting to see you too." We all turned around to see the newcomer. It was Edna Stillman. Edna Stillman? What was a friend of my parents doing here, running into our abduction? It was like seeing an animated Disney character walk into the middle of *Casablanca* or the *Maltese Falcon.* (170)

References to American pop culture icons, such as Disney characters or Bogart, habitually appear in Engel's works, but with a critical difference. In *Murder on Location,* for example, Benny investigates a situation that markedly resembles the plot of *Niagara,* a movie filmed in Niagara Falls, Ontario, and a movie that the novel situates firmly within Canadian borders. Reminding readers that American works often draw on Canadian locales for their momentum, Cooperman continues to invert expectations fostered by American cultural artifacts.

Yet Engel also goes beyond simple nationalist revisions and, in *Dead and Buried,* offers a reminder that the "great white north" was precisely that — white and WASP — and for a long time. Invited to dine at the Grantham Golf Club, Benny recalls: "My father had often been a guest at the club during the years when I was growing up. He joined as soon as the restrictive membership practices of the past had been done away with" (190).

Engel does a great deal to "chop" the hard-boiled nature of many American mystery novels, and he concomitantly weaves ethnicity into his texts. However, the bulk of contemporary hard-boiled Canadian detective fiction is written by women and advances further subversions of the tough-guy American mode. Names like Sparkle Hayter, Elisabeth Bowers, and Tanya Huff are prominent in Canadian crime circles and have made headway in the larger North American market. Published by mainstream presses, these writers attract more general notice than their small-press-published sisters, but this is not to elide how small-press writers have worked to put Canada on the crime map. Canadian Eve Zaremba (published first by Amanita and later by Second Story Press) offered one of the the first lesbian detectives, Helen Keremos, whom Margaret Atwood describes as "a cross between Philip Marlowe and Lily Tomlin" (*Uneasy,* cover blurb). Shortly after Keremos's debut, she was followed by Lauren Wright Douglas's Caitlin Reece (see Manina Jones's article in this volume for further information) and Jackie Manthorne's Harriet Hubbley (published by Gynergy Books), a Maritime-born detective who resides in Montreal. It is also interesting to note that the (in)famous "American" lesbian novelist Katherine V. Forrest was born in Windsor and that the renowned Lia Matera hails from Vancouver.

Canadian critic Barbara Godard draws attention to the attraction detective fiction holds for women writers. As she notes, one "of the major sites of feminist re-visionary activity with respect to fictional genres has been the development of the detective novel" (47). She goes on to say that "the murder mystery is imbricated in an antagonism between truth and verisimilitude" that piques the interest of various feminist writers (47). Certainly, such is the case with Elisabeth Bowers, whose two novels, *Ladies Night* and *No Forwarding Address,* push at the borders of law and criminality. In the opening chapter of *Ladies Night,* the continuum of crime is spotlighted: "Where did it start? Sometimes it's hard to draw the line between the end of one case and the beginning of the next; they seem interlocked like links on a chain. One thing keeps leading to another" (3). Bowers's protagonist, Meg Lacey, a rape victim, began her career in private investigation as a means of fighting back. In *Ladies Night,* Meg focuses on a pornography ring that "stars" young girls in its productions. During her investigation, Meg is introduced to the Vancouver bar scene, wherein young women are encouraged to get drunk on "Ladies Night," which means:

> "Different things, different places."
> At Kinky's it meant that there was no cover charge, and no men on the premises apart from the staff and the stripper. We walked into the bedlam — a mass of pubescent femininity chattering, giggling, screaming above the music, glowing lime-green and gold beneath the revolving stage-lights. And I mean pubescent. As my eyes accustomed to the dimness, I concluded that most of the customers should have been home preparing tomorrow's homework. Instead they were drunk. Uproarious and silly, hysterical with giggles. (36)

Meg is informed that Ladies Night ends at 10 p.m. when the "ticket booth" opens: "ladies get in free. But the men have to pay" (39). The detective is horrified, since, after the many free drinks supplied by the house, the female patrons are "riotous, reckless, sloppy with drink. Eyes glazed, cheeks glowed, limbs gestured wildly" (39). Meg thinks: "They can't let those men in here" (39), but of course they do, and while Meg is able to close down the pornographic ring that uses the bar as a recruiting ground for its operations, she can do nothing about Ladies Night — the exploitative practices of Ladies Night are "legal."

In a different vein, Sparkle Hayter's fiction focuses on the operations of a TV newsroom. Within it, investigative reporter Robin Hudson is in a career slump, having belched on-air at an inopportune moment, and her struggles with her colleagues provide a forum for Hudson's "hard-boiled conceits," a term that Scott Christianson explains is "a particularly pointed or extended metaphor or simile which is usually serious, and which is spoken to the reader directly to convey the detective/narrator's complex sensibility" (133). Robin's wisecracks pepper Hayter's text and make for provocative subversions of the conceit's usual placement in tough-guy, hard-boiled detective novels. Unlike her taciturn male predecessors, Robin asserts, "I always say … it takes seven major muscle groups just to hold my tongue" (*Nice,* 4). When one of her companions reminds her that "as the old saying goes, you get more flies with honey than with vinegar," Robin responds, "Well, if you *really* want flies, you ought to try bullshit…. It's an old folk remedy" (*What's,* 52). At a network cocktail party, the reporter uses a version of the hard-boiled simile to describe one of her senior colleagues, whose "little problem relating to women" she translates as follows: "When he's sober and he comes face to face with a woman in a social setting, he tends to become focussed on her breasts and can't look her in the eye. If she moves from side to side, his head moves from side to side too, like a dog watching a tennis ball" (*What's,* 16).[3] And, where Meg Lacey practises martial arts for personal safety, Robin, who lives in New York, devises ingenious security measures: she grows poison ivy in her window boxes and carries a weapon, a "high-velocity hot-glue gun, with two settings, stream and spray" (*Nice,* 139).

Of course, not all Canadian crime writers write within the hard-boiled tradition. Many authors prefer the police procedural mode, like Medora Sale, whose Toronto police detective John Sanders and his photographer lover Harriet Jeffries investigate various crimes together. In turn, L.R. Wright's work features RCMP officer Karl Alberg and his librarian companion, Cassandra Mitchell, who also team up to crack mysteries.

More in the mode of British "puzzle mysteries" are Gail Bowen's works. Her novel *A Colder Kind of Death* won the Arthur Ellis Award for Best Crime Novel in 1994, and her series follows the adventures of Joanne Kilbourn, an amateur sleuth who, in the process of her inquiries, illuminates the workings of Saskatchewan politics. Another form of politics inspire Marion Foster's writings, since her defence lawyer protagonist, Harriet Fordham Croft, finds that her sexual orientation becomes an issue in the practice of her profession. Similarly, Nora Kelly sets her academic mysteries in a thinly disguised Simon Fraser University, wherein her hero, historian Gillian Adams, confronts diverse forms of sexual harassment in campus life. In the business world, Ellen Godfrey's Jane Tregar is a computer investigator who must fight her way through office politics in order to solve the crimes that confront her. And Suzanne North's *Healthy Wealthy and Dead,* featuring television camerawoman Phoebe Fairfax, also explores corporate politics, at an Alberta health spa that doubles as a murder scene.

The politics of Quebec provide an interesting site for a growing number of American mystery novelists. The recent *Deja Death*, featuring a female forensic pathologist in the vein of Patricia Cornwell, is creating a stir. Kathy Reichs is an American forensic anthropologist who lives and works in Montreal, as does her protagonist, Dr. Temperance Brennan. The Quebec metropolis attracts other American authors, such as Phyllis Knight, whose *Shattered Dreams* takes place during the Montreal jazz festival.

Some Canadian writers like to blend genres. Alison Gordon, for instance, writes baseball mysteries that cross the boundaries between detective and sports fiction. Her hero, Kate Henry, enumerates the benefits of her job: "One of the advantages of being a baseball writer is that it's never difficult to get a conversation going with strangers, especially men. Most of them think a woman sportswriter is a bit like a roller-skating duck, so amazed are they that something in a skirt knows more about jock stuff than they do, which gives an interesting edge to the conversation" (95–96). But life is not all home runs for the Toronto Titans, and Kate is always on hand to help solve the murders that plague the team.

In another amalgam, Tanya Huff commingles hard-boiled crime and fantasy fiction in her novel series starring former police detective Vicki Nelson and her unofficial partner, Henry Fitzroy, a Renaissance vampire. Although Vicki protests, "I don't even watch horror movies. What the hell am I doing starring in one?" (275), she finds herself accepting Fitzroy's help. Since Vicki suffers from a congenital disease that interferes with her eyesight and was the cause of her retirement from the police force, she comes to rely on Fitzroy's acute night vision. Vicki's failing sight is clearly a drawback in private investigation, and while she recognizes the assets Fitzroy offers to her and her firm, she is also jealous of his abilities: "to be able to move freely without fear of misstep or collision, to be able to see movement in the shadows" (290). But with Fitzroy's powers and Vicki's detective skills yoked together, the two make for a formidable team.

Partnerships and communities are important facets of Canadian detective fiction, as the above novels suggest. These same aspects are apparent in the short-story collection *The Ladies' Killing Circle,* edited by Victoria Cameron and Audrey Jessup, which compiles the work of Ottawa's Sisters in Crime writing group, among others. The text ranges from Marguerite McDonald's "Death at Network News," in which a news anchor meets with an early death, to Mary Jane Maffini's "Cotton Armour," detailing an old woman's revenge, to Linda Wiken's "There Goes the Neighbourhood," wherein a wronged wife avenges herself on her husband and his lover. Overall, *The Ladies' Killing Circle* threads together various murderous efforts and intersperses and links them through Joy Hewitt Mann's poems. After displaying the skills of the women and their largely female protagonists, the book ends with Mann's ironic "Mystery Men." The poem reads as follows:

> Here's to the men
> And the mysteries they write.
> We all still enjoy them —
> Especially at night. (171)

In proffering different takes on crime and punishment, this collection manifests a group effort to plot murder. Through their collaborative effort, these local writers provide readers with a bevy of criminal scenarios, mostly set in Ottawa, that reflect women's experiences and mishaps in efforts to achieve a semblance of "justice." Having followed this collection with another, *Cottage Crimes,* the Ottawa writing group continues to collude in their own version of "murder ink."

In a larger sense, as *The Ladies' Killing Circle* demonstrates for the Ottawa region, fictive criminal activities help to put Canada on the investigative map. Through the tellings and retellings, this map is pink indeed (not just because its previous incarnation as a colony of the British Empire was signified by its "red" shade on old maps), now coloured with the bloody offerings of Canadian crime writers. These writers and their work demonstrate that the "gentle" Canada of American imagination can be just as insidious and Machiavellian a locale as any other — even if much of its crime is contained within the pages of mystery novelists. As Mann writes in "Reading Gaol":

> Mysteries are more than books
> With crime in all its stages.
> They keep the murderers safe for us,
> Imprisoned in their pages.

ENDNOTES

1. Walcott's observation was articulated during a conversation at the American Studies Association Conference in Washington, D.C., in October 1997.

2. This statement arose during discussions surrounding *Detective Agency: Women Re-Writing the Hard-Boiled Tradition,* co-authored by Walton and Jones and published in 1997 by the University of California Press.

3. For these examples, I am indebted to Manina Jones's work in our co-authored *Detective Agency: Women Re-Writing the Hard-Boiled Tradition.*

REFERENCES

Bowen, Gail. *A Colder Kind of Death.* Toronto: McClelland and Stewart, 1994.

Bowers, Elisabeth. *Ladies Night.* Toronto: Seal, 1988.

Cameron, Victoria, and Audrey Jessup, eds. *The Ladies' Killing Circle.* Burnstown: General Store Publishing House, 1995.

Christianson, Scott R. "A Heap of Broken Images: Hardboiled Detective Fiction and the Discourse(s) of Modernity." In *The Cunning Craft: Original Essays on Detective Fiction and Contemporary Literary Theory,* ed. Ronald G. Walker and June M. Frazer, 135–48. Macomb, Ill.: Western Illinois University Press, 1990.

Douglas, Lauren Wright. *A Tiger's Heart.* Tallahassee: Naiad, 1992.

Engel, Howard. *Dead and Buried.* Toronto: Penguin, 1991.

———. *Murder on Location.* Toronto: Clarke, Irwin, 1982.

Foster, Marion. *Legal Tender.* Toronto: Second Story Press, 1992.

Godard, Barbara. "Sleuthing: Feminists Re/writing the Detective Novel." *Signature* 1 (1989): 45–70.

Godfrey, Ellen. *Murder behind Locked Doors.* Toronto: Penguin, 1988.

Gordon, Alison. *Safe at Home.* Toronto: McClelland and Stewart, 1990.

Hayter, Sparkle. *Nice Girls Finish Last.* New York: Penguin, 1996.

———. *What's a Girl Gotta Do?* New York: Penguin, 1994.

Huff, Tanya. *Blood Pact.* Toronto: Daw, 1993.

Kelly, Nora. *My Sister's Keeper.* Toronto: HarperCollins, 1992.

Knight, Phyllis. *Shattered Rhythms.* Toronto: HarperCollins, 1994.

Manthorne, Jackie. *Sudden Death.* Charlottetown: Gynergy, 1997.

North, Suzanne. *Healthy Wealthy and Dead.* Edmonton: NeWest, 1994.

Reichs, Kathy. *Déjà Dead.* New York: Scribner, 1997.

Sale, Medora. *Murder in a Good Cause.* Toronto: Viking, 1990.

Skene-Melvin, David. *Canadian Crime Fiction.* Shelburne, Ont.: The Battered Silicon Dispatch Box, 1996.

Walton, Priscilla L., and Manina Jones. *Detective Agency: Women Re-Writing the Hard-Boiled Tradition.* Berkeley: University of California Press, 1997.

Wright, Eric. *Smoke Detector.* Toronto: Collins, 1984.

Wright, L.R. *A Touch of Panic.* Toronto: Seal, 1995.

Zaremba, Eve. *Uneasy Lies.* Toronto: Second Story Press, 1990.

"PHILIP MARLOWE IN DRAG"?

Performing Gender and Genre in Lesbian Detective Novels

Manina Jones

In its October 1995 survey of the popular mystery fiction market, *Publisher's Weekly* magazine observed that "one subgenre flexing considerable muscle is the growing variety of mysteries featuring gay and lesbian protagonists" (Langstaff, 43). This article, under the heading "Unravelling Puzzles, Gaily," identified a manifestation in the mass-market publishing world of a generic transformation that had been developing in small lesbian and feminist presses since the first installment of American M.F. Beal's lesbian private eye series in 1977, with *Angel Dance*, and the 1978 debut of Eve Zaremba's Canadian private eye series, with *A Reason to Kill*, featuring investigator Helen Keremos.[1] By 1990, Bonnie Zimmerman could assert in *The Safe Sea of Women* that the detective novel had replaced science fiction and utopian writing as the quintessential lesbian genre. The 1980s saw an explosion of lesbian crime fiction in which, as Sally R. Munt puts it, "sexy superdykes strode the city streets in their steel-capped DMs, swinging their double-headed axes, slayed patriarchs in their wake" (120). Writers like Australian Claire McNab, Briton Val McDermid, Canadians Zaremba and Lauren Wright Douglas, and Americans Katherine V. Forrest, Mary Wings, Sandra Scoppettone, Elizabeth Pincus, and many others have created popular lesbian series detectives whose generic analogues are the "tough guys" of classic hard-boiled novels by the likes of Raymond Chandler, Dashiell Hammett, and Mickey Spillane.

Zaremba describes her series as compensating for what she saw as a deficiency in such popular narratives, which tended to ignore or offer only negative, criminalized stereotypes of homosexual characters: "For most of my life," Zaremba writes,

> lesbian detectives did not exist and lesbians generally were invisible in genre fiction, except for their rare appearance in character parts of "perverts." So I wanted to write mysteries about a dyke Private Eye. Period. No overt political messages — lesbian, feminist or otherwise. Just a middle-aged lesbian matter-of-factly going about her job as a PI. Of course, that simple ambition has turned out problematic. ("A Canadian Speaks," 45)

As Zaremba's comments imply, the "simple" act of generic appropriation has complex effects due in part to the complications involved in what might be seen as a perverse decision to translate the archetypally male, aggressively heterosexual, and American figure of the private eye into a homosexual Canadian woman, a translation necessarily caught up in the politics of identity and one that provokes Sally Munt's question, "Can this historically monologic, misogynistic, megalomaniac be transformed by a lesbian-feminist reading?" (93).

While I don't want to subscribe in this essay to the prevalent kind of evaluative criticism that simply assesses the political efficacy of the feminist private eye novel, either censuring it for capitulating to "the masculinist imperatives" (Litler) of the genre or lauding its heroine's potential as a feminist role model (e.g., Décuré),[2] my reading of Canadian Lauren Wright Douglas's Caitlin Reece private eye series does begin with my own initial discomfort with that novelist's reproduction of what I thought of as some of the more retrograde features of the American hard-boiled genre. Douglas, whose five detective novels set in Victoria, British Columbia, are published by the lesbian press Naiad, unlike many of the largely heterosexual women detective novelists I had analysed in my recent work on mass-market women's detective fiction, seemed to risk what Ann Wilson identifies as a central problem in occupying the traditionally male subject position of the hard-boiled detective: making the heroine "seem as if she is a man in drag" (148). Maureen Reddy offers a similar warning about women's adaptations of the tough-guy genre, arguing that "far too often, strong women detectives are found filling the (gum) shoes of strong male detectives, with only the gender changed" (6). Or, as Susan Geeson summarizes her case against certain versions of the genre in the essay from which I take the title of this paper, "the feminist PIs are Philip Marlowe in drag" (116). This last statement reminded me of other protestations against the drag aesthetic, like Canadian Sparkle Hayter's insistence that her New York–based journalist detective Robin Hudson "isn't Sam Spade in a dress" (Jones) or American crime novelist Sara Paretsky's description of her initial failed experimentation with the hard-boiled genre. Paretsky, whose V.I. Warshawski series is one of the most successful examples of the hugely popular mass-market version of the female private eye novel, explained in a *Writer's Digest* interview: "At first, my character was basically Philip Marlowe in drag…. She's in her office late at night and a sexy guy with big shoulders and slim hips comes in and gives a false name. He turns out to be the bad guy. I couldn't sustain it — *it was too much of a parody*" (Shepherdson, 38, emphasis added).[3] These writers seem to define the popular mainstream rendering of the feminist private eye novel as bordering on the possibility of drag performance, but always repudiate drag's enactment as exceeding the ideal criteria for generic subversion. As Paretsky's remarks suggest, the mainstream revisionist version of the genre tends to use hard-boiled narrative conventions more for the purposes of gender parity than gender parody.

It seemed to me, however, in considering this chorus of vilification against generic transvestism, that it made it too easy simply to dismiss as excessively conservative or conventional — as I had intuitively done — work by Douglas and others, especially those writing for lesbian presses and audiences — a dismissal that, ironically, would amount to charging lesbian writers with playing the genre too straight. Might such novelists be performing the traditional script of generic conventions differently, playing to and with a different set of readers and expectations, "queering" the codes of both gender and genre by means of parodic re-enactment? As Judith Butler has famously argued, reproducing heterosexual constructs in non-heterosexual contexts highlights "the utterly constructed status of the so-called heterosexual original" (31). Thus, "the notion of an original or primary gender identity is often parodied within the cultural practices of drag, cross-dressing, and the sexual stylization of butch/femme identities" (137).

The hard-boiled detective novel seems a particularly apt stage for such a parodic performance. There are several important ways in which the workings of popular genre writing in general and detective fiction in particular might usefully be employed to reflect on the construction and reproduction of gender categories. For example, like gender, genres are regulated; they portray regulatory social practices that are understood by both performer and audience. Indeed, performer and audience might be said to mutually *generate* both gender and genre by continually negotiating and renegotiating the terms of a largely tacit social contract. Genre fiction's extreme consumer-driven market status foregrounds the ways in which readers, by negatively or positively reinforcing different forms with their patterns of book buying, influence future productions — and this is one reason why it's important to take the distinctive readership of lesbian and feminist press publications into account. While the relations of heterosexuality are routinely naturalized as original gender identities, the analogy with genre is revealing, since it is much more obvious that genre categories are constituted in and by a set of performances for which there is no true original instance. It is unusually clear in category fiction that *any* author's act of composition is always already an act of mimicry; the genre author is *never* truly original. She writes not simply as an individual, but as part of a body of authors who act corporately to define the genre both by their conformity to rules or expectations and by their limited but infinitely variable departures from them. Genre, further, is precisely as Butler describes gender identity — "tenuously constituted in time, instituted in an exterior space through a *stylized repetition of acts*" (140) — and the serial form of much genre fiction reinforces the importance of this stylized repetition through time. Detective fiction, finally, is also a profoundly ethical discourse grounded in conceptions of legal/normal and criminal/deviant behaviour; it is itself thus implicated in the "policing" of identity categories, not the least of which is gender. Indeed, detective fiction is a form of writing that, perhaps more than any other, is governed by conventional rules and categories at the same time as it makes the violation and enforcement of laws its primary theme.

Douglas's character Caitlin Reece offers a particularly interesting series of test cases involving reversals and repetitions of gender and genre codes of conduct: "worse" than being Philip Marlowe in drag, Caitlin's butch persona is, as we shall see, in many ways even more evocative of Mickey Spillane's later extreme right-wing tough guy Mike Hammer, a character famous for his virulent misogyny, homophobia, and violent crime-busting tactics. I'll begin with the notion of style as a linguistic fashion statement, a statement that makes obvious cross-references to other writing that might be interpreted as verbal cross-dressing. Douglas's novels certainly mimic the linguistic style of the clipped, ironic "tough talk" that is the signature of writers in the hard-boiled genre. In *Daughters of Artemis*, for instance, Caitlin identifies herself with a terse list of generic clichés whose redundancy verges on parody: "And as for whose acolyte I am, well I serve my checking account. I'm a private investigator. A gumshoe. A snoop. Someone people pay to do their dirty work" (107). As Scott Christianson recognizes, the hard-boiled style is "an *exercise* of language as power" (136, italics added). It is, then, not simply superficial garb, but a means of *producing* an authoritative subject position, as Caitlin's excessive linguistic self-assertion potentially suggests. Indeed, in the novel *Ninth Life*, Caitlin is jokingly accused of speaking in pretentious slogans, sounding, not like a tough *guy*, but like that woman who is perhaps the most famous hard-boiled male impersonator of all: "'It sounds so bloody pompous,'" says Caitlin's friend, "'Like something Margaret Thatcher would say.' She dissolved into laughter. I grinned a little in agreement" (*Ninth Life,* 63).

The hard-boiled style itself is thus neither original nor monologic; its voice reverberates with voices of the past, creating a sense of *déjà entendu.* As F.R. Jameson has demonstrated of Chandler's language and as becomes obvious in its parodic re-enactment, hard-boiled tough talk is already a pastiche of "odd linguistic scraps, figures of speech, colloquialisms, place names, and local sayings, all laboriously pasted together in an illusion of continuous discourse" (124). In *The Always Anonymous Beast,* Caitlin sizes up Tonia, the new client who will later become her lover, using something approaching a hard-boiled conceit, a figure of speech identified with Chandler and supposedly distinctive to the "complex sensibility" of the hard-boiled detective/narrator (Christianson, 133), but in this case it is attributed to Caitlin's mother: "She could have made big money with her face. When she didn't scowl, it was positively beautiful. At the moment, however, she was scowling ferociously, the glare she was giving me laser-like. *She was the kind of woman my mother said could chew nails and spit battleships.* Tough. Maybe as tough as me" (*Always Anonymous Beast,* 27, emphasis added). The typical objectifying gaze of the private eye is here defiantly returned by the female client, exemplifying, perhaps, what Maggie Humm refers to as the collapsing of simple spectator/consumer practices put into play by the complexities of lesbian subjectivity (211). Indeed, in this novel, Tonia, an activist theorist of pacifism, described here with a martial metaphor, complicates any simple notion of the "femme" lesbian sex-role identity as a simple counterbalance for a "butch" woman.

Throughout Douglas's series, Caitlin proudly advocates a kind of Hammer-esque violent individualism based on an entrepreneurial model. She is, for example, persistently labelled by herself and others as a "thug" and a "heavy" (*Ninth Life,* 43; *Always Anonymous Beast,* 28, 30, 53, 62, 153): "I'm just paid muscle," she observes in *The Daughters of Artemis,* "Curiosity for hire. A thug" (108). The parodic potential of this characterization is implied when Caitlin repeats the word "thug," giving it an erotic homosexual slant, mimicking and mocking its conventional macho connotations. In their initial encounter her lover feels Caitlin's arms and comments in surprise on their strength, Caitlin: "'We thugs are like that,' I [Caitlin] said smiling, my lips against her throat. She laughed …" (*Always Anonymous Beast,* 153). The incident mockingly echoes love scenes like the one in Spillane's *I, the Jury,* in which his lover, her arms bruised from his passionate embrace, admiringly says to Hammer, "You love hard, too, don't you, Mike?" (65). There are also ironic effects achieved by using the erotic language licensed by hard-boiled detective fiction to allow for — indeed, by the rules of genre to *require* — the routine description of lesbian sexual relationships, which are a formulaic aspect of Douglas's novels and which demonstrate the important and distinctive generic connections between lesbian detective fiction and lesbian romance novels.

There is, by the way, a similar potential for a reading of Caitlin's status as a Canadian, as a mimicry of the distinctively American national identity of the hard-boiled private eye and his association with both entrepreneurism and violence. One might have expected from a Canadian PI the kind of "soft-boiled" approach of a writer like Howard Engel, whose mild-mannered detective Benny Cooperman substitutes chopped-egg sandwiches and milk for the traditional private eye's hard liquor. In *Dead and Buried,* for instance, Cooperman muses on the American literary tradition of "the fixer" who comes into a community from outside and then moves off into the sunset when the work is done:

> Maybe Sam Spade and the Lone Ranger are brothers under the skin, but I don't see how that affects me trying to make an honest buck up here north of the world's longest undefended frontier. We don't have that strain of vigilantism in Canada. Dirty Harry's looking for work in Toronto, putting in time until the streets get meaner. He may not have to wait long, but in the interval, the traditions aren't the same. Canadians are bigger consumers of law and order for one thing. (53)

Although she works in Victoria, a setting renowned more for its gingerbread architecture and gardens than for its mean streets, Douglas's detective frequently calls attention both to her outsider status as a woman and a lesbian in relation to traditional Canadian notions of law and order, and to her self-conscious flouting of its principles, commenting, for example, that she carries a concealed .357 in self-conscious contravention of Canadian gun laws, "the toughest in the world," because she has no illusions that she is more powerful than the "bad guys" (*Ninth Life,* 171).

In *Ninth Life*, a description of Caitlin's preparations reproduces the arming scenes typical of hard-boiled writing. However, a version of burlesque play-acting inflects the description; the performance is thrown into relief by Caitlin's final self-conscious flourish of mock femininity, which tends to denaturalize *both* male and female roles:

> I hurried into the bedroom, pulled on a pair of clean levis, a pale yellow cotton turtleneck, and threaded a braided leather belt through the belt loops. From a shoebox in my closet, I took my .357 Magnum, checked the load, and clipped its holster to the back of my jeans. My Harris Tweed blazer draped quite nicely, I thought, checking myself out in the full-length mirror. The gun made nary a bulge. I laced on a pair of well broken-in Reeboks, batted my eyelashes girlishly at my reflection, and ran out of the house. (36)

Later in the novel, the narrative again calls attention to Caitlin's self-conscious reversal of gender roles when the act of negotiating a simple purchase of information from a computer hacker becomes a major production: "Doing business with Francis the Ferret was always such a big deal. His sense of the dramatic meant that I had to bluster and threaten, and he had to demur and protest. Then, after I got really tough and insulted him, he caved in and agreed to do what I want. Me Tarzan, him Jane. This tedious little charade had to be acted out every time we did business." (*Ninth Life,* 87–88). The notion of charade or masquerade is further highlighted in this novel by the fact that the story takes place during the days leading up to Halloween.

Perhaps the most striking version of gender masquerade is developed in the plot of *The Always Anonymous Beast*, in which Caitlin works on behalf of Val, a married television news journalist who is being blackmailed because of a past lesbian relationship; this character is made vulnerable because she is acting out a charade of heterosexuality to protect her public image. The notion of guilt essential to crime fiction is in part reconfigured in this novel to accommodate Val's guilt for her suppressed homosexual feelings, a guilt on which her blackmailer preys: "Val's attitude and the case were inextricably intertwined. Val's guilt not only gave the blackmailer a handle on her professional life, but it gave him power over her personal life as well" (*Always Anonymous Beast,* 10). That guilt takes the symbolic form of the figure of the Dark Lady of Shakespeare's sonnets, which Val had transcribed in a letter to her lover, here a kind of madwoman in the closet who also haunts several other installments of Douglas's series.

In *Goblin Market*, a psychiatrist describes yet another version of gender role-playing, characterizing the mental state of certain types of killers in a manner that reminds me of the way genre fiction itself works by obsessive repetition, at the same time revealing the potentially coercive and even psychopathic nature of prescripted and prescriptive gender roles: these killers have "been obsessively imagining all the details of the fantasy for years, building on it the way a novelist will build a story … they've been playing and replaying a ritualized inner script" that they finally enact, forcing unfortunate women to perform the fatal part of victim (80–81). This psychopathic behaviour is not so different from the so-called heroic actions of the hard-boiled hero, whose execution of a betraying woman is part of the narrative formula. The conclusion of Spillane's *I, the Jury*, for example, is a seduction scene in which Hammer remorselessly guns down the *femme fatale* (interestingly, a psychiatrist) on the line "The roar of the .45 shook the room": "How c-could you?" she had gasped, realizing she was mortally wounded, and Hammer recalls, "I only had a moment before talking to a corpse, but I got it in. 'It was easy,' I said" (174). Butler suggests that "the parodic or imitative effect of gay identities works … to expose heterosexuality as an incessant and *panicked* imitation of its own naturalized idealization" (22–23). If there has ever been a fictional example of a panicked imitation of heterosexuality it is Mike Hammer, whose numerous sexual encounters in each novel obsessively — even psychopathically — act out the co-extensive nature of power and sexuality in heterosexual relationships. For Hammer, sex is often both figuratively and literally "replaced by death and torture" (Symons, 251). It is surely no coincidence, given the dramatic scenario described by the psychiatrist in *Goblin Market*, that in the climactic scene of the novel Caitlin diverts and then thwarts the killer by replaying and recasting a scene from Shakespeare's *The Tempest*, a play in which the killer had in high school played the role of the monster Caliban. Caitlin attracts the killer's attention when she takes on the masterly male voice of the disciplining magician Prospero in a gesture that is an epitome of the reverse discourse of Caitlin's "enforcer" role in the series as a whole. That very enforcer role is virtually announced in one of the opening scenes of *The Daughters of Artemis*, when Caitlin dons "a comfy old red T-shirt with Dirty Harry's famous utterance on the front" (11). Her attire seems almost to respond to Benny Cooperman's assertion of Dirty Harry's lack of employment in Canada.

In collecting these instances, I have perhaps given a misleading impression about the frequency and self-consciousness of Douglas's parodic gestures. She does not use the sustained or flagrantly theatrical post-modern gestures incorporated, for example, into the transvestite, transsexual, translation mystery of a novel like Barbara Wilson's *Gaudí Afternoon*, but it is Douglas's parodic touches that suggest the ways her use of hard-boiled patterns might be read through a parodic lens. One of the features that first struck me in her novels was the way Douglas seems virtually to reproduce from writers like Spillane the detective whose overt function is to act in compensation for the failings of the justice system. In Spillane's *I, the Jury*, Mike Hammer tells a police officer that he will seek retribution for a friend's murder outside the court system:

> By Christ, I'm not letting the killer go through the tedious process of the law. You know what happens, damn it. They get the best lawyer there is and screw up the whole thing and wind up a hero! … No, damn it. A jury is cold and impartial like they're supposed to be, while some snotty lawyer makes them pour tears as he tells how his client was insane at the moment or had to shoot in self-defence. Swell. The law is fine. But this time I'm the law and I'm not going to be cold and impartial. (7)

Caitlin, similarly, emphasizes her rejection of the law: she leaves her position as a lawyer with the Victoria Crown prosecutor's office after watching criminals slip "through the grasp of justice with ridiculous ease" (*Ninth Life,* 35), and a representative speech from *The Daughters of Artemis* seems more like a paraphrase than a parody of Spillane's sentiments:

> Fortunately, I no longer need give a rat's ass for juries or for the rules of evidence. Now, people come to me with the problems which they can't get resolved within the system…. I've discarded such meaningless notions as "right" and "justice" and "fairness." Once I acknowledged that the thin blue line is not sufficient to keep the hordes of bad guys at bay … I decided to hire out my wits, my strength, and my determination to assist those the system can't help. (44)

It is important to remember, however, that this detective responds to the legal system's endemic injustices against women. Douglas also obviously adapts to the role of the avenger the kind of romance pattern most obviously signalled in Raymond Chandler's Philip Marlowe narratives, which are often described in the symbolic terms of medieval quest-crusades on behalf of (apparent) damsels in distress. Caitlin, for example, wears a leather jacket likened to "armour" (*Daughters of Artemis,* 184), and her bravery is compared both with dragon slayers of old (*Always Anonymous Beast,* 176; *Goblin Market,* 165) and the warrior-angel Michael (*Goblin Market,* 138), though, again, the distressed damsels of her investigations are almost always lesbians, who have few advocates within the institutions of justice. At the same time as the novels tap into the obvious appeal of the *un*-masked or "out" lesbian avenger, they occasionally both mock it and acknowledge it as a kind of seductive but potentially dangerous individualist wish-fulfillment fantasy. For example, in *Goblin Market,* Caitlin engages in another exercise of excessive self-identification, observing with chagrin, "Me. Intrepid private investigator, righter of wrongs, protector of the downtrodden, bulwark of the disenfranchised, champion of the have-nots. The idiot who'd let herself be clobbered from behind by a bad guy" (105). In *The Daughters of Artemis*, Caitlin, encountering a group of vigilante women, muses, "A militant sisterhood. Yes indeed, that had a certain appeal. Amazons united against the foe, riding into battle with bows drawn and breasts bared. I snorted. Unfortunately the foes women had to fight today couldn't be felled so easily. But the appeal was there, nonetheless" (124). In that novel, Caitlin actually works to prevent these women from taking extra-legal revenge against a rapist by capturing and castrating him.

Still, what is most troubling about this aspect of the novels is that in allowing for a characterization of the criminal male as a monster, the narratives can outright reject the social and psychological issues surrounding crime and punishment as irrelevant. Like Hammer, Caitlin demonstrates a contempt for "soft-headed psychologists" (*Daughters of Artemis,* 42) who diagnose as mental illness what she considers evil pure and simple; in a gesture that twists hardboiled in the direction of gothic writing, the woman-hating male criminal is invariably cast in Douglas's novels as a monster,[4] and thus the use of violence as retribution against such "gynophobic" (*Always Anonymous Beast,* 35) figures makes a certain kind of contradictory generic sense. It repeats and elicits pleasure from the retributive violence of the hardboiled model.[5] At one point Caitlin admits, "Sometimes, I *did* enjoy the scaring, breaking and shooting. Sometimes, seeing a look of abject terror come into some pimple-faced punk's eyes, and knowing it was I, not he, who had the power — *and that he knew it* — was enjoyable in itself. And it scared the hell out of me" (*Always Anonymous Beast,* 31). At the same time, this also throws into relief the very gendered power dynamic represented by a figure like Mike Hammer and others, since the ultra-masculine villains, in fact, often resemble that character, who has been called a monster masquerading as a hero by one historian of the genre (Symons, 243).

The hard-boiled novel thus has a kind of powerful, attractive logic that is both difficult to resist and difficult for a lesbian writer to replay without interrogation. During one investigation, Caitlin is stalked by a violent offender she once prosecuted. When she confronts an intruder in her apartment,

> [m]y hand seemed to belong to someone else. As if in a dream, I saw the hand's thumb on the hammer, the index finger moving to begin the trigger pull. And as I watched, I felt a dark, gleeful bubble build up inside me, a silent black laugh, and heard a voice yammering: *Kill him pull the trigger blow the little bastard's brains out his other ear he deserves it do the world a favor shoot the son of a bitch no one will ever know shoot him shoot him shoot himmmmmmmmm.* (*Daughters of Artemis,* 81)

The italicized voice here might well be that of Mike Hammer himself, urging Caitlin to conform to the requirements of the genre by pulling the trigger. While she resists the urge in this incident, in a similar situation she later performs according to convention, shooting the unidentified interloper, thus fulfilling a narrative pattern typical of Spillane by killing what turns out to be another woman, a woman who was briefly her lover. Parody, rather than achieving a comic effect, here involves playing out the irresistible logic of the hard-boiled narrative, but exposing its mechanisms by recasting the conventional roles. In effect, this transformation means the troubling conversion of the sexual butch-femme relationship into that of the butch detective–femme *fatale.*

Recasting lesbian characters in traditionally heterosexual roles also clearly acts out in parodic form the homosocial tension *already* a central, if repressed, aspect of the hard-boiled narrative. As David Glover observes, the active, brutal staging of male agency in these traditional novels "is undercut by a profound sense of homosocial unease…. Homosexuality," he concludes, "remains unfinished business for the thriller's male order" (78). While the hard-boiled hero is certainly misogynistic and megalomaniac, then, Sally Munt's description of him as "monologic" is not quite just. It pre-empts the important possibility of drawing on (pun intended) the pleasures and patterns of popular fiction to perform a skewed, subversive repetition that I can't resist referring to as "cocking the Hammer," redressing the ideological problems posed by the masculine genre by re-dressing the hard-boiled tough guy in a drag performance. As Debra Silverman puts it, "the stakes of female drag are high. But at the same time I suggest that if one can fully play the game, the results are rewarding" (72). In lesbian detective fiction, such dialogic play performs an interrogation from within, one in which category fiction's potential to derail what Butler calls the "categorical fiction" of compulsory heterosexuality (32) might call into question the disciplinary practices of identity itself.

ENDNOTES

1. While Zaremba's first novel was published by a mainstream press (Paperjacks), Zaremba comments that this mainstream press debut was "an aberration"; her four subsequent novels have been published by Amanita Press and Second Story Press ("A Canadian Speaks," 45).

2. As Delys Bird and Brenda Walker observe, "That writers of feminist crime fiction walk a women's tightrope, suspended over competing demands and interests, is evident from the quantity of criticism that either applauds their work or berates it for capitulation to the demands of the genre, or worries that political (feminist) correctness produces dull books and poor politics or is of the kind that continues to believe that this is no place — that it is indeed an unsuitable job — for a woman" (28–29).

3. A similar rejection of a drag aesthetic comes from the opening of a *Newsweek* article on the popularity of mysteries featuring a female detective: "Call her Samantha Spade or Philippa Marlowe and she would deck you. A tough new breed of detective is reforming the American mystery novel: smart, self-sufficient, principled, stubborn, funny — and female" (66).

4. The case that launches her career in the private sector involves a rapist-murderer who, according to Caitlin, "copped an insanity plea and got life in a cushy institution up-island. Annie Graves [the victim] got a funeral one rainy Sunday in April. And I got smart. I resigned from the CP's office the day Bergeron's lawyer pleaded him crazy. Because he was no crazier than you or I. He was evil, and that's a whole different story" (35).

5. An example of Spillane's violence: "I snapped the side of the rod across his jaw and laid the flesh open to the bone. He dropped the sap and staggered into the big boy with a scream starting to come up out of his throat only to get it cut off in the middle as I pounded his teeth back into his mouth with the end of the barrel.... He smashed into the door and lay there bubbling. So I kicked him again and he stopped bubbling. I pulled the knucks off his hand then went over and picked up the sap. The punk was vomiting on the floor, trying to claw his way under the sink. For laughs I gave him a taste of his own sap on the back of his hand and felt the bones go into splinters. He wasn't going to be using any tools for a long time" (*The Big Kill*, 41).

REFERENCES

Ames, Katrine, and Ray Sawhill. "Murder Most Foul and Fair." *Newsweek*, 14 May 1990: 66–69.

Bird, Delys, and Brenda Walker. "Introduction." In *Killing Women: Rewriting Detective Fiction,* 1–61. Sydney: Angus & Robertson, 1993.

Butler, Judith. *Gender Trouble: Feminism and the Subversion of Identity*. New York: Routledge, 1990.

Christianson, Scott. "Talkin' Trash and Kickin' Butt: Sue Grafton's Hard-boiled Feminism." In *Feminism in Women's Detective Fiction,* ed. Glenwood Irons, 127–47. Toronto: University of Toronto Press, 1995.

Décuré, Nicole. "V.I. Warshawski, a 'Lady with Guts': Feminist Crime Fiction by Sara Paretsky." *Women's Studies International Forum* 12, no. 2 (1989): 227–38.

Douglas, Lauren Wright. *The Always Anonymous Beast*. Tallahassee: Naiad, 1987.

———. *The Daughters of Artemis*. Tallahassee: Naiad, 1993.

———. *Goblin Market*. Tallahassee: Naiad, 1993.

———. *Ninth Life*. Tallahassee: Naiad, 1990.

———. *A Tiger's Heart*. Tallahassee: Naiad, 1992.

Engel, Howard. *Dead and Buried: A Benny Cooperman Mystery*. Toronto: Penguin, 1991.

Geeson, Susan. "Ain't Misbehavin'." In *Killing Women: Rewriting Detective Fiction*, 111–23. Sydney: Angus & Robertson, 1993.

Glover, David. "The stuff that dreams are made of: Masculinity, femininity and the thriller." In *Gender, Genre and Narrative Pleasure*, ed. Derek Longhurst, 67–83. London: Unwin Hyman, 1989.

Humm, Maggie. "Legal Aliens: Feminist Detective Fiction." In *Border Traffic: Strategies of Contemporary Women Writers*, 185–211. Manchester: Manchester University Press, 1991.

Jameson, F.R. "On Raymond Chandler." In *The Poetics of Murder: Detective Fiction and Literary Theory*, ed. Glenn W. Most and William W. Stowe, 122–48. San Diego: Harcourt Brace Jovanovich, 1983.

Jones, Manina. E-mail interview with Sparkle Hayter. 21 October 1995.

Langstaff, Margaret. "Unravelling Puzzles, Gaily." *Publishers Weekly,* 23 October 1995: 43.

Litler, Alison. "Marele Day's 'Cold Hard Bitch': The Masculinist Imperatives of the Private-Eye Genre." *Journal of Narrative Technique* 21, no. 1 (Winter 1991): 121–35.

Munt, Sally R. *Murder by the Book? Feminism and the Crime Novel.* New York: Routledge, 1994.

Reddy, Maureen T. *Sisters in Crime: Feminism and the Crime Novel.* New York: Continuum, 1988.

Shepherdson, Nancy. "The Writer behind Warshawski." *Writer's Digest*, September 1992: 38–41.

Silverman, Debra. "Making a Spectacle, or Is There a Female Drag?" *Critical Matrix: The Princeton Journal of Women, Gender and Culture* 7, no. 28 (1993): 69–89.

Spillane, Mickey. *The Big Kill.* New York: Signet, 1951.

———. *I, the Jury.* New York: Signet, 1947.

Symons, Julian. *Bloody Murder: From the Detective Story to the Crime Novel: A History.* London: Pan Books, 1992.

Wilson, Ann. "The Female Dick and the Crisis of Heterosexuality." In *Feminism in Women's Detective Fiction*, ed. Glenwood Irons, 148–56. Toronto: University of Toronto Press, 1995.

Wilson, Barbara. *Gaudi Afternoon.* Seattle: Seal Press, 1990.

Zaremba, Eve. "A Canadian Speaks." *Mystery Readers Journal: The Journal of Mystery Readers International* 9, no. 4 (Winter 1993–94): 45–47.

Zimmerman, Bonnie. *The Safe Sea of Women.* Boston: Beacon Press, 1990.

THE BANANA-SKIN
BALLET OF
WILLIAM GIBSON

Derek Foster

Nineteen eighty-four was the year that so many individuals revisited George Orwell's novel of 1948 and wondered how closely his dystopian vision of the future reflected the reality of the present. It was also the year that the novel *Neuromancer* by William Gibson was published. This science fiction story galvanized the term "cyberpunk" in the popular imagination and introduced the term "cyberspace" to a public that would take this imaginative construct and make it flesh. *Neuromancer*, a collage of popular culture influences, was the product of an author who was an obsessive aficionado of late twentieth-century experience. And, if you could stitch a label inside the front jacket of the book, it would proudly declare "Made in Canada."

My argument is that William Gibson produced a vision of the future that is far less an exercise in forecasting than it is a reflection of present-day popular culture and the world around us. His particular brand of science fiction is decidedly influenced by the non-fiction environment in which he found himself writing. This environment, both physically and psychologically, is Canadian. In particular, this Canadian temperament will be demonstrated by highlighting linkages between the fictional musings of Gibson and the non-fictional reflections of Canadian media theorist Marshall McLuhan. McLuhan, in *Understanding Media*, spoke of a "banana-skin pirouette and collapse" (1964, 73) that will occur if we continue to view technology as outside of our bodies and independent of us. Gibson, I suggest, takes a series of these pirouettes and transforms them into a ballet. His writing becomes a kind of dance, sometimes ugly and difficult to watch, but elegant in its evocation of culture and technology and in its awareness of their intertwined effects.

Neuromancer is certainly widely acclaimed. Invoked almost as a divine force, it is the only novel ever to win the holy trinity of science fiction's highest honours: the Hugo, Nebula, and Philip K. Dick awards. As a direct result of this book's influence, it has been suggested that science fiction has lurched "from its cave into the bright sunlight of the modern zeitgest" (Sterling 1987, ix). And while opinions vary as to the originality of Gibson, there is no denying that he changed the direction of science fiction and the influence of the genre itself. The ideas Gibson presented in his novels are now appearing in many other contexts — artistic, sociological, and technical — not the least of which is the fact that every day the Internet progresses closer to Gibson's 1984 vision of the Matrix, his all-encompassing computer network. Today's World Wide Web ensures that Gibson's presentation of virtual worlds has become permanently ingrained as an artifact of our culture.

The effect, then, of Gibson's work is like that of Viagra for the imagination. An injection into the world of science fiction, it wrested the genre from the dysfunctional "space opera" mind set and made everyone stand at attention. Like the slogan of the *Max Headroom* show — starring Canadian actor Matt Frewer — one could see its science fiction style reflecting the non-fiction sensibilities of a world just 20 minutes into the future. Gibson himself has suggested that science fiction may be a signpost of the elements of popular culture that help define our everyday existence: "I don't think science fiction has a lot of predictive capacity, but it's an interesting tool for looking at the world you live in" (in MacNair 1989, 23).

So, rather than an exercise in deliberate prognostication — either the post-apocalyptic grime of traditional hard sci-fi narratives or the metanarrative forecasting of a "third wave" brand of sociological commentary — Gibson's cyberpunk scrawl is a response to a contemporary culture whose phasars are permanently set on stun. In this fashion, his cyberpunk vision becomes, like the science fiction genre itself, something that allows us to "historicize our present by reimagining it as the past of a determinate future" (McHale 1992, 239).

McLuhan echoes this theme: "The future of the future is the present. If you really are curious about the future, just study the present" (in Benedetti and DeHart 1996, 186). It appears that Gibson holds similar sentiments: "[M]y SF is realistic in that I write about what I see around me. That's why SF's role isn't central to my work. My fiction amplifies and distorts my impressions of the world" (in McCaffery 1991, 276). Just as it is my argument here that Gibson's work should not be viewed through the lens of predictive sophistry, Eric McLuhan (in Benedetti and Dehart, 186) noted that "everything [Marshall McLuhan] said wasn't a prediction of what would happen but of what was just happening at the time." Neither Gibson's nor McLuhan's writings tell us how things are going to appear in the future. They try and do something far more difficult; that is, they "predict the present."

Gibson's books are not meant, however, as instruction manuals for the newest Microsoft operating system or as a substitute for the "Idiot's Guide to the Internet." Indeed, whole sections in bookstores are taken up by such volumes, almost all of which have arrived in the wake of Gibson's fiction. Rather, Gibson's fiction provides a glimpse into the harried reality that is the result of the first generation of science fiction producers and consumers who are living in a science fiction world. Gibson produces "poetry of the retrofuture" that is "derived from the illusion that it is fluent in the dialects of the future before they have even emerged" (Csicsery-Ronay 1992, 37). His depiction of society is emblematic of a culture that is captivated with information and high-tech visions of ourselves. These visions are set adrift in a world of our own making that is often unrecognizable as such. Spin together this information culture with a popular culture that already seems strung out on LSD — a chaotic conflagration of fashion, music, architecture that weaves its web of Gothic influence in Gibson's novels — and one is confronted by an intoxicating crash course in cultural mixology.

Consequently, I believe that it is imprudent to suggest that Gibson's fiction relies on any distinction between art and pop, between culture and technology, between the obscene and the sublime, between desire and dread, or even between apathy and aspirations. As

Tabbi notes, the cyberpunk writer's task is that of "leveling distinctions between the technical and the literary, fiction and history, 'high' and 'popular' cultures" (1995, 211). Gibson sets the stage for this approach. Arguably, he did it first, and he did it better than any who have come along since, riding on the coattails of the cyberpunk label. This sense of style, more than any debt to authors who preceded him, is responsible for the success of Gibson's work. This is, at least, according to McCaffery, who notes that this style first characterized the new technological medium that has so strikingly captured the popular imagination,

> the cyberspace of the computer matrix where data dance with human consciousness, where human memory is literalized and mechanized, where multi-national informations systems mutate and breed into startling new structures whose beauty and complexity are unimaginable, mystical, and above all nonhuman. Probably as much as any first novel since Pynchon's *V.* (1963), *Neuromancer* seemed to create a significant synthesis of poetics, pop culture, and technology. (McCaffery 1991, 264)

This collapse of distinctions between pop culture and serious culture is welcomed by Gibson, who hastens to add that he sees himself as a party to "cultural mongrelization": "If you're a writer, the trick is to keep your eyes and ears open well enough to let all this in" (in McCaffery 1991, 266). This statement is reminiscent of another Canadian author's tale of how he became a writer. The late Robertson Davies frequently told of a visit, at an early age, with a witch, who, in order to grant the young boy's wish to become a writer, "turned his eyes inside out." From that day on, he saw the world differently and had no choice but to portray it as such.

Interestingly, both Davies and Gibson used different aspects of Canadiana as inspiration. Gibson, who "wastes very little time shaking his finger or wringing his hands" (Sterling 1987, xi–xii), kept his eyes peeled on kids in video arcades on Vancouver's Granville Street that provided the inspiration for the fixation of cyberspace. He was also attentive to the language of the counter-culture — that of the hippies who left the United States and lived in Canada and the slang of 1969 Toronto dope dealers. All of these were elements of Gibson's contemporary life, strung together to form the illusion of futuristic lingo. Importantly, this style arose out of a country that he reports arriving in and not imagining as being any different from the United States (in McCaffery 1991, 269, 272, 283).

Consequently, I suggest that the style and content of Gibson's work emanate from the Canadian consciousness, for, as an American ex-patriot/expatriate, Gibson has been living as a Canadian. Although Gibson was born in the United States in 1948, he had some problems with the Vietnam War and the U.S. draft board. In search of a counter-cultural lifestyle, he decided to go on an extended leave of absence from his home and native land. He arrived in Toronto at the age of 20, and eventually settled in Vancouver, British Columbia, with his Canadian wife in 1972. There, at the University of British Columbia, he took his first course in science fiction (see Olsen 1992, 5).

But living one's adult life as a Canadian surely must mean more than writing different stories than if one instead had lived in Los Angeles or New York. I suggest that one of the most useful statements in this regard comes from Marshall McLuhan: "Canada is a land of multiple borderlines, psychic, social and geographic. Canadians live at the interface where opposites clash. We have, therefore, no recognizable identity, and are suspicious of those who think they have" (in Nevitt and McLuhan 1994, 285). Arguably, then, Canada has an inferiority complex. It defines itself not on the basis of what it is, but on what it is not — more often than not with reference to the lion that lies to the south of us and threatens to squash us simply by rolling over in its sleep.

Gibson's outlook coincides well with this temperament. As demonstrated by the journeys of his characters on his pages, "the international and the intercultural have become the norm. He suggests that it is thus grossly naive to think of oneself … within any national restriction" (Olsen 1992, 6). And arguably, Canada has no unified culture itself, no manifest destiny linking its occupants, except perhaps policies encouraging official multiculturalism. As such, it may be the perfect environment for visions of society such as those fostered by Gibson.

With this perspective, it is useful to note another similarity between the writings of McLuhan and Gibson. Both authors share a contempt for the "national question." McLuhan saw no need for such a parochial standpoint in an age of instantaneous electronic-information transmission. He was, in fact, "always firm in his belief that the dawn of the 'global village,' this new era of 'universal understanding and unity' required the by-passing of 'national' political communities" (Kroker 1984, 82). Gibson, in turn, adopted a similar attitude: "People still don't understand that the Internet is transnational. Cyberspace has no borders, and that's fine with me because I had my fill of nationalism in the Vietnam War" (Josefsson 1996).

Through the use of new electronic technologies McLuhan foresaw a new age of interdependence that would recreate the world in the image of a global village. Furthermore, this view of technology is a common one within Gibson's genre: "The tools of global integration — the satellite media net, the multinational corporation — fascinate the cyberpunks and figure prominently in their work" (Sterling 1988, xiv). However, seeing world frontiers subsume nationalisms is not the only metaphor of the interface that Gibson and McLuhan share. As Kroker notes, "McLuhan's imagination always played at the interface of biology and technology" (1984, 71).

McLuhan argued that, in the electronic age of media with instantaneous scope and transnational range, people place their physical bodies inside extended nervous systems by means of electric media. Similarly, cyberpunk is described by Porush as the locale where passion and technology collide: "If we have learned that the flesh has a playground, then punk teaches us that the nervous system itself is where it is" (1992, 256). Many of the characters in Gibson's fiction demonstrate a need to extend themselves through the human-machine interface. In this fashion, cyberspace performs one of the primary functions of the electronic age, what McLuhan termed the disembodiment of users, the transformation of people into software (Benedetti and DeHart 1996, 79). This is perhaps most noticeable in the beginning of *Neuromancer* when Case describes his body as "meat"; unable to tap into cyberspace, he becomes trapped in the prison of his flesh.

Speaking of Case's situation in this fashion invokes one of the central slogans of the movie *Videodrome*: "Long live the new flesh!" Csicsery-Ronay Jr. (1992, 39) suggests that the film captures the essence of cyberpunk at least as well as *Neuromancer*. For my purposes, this is quite interesting. David Cronenberg, the director of the film, is Canadian. And one of the major characters in this film is the high priest of television and founder of the Cathode Ray Mission, Professor Brian O'Blivion. This character is a deliberate caricature of Marshall McLuhan, spouting such neologisms as "The television screen is the retina of the mind's eye." Reinforcing the idea that the media are in fact extensions of those who use them, O'Blivion believes that "watching TV will help patch [people] back into the world's mixing board."

We can see, then, that the cyberspace of Gibson's imagination is certainly a gateway to a fascinating universe of complex and transcendent information. It is, however, also a device used to control people and the information that they use for cultural capital. Viewed in this manner, Gibson's sense of technology — not utopian, but not explicitly anti-technological either — is very similar to McLuhan's. Notably, "in *The Medium Is the Massage*, McLuhan spoke of technology in highly ambivalent terms as, simultaneously, containing possibilities for emancipation and domination" (Kroker 1984, 62). Whether or not this ambivalence is characteristically Canadian, one could just as easily imagine Gibson explaining his work in the following manner: "I am an investigator. I make probes ... I talk back to the media and set off on an adventure of exploration. I don't explain. I explore" (McLuhan in Stearn 1967, xiii).

Obviously, then, there are similarities between William Gibson's and Marshall McLuhan's media-saturated sensibilities. Tom Wolfe asked of McLuhan in 1965 "what if he is right?" and 20 years later the world was asking similar questions of Gibson's shockingly dystopic vision of society. Now, more than 15 years after *Neuromancer* was written, when Tom Wolfe can be seen introducing McLuhan as the "seer of cyberspace" in the *VideoMcLuhan* series, linkages between the two men are beseechingly prevalent.

For instance, "Gibson regularly loads his sentences with a blend of high-tech jargon, brand names, street slang, and acronyms that lends an overall sense of urgency, intensity, and at times congestion to his style" (Olsen 1992, 36). Similarly, McLuhan also created a kaleidoscopic spectacle composed from the cultural flotsam and jetsam upon which our century floats. Neologisms, metaphors, and poetic intensity leap from the printed pages of both men. Confronted by a thousand points of light blazing across their writing — both brilliant and disorienting — popular culture has never been the same since the introductions of the terms "the global village" and "cyberspace" and the burning of these images into our collective imaginations.

This is not meant to indicate, of course, that Gibson could not have written what he has if McLuhan had not produced his body of work earlier. I know of no acknowledgment by Gibson that he has even read McLuhan, much less admit a creative debt. Similarities between the writers abound, however, in aspects of both their style and their content. Also interesting is the fact that, as is typical for most Canadians, they both had to go abroad to be recognized as successful. And while McLuhan became a ubiquitous American presence, Gibson did this in reverse. Gibson, a man of dubious nationality, like his characters, exhibits the same quality as McLuhan, "one of the great borderline features of the Canadian, namely his opportunities to 'take over' the United States intellectually" (McLuhan and Powers 1989, 161).

So, while it might be overstating the case to suggest that "cyberpunk came from Canada," I still wish to acknowledge the nationality of both Gibson's and McLuhan's work. While such romanticism may run contrary to these authors' own ideology, it follows a certain precedent: "I have no grasp of how computers really work.... My ignorance had allowed me to romanticize it" (Gibson in Olsen 1992, 3). With the background of Gibson's Canadian "lineage," one also must foreground the importance of popular culture to Gibson's world. This combination of absentee Canadiana and pop culture is colloquially evident in *Idoru*, the protagonist of which is christened Chia Pet McKenzie after "something cycling past on the Shopping Channel ... to the amazement of her absent Canadian father" (Gibson 1996, 14).

What, then, does the future hold for Gibson's futuristic society informed by present-day popular culture? Clues about the lasting significance of Gibson's work may be found in both his and McLuhan's words. In *Neuromancer* we find the passage, "fads swept the youth of the Sprawl at the speed of light; entire subcultures could rise overnight, thrive for a dozen weeks, and then vanish utterly" (1984, 58). It appears, however, that Gibson's vision has longer staying power than this excerpt suggests. Therefore, I appropriate McLuhan's words about quantum and relativity physics and suggest that Gibson's "cyberpunk" fiction and the importance of cyberspace "are not a fad. They have provided new facts about the world, new intelligibility, new insights into the universal fabric" (1951, 3).

Finally, I propose that the key to reading Gibson, and also McLuhan, is to be found in Gibson's own words. In *Mona Lisa Overdrive*, a work that brings the Matrix Trilogy to its conclusion, the reader is advised merely to seek comprehension, not closure: "Once Gentry got going, he used words and constructions that Slick had trouble understanding, but Slick knew from experience that it was easier not to interrupt him; the trick was in pulling some kind of meaning out of the overall flow, skipping over the parts you don't understand" (Gibson 1988, 127). Following in the footsteps of McLuhan, Gibson has managed to ignite prairie fires across our cultural landscape. While not everyone may enjoy his vision, and while it may not presage the exact social or technological development of the next millennium, he has taken a Canadian attitude and enlivened science fiction writing, made it illuminate the world around us, and invigorated our imaginations. As for the flames, I say let them burn.

REFERENCES

Benedetti, Paul, and Nancy DeHart. 1996. *Forward through the Rearview Mirror: Reflections on and by Marshall McLuhan.* Scarborough: Prentice Hall.

Csicsery-Ronay Jr., Istvan. 1992. "Futuristic Flu, or, The Revenge of the Future." In *Fiction 2000: Cyberpunk and the Future of Narrative,* ed. G. Slusser and T. Shippey. Athens, Ga.: University of Georgia.

Gibson, William. 1984. *Neuromancer.* New York: Ace Books.

———. 1988. *Mona Lisa Overdrive.* Toronto, Ont.: Bantam Books.

———. 1996. *Idoru.* New York: G.P. Putnam's Sons.

Josefsson, Dan. 1996. *Interview* (for the Swedish TV news program *Rapport*) [online]. Available: http://www.algonet.se/~danj/gibson1.html

Kroker, Arthur. 1984. *Technology and the Canadian Mind: Innis/McLuhan/Grant.* Montreal: New World Perspectives.

MacNair, Marian. 1989. "Mainframe Voodoo." *Montreal Mirror,* 7–20 April.

McCaffery, Larry. 1991. "An Interview with William Gibson." In *Storming the Reality Studio: A Casebook of Cyberpunk and Postmodern Fiction,* ed. L. McCaffery. Durham: Duke University Press.

McHale, Brian. 1992. *Constructing Postmodernism.* London: Routledge.

McLuhan, Marshall. 1951. *The Mechanical Bride: Folklore of Industrial Man.* Boston: Beacon Press.

———. 1964. *Understanding Media: The Extensions of Man.* New York: Mentor Books.

McLuhan, Marshall, and Bruce Powers. 1989. *The Global Village: Transformations in World Life and Media in the 21st Century.* New York: Oxford University Press.

Nevitt, Barrington, and Maurice McLuhan. 1994. *Who Was Marshall McLuhan?* Toronto: Stoddart.

Olsen, Lance. 1992. *William Gibson.* Mercer Island, Wash.: Starmont House.

Porush, David. 1992. "Frothing the Synaptic Bath: What Puts the Punk in Cyberpunk?" In *Fiction 2000: Cyberpunk and the Future of Narrative*, ed. G. Slusser and T. Shippey. Athens, Ga.: University of Georgia.

Stearn, Emanuel. 1967. *McLuhan: Hot and Cool.* New York: Dial Books.

Sterling, Bruce. 1987. "Preface." In William Gibson, *Burning Chrome*. New York: Ace Books.

———. 1988. "Preface." In *Mirrorshades: The Cyberpunk Anthology,* ed. B. Sterling. New York: Ace Books.

Tabbi, Joseph. 1995. *Postmodern Sublime: Technology and American Writing from Mailer to Cyberpunk*. Ithaca, N.Y.: Cornell University Press.

SPENDING, GETTING, SPENDING

INTRODUCTION

"Born to Shop," the T-shirt read, in big red letters on a black background. It had probably been a joke gift years ago, perhaps a reminder of excesses past. Now such slogan T-shirts crop up in second-hand stores and thrift shops, delivered bunched into plastic bags following closet-cleaning frenzies, one assumes. Donors hope someone else might get some use out of them—or at least garner a sardonic laugh. However, today's second-hand shoppers fall into three distinct categories: those who cannot afford to buy their clothes anywhere else; those who, disgusted by the staggering mounds of goods for sale, reject regular shopping outlets on moral and/or political grounds; and those trendy shoppers who seek retro or vintage goods. For the first category of shoppers, that "Born to Shop" slogan would seem cruel indeed.

Sloganeering shirts are no longer really cutting-edge fashion, but there were thousands of them around for a while, starting in the sixties. Shirts (and nightshirts) bearing the "Born to Shop" slogan were initially meant to be both ironic and self-deprecating: announcing one's unabashed materialism defused it somehow, made it less unattractive. Or so the marketers seemed to assume in the materialist 1980s. Despite the sobering realities of the 1990s, including a plunging dollar and high unemployment, the sentiment expressed by that old T-shirt may be more relevant than ever. Since the advertising boom began in the late 1950s, more than two generations of Canadians have been raised on a steady diet of advertising that successfully creates "wants" among thousands of people whose basic "needs" are already well met. It could be argued that the impetus to "express yourself through spending" might be stronger than ever worldwide because shopping is one of the few avenues of power and self-actualization (however spurious) left to the average person. And there have never been more blatant opportunities to shop, thanks to the increased growth in big-box outlets, television and Internet shopping sites, malls featuring the same chain stores selling the same merchandise nationwide, and the overall globalization of economies everywhere.

The Irish-born poet and dramatist Oscar Wilde (1854–1900), who has recently become somewhat of a commodity himself as a new generation of biographers, playwrights, and consumers rediscovers him, once wrote that a cynic is "a man who knows the price of everything and the value of nothing." He could well be referring to those unfortunate souls we now term "shopaholics," people who get their kicks buying more and more things that they don't really want or need. Like gamblers and alcoholics and other substance abusers, compulsive shoppers have their self-help groups.

This segment of *Pop Can* casts an eye both analytical and fond upon the way that merchandising — and purchasing — is a part of Canadian life and has a force and a scope that demand it be taken seriously as representing a subculture if not a culture unto itself. Journalist Robert Fulford muses upon the appeal of cheap figurines of Elvis (Presley not Costello or Stojko). Professor Candace Fertile calls shopping the "oldest profession" and remembers her earliest, moneyless forays into acquisition. And writer-professor Robert Wilson looks at the post-modernist aspects of the mall experience in his tour of the gargantuan (fiscally troubled but still growing) West Edmonton Mall. Perhaps in laying out floor after floor of shopping delights and time-wasting diversions, the mall's creators were subliminally aware of that other much-cited Wildean line from *Lady Windermere's Fan* — "I can resist everything except temptation."

THE MYSTERY OF THE BATHURST STREET ELVIS

Robert Fulford

It seems natural, if you think about it, that an air of mystery should surround anything connected with Elvis Presley, even a cheap plaster bust 50 centimetres tall. Presley, dead since 1977, keeps making furtive appearances among us, so why shouldn't there be something clandestine about a likeness of him sold at a corner store in Toronto?

For years I've pondered the garish, clumsily painted busts of Presley that sit in the window of Tops Variety, on Bathurst Street. Are they money-making items or just window decoration? Recently I went in and put this question to Walter Musy, one of the owners of the store. "They sell," he said, "very well — about 200 a month." He obviously enjoyed my astonishment. I had no idea Elvis was so hot in the Annex.

If Tops sells 200 a month, that means the homes of Toronto absorb 2400 Presleys a year from just one store. And it's no passing fad. Musy says sales have been steady for years, so Tops has sold about 10 000 since 1992. Buyers cover the demographic spectrum — "All walks of life, young and old, from junkies to doctors. Last Christmas we sent Elvises by courier to Vancouver, Ottawa — and Tokyo. One time a caterer bought 24 of them, for centrepieces on the tables at a wedding banquet." How many are bought "ironically," how many "seriously"? There's no way to tell; perhaps the purchasers themselves wouldn't know for sure.

Who makes them? That's the mystery. "To tell you the truth, I don't know," Musy said. "The man who delivers them won't say who the manufacturer is. All I know is, it's someone in Hamilton." The delivery man, Frank, won't give his last name, either. Also, he won't tell why he won't tell. He just shows up, often, with a few dozen Elvises in neat rows in the back of his station wagon, some in blue, some in gold (blue outsells gold, seven to three). Been doing it for years. Frank gets paid in cash, $15 per Presley; Tops sells them at $19.95, a modest one-third mark-up. Frank also brings gargoyles and statues of Jesus and Mary, but they don't sell like Elvis.

Musy is mildly frustrated by the secret provenance of these art objects, and he has carefully but fruitlessly examined a couple of them, looking for a stamp or a mark. There's insecurity in working with a nameless source: if Frank failed to show up, Musy wouldn't know where to call him. Still, Musy can accommodate a little frustration and insecurity. Not counting overhead, Tops Variety makes about $12 000 a year from Elvis Presley and an artist nobody knows.

THE OLDEST PROFESSION

Shopping

Candace Fertile

My shopping career began in earnest when I was seven. My currency was time and deceit. My boutiques were the garbage cans in the alley behind our apartment house in Edmonton.

I could not believe that people threw out such wonderful stuff. What a deal — something for nothing. Perhaps like the first-time gambler who wins and is forever hooked on that adrenaline rush, my love of shopping began with that first magical exposure, on a day when I was wandering home from school, taking my usual route through back alleys. To my extreme delight, I saw peeking out of a galvanized-steel garbage pail what looked like a blue three-ring binder. Acquisition grabbed my seven-year-old soul, and to this day it hasn't let go, fuelled no doubt by relentless advertising and the creation of more and more stuff that announces to the world who we are. Or perhaps who we want to be.

In that alley, my paper-loving self honed in on that blue binder like a cat streaking up from the basement at the sound of a can opener, and I started to understand the power of objects. As a second-grader, I was (unjustly, I thought) required to use despised scribblers. The covers were barely more substantial than the rather nasty paper within them. The booklets had three staples in the middle holding the whole ugly mess together. I hated these scribblers, and I hated their name. And I particularly hated the fact that the teacher would stalk around the room, checking to see if we were properly holding our pencils (another affront — I longed to use a pen). Periodically she would sneak up and grab our yellow HBs to make sure that we were not gripping them too tightly. Her actions made me clutch my pencil as if it were keeping my heart pumping. And the choke-hold I had on my pencil meant that I frequently made holes in the flimsy paper of the scribbler. With grim regularity the teacher and I would get into a tug-of-war over my pencil.

It was after such a dismal war (I always had to lose) that the bright blue plastic corner of the binder caught my eye. I debated for some time about whether or not I was allowed to look in the can, or if taking something from a garbage can was stealing. I should mention: not only was I polite, but I was also Catholic. I knew God was watching my every move, and should I be so vile as to commit a mortal sin, lightning bolts would descend and incinerate my evil little soul, so that all that would be transported to Hell would be something the size of a barbecue briquette. The possibility of owning a binder seemed worth the risk.

I inched closer, then looked up and down the alley to make sure no one was watching me. I carefully removed the lid, which was already precariously perched to one side, and laid it on the ground. A perfect, blue, three-ring binder glowed at me. I was in Heaven. I picked it up and with disbelief discovered an unopened packet of three-hole paper inside. The narrow blue (not even the more babyish wide) lines on the stark white paper with the margins marked with a thin pink line were everything my crummy scribbler wasn't. This paper and binder were for grownups, not little kids.

I could hardly wait to write in my new binder. With a pen. I felt instantly grown-up, more important, more substantial, the tug-of-war over my pencil forgotten. I had gained a new status. And this emotional boost into the stratosphere was accomplished by the simplest of means: I had acquired a new object. And it was free. No drug would ever reproduce the rush I felt as my concept of myself and the world tilted.

On subsequent shopping expeditions down the back alleys I never found anything as great as the binder and paper, but sometimes I found stuff for my little brother. At two, he would play with just about anything. I enjoyed his delight, and finding free stuff meant saving my allowance. I now suspect my kid-sized version of dumpster-diving sparked my career as a bargain shopper.

Once I found a scarf — a sophisticated, almost sheer, leopard-spotted scarf. It spoke of glamour, beauty, and fashion, with just an edge of wildness. It was a scarf worn by elegant and capable women on television. It was perfect for my mother, who set off for work each morning with her matching high heels and handbag.

Maybe the scarf wasn't even supposed to have been thrown out, but there it was, dangling from a garbage can a few blocks away from home. (In the space of a few weeks, I had increased my territory substantially.) My mother would love this scarf, I thought, but I had no idea how I would explain the acquisition of such a treasure. I didn't have that kind of money. I had finally revealed the binder to her, as it was too difficult trying to write in it without being found out. Even that was hard, as I'd had to commit what I hoped was a venial sin by lying that a friend's older sister had given me the stuff. I knew that wouldn't work again with a scarf. And I still felt a bit singed around the edges from the lie. For a week I had imagined everyone thought I smelled like a campfire. And while I knew what the wrath of God entailed, I was absolutely sure that the wrath of my mother was worse.

I decided to come clean. I took the scarf home, and when my mother got home from work, I presented it to her. She was astonished, and then asked where I got it. I told her. To my bafflement, she burst into gales of laughter, nearly hiccupping herself into a coma while trying to catch her breath.

When she regained control, she announced that my garbage-looting days were over. Nice girls didn't do such things. And there could be dangerous things in the garbage. Like what, I wanted to know, but she wouldn't tell me. These events happened decades ago — I'm sure my mother was worried I'd cut myself on a tin can or broken bottle, not get jabbed by some hypodermic needle. Garbage was safer then, but not safe enough for my mother's daughter to play in it.

But what sticks indelibly in my mind is that my mother carefully washed and ironed the scarf and wore it faithfully, even proudly, a splash of jungle against her ever-so-fashionable green wool coat with the fur around the sleeves. She would fling one end over her shoulder as she headed out the door in the morning, as if to announce her formidable presence in the universe.

Scavenging no longer an option, I had to find another way to satisfy the desire for acquisition now flowing through my veins. Little did I know that I was turning into a good little twentieth-century consumer. According to Lauren Langman, an academic who studies human development:

> In the contemporary world, the signifying and celebrating edifice of consumer culture has become the shopping mall which exists in [a] pseudo-democratic twilight zone between reality and a commercially produced fantasy world of commodified goods, images, and leisure activities that gratify transformed desire and provide packaged self-images to a distinctive form of subjectivity. (40)

[handwritten: ↳ why is desire being transformed? to deflect Chomsky's 80%?]

Langman's thesis certainly helps to explain not only the label consciousness of shoppers but also the desire of many shoppers to become apparent walking billboards for name-brand products. How much difference, if any, is there between my girlish desire for white go-go boots and the current stampede to wear T-shirts emblazoned with "Roots" or "Nike"?

I prefer to think the difference is significant. I could be wrong, in which case, Langman's argument is unassailable. But another academic offers me some hope. In an article in *Vogue* titled "The Professor Wore Prada," Elaine Showalter, professor of English at Princeton and recently president of the Modern Language Association, comments on her love of fashion and shopping. She does so in a humorous way, defending her intellectualism, femininity, and feminism. As she says, "For years I have been trying to make the life of the mind coexist with the day at the mall, and to sneak the *femme* back into feminist" (80). Showalter delineates the various ways female academics (herself included) have dressed in an effort to be taken seriously, and ends her essay by saying, "if you want to deconstruct my feminist criticism, go right ahead. But you'd better not sneer at my angel backpack or step on my blue suede shoes. I've paid my dues dressing 'feminist,' and now I'm going to wear what I like" (92). Showalter's essay is full of the pleasure one can gain from shopping, both the activity of looking and actual purchase. Throughout history and likely before, human beings have been drawn to objects of beauty (although certainly the concepts of beauty change).

[handwritten: beauty for spice of life, not way of life]

The acquisition of objects, beautiful or otherwise, is usually an economic transaction. As a child prevented from plundering garbage bins, I needed a new way to get the stuff I wanted. So from time and deceit as currency, I turned to the more usual one: money. Getting that required work. My first job was ironing for my mother. I had seen a T-shirt in Sears, and my mother refused to buy it for me because, as she said, "You don't need it." It's no wonder that nowadays when I buy yet another object I don't need I think of King Lear's "Oh, reason not the need." The other object that captured my fancy was a particular lava lamp. I loved that lava lamp, but it was out of the realm of financial possibility. And my mother was right about the T-shirt. I didn't need it. I wore a uniform to school, and I had sufficient play clothes. Incessant pestering of my mother resulted in the ironing agreement. I ironed like a demon, encouraging my beleaguered mother to change clothes frequently so I could have something to iron. Eventually I saved enough to buy the T-shirt, and I wore it to shreds. It was the first thing I bought for myself with my own money, and I remember it in every detail. Still. It had short white sleeves, a white back, and a front in four coloured squares of red, yellow, blue, and green. If I had had white go-go boots to match, life would have achieved its pinnacle. (Elaine Showalter, by the way, wore white go-go boots to her Ph.D. defence.)

[handwritten left: desire for beauty used by commerce in order to subjugate]
[handwritten right: self ownership through purchase power]

Since those very early days, my shopping has expanded in terms of money, objects, and range. Like many middle-class Canadians, I have more material goods than some small nations, and I am constantly acquiring more. What is interesting is that none of us needs all these things, but lemming-like we hurl ourselves at the nearest mall, which has acquired the status of a cathedral for some. Or else we seek out independent and unique shops in downtowns and other shopping areas. We go to outlets and discount centres. We are the consumer society of which much has been written. Thorstein Veblen's *The Theory of the Leisure Class* (1934), Christopher Lasch's *The Culture of Narcissism* (1979), and Hilary Radner's *Shopping Around: Feminine Culture and the Pursuit of Pleasure* (1995) are just three of the many works written to explore humans' need to shop even when we are way beyond buying what is necessary for our survival. Veblen's term "conspicuous consumption" indicates that the purchase of many unnecessary items is a performance. It's interesting to imagine what the performance means. If we examine advertising, which certainly fuels consumer desire, we see that Langman's view of buying an identity is accurate. To wear a certain brand (a "Roots" or "Nike" T-shirt is infinitely more desirable to certain groups than, say, a "K-Mart" T-shirt) or to drive a certain car or to drink a certain beer is presumably a statement of who we are. Or is it?

In his essay "The Individual, Consumption Cultures and the Fate of Community," Rob Shields attends to the performative aspect of purchasing and gives consumers some credit: "Many consumers are now ironic, knowing shoppers, conscious of the inequalities of exchange and the arbitrary nature of exchange value. As social actors, they attempt to consume the symbolic values of objects and the mall environment while avoiding the inequalities of exchange" (100). Shields's essay notes that public spaces have changed and that the mall serves as a gathering place. Thus, the activity of shopping (whether or not a purchase is made) plays a significant social role. Shields argues: "It is necessary to recognize that consumption itself is partly determined by the non-rational, cultural element of society. Shopping is not just a functional activity. Consumption has become a communal activity, even a form of solidarity" (110). It appears to me that shopping plays a number of roles, and one of these is certainly a communal one, as Shields argues. But it can also be said that in addition to having a connective importance, shopping — and more specifically the purchased goods — can fulfill people's desires both to join a group and to differentiate themselves from one another. For example, clothing choices are laden with meaning, even if the message is inaccurate.

Shoppers, as Shields notes, are becoming more sophisticated and particular, if the growth in thrift stores is any indication. A CBC newscast in July 1998 noted that the thrift store business is so popular that charities depending on donations have to be much more competitive. We are still conspicuously consuming, but we want a bargain. Certain sections of the population have always needed to shop for sale goods, but the practice is now losing any stigma it might have had. In fact, getting a bargain, or a "steal," marks one as a consummate shopper. Getting a deal has become a selling point for much commercial activity. I'd like to mention sales, for example. Anyone in western Canada familiar with Woodward's $1.49 Day will remember the thrust and parry of grabbing for the goodies on this once-a-month sale extravaganza. The deals were often extraordinary, and people didn't want to miss this opportunity. Encountering sharp elbows was common. In contrast, the former frenzy of Bay Day has abated now that the sale lasts for ages and has lost any special air. No need to dive in a scrum for the merchandise. No, it's all there in stacks, and then we stand in line to pay. Infrequent sales events such as Boxing Day sales create line-ups hours before the stores open. The sale must appear to be an unusual event or it garners little excitement. I once worked at Harrods, and the annual sale was marked by the sound of crashing crockery as maniacal shoppers stormed the aisles.

But what are we doing when we shop, and why do I refer to it as the oldest profession? The answer is simple. Well, sort of. In *Shopping Around: Feminine Culture and the Pursuit of Pleasure*, Hilary Radner argues the following: "Feminine culture emphasizes a process of investment and return, of negotiation, in which the given articulation of pleasure is always measured against its costs, the inevitable price of an invitation that is never extended freely, never absolutely, the terms of which change from day to day, from place to place" (178). While the terms and values change, it is surely the case that a shopper considers the relative costs (whether in time, effort, or money) and the benefits of the object gained. And these judgments will differ from person to person even within the same socio-economic group.

Shopping is our contemporary form of hunting and gathering. Men may have hunted, and women may have gathered, but both processes resulted in maintaining life. And if the effort expended exceeded what was gained — the result was death. Such an obvious relationship between acquisition (shopping in a sense) and survival is still evident in the world today. But in rich countries like Canada, hunting and gathering is largely done at the mall, and our survival is not in question. In "Dressed to Kill," Don Gillmor makes fun of men at a clothing sale, and he uses the metaphor of the hunt:

> The big game is on the suit rack, though. Some of the men simply drape a dozen business suits over one arm and then try to find a little room in which to sort and sniff them, like lions defending their kill. But to bring down a three-button, blue wool crepe 42R Donna Karan (reg. $2,295, now $395) in open country requires keen eyesight, stealth, and a burst of cheetah-like speed…. [Men] are taking home cashmere and silk and cotton that feels like whipped butter. They have hunted well and they are filled with the self-knowledge that comes with risk and death and loss and dramatic savings. (75)

Whether the hunting is done in an exclusive boutique or a thrift store, it's the thrill of the chase that drives shoppers. It could be the lure of low prices, or exclusive merchandise, or the media-created buzz about something completely useless like Cabbage Patch Dolls or Beanie Babies that gets everyone out there, roaming, foraging, stalking, pouncing, occasionally even wrestling another shopper for the item.

Then we bag our prize and take it back to our cave, er, home. I bet those cavepeople never stopped and said to each other, "Listen, honey, I think we have too many acorns or dried fish or fur blankets." I think they were out there scooping up whatever they thought might come in handy for survival.

And so while many of us shop for a variety of reasons, including pleasure, but rarely need (even grocery stores are full of stuff no one needs to survive; in fact, some of that junk probably shortens lives), perhaps somewhere at the heart of the endeavour is a genetic link to our past, when tracking and locating food was essential for survival. Now different needs drive our shopping expeditions. And survival is perceived in ways beyond the merely physical.

[handwritten marginal notes: "but that was natural (eat or die) shop-o-die is not, what of the reasons behind the creation of this sys. of consumption? Is it a prison of commerce's creation? Chimpokemon 'gotta catch'em all' why?"]

[handwritten marginal note: "perception reordered to unnatural by commerce."]

REFERENCES

Gillmor, Don. "Dressed to Kill: What Really Happens When Men Go Hunting for Deep Discounts." *Saturday Night* 113, no. 5 (June 1998): 75.

Langman, Lauren. "Neon Cages: Shopping for Subjectivity." In *Lifestyle Shopping: The Subject of Consumption*, ed. Rob Shields, 40–82. London: Routledge, 1992.

Radner, Hilary. *Shopping Around: Feminine Culture and the Pursuit of Pleasure*. New York: Routledge, 1995.

Shields, Rob. "The Individual, Consumption Cultures and the Fate of Community." In *Lifestyle Shopping: The Subject of Consumption*, ed. Rob Shields, 99–113. London: Routledge, 1992.

Showalter, Elaine. "The Professor Wore Prada." *Vogue*, December 1997: 80, 86, 92.

PLAYING AND BEING PLAYED

Experiencing West

Edmonton Mall's *Hyperspace.*

Robert R. Wilson

One Friday night I stood in front of Chilli Hot Hot, under the twinkling electric night sky, on Bourbon Street in West Edmonton Mall (WEM). Immediately across the way, a woman emerged from the red and green Sherlock Holmes pub firmly guided by a man who was speaking to her even as he seemed to be pushing against her shoulders. She looked as if she were in one of those difficult in-between states, tears and rage in her case, when you are forced to do something that you definitely would prefer not to do. My attention was abruptly attracted to a second man, who was issuing from the pub behind her, a friend or companion of the evening, I supposed. He was a large young man with a blond brush cut, and he was wearing a green flannel sports jacket and a striped shirt open at the neck. His face was contorted in pain, anger too it seemed, and he appeared to be dancing, rising backwards rigidly and stepping forward on his toes. This was an illusion. He was being shoved, one arm twisted up behind his back, by an even larger man I understood to be a bouncer. Once they were out of the pub, the bouncer was joined by the man who had escorted the woman outside; together they threw the large blond man down on the floor next to a battered red London telephone booth, a Sherlock Holmes signature.

As a crowd began to gather, the two men pushed the other down flat against the floor, and one of them knelt beside him and began rhythmically to bang his head against the tile surface. The woman stood back, weeping and talking to herself. The young man on the floor kept saying, "I'm sorry. I'm sorry." A moment later they dragged him to the exit (number 6) and threw him down on the rubber matting between the doors. I didn't try to get any nearer and so I couldn't hear what they were saying to him. I supposed that they were threatening him and perhaps giving him a reprimand. After another couple of minutes, an Edmonton Police cruiser arrived. The man was searched, his hands were tied behind him, and he was then bundled into the back seat of the cruiser. He was still talking, probably still saying, "I'm sorry." I had no idea what he had done, and no one in the group of people who were gawking with me seemed to know either. The woman who had emerged from the pub ahead of him had now disappeared into Bourbon Street's artificial night. There was no way to ask her, even if I had wanted to do so. Perhaps he had been violent or, more likely, had given indications that he might become violent; perhaps he had been insulting or grossly rude to one of the servers. When I asked my companion what she had understood his cringing apologies to mean, she said that he must have been sorry for having had too much fun. That answer, though perhaps rather abstract for the violence witnessed, was the likely reason.

There are limits to the amount of fun you can have under the best conditions, but a commercial pleasure dome, such as West Edmonton Mall, restricts your fun tightly. You wouldn't dance in the mall or in one of the shops (imagine dancing in the Sony Store!), and you wouldn't sing, no matter how splendid your voice, in one of the food fairs. You probably would not last long if, in a moment of exaltation or pure delight, you tried skipping, hopping, or prancing. You can have fun in the mall, but only within the known limits and according to the prescribed manner. There is no allowance for spontaneous behaviour, no tolerance for street theatre, for satire, mockery or dramatic inversion. Within the mall's perpetual ambience of carnival, there is no room for truly carnivalesque behaviour.

Although there are always unexpected events, a sudden show of violence perhaps, an actual crime or an attempt, an unpleasant expression of madness, most malls run smoothly. Viewed from a distance as a well-oiled commercial machine, a mall might even seem boring. Yet malls fascinate. Even people who despise the experience of shopping at malls, thinking of them as hyper-commercial or degrading or as traps to lure the unwary, may find the mall concept compelling. Malls are much like labyrinths or theme parks: they are constructed by humans and they are self-enclosed, often difficult to navigate, and packed with surprises. To understand how malls fascinate, imagine standing outside a room with its door closed, its contents hidden from view. You open the door, cross a threshold, and enter a new and different space, or at least you do so the first time you cross. It is the act of crossing for the first time that promises adventure, difference, and reward. There is a scene in Federico Fellini's 1970 film, *Roma*, in which the workers building a subway beneath Rome break through a curtain of dirt into a space that had once been a room in a Roman villa. The walls are decorated with frescos representing the everyday life of ancient Rome. As the construction workers and the members of Fellini's film crew watch, the frescos vanish into the air. Every room, until you know for certain what is in it (and even then), contains potential mysteries. And, like the underground room in *Roma*, there is nothing in any room that you can be certain will remain unchanged. Part of the capacity of rooms to surprise lies in this uncertainty. This may even be true of the rooms with which you are most familiar, but it is certainly the case with rooms, educational or commercial, that you visit only occasionally. Anyone who has ever shopped in a large mall, or who has been in the habit of going to one for entertainment, will recognize the moment of finding a favourite shop gone, a restaurant or a particularly exciting amusement disappeared.

The idea of a room suggests one source of a mall's attractiveness. It points to a universal human experience, crossing over and entering, which may explain how malls assert their commercial power. A second explanatory idea, diametrically opposed to the first, has to do with understanding malls as a peculiar kind of space. The idea of a totally strange space, one so bizarrely involuted and disorienting that you might find yourself lost within it, plays an important role in attempts to make sense out of this post-modern phenomenon. In this view, malls are something new but also very much a part of the general approach to architecture that has emphasized perplexity, illusion, and all the potential for misdirection that bizarre spaces can offer.

I am beginning this essay on West Edmonton Mall within a context that also considers other commercial malls and with two incompatible hypotheses. In itself, this might seem like a post-modern effort. However, as I shall make clear, I favour the first idea — that malls are best explained in terms of universal human experience, both in the actual world and in literature. I shall return to the post-modern theory of strangeness and uncanny space, but I shall begin with the (far from) simple idea of a room.

When you think about going into a strange room, one that may contain unimagined pleasures or horrifying threats, you must envision both a space and also a point of crossing, an entrance. This might be a door, a hatch, a flap, a curtain or merely an open rectangle of light or darkness. It might even be, as in old-fashioned fun houses, a short series of turns, the arm and elbow of a rudimentary maze. Whatever shape it takes, the crossing-point, over the threshold or under the lintel, leads into the possibilities of the room. The first step into the room involves the decision to cross, to accept the challenge the threshold poses. This is illustrated by the liturgy and doctrine of religions, which usually lay claim to a sacred space or to a number of rituals that, whenever they are enacted, create a separate and holy place. Crossing over or entering seems to be a fundamental aspect of all religious experience. Acknowledging this is not to claim that contemporary malls, such as West Edmonton Mall in Alberta or the Mall of America in Minnesota, are sacred spaces or in any significant way related to religious experience.[1] The analogy of sacred space does, however, suggest that the builders of malls know very well how attractive and exciting a self-enclosed space can be and what a powerful aura may accompany crossing into it. A mall, such as West Edmonton Mall, re-enacts the possibilities of enclosed space, holding out the opportunities such spaces have always promised. Each time you cross into one, leaving the world behind in the parking lot, even if it is only to browse or hang out, you enter the promise of alternative space: difference, excitement, even fun.[2]

European literature overflows with narratives about people, often children, who have crossed a boundary of some sort and found themselves within an alternative reality, a bizarre land of existential puzzles. Quite often it turns out to be a land that follows different physical principles: horses and other animals can fly; magic is normal. In contemporary science fiction versions of the land across the threshold, faster-than-light speeds are possible (from the standpoint of fiction, a magical flying horse or carpet and a faster-than-light spacecraft are not greatly dissimilar); both space and time behave differently; and the inhabitants may be distinctly non-human. Folk tales recount crossings-over into supernatural worlds populated by fairies, elves, or tiny garden sprites, all with powers that, on the human side of the boundary, are impossible to obtain. In the sixteenth century, Edmund Spenser transformed this kind of folk lore into a long narrative poem in which characters move from England to "Faerieland" across a boundary that is indefinite and largely indeterminate, although associated vaguely with the Irish Sea as Faerieland itself, through the force of allegory, is identified with Ireland. Many stories written for children involve trips across borders (a looking-glass, for example, is a kind of territorial boundary) into places like Oz, Narnia, or Middle-Earth. Games, like fiction, also possess borders and indicate thresholds to cross. Part of the appeal of any game, whether played on a board, on a field, or (like Dungeons & Dragons and other role-simulation games) in the head, is the experience of crossing into a separate and self-contained space that allows, according to its rule structure, an alternative reality.

The two experiences, playing games and reading fantasy, are often combined in fictions in which characters find themselves entrapped within a game. Both Chris Van Allsburg's

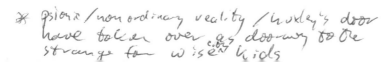

Weaveworld

1981 novel *Jumanji* and Joe Johnston's rather different 1995 film version explore this narrative path insightfully: the game is a self-contained alternative world, following its own principles, that can be accessed through playing it. Players, like readers in their similar experience, can be absorbed in, caught up in, lost in, "swallowed" by the game; they can be run away with. In all kinds of ways, players are submerged in and transformed by the mental activity of games. Even when the game is extremely physical, hockey or football, say, players find themselves absorbed in the play, so wholly caught up in the game's mental dimension that the ordinary world might be said to have ceased to exist for them. For all of these related experiences, the initial moment is the crossing of a threshold. Once you make that first move, you find yourself in what Johan Huizinga calls the "magic turf," the closed space — "hedged off from the everyday surroundings" — in which special rules obtain and play proceeds (Huizinga, 19). The child's invocation "Let's pretend" is an invitation to an experience of make-believe, but it is also an invitation to a voyage. Make-believe domains are what make both games and, more complexly perhaps, literature exciting. Their possibility is also what gives allure to self-enclosed spaces such as malls. Behind the construction of malls lie two fundamental notions: that people universally desire alternative worlds, self-contained experiences that are different and ordinarily unavailable, and that they will recognize such a world when they encounter it. This is one reason why malls such as West Edmonton Mall often seem to be competing not only with downtown shopping centres but with museums and zoos, as well as with, much more obviously, theme parks. The more eye-catching things you can pack into a mall without seriously curtailing retail space, the better.[3] Why these beyond-the-threshold experiences are so fascinating, so hard to resist, is a difficult question, but the answer may have much to do with the obvious truth that all human life is marked by the crossings of metaphorical thresholds such as birth and death.

A mall is a large collection of different rooms, each promising pleasure or satisfaction, but it is also a room in itself. A modern North American mall is a radically self-contained structure. In this respect, it is both like and unlike the arcade, a commercial edifice that became popular in Europe and South America during the nineteenth century. Following its etymology as an architectural term signifying a long walkway beneath arches, the arcade is typically a long, narrow commercial space that you can enter from the street. Once you are inside, you walk along a large central corridor flanked by shops and cafés. Sometimes the high ceiling is glass, recalling the architecture of nineteenth-century European railway stations, but more usually it is only the underside of an office building's higher floors. Often there is a second level, also with shops but less spacious and less elegant, looking down into the central corridor. An arcade creates the possibility of enclosed and continuous shopping with few distractions other than the chance to enjoy a coffee or cake. It has always been easy for shoppers to enjoy the comparative quiet of an arcade, even to lose themselves for a moment or two, and to take delight in the experience. An early twentieth-century cultural critic, Walter Benjamin, remarks upon the "eternal nowness" of an arcade. You could forget things in an arcade and feel yourself swallowed up in the moment, as if the world (the outside, the "left-behind") had disappeared. In that respect, the arcade anticipated the mall, which also offers the pleasures of complete nowness. However, there is an important difference: the mall is actually self-contained, not merely so as an act of imagination. To reach an arcade, you step in from the street; to reach a mall, you drive, park your car, and walk through an entrance.[4] West Edmonton Mall, a huge space occupied by several large buildings of different sizes, sits behind thousands of parking spaces, most of them in multiple tiers.

Its physical separation — standing apart from the surrounding city in its own vastness and reachable only across its parking lots — indicates an essential aspect of contemporary malls. They advertise their physical isolation and promise to provide a total shopping-entertainment experience. They proclaim their apartness.

Looking west along the North Saskatchewan river valley towards West Edmonton Mall from the balcony of an apartment in the city's central core 10 kilometres away, you will see on the horizon several differently formed structures, but three stand out. One is an oddly shaped hump, high and apparently quite narrow, which houses the "Mindbender," a 14-storey, triple-loop roller-coaster with terrifying down-swoops. Another is the mall's "Fantasyland" hotel, a black-glass post-modern extravaganza with 118 "theme" rooms (out of a total of 354) that are designed around a number of different motifs — the Truck Room, the Canadian Rail Room, and Polynesian, African, Roman, Arabian, Hollywood, and Victorian Coach Rooms. And, if that were not enough, there is also an Igloo Room.[5] The largest of the three structures is a glass dome resembling an aeroplane hanger; this is the mall's Waterpark, which features a wave pool with regular machine-generated waves, on which surfing is possible, and 22 slides of varying heights, ranging up to 26 metres. The Alberta-born French novelist Nancy Huston writes that this is the most popular tourist attraction in Edmonton (she is probably not correct in saying this, but the mall as a whole would be) and that her Parisian children were "goggle-eyed" when they saw it (67). The Waterpark, the hotel, and the "Galaxyland" amusement park, of which the Mindbender is only one of 25 rides, all support the illusion that West Edmonton Mall is a self-enclosed experience, full of fabulous possibilities that could never be found, and hardly even approximated, elsewhere. The mall indicates a pattern for other contemporary malls, including the Mall of America: large, crowded (even overpacked), and diverse. People might be drawn there for the vast range of possible experiences, perhaps above all for the surprises, the hint of the fabulous; but once there, they generally want to consume in a big way. In one sense, notwithstanding the varied possibilities for fun, when people cross the threshold into a mall they are being led into a commercial trap.

West Edmonton Mall's size and diversity point the argument back to the second hypothesis concerning the fascination of malls. They are huge, packed, diverse, and entrapping, but they are so in a wholly new way. The sense of "eternal nowness" Benjamin saw in the traditional arcade is further heightened, both intensified and distorted, by the almost-overpowering impression the mall gives of an artificial paradise, a pleasure dome in which time has not merely stopped but has never begun. You do not step in off the street to visit Xanadu; rather, you must travel there as if to an extraordinary, even supernatural, place. Travelling through the United States, Umberto Eco found the repeated phenomena of roadside museums — those attention-grabbing stops ("See IT!" "Don't miss IT!") that appear in almost mind-boggling multiplicity — to be one of the outstanding characteristics of American culture. This phenomenon is a kind of hyperreality, Eco argues, in that obvious fakes, indeed profound falsifications of reality, are taken to be more attractive, more see-able even, than the reality they mimic. Canadian culture, though perhaps more muted in its promotional riffs, is hardly less devoted to hyperreality and the celebration of fakes. In that sense, West Edmonton Mall can be seen as a spectacular mirror world of fakery, in which "reality," normality, and even rationality are all left outside in the parking lot. An important dimension of post-modernism, it could be argued, lies in its preference for fakes of all kinds, for deceptions and illusions.[6]

This view takes on an even more radical form in the writings of Jean Baudrillard, who argues, within the context of an even more hyper version of hyperreality, that illusion actually displaces reality in North America. American reality, he writes, was there before the TV screen was invented, but "everything about the way it is today suggests it was invented with the screen in mind, that it is the refraction of a giant screen" (55). Though you might imagine that TV falsifies everything that it images, it actually confers "reality" upon life. Hence, everything exists as if it had been made for TV or "with the screen in mind." North America is a society of "complexity, hybridity, and the greatest intermingling" (Baudrillard, 7) of distinct levels of reality in which simulacra, whether physical fakes or optical illusions, have come to stand in for what was once known as "reality." The typical post-modern building will be what West Edmonton Mall so wonderfully, if bizarrely, is: a nest of illusions that markets illusions.

Fredric Jameson has argued that the architecture of our time, a post-modern or "late" capitalistic age, has built interior spaces for which nothing in human history has prepared us. They are nearly unimaginable, or at least, as Jameson argues, human imagination has not kept pace with the architectural evolution of enclosed space. The new architecture, he observes, has created paradoxical and difficult-to-navigate enclosed spaces that require us to "grow new organs, to expand our sensorium and our body to some new, yet unimaginable, perhaps ultimately impossible, dimensions" (39). You can easily become lost in such "hyperspace" (44). Even in a definite, if highly complex, space such as West Edmonton Mall (packed with mirrors to enhance its House of Illusions effect), with its many maps, its numbers, and its security force, it is all too possible to lose your orientation, to begin to wander, and ultimately not to know where you are.

Jameson thinks that disorientation is an inevitable consequence of the post-modern imagination, but one that a new generation, with an increased at-oneness with computer technology, will learn to overcome. For Baudrillard, all of North American society is a game of make-believe, a gargantuan simulation in which "Let's pretend" constitutes a metaphysical principle.

There are, as I have tried to show, two distinct, even opposed, ways of looking at a cultural spectacle such as West Edmonton Mall. On the one hand, it can be seen as drawing upon the attractiveness of a room (crossing thresholds) that seems basic to, even co-terminus with, all human experience, but especially religious and spiritual experience. On the other hand, it can be seen as exemplifying a uniquely contemporary experience (involuted and confusing space) that seems basic to all post-modern architecture and marketing. In the first view, a mall such as WEM will seem familiar even before you enter it simply because the kind of promise that it holds forth is itself familiar, the sort of thing that human beings have always sought. In the second view, the mall will seem inherently unfamiliar, even if you have gone there before or have seen other, similar places, because its crowded and illusion-packed spaces differ from the normal reality you have just stepped out of and require you to grow "new organs" of perception in order to understand them.

As I have already remarked, I prefer the first hypothesis. It makes sense to see continuity in human experience and, especially when fascination and attractiveness are part of the equation, to look for common explanations. Yet, like the diverging possibilities within WEM, the different paths that beckon once you have crossed its threshold suggest the second way of looking at contemporary malls, the way that also encompasses theme parks and other commercial structures such as casinos and museums. What the second view underscores most powerfully is the playlessness of post-modern constructions. They are playful in their design (full of *trompe l'oeil* and other illusions), and they offer opportunities for a certain kind of regulated "play" (like that offered at amusement parks, waterparks, and submarine rides), but they preclude spontaneous play. There is little scope for make-believe; instead, the play has been made in advance (prefabricated "made-believe"), designed and packaged for you to step into. You will be played upon much more than you will play. There is nothing at all that resembles the "magic turf" that Huizinga argues is the essential quality of all genuine play. Remember the anecdote with which I began this essay and try to evoke in your mind's eye the scene of the young man being bounced from Sherlock Holmes. Imagine that in the pub he had become exuberant, boisterous, or raucous. One moment he was having fun, being sponta- neous and playful; the next, he had become rowdy. And at that moment, he was having too much fun, more fun than his environment allowed. He would begin saying "I'm sorry," over and over, as the bouncer twisted his arm upwards and hustled him into a frog-step. A huge mall like West Edmonton Mall, much as a casino (a notoriously serious, even dour, place) or a theme park, creates the impression of play but rigorously limits its possibilities. Play (which is a link on WEM's Web site) both exists and fails to exist at the mall. This is a problem for those who hope to analyse and interpret the mall experience, but it is also a problem, one that must be understood if not actually solved, for every single mall-goer. How much fun can you have? Within all the illusions of play, how playful can you be?

ENDNOTES

1. Many people find the Mall of America to be a more elegant mall. It has a number of classy shops and its vast central atrium, dominated by the inflated figure of Snoopy, has become a familiar image since the mall opened in 1992. However, West Edmonton Mall, built in three phases between 1981 and 1985, is still the world's largest mall. Its own publicity claims that it is still listed in the *Guinness Book of Records* as the "largest shopping mall in the world." It contains more than "eight hundred stores and services including eight major department stores" (the Bay shows up twice at WEM). There are over a hundred places to eat (many in the two food fairs) and 19 cinemas. WEM has a large amusement park, a Waterpark (the size of five NFL fields), an NHL-size ice rink, two theme streets (Bourbon Street and the sophisticated Europa Boulevard), numerous fountains, and (the old joke still holds) more submarines (four) than the Canadian Navy. On the same lake (the "world's largest indoor lake") that the submarines navigate along tracks beneath the surface, there is a replica of Columbus's ship the *Santa Maria,* sponsored (appropriately) by Kodak, which can be rented for weddings and receptions. WEM has parking for more than 20 000 vehicles, includ- ing RVs and trailers. (I have talked to children at the mall who claimed that they were spending their summer vacations camped with their parents in one of the lots.) The mall is 483 000 square metres (or 5 200 000 square feet) in expanse. Entering the mall, a visitor may feel that it is too vast, too crowded, already too much. Its sheer physical size can be overwhelming, and some visitors, not otherwise disabled, feel that they must move about on the electric scooters that can be rented. However, lost or confused visitors will be rescued. WEM's self-described "cutting-edge" security system maintains an emergency telephone system throughout the mall and promises rapid re- sponse when called upon. The security force watches over WEM by closed-circuit TV, by foot pa- trol, and, during the summer, by a "security bike unit" that protects the parking lots. (To be a member of WEM's security force, you must have a university degree in criminology, a college diploma in law enforcement, or considerable prior police experience.) There are many rumours about the kinds of crimes committed at WEM, but the most spectacular, once reported by the *Edmonton Journal*, that mall rats (human variety) and vagrants live in the subterranean utility ducts, may not be true. WEM has established a glitzy Web site, accorded "*Gold* status" by *NetGuide,* with internal links to many of the mall's shops and services, including Security. You can reach the site at http://www.westedmall.com.

2. No statistics will tell you how much fun people actually do have in malls such as WEM. However, it is a primary tourist destination for visitors to Alberta and probably attracts some people to the province who would not have come merely to see the Rocky Mountains or the Badlands. Local residents often claim to find the mall boring or unexciting, but it seems clear that many people, seeing it for the first time, are enchanted. For several years, I voluntarily took visitors to the University of Alberta's Arts Faculty on tours, sharing my personal interest in the elaborate illusiveness of malls. I could see that they always found the mall fascinating — perhaps no other word would describe as well the response of these educated, articulate visitors. One famous woman scholar, whom I had picked up from the airport, insisted that I take her to WEM *before* I took her to her hotel near the university. An Egyptian-American semiotician, to my dismay, spent more than nine hours in WEM engrossed in studying its sign systems, seeming to love every moment. An English social critic insisted that I play games in one of the video arcades with her. We sat next to each other and raced cars over dual computer screens for nearly an hour. Another scholar desperately wanted to ride the Drop of Doom, a 13-storey free-fall ride, and so we crashed towards earth together at a literally breath-stifling speed. Still another scholar, the author of a well-known book on postmodernism, demanded a private tour of the Fantasyland Hotel, which had to be diplomatically arranged. WEM changes all the time, and attractions that catch the attention of visitors can disappear overnight. IKEA has now been replaced by Red's, a vast pleasure dome (replicating in itself what the mall promises to be as a whole) that boasts, among many other attractions, five beers that are brewed on site. Once there were two enclosed kinetic sculptures, large glass containers crowded with bizarre combinations of elevators, doors, moving ladders, chutes, and collection funnels in which innumerable coloured balls were kept endlessly moving up and down. The visiting semiotician watched one of them for 45 minutes, so long indeed that I decided *not* to show him the other kinetic sculpture. Those sculptures, so fascinating and so in keeping with the post-modern spirit of WEM, have now, alas, vanished.

3. WEM still has several pools and aquaria with gold fish and exotic tropical fish. It also has a dolphin lagoon with four Atlantic bottlenose dolphins, Mavis, Maria, Gary, and Howard, who perform several times a day. At one time, the mall had other live creatures on display, including a pony for petting and several aviaries. Negative criticism from animal lovers forced WEM to stop displaying animals and birds. The last aviary, which had contained pheasants and peacocks in a relatively large area, has been removed, replaced by a two-storey Body Shop franchise. WEM has always had some museum functions, including a rock and mineral collection. There are replicas of the British Crown Jewels, a seven-foot Chinese pagoda, and seven porcelain vases from the Ching Dynasty. All of these attention-grabbers, although presented in terms of their educational purposes, add to the impression of the mall experience as something special and quite unlike anything possible outside, beyond the parking lots. The display windows of shops also have a vaguely museum-like purpose, and even some of WEM's entertainment locations, such as the Hard Rock Café, Red's, or Hooters, for example, have their own lines of logo-bearing paraphernalia that are displayed as if they were significant collections of valuable objects. Of course, all these museum simulacra are intended to attract your eye, making a claim upon, but never detracting significantly from, your available time for shopping.

4. West Edmonton Mall numbers its entrances. There are 58 of them. It is possible to arrange to meet a friend at a certain entrance simply by using a number: "Let's meet at entrance 33," for example. Most people probably recall where they have parked their cars by the number of the nearest entrance. The numbers, which are large and easily visible, play a significant role in establishing the set-apartness of the mall. An arcade usually occupies a city block as the lower floor or two of a commercial building. Its entrances, fewer than a mall's, lead out onto the streets. People often use arcades as shortcuts, something no one could do with a mall. When I lived in Santiago de Chile, a city with several European-type arcades, I habitually used a central downtown arcade as a way of crossing from one street to another. Today, trying to remember that arcade, I

find it impossible to recall even a single shop. All I can remember is its vaguely "old" style and its happy function as a shortcut between two places. The underground shopping areas in Toronto and Montreal are more like arcades than malls, since they are reached from the street or a Metro stop and are not actually self-enclosed. Large numbers of people traverse *through* the underground spaces towards business destinations. However, Toronto's underground shopping passageways, stretching from Union Station north to the Eaton Centre, are both interconnecting and diverging, offering the experience of wandering in a labyrinth. I have often enjoyed using Toronto's underground corridors both as shortcuts and as places to walk aimlessly, but I have rarely bought anything there. Toronto's underground shopping system resembles a labyrinth as an accident of its historical development and serves its clientele more or less as an arcade would. It is not a mall.

[handwritten margin note: It is a labyrinth leading to a fairy land.]

5. The illusions are carefully maintained within each room. The Truck Rooms (celebrations of rural life) have a number of country motifs, country/western music is played continuously, and the bed is cleverly placed within the bed of an actual pick-up truck. (Similarly, in the Victorian Coach Rooms, the bed is inside a black and gilt open carriage.) In the Canadian Rail Rooms, a fibreglass maitre d', holding a tray bearing a towel-draped bottle of wine in his left hand, watches the bed. (A member of the hotel's housekeeping staff once told me that in more than half the cases the cleaners find that the eyes of the maitre d' have been blindfolded with a bathroom towel.) The Roman Rooms have a circular bed, statues, and a mirror over the beds. The Igloo Rooms are decorated in white with imitation snow, and the bed is inside a cut-away igloo that is guarded by a fibreglass Husky. All the rooms, whatever the theme, contribute to the overall experience of make-believe that characterizes the mall. You can keep on playing make-believe even while sleeping.

6. Although European thinkers, such as Eco, like to associate the delight in fakes and the glorification of illusions with North American culture, Europe has always possessed an abundance of fakes and a pervasive delight in illusory experience. The history of amusement parks could not be written without paying considerable attention to such self-contained walled parks as the Tivoli Gardens in Copenhagen, which first opened in 1843. A few years ago, the British Museum mounted an extremely popular exhibition of the many fakes it had acquired over the years (for the catalogue for the show, see Jones).

REFERENCES

Baudrillard, Jean. *America*. Trans. Chris Turner. 1986; London: Verso, 1988.

Eco, Umberto. *Travels in Hyperreality: Essays*. Trans. William Weaver. London: Picador-Pan Books, 1987.

Huizinga, Johan. *Homo Ludens: A Study of the Play Element in Culture*. 1938; Boston: Beacon Press, 1955.

Huston, Nancy. "A Bucking Nightmare." *Saturday Night,* June 1997: 61–70.

Jameson, Fredric. *Post-modernism, or, The Cultural Logic of Late Capitalism*. Durham, N.C.: Duke University Press, 1991.

Jones, Mark. *FAKE? The Art of Deception*. Berkeley and Los Angeles: University of California Press, 1990.

THE MANY
FORMS OF
MEDIA

INTRODUCTION

When larger-than-life characters from a television satire invade the marbled corridors and carpeted offices of the House of Commons to put political leaders, including the prime minister of Canada, on the spot before an audience of two million viewers, it's difficult to dismiss the power of the media.

Some critics have called CBC's popular *This Hour Has 22 Minutes* the unofficial opposition for its relentless skewering of political pomposity and public tomfoolery. All four of the show's principals — Mary Walsh, Cathy Jones, Greg Thomey, and Rick Mercer — come from Newfoundland, a place with a historic but madcap respect for the voice of the people and the power of language. Even the show's name pays tribute to a formerly powerful television show, *This Hour Has Seven Days,* a controversial current affairs program that the CBC terminated in 1966 because its mix of satire and investigative reporting cut too deeply into Establishment fatuousness. At its peak, *Seven Days* reached an audience of 3.25 million viewers, almost one-fifth of the population of the time. Unlike the near-schmoozing that goes on between *This Hour Has 22 Minutes* and contemporary politicians — Reform leader Preston Manning tends to giggle and look absolutely tickled pink when Walsh's irrepressible persona Marg Delahunty pounces on him — 1960s politicians lived in terror of being accosted by *Seven Days*'s producer-host Patrick Watson. In the book *Mondo Canuck: A Canadian Pop Culture Odyssey*, Geoff Pevere reports that then prime minister Lester Pearson ordered his cabinet ministers *not* to appear on the show, no matter what the issue.

The term "media" is plural in more ways than one: the media today embrace many formats besides the obvious ones of newspapers, magazines, television, and radio. Rock videos, which purvey slick images, mini-dramas, and political content, are a branch of media, as are Web sites and online journals. And never has the Canadian public been more media-savvy. Today's six-year-old can both program the family VCR and cruise the Internet for bedtime reading, some of which might greatly shock his or her parents.

In the following pages, Miles Kronby, who left Toronto to work with the online version of the *New York Times,* explores what it means to be "cool" in today's techno-culture. Victoria professor Aspasia Kotsopoulos explains how the imagined community of Lucy Maud Montgomery has been further transformed by television. Shirley Anne Off examines how the struggle for audience share and advertising dollars affected the early idealism of the Women's Television Network. Carleton professor Michael Dorland looks back on his early days as a starving tabloid journalist. And finally, Toronto critic Alice Van Wart explores how Michael Ondaatje's *The English Patient* was changed from book to movie — and what was lost and gained in that process.

WHAT'S COOL

Miles Kronby

I lost my cool, or at least reassessed it, on Valentine's Day, 1996. The Webzine I edited, the *Review*, had been invited to join a competition called "The Coolest Site of Valentine's Day." The competition was sponsored by the company that bestows the "Cool Site of the Day," a prestigious and valuable online award. A month before, when the *Review* had been chosen Cool Site of the Day, the world — that is, tens of thousands of people with nothing better to do — had beaten a path to our server. Our hit count went through the roof. We figured that "The Coolest Site of Valentine's Day" competition would renew the buzz, so we signed right up.

We built a moody little site called "Is the Net an Erotic Medium?" It consisted of two short essays that said yes ("The torture of waiting, of disappointment, is erotogenic at 98.6 degrees fahrenheit or 14.4 Kbps …") and also an article by a friend of ours describing the weekend he finally spent, in person, with the lover he had met online. Accompanying that article was a QuickTime VR download of a snowy night in an empty square in Greenwich Village, which Jim had e-mailed to his lover as a kind of heartbreak offering after they broke up. Just before Valentine's Day, the Cool Site home page offered links to the three sites in the competition: ours, a site that looked sort of like a head shop and had messages on it about love, and a site that foretold your romantic fate using an animation of one of those origami fortune-tellers that kids like to make. The competition was decided by popular vote. The winner was announced on February 14th. The fortune-teller narrowly edged out the head shop. Our site came in a distant third, uncool by popular vote, and we had a laugh about it as the streaky snowflakes whirled around in the black bubble of Jim's QuickTime VR.

That's when I got interested in what "cool" actually means and in how it became the prevailing — even canonical — term of praise in digital media. On Netscape's home page, the button labelled "What's Cool" emphasizes the *what* rather than the *cool*. It tells you what is cool (a collection of mostly big-budget sites, and "The Cool Site of the Day"), but leaves it up to you to figure out what cool is. One thing about "cool" online is its ubiquitousness. A search on Alta Vista turned up about 700 000 Web pages containing the word "cool." In Usenet, about 90 000 messages invoked "cool." These ranged from the technical ("How do people get the cool shadowing effects on their GIFs?") to the sacred/profane ("Christian Punk is cool!"). Online, "cool" almost holds its own with its close cousin "good" (a million). Offline, it's a different story. A Lexis/Nexis search of the *New York Times* database turned up 340 000 uses of "good" and only 27 000 of "cool." In traditional media, it appears, "cool" is marginal; in new media, it's basically in charge. As the *New York Times* reported around the time Windows '95 was launched, "Amid all his earnest patter about personal computers being tools of empowerment, Bill Gates, the billionaire chairman of Microsoft, offered CNN's Larry King three words that finally touched on what all the fuss over a software program was really about. 'Software is cool,' Mr. Gates said" (27 August 1995).

By this, Bill Gates was saying that software is trendy, exciting, fun. But his statement is also true in another sense. Software fits the *Oxford English Dictionary*'s definition of "cool": "not heated by passion or emotion; unexcited, dispassionate; deliberate, not hasty; undisturbed, calm." Software is controlled by unbreakable rules, patiently waiting for a signal that's either "on" or "off," oblivious to everything else. The messages it sends you — for instance, "Error 14: Unable to locate driver. Restart?" — are the essence of dispassionate cool, which, as it happens, makes you feel murderous. (Such messages usually arrive in perversely named "Dialogue Boxes." When all you can do is click "OK" and accept your fate, it hardly feels like a dialogue.) Yet these same qualities make software seem, in another sense, the opposite of cool. Jazz musicians in the 1940s brought the word "cool," and perhaps the attitude, into the mainstream. And isn't jazz in many ways the opposite of software? Cool jazz is relaxed, spontaneous, improvised. Software is fussy, predictable, and rigidly defined, vastly more so than even *classical* music. It used to be that techies themselves, for all their creativity, were considered as uncool, as geeky, as unsexy as software itself. But Gates could grin at Larry King. The makeover is almost complete: nerds weren't hip, but now they're rich. With their new prosperity, they've acquired cool, a word and trait they always wanted.

When software becomes more and more cool in the Bill Gates sense — that is, richer in multimedia and more like TV — it becomes less cool in the way that Marshall McLuhan famously used the word. "Cool media," he wrote in *Understanding Media* in 1964, "are high in participation or completion by the audience." To McLuhan, print is a cooler medium than TV because print requires readers to participate by translating the words they read into pictures in their head. The images contained in print are completed by readers' imaginations. By contrast, wrote McLuhan, "A hot medium is one that extends one single sense in 'high definition.' High definition is the state of being well filled with data. A photograph is, visually, 'high definition.' A cartoon is 'low definition,' [i.e., 'cool'] simply because very little visual information is provided." Currently, the Internet is a much cooler medium than TV, in the McLuhan sense, because the Net can't support "high definition" media. A photograph or a sound can't be "well filled with data" if you want it to travel through the Net and squeeze through a standard modem in a reasonable amount of time.

So when Web surfers bent on speed set their browsers to "do not load images," they make the Web even cooler. Similarly, people who produce Web sites often like to convert images from colour to black and white. Compared to a colour photograph, a black-and-white image requires fewer bits of data to express its visual information. A computer is spared having to describe all the different colours in a sunset, for instance, when those colours have been reduced to a much smaller palette of greys. "Cool" black-and-white images move faster over the Net and leave more to the imagination, but fewer people want to look at them. The challenge of turning the Net into a mass medium has largely been the struggle to make it cooler in the commercial sense (the Bill Gates sense) by making it less cool in the McLuhan sense: to load it with data, with pictures and sounds that are rich and realistic rather than grainy and impressionistic.

A couple of years after McLuhan published *Understanding Media*, Susan Sontag identified what she called the "new sensibility" in American art, with its insistence on coolness. In her words you can almost hear "new media" booting up:

> The model arts of our time are actually those with much less content [than literature], and a much cooler mode of moral judgement — like music, films, dance, architecture, painting, sculpture. The practice of these arts — all of which draw profusely, naturally, and without embarrassment, upon science and technology — are the locus of the new sensibility. (Sontag, "One Culture and the New Sensibility" [1965], in *Against Interpretation* [New York: Anchor Books/Doubleday, 1990], 296)

This "cooler mode" is evident, Sontag claims, in John Cage's music, Merce Cunningham's dance, and Mark Rothko's painting. All this is abstract and arty stuff, and it wouldn't get a much warmer welcome on the popular areas of the Web today than it would on prime-time TV. Yet what Sontag saw in 1965 as a budding relationship between science and the non-literary arts is full blown on the Web. Much of new media's coolness, its excitement and popularity, comes from the tricks that result from collaboration between artists and engineers: streaming audio and video and clever uses of databases. A chief response provoked by cool things — like the response to, say, a 100-foot-high sculpture of a shovel, its spade stuck at a digging angle into the ground — is "How did they do that?"

In the same article, Sontag describes what almost sounds like virtual reality — that Holy Grail, or maybe red herring, of new media: "The new sensibility understands art as the extension of life — this being understood as the representation of (new) modes of vivacity.... For we are what we are able to see (hear, taste, smell, feel) even more powerfully and profoundly than we are what furniture of ideas we have stocked in our heads."

The dream of virtual reality is nearly the same thing: to create illusions so powerful that the user believes he or she can see, hear, taste, smell, and feel them as if they were real. For many new media creators, VR represents the ultimate in cool, a giant leap beyond static text and pictures. (In the McLuhan sense, again, it would also be the ultimate in "hot": massive amounts of data with no gaps for the audience to complete for themselves.) The Coolest Site of Valentine's Day, the image of the origami fortune-teller, was like a stone-axe version of VR. When you clicked the screen, the image of the fortune-teller split open to show a message. The coolness and cuteness of that effect, like the coolness in Sontag's "new sensibility," involves a preference for simulation and representation over interpretation.

That preference became celebrated in the art of Andy Warhol. "I've always had this philosophy of: it doesn't really matter," Warhol once said. Almost all of his work — the Campbell's soup cans, the portraits of Marilyn, his strange films — express a philosophy of dispassion. "And no one in the history of cool," wrote Calvin Tomkins in 1976, "has ever been cooler than Andy." Warhol created icons and turned himself into one, and his cool was nearly digital. He was a new media producer working in old media, sampling and colourizing familiar images, replicating those images (on canvas) again and again. Today's image-manipulation software, applications such as "Photoshop," allow anyone to ape Warhol, but Warhol got rich off his work. Partly because of Warhol, commercial has *become* cool: these days music videos not only sell music, but *are* music. The Web, swarming with corporate sites, is a test lab for new and mutant strains of "advertorial" (advertising plus editorial, minus remorse). Warhol was a pioneer. A fine line separates his commercial illustrations, mostly for department stores in New York, from the pop art that turned him into a star. In both cases, he started with familiar commodities: shoes, lipstick, bras, handbags, soup cans, Marilyn Monroe. He drew the shoes and bras in a blotted line, sometimes surrounded by little cherubs. He lifted an image of Marilyn's face from the movies and recast it in a wash of colour. He freed each of these objects from all traces of their familiar context, and in doing so he made them as self-contained, as autonomous, as cool as himself.

So picture this: Bill Gates admiring the flat-panel high-definition digital art screens on the walls of his new house. Imagine a line of paintings — flawless reproductions of Renaissance religious scenes — glowing on the screens. The Richest Man in the World slides his finger along a bronze strip set into a wall (or whispers the name of a flower) and each crucifixion morphs into a Van Gogh sunflower. Bill Gates cocks his head slightly. His finger returns to the bronze strip: the arrangement of sunflowers becomes a virtual regatta of Thomas Eakins's rowers. Once more, finger to bronze — and a crisp series of Andy Warhol's Marilyn flicks into place. The face of Marilyn: bright eyes, eager smile, again and again and again. Perfect. Bill Gates adjusts his glasses. He presses the strip just so: Marilyn's colour grows softer, less garish, its greens turn to blues. More perfect. Software *is* cool.

The coolness of software has much in common with the coolness of Warhol's pictures and the coolness of Bill Gates's house, a house in which everyone has his or her own soundtrack. According to legend, the audio speakers throughout the Gates compound are programmed to track the movements of each resident or guest. As you walk around, you're accompanied by your choice in music, which is passed along from speaker to speaker. That could be nice, like a weightless and invisible Walkman, or it could be like having a troubadour chase you around the house. Either way, it sets you apart. The music is for you alone. As in the breakthrough CD-ROM puzzle-game Myst, you're on your own. Myst is a beautiful place, soothing and melancholy, full of rooms and courtyards as tastefully loaded with gadgets as the Gates compound promises to be. When you explore Myst you become the only living person there, the centre of its world. Myst, then, puts its own strange spin on one of software's great promises. Of all the media since Copernicus that have helped us reclaim that comfy feeling of being at the centre of the universe, digital media probably do it best.

By contrast, a TV station makes itself the centre of its universe, and each viewer merely reflects its light. Broadcast media such as TV and radio pretend to talk to us — "Aren't you tired of the same old breakfast cereals?" — but we know they're bluffing. They're not even sure we're out there. Personal computers are different. We *interact* with them, and they remember our preferences. They await our commands. They attempt, awkwardly, to call us by name — "You have new mail, Kronby" — and to engage us in (phony) dialogues. "Help Wizards," *deus ex machina*, appear with suggestions if we get confused. When we use computers to socialize, in forums or chat rooms, they place us in the centre of the crowd and the screen. And they allow us, if we wish, to keep a cool and mysterious distance from everyone else who's there.

Digital media offer a vast range of new ways for us to connect with others, but at all times they put us in control. They lure us, too, with their seeming ease in what author Douglas Rushkoff cheerfully calls "the unnerving discontinuity of the modern age." Such discontinuity results from, among other things, a glut of trivial information and the erosion of traditional narratives — narratives such as "a job for life," "a nuclear family," "a cohesive neighborhood or community," "God." As these narratives become less pertinent, when the fabric that gave previous generations a sense of meaning unravels, we are left in an apparent chaos of "media," of fractured images and jingles. Traditional media seem uncomfortable in that chaos, which is one reason we rarely describe them as cool. The structure of the novel resists discontinuity: its plot tries to impose order on the world of its characters. The novel's linearity is consistent with, and grows out of, the basic structure of prose: a novel is built of words, and words generally make sense when arranged in long, continuous strings. A painting isn't linear, but it, too, is inherently stable. Paint is a commitment. Once dry, it can be covered up but not taken back. Things that are cool aren't so dependent on continuity or context. A one-liner, a special effect, a TV commercial, a theme hotel in Vegas, a neat bit of clip art: you can cut them from one place and paste them on another and everything's cool.

Software and digital media, made only of "bits," are pretty much built for and of discontinuity. The electrical impulses at the heart of new media can change their form, and their directions, instantly. "On" can turn "off," and "off" can turn "on." Bits have no weight; they travel light. A bit does not commit. With software, whether you're putting together a spreadsheet or writing an essay or composing a song or drawing a picture, you can change your work — and undo your changes — and leave no trace of what came before. No sweat. The computer doesn't even seem to work at it. It just hums, quietly. We often talk about a computer's "memory," but in a way it doesn't have one. What it does in the future is not affected by what it did in the past. A computer disk can just as easily store words or numbers or pictures or music, while in fact storing none of these. It only stores bits. What it makes from those bits is up to us. And what we make from those bits is what we want to become: vital, valuable, autonomous, infinitely adaptable, effortlessly cool.

HER ~~OUR~~ AVONLEA

Imagining Community in

an Imaginary Past

Aspasia Kotsopoulos

A single female who likes Bronte and cats, lots of cats.

According to its creators at Sullivan Entertainment, *Road to Avonlea* is based on the spirit of Lucy Maud Montgomery's tales of rural Prince Edward Island at the turn of the century. On the one hand, the characters, settings, and situations created by Montgomery serve as the basis for the television series. On the other hand, the creators of the series have taken a certain amount of poetic licence with Montgomery's original text. This disjuncture between the original text and its subsequent interpretation for television reveals certain desires, anxieties, and fears contemporary with our own times rather than Montgomery's. Indeed, *Road to Avonlea*'s dramatization of contemporary concerns in a period setting produces "a modern past," a pastiche of present-day anxieties and olden-day artifacts. Andrew Higson coined the term "modern past" (113) to describe recent British costume drama. While *Road to Avonlea* is a Canadian television series rather than a British film, Higson's term aptly describes the show and its interest as a cultural text. *CRAP.*

Moreover, the popularity of this Canadian series within Canada also makes it of cultural interest. Every Sunday night for seven years, approximately 2.5 million Canadians tuned in to CBC for each first-run episode of *Road to Avonlea*, and about 1.5 million viewed every rerun. CBC strategically placed the show at the head of its Sunday night "Family Hour" as a lure for further Sunday night viewing, indicating the corporation's confidence in the series. Indeed, *Road to Avonlea* stands as one of CBC's most successful and longest-running dramatic series. At $15–$16.6 million per season, it is also the most expensive television production ever mounted in Canada, with funding from the CBC, Telefilm, and Disney. Each hour-long episode cost just over $1 million to produce.

Toronto-based Sullivan Entertainment, the producer of *Road to Avonlea*, seems to have found a niche market when it comes to creating Canadian period pieces for television, having mined the Montgomery oeuvre with telefilms of *Anne of Green Gables* (1985), which included a sequel (1987), and *Lantern Hill* (1991), as well as other movies for television — for example, *Under the Piano* (1996) and *Promise the Moon* (1997). Additionally, Sullivan

Entertainment's new Depression-era series, *Wind at My Back,* premiered in the fall of 1997 in *Road to Avonlea*'s old time-slot.

Road to Avonlea, which had its premiere on January 7, 1990, centres around the King family and their friends, neighbours, and relations in the pastoral turn-of-the-century community of Avonlea, Prince Edward Island. *Road to Avonlea* starts out as more a drama for children than for adults because the early stories revolve around young Montreal heiress Sara Stanley, detailing her adjustment to her new life in Avonlea with her spinster-schoolteacher aunt, Hetty King, and her cousins, Felicity, Felix, and Cecily, who also figure prominently in these episodes. By the fifth season, however, both the tone and the focus of the series change somewhat from the light-hearted drama about childhood pranks and misadventures of the earlier episodes. More and more, the adults come to share the spotlight with the children in stories of romance and tragedy. Additionally, as the child actors grow up, so do the Avonlea children, and the series begins to deal with painful coming-of-age issues. *Road to Avonlea* ran for seven seasons, the final episode airing March 31, 1996, and along the way, it garnered many awards and many fans, both in Canada and in over 140 countries abroad.

From the start, *Road to Avonlea*'s setting marked it as different from other shows on television, making the fantasy it presented to viewers unique. To the best of my knowledge, *Road to Avonlea* was the only ongoing series (as opposed to mini-series) that was a period piece, with the exception of *Little House on the Prairie* and *Dr. Quinn, Medicine Woman*, whose frontier settings arguably give them more in common with the western. While there have been contemporary television westerns that could qualify as period pieces, *Road to Avonlea* is significantly different from them, as it focuses on the feminine world of feelings and relationships and not on the masculine world of law and order. This focus gives the series an intimacy rarely found on other shows, perhaps with the exception of daytime soap operas.

Though a weekly series rather than a daily soap, *Road to Avonlea* is similar to the latter in its use of plot and character. In soap opera, the plot moves slowly because the emphasis is on the characters, their development, their thoughts and feelings, and, perhaps most importantly, their interactions with each other. *Road to Avonlea* works in a similar fashion: the stories are usually simple and always secondary to the characters, giving them the opportunity to display their complexities and idiosyncrasies on a weekly basis. In each episode, the *Avonlea* characters struggle with personal choices and deal with changes in their lives and their community. Like the uncomplicated plots, the period setting acts as an unobtrusive backdrop for the exploration of character motivations and emotional conflicts.

The recent revival in period pieces or costume dramas owes a debt to second-wave feminism, which, in an attempt to reclaim women's past, has brought attention to forgotten texts written by women. Period pieces, often adapted from women's literature, address questions of female identity and female desire. Films like *My Brilliant Career* (1979) and the recent screen adaptations of *Little Women* (1994) and *Emma* (1996) tap into this tradition and create an affinity between women's past and present struggles. *Road to Avonlea* belongs to this tradition. Women play a central role in the *Avonlea* community. They participate in town-hall debates about the good of the community; they run households, farms, and businesses; they have rewarding careers; and they hold considerable opinion-making power and are held in high respect. You could even be a single, middle-aged, working woman like Aunt Hetty and rarely have anyone comment disparagingly upon your spinster status.

The show gives considerable attention to relationships, often intergenerational, between women, which is rare for television and film. What's rarer still is that the women's relationships, for the most part, are not based on competition. Episodes focus on the deepening of the relationship between Hetty King and her young charge, Sara Stanley, on the difficulties and rewards of sisterhood (as in the stories centred around Hetty and Olivia), and on the trials and tribulations of Janet King and her daughters, Felicity and Cecily. These younger women, along with Sara, become a focus of the show. In the last two seasons, cousins Sara and Felicity face difficult decisions. Sara struggles with the decision of whether to leave the island community she has grown to love in order to study in Europe. Felicity becomes one of the first female medical students in Canada and encounters sexism for the first time. She also has to choose between her dreams of an education and the man she loves, who has his own dreams to pursue. Meanwhile, Cecily convinces her father to train her to run the family farm and to pass the beloved farm down to her, challenging the family's tradition of male inheritance. These representations are departures from the usual images of young women in mainstream media.

While *Road to Avonlea*'s historical setting might suggest a conservative viewpoint, the show's implicit liberal feminism challenges this possibility and merges modern feminist values with a rural romantic past. Even relationships between men and women are among the most equitable on television. *Avonlea* men who are sexist usually learn a hard lesson, as Felix does after he boasts to his male friends about his "relationship" with best friend Izzy Pettibone. Janet and Alec King are the perfect married couple, still in love and communicating after all these years and four kids later. Moreover, Alec never throws his patriarchal weight around. Instead, he teaches his children to talk their problems out. The Kings are the ideal family, resolving conflict through communication. If the picture sounds saccharine sweet, it is. But there is another side to this rural historical romance that needs exploring: the series suppresses differences and history in its effort to create a utopian vision of the past.

GENRE AND HISTORICAL SETTING

I call *Road to Avonlea* a period piece or a costume drama. The term "period piece" refers to a cultural production that is set in the past, usually the distant past, and can be a film, a play, a television series, or a novel. Time and its relationship to the cultural producer are important in defining the period piece. For example, Jane Austen's novel *Sense and Sensibility* is not a period piece because it is set in the time in which Austen wrote it: it is a contemporary interpretation of her times. But the 1995 screen adaptation of *Sense and Sensibility* starring Emma Thompson is a period piece because it is a contemporary interpretation of a time past. Similarly, *Road to Avonlea* is a period piece, as are most of Montgomery's works, perhaps with the exception of her earliest ones written in the teens of this century. (In fact, the kind of world Montgomery was writing about when she began her *Avonlea* stories had already nearly vanished and had certainly disappeared well before the end of her career.)

The costume drama is a type of period piece, as is the historical film. Elaborating from Jean Gili's work, Marcia Landy provides a useful definition of the costume drama as a type of film distinct from the historical film: "Unlike the historical films, which claim to re-enact the lives and actions of prominent individuals [e.g., military heroes, monarchs, composers] with some accuracy, the costume dramas are fictional and play loosely with historical contexts, transposing history into romance" (*British Genres*, 210). Landy's distinction between historical film and costume drama derives from the different ways in which these two genres treat history. Both genres are reconstructions of the past and must be seen as fictions. However, the historical film offers dramatizations of actual events and personages from the past, while the costume drama uses all the outward trappings of the historical film (i.e., the period setting, the costumes, the *mise en scène*) but does not have any claims to "documenting" historical events or the lives of historical figures. Characters and situations are purely imaginary in costume drama, with the historical setting functioning as a dramatic, and even exotic, backdrop for romance and sometimes adventure and intrigue.

Along these lines, Sue Harper argues that the costume drama produces "a vision of 'history' as a country where only feelings reside, not socio-political conflicts" (179–81). She maintains that the loose treatment of history allows viewers to appropriate issues explored in the costume drama as contemporary to their own. Such discussions of the costume drama seem to demand a recognition of this genre as a particular kind of fantasy, one in which contemporary desires, anxieties, and fears find safe expression through displacement into a period setting. As Landy says, "The specific time of the events recedes, and they become … transhistorical and timeless and, therefore, as relevant for the present as for the past" (*Looking Backward*, 135). In this way, the costume drama creates a sense of continuity between past and present through the portrayal of concerns that have contemporary resonance — for instance, concerns about gender and family or about duty and community (cf. Bruzzi, 233–35, and Landy, 126).

For this reason, Higson, writing on the British heritage film, a type of costume drama, calls the past that such films construct "an imaginary object" invented from the point of view of the present to evoke "pastness." Higson states that "the evocation of pastness is accomplished by a look, a style, the loving recreation of period details — not by any critical historical perspective. The self-conscious visual perfectionism of these films and their fetishization of period details create a fascinating but self-enclosed world" (113). In the process, the past is purged of socio-political conflict, making it suitable for visual display via a lavish *mise en scène* and a pictorial camera style that brings with it "all the connotations of art photography, aesthetic refinement, and set-piece images" and that often exceeds narrative motivation (112–13, 117).

But this is not to argue that cultural productions such as *Road to Avonlea* are purely escapist and trivial confections, devoid of any meaning or relevance. According to Landy, although costume dramas "do not make a serious effort to treat historical events with any accuracy, they are nonetheless engaged in the process of constructing or rewriting the past" (*Looking Backward*, 127–28). This process of "constructing" or "rewriting" raises questions around fantasy, specifically the role of present-day fears and wishes in contemporary imaginings of the past. Indeed, fantasy would appear to be a key element of Higson's notion of a modern past, an imagined distant time born out of contemporary desires.

While *Road to Avonlea* is a television series rather than a film, I believe the above discussion of costume drama aptly defines the series and, in particular, its relationship to period setting. The show presents us with a vision of a past that is based on style, not on historical context. There are too few clues that this is Canada at the turn of the century because history never intrudes on the lives of the characters. (Talk about island living.) Costumes, sets, and props give the sense of an era rather than concrete historical facts; in other words, "history" serves as a backdrop. The phantasmatic, pastoral world of *Road to Avonlea* makes the past appear non-specific and therefore timeless. What we get is a nostalgic, sanitized vision of pastness.

The timelessness of *Road to Avonlea* and period pieces like it contributes to a sense of continuity with the past, which renders these fantasies safe and appealing, particularly in times of economic insecurity and social instability. The timelessness of values such as love, family, and community creates a fantasy of security that goes against perceived contemporary uncertainties. Moreover, the familiarity of the themes portrayed gives viewers an entry into the fictional world of Avonlea. To illustrate, narrative tensions that develop in the final season resonate strongly with contemporary meanings, suggesting that *Road to Avonlea* has more to say about the contemporary contexts of its production and reception than about life in Prince Edward Island in the early part of the twentieth century.

COMMUNITY VERSUS PROGRESS

Road to Avonlea's island setting is as meaningful as its period setting, with the island representing a haven from the rest of the world, a safe place to be protected from external (usually negative) influences. Not surprisingly, any social conflict that emerges on *Road to Avonlea* occurs either on the mainland, as with Felicity's experience of sexism at medical school, or when strangers from the mainland disrupt the community's harmony.

The final season increasingly presents an image of a way of life under siege by outside forces threatening to destroy both community and family. The series's fantasy of local control and of individuals having a positive effect on their community gives way to fears of loss of control and the destruction of a way of life owing to encroaching "modernization." The series's finale in particular offers a poignant swan-song meditation on notions of community and duty, history and progress, which centres around the Avonlea cannery, destroyed by fire in a previous episode. The town's economic welfare depends upon the cannery, which, as Hetty puts it, represents Avonlea's bread and butter.

The Avonlea cannery crisis exemplifies the concern with changes to Avonlea and with the threat these changes pose to community. Consistently, the figure of Hetty has represented stubborn opposition to these changes, that is, to the dissolution of the Avonlea community in the name of profit and modernization. The cannery crisis effectively crystallizes these issues and points up ideological contradictions between humanist concerns with individual welfare and community obligation and the aims of capitalism and progress, which do not always work in the interests of individuals or communities.

In the final episode, cannery owners Jasper and Olivia Dale struggle with their sense of duty towards the community. As Olivia says to the banker Stuart Macrae, "These people are counting on us." But Stuart (who, significantly, is not an islander by origin) explains to the couple that that kind of thinking doesn't hold up in the modern world. He points out that the most up-to-date cannery that money can buy is already up and running, right in the next town. This cannery, he says, is competitive and has cornered the Avonlea cannery's suppliers, markets, and even workers. Reluctantly, Jasper and Olivia accept Stuart's advice not to rebuild. Upon learning of this threat to the future of Avonlea, Hetty exclaims, "Here we have profiteers sneaking about our land, stealing away the very heart of Avonlea with their clever machinery and their roguish notions of progress, and you choose this moment to turn your back on us!"

Hetty's analysis of the situation shifts the narrative towards risky ground where modern capitalism collides with responsibility to community, revealing the two as incompatible. At the same time, however, the narrative works to naturalize capitalism and its effects. Olivia's common-sensical understanding of change as an inevitable part of life effectively subdues any critique of capitalism that the narrative may be veering towards. In the process, Hetty's opposition to profiteers is gradually defused, becoming the fuming of a woman unable to cope with change, defined in this episode as a basic aspect of human existence. The result is that the clash between capitalism and community is transformed melodramatically into a familial conflict between the generations, between people like the spinster Hetty, who is stubbornly resistant to "change," and younger people like her sister Olivia, who rolls with the punches or makes lemonade out of a lemon (to paraphrase this character's words). For Olivia, making lemonade involves moving to England, after Jasper accepts a job there. The narrative represents the loss of community and the concomitant fragmentation of the extended family — Hetty's main fears — and these are portrayed as inevitable and natural, not as the by-products of changes wrought on Avonlea by early twentieth-century capitalism. Change is de-historicized and essentialized so that it becomes impossible to judge changes as "good" or "bad"; there is only the inevitability of "change," to which individuals must resign themselves.

To return to the notion of a modern past, the Avonlea cannery crisis and the threat posed to the island community by roguish notions of progress articulate anxieties about social and economic circumstances in present-day Canada. The human meaning of job loss and the destruction of community as a result of company closure cannot be restricted to *Road to Avonlea*'s turn-of-the-century P.E.I. setting. In this way, the Avonlea cannery crisis operates allegorically. Indeed, Landy explains that costume dramas "work in allegorical fashion to dramatize contemporary reality by making an analogue with the remote past in the interests of continuity, or, conversely, the history may serve as an excuse to be critical where direct discourse may fail" (*British Genres*, 55). Just how far *Road to Avonlea* goes in being "critical" of the present is questionable, even though the issues it addresses and the appeal it has had for viewers are suggestive of, if nothing else, a dissatisfaction with something that cannot be named and a longing for something other than what is.

READINGS OF NOSTALGIA

The phenomenon of nostalgia, discussed as both a psychological and a cultural manifestation, has been defined as "a longing for what is past, a painful yearning for a time gone by" (Jacoby, 5). Certainly, much of *Road to Avonlea* is suffused with nostalgia, but this is particularly the case in the final episode, where nostalgia takes on double meanings: it refers not only to a yearning for a time past (imaginary though it may be), but to a longing for a television series that is also past. The character of Hetty best expresses the sense of nostalgia both in the series and for the series. Significantly, when all is said and done, Hetty still gets the last word on *Road to Avonlea,* despite her characterization as a troublesome figure resistant to change. At the wedding reception for Gus and Felicity, Hetty makes a speech about her "fuming over changes happening to the town" and over people leaving. She concludes with a toast, which ends the series: "Wherever you wander, rest easy, you'll have a place to come home to. Avonlea. To our Avonlea." Hetty's toast is directed just as much to the viewers watching the show as it is to the characters on the series. Without making too much of the final episode's self-reflexivity, it is fairly safe to assume that Avonlea is home not only to the series characters, but also to its viewers. So what does it mean to come home to Avonlea?

Along these lines, Pam Cook has explored the role of nostalgia in popular imaginings and in the formation of national identities. Cook states that nationalism can be seen to "(appeal) to a fundamental desire to find a 'home,' an imagined place where unified, stable identities nurtured by common interests can flourish." She points out that the stabilization of identities and the search for common interests require homogenization and a covering over of past atrocities (2). As Cook says, "'Home' is, in fact, a haunted house" (39). Certainly, this is the case in *Road to Avonlea*. The sheer homogeneity of the Avonlea community makes social harmony easy to maintain, as does the suppression of histories for indigenous people, working people, and non-Anglo Canadians. For instance, class differences either do not exist in Avonlea or, when they do, they are used to make the Kings look kindly and charitable. (The impromptu Christmas they put together for the lower-class kid dying of tuberculosis is a classic example. The boy dies, and they all have the opportunity to feel good about themselves and their secure middle-class lives.) The fact that the working class live in another part of town, which we rarely see, also makes the fantasy of social cohesion possible. It's a good thing itinerant worker Gus Pike decides to become more respectable (i.e., middle class) by learning to read and to hold down a job; otherwise, he never would have had the chance to romance a daughter of the middle classes like Felicity.

Cook says that the critique of nostalgia found in leftist discussions of national identity follows this line of thinking, whereby "[t]he longing for an imaginary golden age is often perceived to be embedded in regressive myths of community from which traditional group and national identities are constructed." "Such longings," she argues, "are generally seen as culturally conservative, obstructing the way to the formation of modern, progressive identities" (25–26). But Cook proposes an alternative, one that may lead us to rethink the images of the past found in *Road to Avonlea*. Cook says:

> It is rarely considered that nostalgia might play a productive role in national identity, releasing the desire for social change or resistance…. Rather than a refusal of nostalgia, it seems more pertinent to investigate the powerful emotional appeal of reliving the past and the part this plays in popular imaginings of community and resistance at specific historical moments. (26)

Earlier I said that *Road to Avonlea* expresses a dissatisfaction with something that cannot be named and a longing for something other than what is. Arguably, this inability to name is something that places the series outside the realm of critical comment, in the sense of offering a cogent social analysis. For instance, the final episode uses common-sensical truisms about change to explain away the social ills associated with capitalism and progress. Nonetheless, the nostalgia expressed in the series, which, in keeping with Cook's understanding, I would characterize as a longing for home, is suggestive, particularly as it centres around the desire for community and, in the final season, around the very struggle for the survival of community in the face of perilous economic circumstances that speak to the contemporary Canadian viewers of the series. With its themes of home, community, and belonging, *Road to Avonlea* does indeed remain true to the spirit of Montgomery's original texts. While these themes remain the same, they nonetheless take on different meanings relevant to the late twentieth-century contexts of *Road to Avonlea*'s production and reception. In *Road to Avonlea*'s final season, nostalgia, such as that evoked by the series's period setting, provides an avenue for the expression of contemporary fears: the fear of loss of local control because of the interests of capital, the fear of job loss and loss of community because of company closure, the fear that one may not be able to do what is right by people because of economic forces beyond one's control. Significantly, each of these fears finds its corollary in a desire: the desire for local control, for community, for doing what is right by people. In expressing these desires, *Road to Avonlea* suggests the resistant, perhaps even progressive, possibilities inherent in imagining community in an imaginary past.

The series concludes nine months before the outbreak of the First World War, with Avonlea poised at the brink of events that would change the community forever. Of course, the citizens of the insulated Avonlea are completely unaware of European tensions. The fantasy ends before history can intrude upon the characters' lives. But to see *Road to Avonlea* as concluding at the end of a "last great period of innocence" is to miss the point. Instead, *Road to Avonlea*'s demise signifies the end of a fantasy that is no longer tenable in the increasingly difficult and uncertain times inhabited by the middle-class Canadian audience.[1] The show's fantasy of middle-class plenty and harmony becomes harder to sustain as the years pass. That 1996 marks *Road to Avonlea*'s final season is a sign of the times we live in, not those of the series's characters. In the following year, Sullivan Entertainment filled the Sunday-evening void left behind by *Road to Avonlea* with *Wind at My Back,* a series that chronicles the struggles of an Ontario family torn apart by economic hardships during the Great Depression. A sign of the times, indeed.[2]

See sources high Simpsons for real social commentary.

ENDNOTES

1. By the time of publication, a *Road to Avonlea* telefilm taking place during the First World War was produced. It aired December 1998 on CBC.

2. This essay is based on a commentary appearing in *Pacific Current* magazine (April-May 1996) and a paper presented at the Console-ing Passions: Television, Video and Feminism conference, held at Concordia University (May 1997).

REFERENCES

Bruzzi, Stella. "Jane Campion: Costume Drama and Reclaiming Women's Past." In *Women and Film: A Sight and Sound Reader,* ed. Pam Cook and Philip Dodd, 232–42. Philadelphia: Temple University Press, 1993.

Cook, Pam. *Fashioning the Nation: Costume and Identity in British Cinema.* London: British Film Institute, 1996.

Harper, Sue. "Historical Pleasures: Gainsborough Costume Melodrama." In *Home Is Where the Heart Is: Studies in Melodrama and the Woman's Film,* ed. Christine Gledhill, 167–96. London: British Film Institute, 1987.

Higson, Andrew. "Re-presenting the National Past: Nostalgia and Pastiche in the Heritage Film." In *Fires Were Started: British Genres and Thatcherism,* ed. Lester Friedman, 109–29. Minneapolis: University of Minnesota Press, 1993.

Jacoby, Mario. *The Longing for Paradise: Psychological Perspectives on an Archetype,* trans. Myron B. Gubitz. Boston: Sigo Press, 1985.

Landy, Marcia. *British Genres: Cinema and Society, 1930–1960.* Princeton: Princeton University Press, 1991.

―――. "Looking Backward: Versions of History and Common Sense in Recent British Drama." In Marcia Landy, *Film, Politics and Gramsci,* 123–54. Minneapolis and London: University of Minnesota Press, 1994.

THE WOMEN'S TELEVISION NETWORK

By, For, and About Women

... or was that Ratings?

Shirley Anne Off

The Women's Television Network (WTN),[1] Canada's first specialty cable channel for women, initially proposed that it would be "a broadcast service *for women, by women, about women and their worlds*"[2] (emphasis in original). Even though WTN claimed that it would "change the broadcasting system overnight,"[3] by the second season of broadcasting, the conventions, demands, and limitations of the commercial popular television industry were apparent. This discussion of WTN considers two "moments" in the channel's history: the CRTC (Canadian Radio-television and Telecommunications Commission) application and licensing stage (1993–94) and the first two seasons of broadcasting (January to August 1995 and September to April 1996).[4]

WTN began broadcasting on Canadian airwaves on 1 January 1995 as one of ten new specialty cable channels licensed by the CRTC. WTN's arrival on the Canadian broadcasting scene came on the heels of 15 years of debate over the media's sex-role stereotyping of women and after the establishment of a new equity clause in the 1991 Broadcasting Act.[5] Thus, WTN emerged after three national women's organizations called for the establishment of a women's channel and after 50 years of commercial television cultivating and cashing in on female viewers.[6]

By proposing to be a channel that would address concerns over the sex-role stereotyping of women and that would rely on advertising and cable-fee revenues, WTN embraced two contradictory mandates. One mandate was political — to respond to the argument put forth by feminist organizations and scholars that women are objectified and stereotyped by the popular media. The other was commercial — to establish a privately owned, profit-oriented cable television channel squarely targeted at the female audience, an audience that, in turn, would be sold to advertisers.[7] In reality, by the end of the second season WTN was clearly privileging conservative women's programming over innovative programming and prioritizing the commercial imperatives of the business over the social benefits described to the CRTC in the application.

WTN's desire to attract female viewers, in and of itself, is not remarkable. Since the dawn of television in the 1940s, women have been considered and have proved to be a lucrative audience. As Spigel and Mann write, "Television has always had its eye on women."[8] The commercial television industry has primarily seen women in terms of their roles as primary care-givers and consumers of household products and therefore as an appealing target audience for advertisers. Television has actively sought to categorize viewers as masculine and feminine subjects — otherwise known as the gendering of the audience. Techniques aimed at gendering the audience include gender-specific scheduling practices (i.e., daytime lineup for women) and programming genres (sports, news, and police drama for male viewers; soap operas, family dramas, and domestic advice shows for female viewers). What is new about WTN is that, for the first time in Canada, an entire channel with an entire programming schedule — rather than specific programs or blocks of programs — is squarely aimed at female viewers.

SITUATING WTN

How do we situate WTN in light of feminist television theory and in relation to previous experiments with alternative women's television? First, popular television has always been interested in women and has often been at odds about how to represent women. On the one hand, it reproduces many of the dominant and sexist attitudes in society, rarely taking chances to challenge or disrupt these representations. On the other hand, television seeks to keep the female audience interested by incorporating new and sometimes progressive images of women. The 1980s police drama *Cagney and Lacey* is one example of an attempt by popular television to incorporate progressive images of women into a traditional masculine television genre: the police drama.[9] For the most part, this change in attitude towards the portrayal of women in the media began in the 1960s with the rise of second-wave feminism. Since that time, feminist media scholars and producers have made explicit efforts to challenge the sex-role stereotyping of women and demand that women author their own images. Because of its mass popular appeal, television has been viewed as a critical site of intervention — a place where programming, designed to serve the interests of women, could be defined, created, and viewed by women.

Secondly, a number of experienced feminist television producers and respected scholars[10] consider television to be an "impenetrable citadel"[11] — one that poses too many limitations and negative consequences for women. One argument is that television involves too many institutional conventions and controls that subsequently limit women's ability to "negotiate for themselves alternative visions, definitions, ways of being."[12] Another states that the broadcasting industry is "too dependent on large audiences to generate enormous amounts of advertising revenue ... [too] bureaucratized and dependent on complex technology ... [limiting] the possibilities of a feminist television channel or station."[13] Yet another argues that the industry's reliance on ratings for proof of a program's success discourages innovative programming.[14] In fact, past case studies have shown that television series made by all-women production teams that attempt to escape generic conventions have been "allowed to fail and ... stored away ... as 'interesting experiments.'"[15] Despite these criticisms, television still attracts large audiences of women to its programming and the industry continues to devise strategies to cultivate this lucrative audience.

Thirdly, the rise of the cable television industry has prompted both optimistic and pessimistic theories on its potential to challenge conventional television practices. Some argue that cable television will result in better programming because of the increased competition for programming from independent producers.[16] Others suggest that cable television has the capacity to push the "boundaries of representation,"[17] while others believe that the cable industry is merely "'a franchise' to make even more money" and acts as a "conduit for recycled [and inexpensive] entertainment programming."[18]

In Canada, the new cable industry also provides the CRTC with the opportunity to respond to the requirements of the 1991 Broadcasting Act's equity clause concerning equal opportunities for women, minority groups, and aboriginal peoples. In the application, WTN clearly declared that it would honour and meet these new requirements by providing jobs for women in the industry and that it would also address sex-role stereotyping of women.

WTN: THE CRTC APPLICATION

In WTN's application for a broadcasting licence, it challenged the traditional methods of attracting the women's viewing audience in two ways. First, WTN was to be a channel that was by, for, and about women. WTN proposed that it would meet this goal by ensuring that the network's top executives would be women and that they would make the decisions about what went on the air, that programming would be created by and feature stories about women, that the issues dealt with would be of interest to women, and that women would be the primary target audience. The channel's supporting research argued that "female creative control would better serve women's communication needs at this time; and that a woman's television channel would better address equity issues than existing broadcasters."[19]

Secondly, the channel proposed a programming schedule unlike any other. WTN argued that the existing television choices did not meet the needs of women and that women's information programming was relegated to the daytime schedule and was not available to women who work outside the home. Unlike conventional network broadcasters, WTN proposed a programming schedule that would feature women's informational programming not only during the conventional daytime lineup, but during prime time. In addition, the entertainment programming aired during prime time (and throughout the schedule) would challenge sex-role stereotyping, would feature strong lead female characters, would not portray gratuitous violence, would ensure that dramatic violence was viewed within a context of social reality, and would focus on issues of importance to women.

WTN argued that it would establish a unique spot on the television spectrum where Canadian women could see positive images of themselves, could gain access to important and relevant information not otherwise found on television, and could view original programming designed especially with women's unique television and communication needs in mind.[20] WTN argued that its programming would "add important and wider social benefits to the broadcasting system."[21] Based on the application made to the CRTC, WTN was granted a licence to begin broadcasting Canada's first cable service for women, by women, and about women and their worlds.

ADJUSTING THE IMAGE — WTN'S FIRST
TWO SEASONS OF BROADCASTING

The next "moment" in WTN's development occurred over the first two seasons of broadcasting, which took place from January to August 1995 and September 1995 to April 1996. It didn't help that the channel was racked with problems in the period leading up to the launch of the channel, including a consumer backlash against the cable companies, increased competition from specialty services, and hostile media commentators. The effects on the original vision for the channel were multifold. On one level, spokespeople for WTN distanced themselves from anything controversial, stating that the channel was "neither radically feminist nor powder-puff fluff. It's simply market-driven."[22] Linda Rankin, the channel's first president, was careful to explain that WTN's vision was not informed by "radicals" and added that "in our travels across the country there was overwhelming support for making something different happen. They were not from wild-eyed radicals. They were just from plain ordinary women like me."[23] However, prior to submitting its application to the CRTC, WTN had solicited letters of support from the feminist community and relied heavily on feminist media research to support the argument that women had unique communication and television needs that were not being met. The later distancing of WTN from "anything feminist" revealed the channel's about-face when confronted with the demands, limitations, and constraints of the television industry, its advertisers, and its critics.

This new public relations strategy was coupled with a name change. Rather than continuing to use the name "The Women's Television Network," the channel became known as "WTN." Jacqueline Cook, vice-president of marketing, stated that the name strategy would ensure that the channel's on-air name did not explicitly refer to women. This way WTN could be "soft and inclusive and subtle and not in your face."[24] She also added that the new programming strategy now focused on being *by, for, **or** about women,* rather than the original *by, for, **and** about women.* According to Cook, the application had just been a concept — the originators of the channel had been too idealistic about what they could accomplish.

Rather than continuing to invest time and money in originally produced independent programming by women, as originally proposed, by the end of the first three months of broadcasting the network had allowed the programming schedule to be dominated by foreign acquisitions of reruns and by recycled programming from other sources. These shows included *The Mary Tyler Moore Show* and *Rhoda* (1970s) and *Kate and Allie* and *Cagney and Lacey* (1980s). *The Mary Tyler Moore Show,* for example, had the highest repeat pattern on the schedule, appearing 14 times a week.

By the beginning of the second season, WTN had entrenched its new programming strategy, emphasizing prime-time entertainment over informational programming. Informational programming was relegated to the less-watched late-night, daytime, or weekend schedules, and in its place was more 1970s and 1980s recycled entertainment programming. The lineup and publicity materials featured more situation comedies, dramatic series, made-for-TV movies and classic films. Gone was the emphasis on documentaries, foreign or independent films, and unique women's informational programming. While images of women still dominated the screen — as leading ladies and spokespeople — gone were many of the female producers, directors, and artists who were highlighted in the application and during the first few months of broadcasting.

The primary strategy of the new season's programming was to create a prime-time lineup with broad audience appeal. Despite stating in its application that it would not "jeopardize the mission, vision and values of the service"[25] for the sake of advertisers, WTN was now programming "television that was attractive to a large group of viewers and not a group with a narrow focus."[26] What this meant, however, was that some (but not all) of the more innovative informational programming was cancelled and replaced by more familiar and conventional women's informational programming. This new lineup included domestic advice, beauty, and fashion programs along with reruns of syndicated talk shows. The commercial imperatives of the channel — to attract a broad audience with advertiser appeal — and the generic conventions of profit-oriented television were prioritized over the WTN's original intention to provide a unique Canadian broadcasting service. In essence, WTN was abandoning its vision of unique programming for women and was beginning to rely heavily on tried-and-true methods of attracting a women's television audience.

The application to the CRTC had emphasized innovative and risky programs — in some cases, television formats not traditionally aimed at a women's television audience. However, by the second season, WTN had clearly become reluctant to schedule anything too risky or controversial. There was a reliance on well-established generic conventions and existing television aesthetics, and a focus on ratings as the measure of a successful program. These practices, while essential to the commercial imperatives of the channel, can limit the possibilities of experimental or innovative programming for women. Although WTN had stated in its pre-launch publicity that women "watch more than day-time TV, [women are] more than cooking shows, gardening shows, fashion shows, talk shows and soap operas,"[27] the network began scheduling programming along these very lines. These changes did not go unnoticed by the popular press or the public. The *Ottawa Citizen* wrote that the addition of fashion, lifestyle, and home-decorating programs were "precisely the kinds of 'stereotypical' women's programming that WTN ... vowed would not be on the channel."[28]

WTN had devised a programming schedule for its second season that would satisfy advertisers and investors and would reap, it was hoped, higher revenues. Jacqueline Cook stated that the new programming "package" was designed to be more entertaining in order to attract a broader audience and to ease advertisers' concerns because "investors and advertisers attempt to avoid a thing called risk. And risk can be as simple as we don't know [what this is]. So, if you have a schedule of programming that no one knows, then it looks too risky."[29]

During the application stage, WTN presented itself as a privately owned commercial cable channel with a public service mandate, a mandate to create a unique and alternative viewing space for women on the Canadian television spectrum. It initially proposed to be by, for, and about women and their worlds. However, by the time the channel reached the air, this mandate had already shifted. Only a few of the original programming concepts designed to embody the vision and values of the channel made it to air. Most important, ratings had become the key factor in the decision whether a show should remain on the air. Jacqueline Cook stated, "We use ratings. Ratings are not just a yardstick for how attractive we are to advertisers but [are] also our most immediate and measurable yardstick for what viewers think of us and how many of them there are."[30] A show's value no longer lay in its social benefits, but rather in its ratings and appeal to advertisers. The audience being cultivated was not the diverse and unsatisfied female audience described to the CRTC, but rather the broad, large, affluent, and consumer-based female audience so important to advertisers.

The following statement by the vice-president of marketing illustrates that by the second season WTN's goal was no longer, as had been stated in the application, to "change the broadcasting system overnight": "Our goal is to ... build on what has become successful, continue to help refine ... what we mean by WTN. Have people refer to us as WTN. Make sure everybody feels they are welcome to watch."[31]

Whether or not the first three years of WTN's development demonstrate that television is an impenetrable citadel or a safe harbour, WTN certainly illustrates on a case-specific level that when a channel encounters the generic, fiscal, and production conventions of the commercial television industry, the industry's commercial imperatives become prioritized.

ENDNOTES

1. The corporate name of WTN is Lifestyle Television Limited. Throughout the application and hearing process before the Canadian Radio-television and Telecommunications Commission process (September 1993–July 1994), the channel was referred to as Lifestyle Television by the applicant, the CRTC, and the press. However, the on-air name of the channel became the Women's Television Network in September 1994 during the pre-launch publicity for the channel and was changed to WTN in October 1995.

2. Lifestyle Television, Application, Part 1, section 4.

3. Lifestyle Television, September 15, 1993, "Application by Linda Rankin on behalf of a company to be incorporated (Lifestyle Television Inc.) for a new national English language Canadian specialty service," Executive Summary (original document).

4. For a detailed discussion of these "moments" in WTN's history and development, please see Shirley Anne Off, "Defining the 'W' in WTN: A Feminist Case Study of the Women's Television Network (1993–1996)" (master's thesis, Carleton University, 1996).

5. The relevant section, Clause 3(d)(iii), of the 1991 Broadcasting Act reads: "It is hereby declared as the broadcasting policy for Canada that … (d) the Canadian broadcasting system should … (iii) *through its programming and the employment opportunities arising out of its operations*, serve the needs and interests, and reflect the circumstances and aspirations, of Canadian men, women, and children, including equal rights, the linguistic duality and multicultural and multiracial nature of Canadian society and the special place of aboriginal peoples within that society" (emphasis added).

6. In the two years prior to the licensing of WTN, the National Action Committee on the Status of Women, Toronto Women in Film and Television, and the Royal Commission on the Status of Women all called for the establishment of a women's television channel with the hope of improving professional opportunities for women in the industry and the representation of images of women on television.

7. At the time of the application, the controlling investor was Moffat Communications (holding 65 per cent of shares) — owners of CKY, the CTV-affiliate in Winnipeg, and various other broadcast holdings. Other investors included Michael Ihnat and Ron Rhodes (10 and 12 per cent respectively), a group of women investors (8 per cent), and WTN's president and CEO (5 per cent).

8. Lynn Spigel and Denise Mann, eds., *Private Screenings: Television and the Female Consumer* (Minneapolis: University of Minnesota Press, 1992), vii.

9. Julie D'Acci, *Defining Women: The Case of* Cagney and Lacey. Chapel Hill: University of North Carolina Press, 1994.

10. These producers and scholars include Helen Baehr, A. Spindler Brown, Rosalind Coward, Gillian Dyer, Ella Taylor, and Linda Steiner.

11. Helen Baehr and Annette Spindler Brown, "Firing a Broadside: A Feminist Intervention into Mainstream TV," in *Boxed In: Women and Television,* ed. H. Baehr and G. Dyer (New York: Pandora, 1987), 117.

12. Linda Steiner, "The History and Structure of Women's Alternative Media," in *Women Making Meaning: New Feminist Directions in Communications,* ed. L. Rakow (New York: Ballantine Books, 1992), 121.

13. Ibid., 135.

14. Ella Taylor, *Prime-Time Families* (Los Angeles: University of California Press, 1989), 50.

15. Rosalind Coward, "Women's Programmes: Why Not?" in *Boxed In: Women and Television,* ed. H. Baehr and G. Dyer (New York: Pandora, 1987), 100.

16. M. Cantor and J. Cantor, *Prime-Time Television: Content and Control* (London: Sage, 1992), 61.

17. Julie D'Acci, *Defining Women,* 27.

18. Janet Wasko, *Hollywood in the Information Age* (Great Britain: University of Texas Press, 1994), 71, 112.

19. Lifestyle Television, Application, Appendix B: 4-41.

20. Lifestyle Television Application, Part 4.

21. Lifestyle Television, Application, Part 3:18.

22. Canadian Press, "President defends women's channel," *Calgary Herald*, 8 January 1995: A11.

23. Terry Weber, "The women's TV channel faces undeserved hostility," *Toronto Star,* 28 March 1995: E3.

24. Interview with Jacqueline Cook, vice-president of marketing, Lifestyle Television Ltd. (WTN), 16 February 1996.

25. Lifestyle Television, Application, Part 4:25.

26. Interview with Jacqueline Cook.

27. Barbara Barde, vice-president of programming, Lifestyle Television Ltd. (WTN), quoted in Suzanne Matczuk, "Women's Television Network: A Narrow-Cast Celebration," *Interchange,* January 1995: 6–7.

28. Tony Atherton, "Canadian cable channels TUNE UP to stay alive," *Ottawa Citizen*, 23 December 1995: H1.

29. Interview with Jacqueline Cook.

30. Ibid.

31. Ibid.

THE LAST CIRCLE OF JOURNALISM HELL

The Bargain Basement

of the Tabloids

Michael Dorland

Give me your poor, your huddled masses, yearning …

The Statue of Liberty

I was broke and desperately in need of a job. I had just quit Ph.D. studies at the University of London and returned to Montreal. There was an ad in the paper: "Writers Wanted!" I thought of myself as a writer, especially now, after my farewell to scholarship.

The ad led to a nondescript grey office building on St. Catherine Street, near Guy. The name of the company was Globe Communications and they published tabloid newspapers, one of which I'd known of since my teens: *Midnight*. This was a black-and-white and lurid tabloid that I'd often seen read by commuters on the train to my father's house, half an hour out of the city. It had enormous headlines, like "Mom Boils Baby in Oil," and appropriately gruesome photographs.

The fatalities of family and class had marked me out for either the professoriat or the diplomatic corps. Secret dreams of journalism had fed what seemed like a more glamorous career orientation. Self-nurtured on books about Edward R. Murrow, on Walter Cronkite's *The 20th Century*, and on the dispatches by the heroic reporters of the United Press International, I found that strolling into the *Midnight* editorial offices was not exactly the grand entry into the business that I had foreseen. But a newsroom was still a newsroom: typewriters clattering, yellowing newspapers piled about, furious activity, and maybe a job if I passed the "writing test."

My Virgil was a soft-spoken Brit who wrote astrological advice under the name of Madame Blavatska, or something like that, and later went on to a moderately successful career as a TV psychic. He took me into an office — grey metal desk, grey Olympic typewriter — and handed me a legal-sized folder. It contained a photo of a well-endowed and unclothed female and a single sheet of paper with suggested titles: "I Change Men Like I Change Panties," "Only Six Lovers at a Time Can Satisfy This Lusty Gal," and several others along those lines.

"Go to it," said Geoff. "Go to what?" I gulped, not at all certain what I was supposed to do next. "Write us three stories using those headlines." "That's it?" "That's it: the photo is for inspirational purposes."

So I sat down at the typewriter, fed it some sheets of very cheap paper, stared at the photo briefly, and pounded out some sort of prose.

The phone call came the next day. It was Geoff. "Congratulations! You've passed the writing test. Report for work tomorrow at 8:30; salary's $250 a week." I'd just landed my first job as, well, a journalist.

At a time when there were few university journalism schools in Canada (and well into the 1970s even these were viewed with suspicion and ill-disguised contempt in the business), Midnight-Globe was probably the leading j-school in the country. Many name journalists had gotten their start there. The alternative tickets into metropolitan dailies were either to be British and to have worked (or claimed to have) on Fleet Street or to work your way up from small-town papers. Working for Midnight-Globe meant you were not only working in a major Canadian metropolis right off the start, but you learned how to write to deadline, how to make up a page and crop photos, how to do phone interviews, and how to talk to a diverse and unusual collection of "sources," ranging from the local sheriff, to eyewitnesses of UFO sightings, to people speaking from beyond the grave.

Although physically located in Canada, Globe Corp. was in fact the tip of a complex corporate structure. The company was registered in Delaware, with postal addresses along the U.S.-Canada border. Most of its news-gathering took place in the United States and mostly by phone. You learned to work those phones like a piano virtuoso, and there was seemingly nowhere you could not go by telephone. Calling the White House was nothing. I phoned in once into the midst of a hostage-taking in Washington and had the "perp" on the line for an exclusive interview, or rather it would have been an exclusive had we been a daily; we were a weekly, and by the time we got to press, the Washington police had either killed or arrested him. But all that came later.

First, one had to climb up the rungs of the tabloid universe, the bottom rung of which consisted of many variations of the "writing test." Two tabs, the *National Spotlight* and the *National Close-Up*, made up the bottom of the Globe edifice. Their circulation was around 50 000 copies each and the readership seemed primarily to consist of convicted felons whose jail-cell fantasies it was our job to aliment with endless stories of "lesbian" sex, group sex, sex with animals, and the ongoing adventures of various fearless heroines who, in addition to having a lot of sex with pretty much anything that moved, also reflected the fetishisms and obsessions of whoever had to write the columns, a job that rotated through the writer pool. We writers were a half-dozen wanna-be novelists (each with our current novel hidden in our desks that we'd work on after completing our daily quota of *Spotlight* or *Close-Up* material). Most of the writers were American draft-dodgers; others, like myself, had dropped out of graduate school; some were musicians; one claimed to be a Russian spy. Most went on to editorial and executive careers in daily journalism; the others disappeared; a few committed suicide; and at least four published novelists that I know of came out of that pool.

The next rung up consisted of a half-dozen "True Detective" and "True Crime" magazines. Most of these stories were farmed out to freelancers; Globe did the editorial work and publishing, collected the crime-scene photos, and kept in contact with the cops, often the first to phone in details of a story. The editor was himself an ex-cop from Texas. He cubby-holed himself away in a small office, and his assistant would sometimes sneak us in to look at the crime-scene pictures of assorted murders.

In the strictly tabloid hierarchy, the rung up from spinning sex-fantasies — an activity whose tedium led to increasingly surreal depictions of sexual acrobatics that eventually brought the company lawyers in to read the fine print of the laws governing the depiction of sex, always a sobering episode but only briefly restraining weary imaginations — was to move out of the body entirely and into the realm of the supernatural. This was the domain of two other tabs, edited by a former Joyce scholar utterly devoted to his day job, which he executed with sensitivity and imagination. The realm of the supernatural also overlapped to some degree with the realm of stardom. At Globe, stardom involved a strict hierarchy: lesser stars could be written about by the various lower-level tabs (though not the skin tabs, which were entirely fictional); some stars could not be written about at all under any circumstances, either because they had successfully sued the company or threatened to; and then there were the stars who were the exclusive preserve of the flagship paper, the former *Midnight*, now better known to supermarket shoppers as *The Globe*.

During my tenure, the top stars were Jackie Onassis, Aristotle Onassis, and the ghost of Jack Kennedy, and only the paper's top writers, in this case, a former sportswriter out of Miami, could be trusted to write Jackie and Ari stories with the right emotional finesse. The late JFK was easier to contact: once, the editor-in-chief dragged a wheelchair and a photographer atop Mount Royal, climbed into the wheelchair swaddled in gauze; the photographer took a long shot and the photo ran as a Midnight-Globe exclusive: "JFK ALIVE ON ARI O'S ISLE OF SKORPIOS!"

Midnight was originally the brain-child of a Lebanese carpet-dealer who emigrated to Montreal and became a tabloid publisher. The days of his ownership made up the stories of Camelot at the paper: newsroom open 24 hours a day, everyone stoned on LSD, the owner dropping by with cases of steaks to feed his scribes (he'd gone on to cattle-ranching). In the 1960s, *Midnight* was bought by two McGill students, one an accountant, who is still the owner of the enterprise, and the other perhaps the only person the accountant could trust absolutely, who became *Midnight*'s editor-in-chief.

A great messy bear of a man, half-blind and thus, perhaps, his resulting love of 180-point headlines, Johnny was a tabloid genius. He could concoct the most amazing whoppers from the slenderest of facts. With the exception of the skin tabs, the type of journalism practised at Globe might be described as creative embellishment: a story did have some basis in fact, even if that basis was slender. If someone told you they'd been picked up by a UFO, then that was true because the story had attribution. If you were going to be really picky, then you needed confirmation by at least one other source that the story was true — so the brother of the person who had been picked up by a UFO would do. Stories involving stars had to be based on a creative reading of something a gossip columnist wrote or on the interpretation of a photo. Thus, it was one of the Globe papers that first made headlines out of the weight problems of the later Elvis.

In addition to selling fantasies about the living, the dead, and the fictional, lesser Globe companies under a variety of names sold talismans, amulets, and good luck charms to the truly desperate. For a dollar (prices were usually low), an ancient Egyptian ankh could be purchased that would surely reverse your bad luck, your love life, or whatever ailed you. I remember once walking into a room in which a number of people in green eye-shades were counting what seemed truly a mountain of greenbacks sent in by the despairing. It was like being in a Vegas counting room.

And so it went. The papers came out every week; the money poured in. Eventually Globe Corp. moved to southern Florida, a right-to-work state where they would not be bothered by the various unionization drives that rocked the company under Quebec's more favourable labour laws, and set up shop near their great rival, the *National Enquirer*.

I spent a total of five years working there, leaving once for corporate communications at Bell Canada, a job I lasted in for six months, returning to Globe for another two years before finally making the jump to the *Montreal Star*, a newspaper I'd been trying to get into since age 16. Not long after coming to the *Star*, actor John Wayne died, and the overnight shift toiled mightily to produce a special commemorative colour supplement to honour the tragic passing of "the Duke."

I'd seen the future of daily journalism working at Globe, but was too young and too dumb to realize it then. Had I known, I could be working in Florida; I could have been on stories like the OJ Trial of the Century or the JonBenet Ramsay case.... Instead, I am a professor of journalism and communication at Carleton. "Le journalisme mène à tout — pourvu qu'on en sorte," once said a former premier of Quebec and ex-journalist. Journalism leads everywhere, so long as you can get out of it. It's the "getting out of" that's the tricky part.

TURNING *THE ENGLISH PATIENT* INTO A FILM

Alice Van Wart

> *Full fathom five thy father lies;*
>
> *Of his bones are coral made:*
>
> *Those are pearls that were his eyes*
>
> *Nothing of him doth fade,*
>
> *But doth suffer a sea-change*
>
> *into something rich and strange.*

Shakespeare, The Tempest

Rarely do successful literary works turn into equally successful films. *The English Patient,* based on Michael Ondaatje's hugely successful lyrical novel, is one of those films. The success of the film, however, is not because of the richness of the novel, but despite it.

Ondaatje's novel is intricately layered and episodic. It intertwines several plots, exploring through shifting points of view the devastation of war on human life. Its power lies not in its plot development, or even, finally, in its characters, but in Ondaatje's luminous prose. With the poet's eye and his skill with language, Ondaatje suggests rather than creates character and place. In his use of language he evokes the force of feeling and the poignant sense of what could have been.

The film, on the other hand, is tightly structured around a strong narrative line centred on character and event and moving from beginning to middle to end. Sensitive to the novel's language and its interior world, the film's screenwriter and director, Anthony Minghella, rightly uses the literary work as raw material only. His film is a loose translation of the novel. By using the resources of film, he achieves an approximation of the essence of the literary work. The film's adaptation succeeds precisely because of the changes the film's screenwriter and director makes. He transposes the novel into a rich new form that works on its own terms. In 1996 *The English Patient* was nominated for several Academy Awards.

In the short history of cinema, few Academy Award–winning films have been adapted from novels. *Birth of a Nation,* the 1915 Oscar winner, considered both the best silent film and cinema's first and still most famous epic, was an adaptation of a novel. So was the hugely successful Oscar winner, *Gone With the Wind,* in 1939. More recently, in 1995, *Sense and Sensibility,* adapted by Emma Thompson, was nominated for best picture, and it won her an Oscar for best screenplay.

For each of the few successful adaptations of novels into film, however, there are many more failures. Hollywood's attempt to turn Nathaniel Hawthorne's *The Scarlet Letter* into a film was an unmitigated failure. The screen version bore little resemblance to Hawthorne's soul-chilling tale of adultery in turn-of-the-century, puritanical New England. Jane Campion's screen adaptation of Henry James's *Portrait of a Lady* fared only somewhat better. Campion partially succeeds in her attempts to convey the formality and sense of artifice that are integral to James's novel, but she fails in the translation of her central character. Unable to use the device of a narrator's careful and detailed observation of Isabel Archer, Campion has not provided some kind of objective correlative to suggest what lies behind Isabel Archer's perpetually blank expression.

Similarly, David Cronenberg's attempt to eroticize J.G. Ballard's novel *Crash* falls far short of the novel's chilling psychological intentions, where a growing obsession becomes a ritualistic fetish with dire consequences. Cronenberg's film, devoid of psychological insight or motivation, is a shell of the novel, not much more than a grim reminder to wear a seat belt, drive safely, and at least park the car if you're going to have sex in it.

Why do some novels succeed as films and others die at the titles? Jane Austen's novels seem to translate into film with tremendous success at the box office — even though they were written 200 years ago and have no car-chase scenes, no violence, and no sex. They do, however, have strong central characters and strong plots with twists, reversals, jokes, humour, and social concerns not so different from those of today — love, marriage, and money. Yet their success on the screen doesn't mean that Austen's films are easy to adapt; it means that there is enough in them of the kind of material that is needed to make a good film. Even with this right kind of material, the screenwriter of Austen's work still has to turn exposition into dramatic scenes, translate description into visual image, and convert prose scenes into dialogue. Because of film's constraint of time, the development of both character and situation probably requires some condensation. There are also matters concerning the eighteenth century that a modern audience might not understand and that therefore have to be dealt with.

In short, total fidelity to Austen's words is next to impossible and, given their beauty and complexity, not even desirable. Essentially, the film becomes something else. The subject may be similar, but the content, by definition and form, is different.

Although both novel and film may share the intention of telling a story, the way they tell their story is radically different. Being different mediums, they are bound by different conventions determined by very different origins, different production processes, and different audiences. Inherent in these differences lie the limitations and advantages of each art form and the qualities that distinguish the one form from the other.[1]

The history of the modern novel reaches back to the eighteenth century and to the invention of the printing press. Rooted in the abstract system of the printed word and practised by an individual writer, the creative act of novel writing has always been a solitary one, limited only by imagination and language itself. The final product of a single imagination is turned from manuscript to book form by a publishing house that buys, prints, and sells the product. The audience for novels, at least compared to that for film, is relatively small.

Film is a relatively new medium. Its history lies in the literal system of the visual image and corresponds to the invention of the motion picture camera about a hundred years ago. For its production, it is dependent on technology and involves a writer, director, producer, and technical crew, at a minimum. A film is a cooperative production often guided by market demands and finally supported by a mass audience.

Although both novel and film intentionally construct or reproduce reality in a symbolic or abbreviated approximation of the world, both are finally artistic forms. Each form artificially constructs (hence artifice) space, time, psychological conditions, the historical world, as well as the symbolic and the moral world. This construction determines the inner landscape and outer form of the work. The construction of each medium represents a complex, yet different, way of apprehending the universe and rendering states of consciousness, while evoking an immediate or cumulative emotional response.

As a linguistic medium, the novel is conceptual and discursive in form. Film, a visual medium, is perceptual and presentational. To create its universe, the novel depends on words that will stand between the perceiver and the symbolized perception; film depends primarily on the visual image and the rendering of spatial movement. With film, perception itself is immediate and not mediated. Both novel and film manipulate time in the telling of story, but the informing principle in the novel is time itself, whereas that of film is space. The novel takes its space for granted and forms its narrative in a complex presentation of past, present, and future times. The film takes its time for granted and forms its narrative in arrangements of space.

The novel is a highly flexible form implicated in history and myth, concerned with representation, yet with an historical bias towards self-referentiality and self-questioning. It draws upon a long tradition of mythical, historical, and romantic patterns for the articulation of its narratives. As a verbal invention, the novel is symbolic and mediated.

Translated through the process of thought, words create images of things, feelings, and concepts expressed largely through figures of speech, primarily metaphor and metonymy. The writer uses voice and point of view to tell a story, and the particular point of view — first person or third person omniscient or selected or even, though not commonly, second person — determines the telling of the story and the reader's understanding of it.

Film is restricted in creating linguistic tropes — except for dialogue — and uses instead visual images to create its world. The camera itself is more or less omniscient. The process of editing or splicing together the visual images captured on film, each one carefully considered and deliberately intended, is what shapes the film's point of view.

The quality of the image in conjunction with the editing together of these images determines the quality and the form of the film. The central cinematic analogy to the metaphor is montage, or the cutting and linking together of a variety of shots along with the subsidiary elements of dialogue, sound effects, and music.

Sound, music, and other aural effects, important in film, are an extension of the technique of editing. Each shot in a film takes its meaning from preceding shots and future expectations.

Sound is an important element in film, in essence the emblem of subjective mood. It is edited to the visual image through counterpoint (used to emphasize or underline) and through contrapuntal (used to point up hidden meaning). Ultimately, the demands of the visual image will determine the kind of sound or music used. The sound track is usually laid on as a separate line (though not always) after the series of images are linked together.

Consciousness and particularly the act of consciousness itself absorb the signs of language and the photographed image differently. Language can create complex emotional states and meanings, and it better suits the rendition of mental states — dreams, imagination, memory — than does the image. Images can approximate these states with the help of cinematic conventions such as flashback or the speeding up or slowing down of images. At best, the manipulation of images can convey interiority or consciousness; it cannot create, as language can, conceptual consciousness itself.

Given, then, the different, sometimes conflicting conventions and radically different orientations of novel and film, the filmmaker or film adapter will need to make serious adjustments when moving between these mediums. By necessity, those very characteristics that make the novel "novelistic" will probably have to be abandoned, and the adaptation will likely also include other deletions, additions, and major alterations.

But what about films that distort or change the novelist's intention and meaning (as far as we can know it)? Often this abandonment is so severe, in a strict sense, that the new creation bears little resemblance to the original. An example of this is the film version of *The Scarlet Letter,* which completely loses the novel's allegorical purpose. Without this dimension, the film lacks social and moral implication, the underpinning of the novel's very complexity. Campion's film version of *Portrait of a Lady* may have seemed virtuously to the point compared to the author's discursive story, but to think so is to miss what makes James's novels distinctive. In a James novel, it is not the point that is important, but the getting there.

Even if these failures were the failures of the screenwriters and not a result of the difficulties of moving from one medium to the other, film cannot duplicate the novel. At best, a film adaptation can approximate in its translation. At worst, it will offer only a paraphrase.

Given these integral differences, by what standards do we measure the success or failure of a cinematic adaptation of a novel? Is the original work the primary standard by which the success of the adaptation is measured? Given the inherent differences in their forms, should it be?

In his adaptation of *The English Patient,* Minghella demonstrates his understanding that there are certain things a novel can do that a film cannot, and he avoids novelistic techniques in his film. To show what a film can do much better than the novel, he radically restructures the novel's story and focus, using only parts of the novel. In fact, he cuts the novel's central thread almost entirely, the relationship between Hanna and Kip, onto which the other stories are stitched. Instead, the relationship between Katherine and the Count Almasy, a small part of the novel's narrative, becomes the film's central story.

In his novel, Ondaatje only briefly explores the affair that is the film's primary concern. There is no sandstorm in the novel to dramatically bring the lovers together as there is in the film. Nor does the novel tell us how Clifton learns of his wife's affair. Minghella extends and expands the development of this affair, thus emphasizing Katherine's and Almasy's betrayal of Clifton, as well as the extent of their passion.

Of necessity, Minghella considerably condenses the peripatetic nature of the novel's story. After radically shifting its focus, he recreates the sequence of events as a flashback that emerges from the first scene — a plane flying over the desert is shot from the sky, and a man parachutes down, holding a woman, both of them burning.

The flashback is the film's story, the development of the affair between this man and woman. Their affair provokes her husband to attempt to kill Almasy, which leads to Katherine being hurt and to Almasy carrying her to the cave for safety. In the novel, there is little about the cave, whose importance in the film is early foreshadowed. In order to find help for Katherine, Almasy has to walk through the desert for several days. Because he doesn't have his correct papers, he is arrested. By the time he makes his way back to Katherine, she is dead. Again he carries her body, this time to his airplane to fly her out of the desert. He is shot down in his attempt. The film comes full circle.

Minghella's linear restructuring, his cause-and-effect action, gives the film both its momentum and its drama. By refocusing the narrative, he is able to frame his story by beginning with the final consequences: a badly burned man in a villa in Italy at the end of the war is being attended by a disillusioned nurse who is resisting a relationship with Kip, a Sikh sapper. In the novel, Kip and Hanna are instrumental in conveying the sense of the fundamental tragedy of war as an historical force. In the film, they only help further reinforce the sense of what is dramatically portrayed in the love story between Katherine and Almasy.

One of the strengths of the novel, impossible to achieve in the film, is the shifting among its characters of the narrative point of view. These shifts weave the various stories and adventures into an intricate form. In the first half of the novel, Almasy remains an unidentified mystery. To shift the focus in the film to Almasy's story, Minghella uses clues only hinted at in the novel to create the events in the film that bring about the love affair between Katherine and Almasy. He enlarges the time frame and heightens the tensions of pre-war Cairo society and the lovers' time spent there. He develops the friendship between the explorers Madox, Geoffrey Clifton, and the cartographer Almasy, as well as the duplicity among these characters.

The power of the novel resides in its power to pull the reader into its story so that the story's voice and language become the reader's. The reader inhabits its characters and the novel's space and time. Film cannot reach into consciousness in the way a novel can; nor can characters be known in film in the same way they can be known in a novel. Film goes beyond individuality: we can identify with the characters, but we can never be them; we may understand their world, but we can never be in it.

Film is free of adjectives and adverbs. What makes film cinematic are the images so carefully chosen to visualize the story. These images work to give meaning to the smallest, even the most familiar, gesture, inflating it into an attitude, opening it to interpretation. They retain a multiplicity of possible meanings. In the split second of a cut or in the few seconds of a dissolve, the images in film show the very unpredictability of reality itself as they transport or take the viewer to what is being shown. Rather than convey destiny, film shows it as it occurs. In this respect, film is immediate and visceral. No other form of narrative gets so close to the variety, the texture, and the skin of everyday life; therein lies its unique power and the power behind Minghella's adaptation of *The English Patient*.

The final standard, then, for films based on novels, regardless of thematic and formal changes in the translation, is not how well the film recreates the novel's story, but whether or not the film stands as an autonomous work of art. The screenwriter and the director have every right to take liberties with their literary models. Their purpose is not so much to respect the intentions of the novel as to transform its dramatic, emotional, and metaphorical elements into a new medium, thereby respecting less the vision of the novel than that of the film.

ENDNOTE

1. The discussion of theoretical issues concerning the novel and film for the purposes of this essay is general and oversimplified. I would like to acknowledge George Bluestone's *Novels into Film: The Metamorphosis of Fiction into Cinema* (Berkeley: University of California Press, 1961). His seminal study began my own thinking on this topic.

P a r t

4

THE SPORTING
LIFE LIVES

INTRODUCTION

First he won it, then he lost it. Even Canadians determinedly blind to the power of sports as a slice of popular culture couldn't ignore the furore everywhere during the first two weeks of February 1998.

When 26-year-old Ross Rebagliati of Whistler, B.C., became the first snowboarder to win an Olympic gold medal at the Nagano Games, Canadians of all ages were delighted — even euphoric. And the media revelled in the story, interviewing everyone from Rebagliati's grandmother to his young sister, also a snowboard athlete. Then, within days, the glory-noise slithered to a crashing halt — the International Olympic Committee voted 3 to 2 (with two abstentions) to strip Rebagliati of his medal because he failed both parts of athletes' drug tests. Rebagliati had tested positive for marijuana!

Sports enthusiasts immediately flashed back to the 1988 Seoul Olympics when Toronto sprinter Ben Johnson was stripped of his gold medal and world record for using the anabolic steroid stanozolol, a performance-enhancing substance. That event had evoked an out-pouring of national soul-searching and racial distress. Sports columnists had agonized at length then on the nature of athletic heroism and threatened to do so again.

But on the heels of the shock about Rebagliati's predicament came the jokes: since when, duuuh, man, uh, was marijuana a drug that speeded up anyone's performance, uunh, or added an edge to their skill? And on the tail-end of that came the debate about ethics: what kind of a message did Rebagliati's lifestyle choices send to young sports fans? Wasn't mar-ijuana, after all, still illegal, whether it speeded up or slowed down a turn on the slopes?

123

Fortunately, before anyone could get too exercised over either perspective, Canadian officials appealed the IOC decision.

Within less than a week, the snowboarder had his gold medal back. And his agent, Ron Perrick, made headlines by saying Rebagliati was now on the road to worldwide fame as a cultural icon and representative of the alternative image favoured in snowboarding circles. In short, the marijuana brouhaha had increased the snowboarder's chances for endorsements and spin-off fame. And, as billboards and ads now attest, the fame has come to pass.

Canadians have a reputation for restraint and taciturnity, but anyone who's attended even a peewee-league hockey game knows that they unleash their passion over sports, particularly, it would seem, sports involving snow and ice. The traditional panoply of Canadian sports includes hockey, football, basketball, golf, baseball, curling — and, in some centres, lacrosse and soccer.

In this section of *Pop Can,* Michael Zeitlin explores the Canadian form within the Canadian Football League as "revenge of Canadian form upon American consumer consciousness," while Gamal Abdel-Shehid probes the images of black male culture encapsulated within the structure of the Toronto Raptors. And of course, the section would not be complete without two articles on hockey — Winnipeg writer Gary Genosko sees hockey as an "all terrain" vehicle for exploring Canada, and Ottawa critic Tom McSorley imagines a conversation (one that *should* have happened) between Wayne Gretzky and one of Canada's greatest thinkers, Harold Innis.

THE CFL AND CANADIAN FORM

Michael Zeitlin

They own the corporations, the processing plants, the mineral rights, a huge share of the Canadian earth. The colonialist theme, the theme of exploitation, of greatest possible utilization. They are right next to us, sending their contaminants, their pollutants, their noxious industrial waste into our rivers, lakes and air. The theme of power's ignorance and blindness and contempt. We are in the path of their television programs, their movies and music, the whole enormous rot and glut and blare of their culture. The theme of cancer and its spread.

Don DeLillo, The Names

In the beginning there was "NFL Football."[1] This remains the dominant prototype, a game globally mass-marketed, addictive as sugar-coated breakfast cereal, and utterly predictable (there are only four teams: the Dallas Cowboys™, the San Francisco Forty-Niners™, the Green Bay Packers™, and the Denver Broncos). No other teams are allowed to win the Super Bowl (as the Buffalo Bills can tell you). And so it is against NFL Football that the Canadian game asserts its antediluvian forms of difference, its bizarre resistance to total commodification. The field is inconceivably wide and 10 yards longer (hence all the passing). The goal pylons stand portentous, like isolated barren trees on the Saskatchewan prairie. Above them sweep the wind, snow, and rain of the Northern wilderness (that's why the Grey Cup is played in November: to play in January would be nearly fatal for players and crowd alike).[2] At ground level the wooden posts are a menace, pure points of collision amid 24 crisscrossing men (some would say the Americans had the good sense, after what might seem the necessary accumulated sacrifice in snapped spinal cords, to reduce the posts to one Y-shaped stem and move the whole looming structure to the back of the "End Zone"). *Twenty-four* crisscrossing men did you say? Yes, there are 12 men per side. Twelve — the numeral itself responds to what appears to be the anti-modern propensity of the game: 12 lost tribes, 12 disciples, 12 rowing Argonauts, 12 Anglo Saxons tromping over the heath. To Americans, the twelfth man is a source of real anxiety: it would be like waking up with an extra digit — what to *do* with it, where to *put* it, how to *use* it? Indeed, the game seems admirably designed especially to confuse Americans. What other football league in the history of the world would have not only *two* tight ends per team but also *two* teams named the "Roughriders"? (OK, one of them spells it "Rough Riders.") Since it is unnecessary to mention the sheer weirdness of there being only three downs with which to accomplish 10 yards, I will not do so.

Then there is the master signifier itself (something small and unnoticed until, magically animated, tumescent, it looms suddenly large): I refer, of course, to "the single point," which enters like an irruption of the archaic into the heart of Late Capitalism. With no time on the clock, lives can be turned around, championships can be won, cities can be transfigured, all on the mere contingent bounce of a leather obloid, punted. And so the game builds its own "uncertainty principle" into the heart of its very structure, showing its contempt for prefabricated plots. Anything *can* happen. More: even with *no time on the clock*, I mean nothing but zeros, there can be time for *one more play*. Only in the CFL is it never over, even when it's over.

If there's something primal, oneiric, and unruly at the heart of the Canadian game, there is also something admirably un-NFL about the way it foregrounds the fluidity of its essential forms. Indeed, there is nothing more subversive about Canadian football than its refusal, before the start of each play, to arrange itself into that "set" tableau by which American football announces its affiliation with paramilitary forms of authority and obedience. Before the ball is hupped north of the border, all may proceed in motion except five down linemen: that leaves six others (not including the quarterback) to seduce, feint, and mesmerize the defence with taunting patterns of motion and camouflage and individual acts of creative self-expression.[3] The effect is to multiply, well nigh vertiginously, the possible forms by which reality in the next five seconds may actualize itself downfield: seven of the twelve players are eligible receivers! (Canada is a more open, a more diverse, a more multicultural society.)

And so, as we read the signatures in this way, the game of Canadian football becomes nothing less than a dramatic form of resistance as well as a creative form of national self-assertion. But, as the theorists tell us, form is primarily defensive, and in this instance, for good reason: as everybody knows, American players dominate the *content* of the game. Or at least they register that effect on the minds of those who market and consume it: Raghib The Rocket, Doug Flutie, Mike "Pinball" Clemons. That is to say, Pure Darwinism unconstrained by Law (or quotas) would lead to utter subjugation: hence the rule — call it a form of affirmative action — that every team must place 20 Canadians on the roster.[4] Of course, this is an unmistakable sign of a predominating Canadian fear, the fear of invasion, of occupation, of displacement.

Who can forget the CFL's noble yet comical attempt (as if in direct response to that fear) at a counter-insurgency just a few short years ago, its sinister plan to expand itself *into* the United States of America? (The sheer audacity of this ambition alone boggles the mind: think, perhaps, of Lithuania "expanding" itself into the Soviet Union, dead metaphor though it be.) The very names of the two new "Canadian" teams should have been a warning. First there was the San Antonio Texans (Texas, born in that rapacious land-grabbing episode known as the Mexican War). Then there was the Sacramento Gold Miners (California, forged in the dream of instant wealth and pure treasure). What could the CFL commissioner and team owners have been thinking? Between them, Texas and California have done more to cash the cheque of American Imperialism and its motto, "What was yours is mine," than all the other States of the Union combined, almost. And so the CFL came *this close* to being completely assimilated into the American apparatus. First, the teams from Sacramento and Texas, surrounded as they were with their own indigenous and prodigious football talent, which the colleges and universities of these great states produce year after year, sought to abolish the quota system that demanded the fielding of 20 Canadians per team. Second, these American teams wanted to do away with the ultimate signifier of a CFL identity founded upon difference, the three-down rule. Playing with three downs south of the border was an un-American activity and so could not have survived for very long. However, Texas and Sacramento went bankrupt before they had a chance to obliterate the CFL entirely. Call it the sweet revenge of Canadian form upon American consumer consciousness.

We can now see that this entire tragicomic episode was merely a small part of a larger conceptual crisis of unprecedented historical complexity in the field of professional sports in North America: the idea of national identity was rapidly becoming a moribund impediment to the free flows of capital (and television rights). "Canada" had won the World Series (with American and Dominican players). "America" had been winning the Stanley Cup for some time (with Canadian and Québécois players, a few scattered Yanks among them). Everything was getting all mixed up; the lines refused to stay in place; the scenario of "Us vs. Them" was verging towards a dangerous evacuation of essential meaning. Whether this was good or bad — the dream of universal brotherhood or the nightmare of miscegenation — would appear to be a matter of perspective.

No, it is not the nationality of the players or even the audience that matters: it's the triumph of a radically un-American form. If "Canada" is to retain any meaning as a site of resistance to and insulation against the Disneyfication of the globe ("We're all one beat away from becoming elevator music," Don DeLillo has said), let us fight fight fight to preserve the CFL, whose symbolic value as insolent, dissident, resistant form remains a thing of beauty.[5]

ENDNOTES

1. That's what "they" want you to believe. It is a lie. First there was boar hunting, then a kind of game with an inflated pig bladder, then rugby, then NFL football.

2. I repress the ugly fact that the Dome, like the Shopping Mall, threatens, like Wallace Stevens's jar in Tennessee, to take dominion everywhere. But anyway …

3. All that is asked is that the players refrain from crossing the line of scrimmage, *although they may threaten to do so*, before the ball actually moves.

4. American superiority remains a pure and complex mystery; certainly it is no mere vulgar matter of race or physique — as everybody knows, Doug, Mike, and Raghib are short little guys.

5. When Dr. Paul Litt (Ph.D., Canadian History) read a draft of this piece, he wrote: "The only thing missing is a lyrical evocation of the feel, smells, and sights of a real turf CFL field mid-game in late October in comparison to the NFL's postage stamps of indoor-outdoor polyester carpeting melting under TV lights." Since I couldn't agree more, I would hope that my esteemed reader would have provided these things for herself. My thanks to Dr. Litt and also to Andrew Baerg, who reminded me of the biggest and most obvious thing: that the CFL uses a differently sized ball, the J5V.

"WHO GOT NEXT?"

Raptor Morality and

Black Public Masculinity

in Canada[1]

Gamal Abdel-Shehid

Recently, a lot of people have expressed concern over the failure of official narratives of Canada to represent the experiences of many of the country's citizens. These post-colonial critiques of the Great White North have largely focused on the experiences of those who exist outside those narratives, First Nations peoples and Canadians who trace their heritage to parts of the Third World. Such critiques have been vital to challenging the myths of Canada. In the area of writing, this crisis in representation was captured during the 1993 "Writing Thru' Race" conference held in Vancouver. The furore that such a conference generated amongst conservative white writers was evidence of the fact that taken-for-granted notions of "what is Canada" were extremely ethnocentric at best.[2] In the world of sports, similar dislocations are at work. No longer is hockey the sport that defines Canada. However, little work has been done in this area. I hope to help to redress this with this post-colonial exploration of the cultural politics of basketball in Toronto, paying attention to the Raptors' emergence.

To begin, I want to describe two phenomena relating to the recent history of basketball in Toronto. The first is a page that appeared in the *Toronto Star* on 6 December 1995. The page featured two stories about two different black men. Their realities, we learned, could not have been more different. On the top part of the page was a picture of Clinton Gayle, a young black man convicted of shooting and killing Metropolitan Toronto Police Constable Todd Baylis. The story is about the previous day's trial hearing, during which Metro police officer Michele Leone, Baylis's partner the night he was killed, pointed his finger at Gayle and positively identified him as the man who shot and killed Baylis. The *Toronto Star* noted that Leone's arm "shook" and his "finger quivered" as he pointed to Gayle. Moreover, during the moment that Leone identified Gayle, "the accused (Gayle) sat impassive in the prisoner's dock."

Beneath this story, there appeared another picture of a black man, that of Sheldon Aberdeen, who died in his high school in Toronto[3] of "an apparent heart condition" after a basketball practice. The Aberdeen story told of the funeral held the day before. Moreover, the writer noted that, at the funeral, Aberdeen had been named an honorary member of the city's new NBA team, the Toronto Raptors.[4] James Williams, the African-American coordinator of the Raptors' community outreach program, had presented Aberdeen's family with a letter detailing this. In addition, the story noted that Aberdeen's family was presented with "an official basketball, signed by all Raptor players."

The second phenomenon involves a curious dialogue between geography, politics, blackness, and history that has recently been commented on by Andrew Thornton.[5] He pointed out the ironic fact that the site of the annual Raptorfest (a three-on-three tournament, hosted by the Raptors, which is becoming one of the most important sports spectacles in Toronto) on University Avenue in front of the Royal Ontario Museum (ROM) is the same stretch of turf that saw massive anti-racist demonstrations by members of Toronto's black community against the ROM's 1991 "Into the Heart of Africa" exhibit. This protest had gone on for several days and culminated in the violent arrests of eleven protesters, all black, and their subsequent trial.[6]

In making note of these phenomena, I do not wish to speculate on the intentions of either the Raptors or the layout people at the *Toronto Star*. Instead, I use these examples as illustrative of a process. This process is the struggle over "who's got next run" in terms of representing a black public masculinity in Toronto. Both phenomena point to the place and prominence of the colour purple[7] in the (re)colouring of Toronto's landscape of blackness. I show how public forms of racialized masculinity are tied to questions of capital accumulation, globalization, and the quest for markets, and explain what this tells us about the limits, or borders, of the relations between Canadian nationalism, gender, and blackness. Moreover, I want to make a political argument for a necessary suspicion and activism against certain versions of American imperial masculinity, regardless of colour.

BASKETBALL AS A SPORT OF DIFFERENCE IN CANADA

It is important to identify the place that the Raptors rumbled into when they played their first basketball game in Toronto in November 1995 — SkyDome. This provides a background to how and why the Raptors market themselves as they do. At that first game of the first season, the Raptors were not the most welcome bunch in town. Despite the myth that has basketball invented by a Canadian, Dr. James Naismith, basketball was seen by Toronto's sports establishment as a *sport of difference* in a "hockey town."

Several writers have contributed to the narrative that names hockey as *the* sport of the imagined community that is Canada. Both hockey and Canada, according to the tradition, involve "(white) man's" persistent struggle against the elements, his attempt to carve out a virile masculinist home in the midst of a cold and hostile land. According to Kidd and MacFarlane, "hockey captures the essence of the Canadian experience in the New World. In a land so inescapably cold, hockey is the dance of life, an affirmation that despite the deathly chill of winter we are alive" (1972, 4).

In addition to being touted for its invigorating qualities, hockey was thought to represent the absolute and discernible difference between Canadians and "our" neighbours, the Americans. In terms of gender, a mythical Canadian heterosexual machismo is fashioned through hockey. According to "new right" CBC broadcaster Don Cherry, hockey imparts to Canadian boys a sense of who they are. It teaches Canadian boys how to beat up on anyone who is different, the "pansy" European players, for example, as a way to establish "our" identity.

There are other important "Canadian sports," such as rowing, lacrosse, and curling, but these exist on a second tier below hockey. There is, if you will, a third level of sports (basketball, track and field, boxing) in Canada. These sports have only recently been recognized on the medal podium in Canada, and it could be argued that this is because of their "colour." These "black" sports, by virtue of the fact that they are played by immigrants or by people who look like immigrants, have largely been narrated as *un*-Canadian sports. By extension, their participants have not been narrated within the national sporting iconography.

Athletes who excel in these sports are often seen as a threat to, rather than a reaffirmation of, our Canadianness. Otherwise, their accomplishments are merely ignored. A few examples demonstrate this reality. First, witness the complaints made by members of Canada's Olympic gold medal–winning 4 x 100 men's relay team. These complaints centred around the fact that, in spite of reaching the pinnacle of their sport, which should have made them attractive to advertisers, the team received hardly any advertising revenue. Second, witness the continuous migration of black athletes, mirroring the migration of other black Canadian cultural producers, to the United States or England in search of more support and recognition.[8]

The fact that black athletes are seen as potentially disruptive of the national sporting fabric is evident in "common-sense racist"[9] understandings of basketball in recent years. Congruent to basketball's recent boom in popularity, there have been corresponding attempts to demonize it, both officially and unofficially. First, at the high school level, the meteoric rise in popularity of hoops in Toronto has been met with various attempts to repress the sport. For example, several school basketball programs have been shut down because principals cite basketball as a sport that is ungovernable. Furthermore, there has been the inauguration of unprecedented "Violence in Sports Workshops" that try to target and "tame" basketball's attitude. These workshops are all the more bizarre given that hockey, with its legendary violence, has historically merited no such conferences. In addition, in 1995, the Toronto Board of Basketball passed a series of restrictive rules governing the conduct and dress of ballplayers, including such absurd regulations as prohibiting players from wearing cut-off T-shirts to games and from bumping chests after a basket.[10] At the media level, there have been several articles on violence in basketball. These note the growing popularity of the NBA and cite the antics of superstars like Dennis Rodman as a bad influence on young boys.[11] In other cases, authors describe the good old days, before West Indians played basketball in Toronto, as being safe and friendly.[12] Third, at the level of the Canadian National Basketball team, in the winter of 1994 Basketball Canada issued a report exonerating Ken Shields of charges of racism. In its justification, the authors of the report attributed the small number of black ballplayers in Canada's national program, not to racist practices or beliefs within the national team, but to black and "inner-city" ballplayers' inability to adapt to Canadian basketball standards.[13]

These instances point to a general attempt by Toronto's sports establishment(s) to narrate basketball as a sport of both difference and trouble within Canada. However, these efforts have not deterred ballplayers, young and old, male and female, black, white, and other, from looking for the next run.

NEGOTIATING DIFFERENCE: INTRODUCING … YOUR TORONTO RAPTORS!

Far from being a subaltern sport in the city, basketball is now a popular and big-time sport in both Toronto and its suburbs. The popularity of hoop cultural styles, worn by young men and women regardless of their colour, is evidence of this growth.[14] Further evidence is the fact that Toronto's largest sports spectacle of this past year was not a hockey or baseball game, but the Toronto Raptors–Chicago Bulls game on 10 December 1996 at SkyDome.

Toronto, in fact, is gaining notoriety on the world basketball map, as seen by the signing up of Trinidadian-born Torontonian Jamaal Magliore for the high-profile University of Kentucky basketball program; the staging of the World Championship of Basketball in Toronto in 1994; and the first Nike "Exposure Camp," recently held in Scarborough.[15]

As a longtime basketball fan, I've found these changes exciting and inspiring. Yet this growth has its tensions. Primarily, there is a tension around what kind(s) of black public masculinity is (are) possible in Toronto. There has been a price to pay for the rise of popularity of hoops in the city. This price is a result of basketball's movement from a sport of difference to the coolest game on the block. At the same time that basketball has been taking off and enjoying immense popularity in Toronto and beyond, we have seen a new discourse emerging around basketball and black public masculinities to replace, or overlay, what could be called indigenous forms of representation. I call this new discourse "Raptor morality," as seen with respect to the Raptor vignettes I began with. This is largely a morality rooted in ritualistic, African-American, bourgeois aesthetics and politics; it represents a hardening or petrification of the political possibilities of black public masculinity.

"THIS IS A PUBLIC SERVICE ANNOUNCEMENT, PAID FOR BY THE NBA ..."

In both vignettes at the start of this essay, what is crucial about the Raptor image is that it acts like an alternative to conventional representations of blackness as trouble. The Raptor allays or responds to racist fears about "violent" black masculinities. In the first case, the pervasive face of a "cop-killer,"[16] or "gangsta," is shown on the same page as Aberdeen's story. In contrast to Gayle, Aberdeen is the boy who worked hard and was a good kid. It is for this reason that the Raptors chose to immortalize him. Comments made at the boy's funeral indicated why the team brought him into the Raptor family by making him an honorary Raptor, the first and only such designation. According to the *Toronto Star*, "Williams said the teen's life mirrored his own and that of Raptor general manager Isiah Thomas, who both came from poor families in Chicago, but through their dreams and aspirations overcame their hardships" (December 6, 1995).

The story continues to quote Williams, who noted that Aberdeen's "spirit and what he exemplified in his character are examples of what we want the team to be." Also, Aberdeen's teacher, Neil Langley, is quoted as saying that Aberdeen was "generous and honourable and cared about others." The symbolic linking of Aberdeen, hard work, and basketball is symptomatic of a Raptor morality in the making. The fact that the Raptors attended Aberdeen's funeral attests to the fact that, in order to establish themselves, they had a certain kind of community in mind. This community is not simply "black," but rather it is a community of hard workers and good students who are also black.[17]

In the second case, the ground shared by the Raptorfest and demonstrators representing the Coalition for the Truth about Africa (CFTA) against the ROM suggests the struggle over what public displays of black masculinity are possible. The Raptorfest — replete with blow-up Raptors and booths selling products made by Nike, KFC, and Gatorade — is a two-day advertisement/carnival for the Toronto Raptors. This past year, over 600 teams participated, which amounts to almost 2000 players, mostly black and male.

Whether or not the Raptors deliberately chose this venue because of the earlier demonstrations, the steps of the ROM are familiar terrain to many anti-racist activists in the city. Moreover, the ironic fact that this area saw both one of the most charged anti-racist protests the city has seen and one of the most vulgar displays of (black)[18] capitalism underscores the tension I spoke of earlier and stresses how important the next run is. In the Raptors' case, it seems they are only willing to sponsor black runs buttressed by corporate heavyweights and without the slightest hint of an anti-racist, or anti-capitalist, sensibility.

Raptor morality is not new. It is a fairly long-standing way of representing black masculinity within capitalist sports cultures. Specifically, Raptor morality is an example of the aesthetic of black masculinity popularized recently in the documentary *Hoop Dreams* and in fictional films such as *Sunset Park* and *White Men Can't Jump*. This aesthetic ties together notions of capitalism, black masculinity, a failed nuclear family, basketball, and the inner-city.[19] The kind of black man that the Hoop Dreams aesthetic puts forth is a determined one, a man who is fiercely individualistic and committed to the dream of "making it" through the brutal channels of professional sports. One author, bell hooks, makes this observation: "Ultimately, *Hoop Dreams* offers a conservative vision of the conditions of 'making it' in the United States" (1995, 23).

What grounds this aesthetic is the belief in the redemptive values of competitive individualism. In describing the attitudes of one of the main characters in the documentary, hooks goes on to say: "An almost religious belief in the power of competition to bring success permeates American life. The ethic of competition is so passionately upheld and valued in (Arthur) Agee's family that it intensifies the schism between him and his dad" (1995, 23).

In place of a collective struggle to combat racism, police brutality, and class exploitation, the Raptors offer a "hoop morality," one oriented to individualistic ideals of community. Unlike those who hold popular assumptions about the redemptive or communitarian ideals of such dreams, hooks refers to this morality as representing "dreams of conquest."

It is this morality, this dream/vision of blackness, that the Raptors hope to establish in Toronto. Attending Sheldon Aberdeen's funeral was one action of this morality. This is further exemplified in the work of the Raptor Foundation, a very public organization designed to help promote the Raptors in the city. In one of their most recent events, a press conference for the NBA Team Up program, Damon Stoudamire, Raptors' superstar, was quoted as saying: "You gotta work hard and stay out of trouble if you want to be successful."[20]

RAPTOR MORALITY AND THE COMMODIFICATION OF PUBLIC BLACKNESS

Recently, commentators have discussed the commodification of blackness as a feature of black popular culture.[21] In sports, this is evident in the multimillion-dollar salaries (not to mention the shoe contracts) paid out to black players, coaches, and broadcasters. The NBA has been at the forefront of this commodification of blackness, marketing a certain kind of blackness as entertainment and doing so with immense skill.[22] What distinguishes the NBA is its community outreach programs and its emphasis on fun for the entire family. More than any other league, the NBA tries, and has thus far been successful, to market basketball as everybody's sport. This is curious, since the NBA is an almost all-black league in a racist culture.[23] It would follow that its sport would be marginalized and literally seen as a sport of difference. However, this is not the case. The success of the Raptors and of the NBA is due not so much to a tidal wave of anti-racism in America and Canada as to the NBA's skillful use of the Hoop Dreams aesthetic and its cultivation of the "Hoop Dreamer." The Raptors' success attests to the ways in which forms of capital have relied on pop cultural notions of blackness to sell an image to everyone, regardless of the level of race consciousness. While this formula for success clearly motivates all sports franchises, the case of Toronto poses particular challenges to the NBA's marketing project. This is so because Toronto is perhaps the first hockey town to have an NBA team.

The NBA could not simply trust that an indigenous "base" of basketball fans would come to the games in Toronto. For this reason, the Raptors' public profile is all the more important. As a result of basketball's initial representation as a sport of difference, the cultivation of the Hoop Dreamer becomes all the more imperative to establishing the Raptors in the city. In an essay on the American liberal passion for black suffering, James Baldwin suggested that while the figures of Bigger Thomas and Uncle Tom may seem opposite characters in the legend of American fiction, the opposite is true. In both cases, the fictional black man is a character who draws empathy but who, in many senses, is a parody.

To sell tickets, the Raptors must market a certain essentialist version of black public masculinity that accords with rigid caricatures of black masculinity. The Raptors must meet a demand among sports consumers for pathos and drama. They also have to produce a kind of commodified public blackness that is firmly rooted within American liberal notions of what blackness is really like. As evidenced in the Aberdeen funeral and the Raptorfest, the apolitical, or rather conservative, Hoop Dreamer becomes consumable by everyone. Thus, Raptor spectacles try to present a story that is tangible to fans, black and white. It is this story, this Hoop Dreams aesthetic, that draws heavily on anthropological traditions of voyeurism, or of gazing at the other, and this accounts for the exceedingly private nature of Raptors' public travails.

DREAMS OF AMERICANADA: BLACKNESS, NATION, AND THE PUBLIC SPHERE

The establishment of a Hoop Dreams aesthetic or Raptor morality in Toronto is important for two reasons. First, this aesthetic names the kind of blackness that the Raptors attempt to narrate and locates this narration within the context of traditional Canadian attempts to write black experiences out of the nation's history. Such a placement suggests that there is a link between state narratives of blackness and the cultivation of the Hoop Dreamer. Second, it shows how capital is informed and organized through conventional notions of blackness. The whiteness of official narratives of Canada enables the establishment of the Raptor morality. Two examples illustrate my claims. First, in 1988, after Ben Johnson was stripped of his gold medal following a positive drug test, he was metaphorically transformed from a Canadian hero into just another Jamaican immigrant. As one Canadian Olympian remarked to black Canadian sprinter Angela Issajenko at the time, "You can have Ben back now, he is not a Canadian now."[24] The second example is the "Just Desserts Case." According to Rinaldo Walcott, the accused killers of Georgina "Vivi" Leimonis were described by virtue of their clothing as somehow gangstas "leaking from South (U.S.) to North (Canada)."[25] Both of these examples register something about the Canadian tendency to represent black masculinity as trouble.

For conservatives, the ideological advantage of such a reading in Canada is that it projects blackness to beyond the nation's borders. Thus, Canada becomes synonymous with white and the outside becomes synonymous with non-white. Moreover, the border becomes the place that demarcates goodness (whiteness) from evil (blackness). Within this frame, a "good Negro," let us say Ben Johnson pre-Seoul, is good not because of something indigenous in him, but only because of his acceptance of "Canadian" values. Therefore, black masculinity, according to official discourse, is seen as being outside the country, or outside the city. If it is seen as being inside, it is often seen as an accident waiting to happen.

This logic operates in representations of Clinton Gayle, whose Jamaican heritage was not missed by crime reporters in the city; they viewed it as another indication of the crime-Jamaica connection. Naming Gayle as a "cop-killer" locates him as a gangsta and accords with the common racist practice of projecting all of society's ills onto the figure of the tough gangsta rapper. The effect of this is to reinforce the idea that black folks are not Canadian. Gayle is framed as either Jamaican or American — he is *out-law*, external to Canada's political/juridical boundaries.

Such representations, unless challenged, make the space for black public masculinity very narrow. Adherence to such representations is an admission that it is impossible for black public masculinity in Toronto to have something it can truly call its own. Such a belief, or memory, about what it is to be a black man in Toronto necessarily excludes other stories of blackness — for example, histories of struggle (for example, the CFTA protests; resistance to racist cops in Toronto). Further, it erases the multiplicity of black experiences in Toronto and their relevance to Toronto and to anyone who lives in it.

The fact that blackness, and in this case black masculinity, is seen in Canada as a border in the public sphere in effect makes the black public sphere in Canada almost a no-man's-land. Official Canadian sports culture is a white thing, whereby images of the land are tied to the bodies of white men and women.

However, it is not fair to say that black men are invisible to the nation. While there has been a vacancy in representations of black masculinity, that has clearly changed, as I stated earlier. The Hoop Dreamer is, within the official terms of the Canadian discourse on "race," the only possible "positive" Canadian rendition of black masculinity. The Raptors' official presence at the Sheldon Aberdeen funeral, the Raptorfest, and the many public appearances by people like Damon Stoudamire telling children, mostly boys, to "stay in school" — all these represent the attempt to translate an American version of black masculinity into the Canadian context. But more importantly, they attest to the relationship of complicity between Canadian multiculturalism and bourgeois "dreams of conquest."

With respect to both the Aberdeen funeral and the Raptorfest, experiences of black masculinity in Toronto are read through the American lens of the Hoop Dream. By contrast, the CFTA protests and the reality of the Clinton Gayle trial, if taken seriously, force us to examine the very foundation of what Canada is and what it has historically meant to non-white peoples. To Raptor-ize the Sheldon Aberdeen funeral is a way of writing over a certain version of Canadian history.

Such a tension, between the borders of blackness and the borders of the nation, attests to the struggle over who has the next run in the city and, moreover, to the fundamentally political nature of such a struggle. It appears that the Raptors themselves are content to overlay Canadian histories of blackness, and in so doing, they see/promote life as a Hoop Dream, as their way of "cementing" themselves to the nation's playgrounds.[26]

This reality is also exemplified by the ironic popular appeal of the Raptors' vice-president and general manager, Isiah Thomas. Thomas's appeal is widespread, as evidenced by his current status as somewhat of a darling among members of the Canadian business media and the Toronto sports establishment, and by the favour in which he is held by members of the black community in Toronto. However, I call Isiah's popular appeal ironic because he does-n't live in Toronto! In fact, his home is in Detroit, and he goes home on weekends and whenever possible during the off-season.

Such a curious phenomenon points to the inability of indigenous black Canadian public masculinities to (officially) come forward. It is more "Canadian" to borrow an American ver-sion of blackness, that of the Hoop Dreamer, than to probe the question of what it means to be black in Canada. This tells us something about how current black public masculinities are imagined in Canada and points to what may be a shift in the contours of such an imagining. Moreover, it also points to Toronto's sports fans' and athletes' all-too-familiar practice of "going south" for representations of black masculinity. The success of the Hoop Dreams nar-rative, now remade as Raptor morality and embodied in the representation of Isiah Thomas as antidote to the gangsta, is evidence of three things: first, the inability of Canadian state nar-ratives to produce local versions of black masculinity; second, the power of certain kinds of blackness to travel across borders with greater ease than others; and last but definitely not least, the cultural politics of young black men who take up this Raptor morality.

PLAYING WITH MODERNITY: RAPTOR MORALITY AND THE NEW BLACK NATION

I'd now like to explain why and how Raptor morality has caught on in Canada, or at least Toronto, and my focus will be the practices of young black ballplayers in the city.[27] I take my cue from Homi Bhabha, whose insights on nation and narration are instructive here. Bhabha likens nations to narratives and, in so doing, shows that discourses of the nation are made possible through the pedagogical instruction to "be a national citizen," but also through the "performance" of such an identity. He writes: "In the production of the nation as narration there is a split between the continuist, accumulative temporality of the peda-gogical, and the repetitious, recursive strategy of the performative. It is through this process of splitting that the conceptual ambivalence of modern society becomes the site of writing the nation" (1994, 145–46).

Thus, nationalism is only possible through the repetition of the rituals of nationalism. If these rituals are interrupted, and they often are, they reveal the limits of the modern nation; for example, the historical marginalization of non-white peoples in Canada's official narrative and the practices of many non-white Canadians that are counter to the narrative represent "this process of splitting."

However, the success and the institutional solidity of the Raptors point to another process, the familiar imperialistic project known as Americanism. While it is clear that blacks have been written out of the official text that is Canada, the Raptors represent the most success-ful attempt to date to write blacks in. However, the narration that the Raptors are involved in is that of a new black nation, and, more to the point, it is American. Thus, in reading Bhabha's observations about performativity through the lens of black modernism, we are forced to consider the performance of Raptor fans as evidence of a persistent social desire to redraw national boundaries.

Given that it is only through the willingness of young brothers to perform a certain black-ness corresponding to that sanctioned through the Hoop Dreamer, something evident in gyms throughout the city, I suggest that paying attention to the bourgeois revolution of blackness, embodied in the entrenchment of a certain class of black folks in Canada and the United States, is crucial to understanding the Raptors' success.[28] We cannot simply read the Raptors' success as attributable to a wave of anti-racism, as I stated earlier; nor can we read it solely through Bhabha's framework. The margin of the modern nation is not where young black fans are asking what this nation is all about; the place is now implicated in another nation.

This movement is thoroughly modernist. In placing Raptor morality within the narrative of black capitalism, or modernism, the work of Arjun Appadurai is suggestive, more specifically his discussion of cricket in the former British Empire. In discussing the way that cricket became hegemonic in India, Appadurai suggests that the ability of colonized subjects in India to play the game of the colonizers affords them a certain power. He writes: "Transformed into a national process by the process of spectacle … cricket has become a matter of mass entertainment and *mobility* for some" (1997, 106).

Appadurai's linking of sports and subaltern masculinity can be applied to the context of the Raptors. The Raptors' success is clearly wrapped up with young black males' identifying and performing the dream of "going south," both literally and figuratively.[29] This process is the performance and repetition of a certain notion of identity, namely a bourgeois African-American version of blackness. Thus, being a Raptor fan, for many, is to participate in an American way of seeing and understanding basketball and blackness. In other words, it suggests a kind of mobility and a way of responding to the whiteness of Canada's official narrative.

Moreover, there is a power dynamic at work. Appadurai notes:

> But because cricket, through the enormous convergence of state, media, and private-sector interests, has come to be identified with "India," with "Indian" skill, "Indian" guts, "Indian" team spirit, and "Indian" victories, the bodily pleasure that is at the core of the male viewing experience is simultaneously part of the *erotics of nationhood*…. The erotic pleasure of watching cricket for Indian male subjects is the *pleasure of agency* in an imagined community, which in many other arenas is violently contested. (1997, 111; my emphasis)

These insights point to how transborder sporting communities are made. Specifically, they underline the importance of capitalist forms of sporting spectacle to questions of identity. For Appadurai, initiation into cricket's imagined community is a bodily/erotic experience that provides a chance to play with the "means of modernity." If we substitute the word "Indian" with the word "black" in the above quote, we get a sense of how Raptor morality works and what tropes it relies on. In many representations, notions of skill, guts, and team spirit are presented by the Raptors as elements of black style. Thus, performing Raptor morality is performing blackness, or black masculinity, the same kind of sporting black masculinity embodied in *Sunset Park* and *Boyz N the Hood*.

The Raptors are drawing on the immense popularity of basketball throughout the world. The success of Dream Team 1992 and the immense popularity and wealth of stars like Jordan, Pigpen, Rodman, and Shaq are signs of the success of a bourgeois revolution of black public masculinity. This reality suggests a new (modernist) configuration of blackness. Such high-profile successes suggest that attempts by young brothers to perform Raptor morality in gyms throughout the city are in part about power. The desire to be "like Mike" is, in the words of Appadurai, a desire to partake in the "erotics of (black) nationhood."

Given Canadian fears about blackness and black presences within the national borders, it should come as no surprise that the kind of blackness that would settle here would be a very modernist or conservative one, reliant on a series of tropes about what blackness is "really like." However, the real possibility of an American modernist version of black masculinity settling in Toronto, and the ease with which it is reproduced among black fans in the city, indicates the power of hegemonic and imperialistic notions of blackness, which the Raptors are reproducing in their marketing of the team. The Raptors' success underscores the power that capitalist sporting institutions hold in the (re)formation of national identity.

CONCLUSION

The battle over who's got the next run in Toronto continues. The Raptors have landed on the cityscape in a very permanent way. Yet we must be careful not to celebrate the arrival of the NBA in Toronto as the epiphany of "integration" of the national sporting landscape. Rather, by paying attention to where the Raptors place themselves, namely, where and how we see purple, we may understand their attempts at permanence as attempts to overlay black Canadian histories and struggles. In the place that Brand calls the "tough geography" that is Canada for many black people, the Raptors provide the blacktop and the myth of the Hoop Dreamer. In this regard, the Raptor morality is ruled by what Baldwin called "a theology of terror." Concomitant with this myth is the conservatism displayed in such admonitions as "Stay in school," "Say no to drugs," and so on. Thus, the Raptor, appearing when and how it does, is the attempt to (re)colour the national landscape by means of replacing one Americanism — the nightmare of the Hood, with another — the Hoop Dream. Indigenous black masculinities are overlaid, in keeping with official narratives that name the nation white. In addition, political forms of resistance, something indigenous to black Canada if nothing else, are overlaid. Thus, it is hard to call the Raptors' arrival in Toronto something that helps cement a "positive" blackness on the sporting landscape.

ENDNOTES

1. The title of the paper refers to a vernacular reference heard in gyms or playgrounds where pick-up basketball is played in the city. If, on the court, there are already two teams playing and on the sidelines there is one or more players waiting to play, the first person who loudly announces "I got next" or "I got next run" gets the right to play in the next game and has the right to choose her players.

2. For more on "Writing Thru' Race," see McFarlane 1997 and Brand 1994.

3. Bloor Collegiate.

4. NBA is the acronym for the National Basketball Association. Hereinafter, I will refer to Toronto's team as "the Raptors."

5. Please see Thornton 1997.

6. For more background on the protests, please see Mackey 1995.

7. The Raptors uniforms are purple, red, and white.

8. Regarding the migratory practices of black Canadian musicians, please see Walcott 1997, especially chapter 4. With reference to boxing, Lennox Lewis is an example. Lewis, a gold medallist in Seoul and Canada's most decorated boxer in a generation, left Canada for England because of lack of financial support and unfriendly media.

9. I borrow this term from Lawrence 1982.

10. This information was gained through the Official Rule Book and conversations with black referees in Toronto.

11. See James Christie, *Globe and Mail,* 13 February 1995.

12. An example of this type of article is Joyce 1994.

13. Please see Basketball Canada 1994. See also Abdel-Shehid 1997.

14. Recently, Nike has come to be synonymous with the rise in popularity of the NBA, given the popularity of its icon, Michael Jordan, and its P.L.A.Y. program. For more on Nike and basketball, please see Cole 1996.

15. With reference to the Nike camp, see *Toronto Star*, 19 September 1997: E12.

16. Throughout Gayle's trial, the Toronto media called him a "cop-killer," which was a riff on the rap song by Ice-T. For more on this, see Abdel-Shehid 1996, Walcott 1995, and below.

17. While the Raptors were absent at the trial of Gayle, it is worth mentioning that Raptor community personnel do not generally attend anti-racist rallies either.

18. I put "black" in parentheses because at the time of the 1997 Raptorfest, Isiah Thomas, the Raptors' general manager, had an agreement in principle to buy the Raptors from its white owner, Alan Slaight. However, since then, Slaight withdrew his offer of sale of the team. Thomas retained the 9 per cent share of the team that he has owned since the team's inception.

19. For more on Hoop Dreams anthropology, please see Abdel-Shehid 1997.

20. See Thornton 1997.

21. See the essays in Dent 1992.

22. On the connection between blackness, entertainment, and sports, Isiah Thomas, then general manager of the Raptors, recently commented that Tracy McGrady, one of the Raptors' players, "understands that this is a business but it's also entertaining." See *Toronto Star*, 16 October 1995, C4.

23. I borrow this term from Goldberg 1993.

24. See *Globe and Mail*, 13 October 1988.

25. Walcott 1995, 52.

26. For more on the tensions between borrowed blackness and the cement of the nation in Canada, see Walcott 1997, chapter 7.

27. In doing so, I recognize that the category "black," like all identities, is not in any way complete or closed. In addition to what could be described as black fans in the city, I will provisionally include in my analysis many non-white boys and men such as South Asians, Asians, and Latin Americans. But this is a far too complicated issue to take up in this paper.

28. For information on the rise of neo-conservatism in the United States, please see Baker 1995. For information on the neo-conservatism of the black Canadian bourgeoisie, please see discussion of the Third Cinema in Canada in Walcott 1997.

29. For more on "going south," please see James 1997b.

REFERENCES

Abdel-Shehid, G. 1996. "Can't Forget Ben: Sports, Racialised Masculinities and Canadian Nationalism." Paper presented at Graduate Social and Political Thought Conference, York University.

———. 1997. "In Place of Race, Space: Basketball in Canada and the Absence of Racism." In *Sport in the City*, ed. R. Wilcox et al.

Appadurai, A. 1997. *Modernity at Large*. Minneapolis: University of Minnesota Press.

Baker Jr., H.A. 1995. "Critical Memory and the Black Public Sphere." In *The Black Public Sphere,* ed. Black Public Sphere Collective. Chicago: University of Chicago Press.

Baldwin, J. 1968. "Everybody's Protest Novel." In J. Baldwin, *Notes of a Native Son*. Boston: Beacon Press.

Basketball Canada. 1994. "The Report of the Review Committee, Men's National Basketball Team." Toronto, December.

Bhabha, H.K. 1994. "Dissemination: Time, Narrative and the Margins of the Modern Nation." In H.K. Bhabha, *The Location of Culture*. London: Routledge.

Brand, D. 1994. *Bread out of Stone*. Toronto: Coach House Press.

Cole, C. 1996. "American Jordan; P.L.A.Y., Consensus, and Punishment." Unpublished paper.

Dent, G., ed. 1992. *Black Popular Culture*. Seattle: Bay Press.

Dryden, K., and R. MacGregor. 1989. *Home Game: Hockey and Life in Canada*. Toronto: McClelland and Stewart.

Globe and Mail, 13 October 1988; 13 February 1995.

Goldberg, D.T. 1993. *Racist Culture*. Oxford: Blackwell.

Hall, S. 1988. "New Ethnicities." In *Black Film/British Cinema*. ICA Document 7.

hooks, b. 1995. "Dreams of Conquest." *Sight and Sound* 5, no. 4: 22–23.

James, C.E. 1997a. "The Long Shot: Chasing the Dream through Basketball." In *Re/Vising,* ed. V. D'Oyley and C.E. James. North York: Captus Press.

———. 1997b. "Going South: Black Student Athletes' Scholarship Aspirations." Paper presented at the Annual Meeting of the North American Society for the Sociology of Sport, Toronto, Canada.

Joyce, G. 1994. "Court Battles." *Toronto Life*, March: 31–35.

Kidd, B., and J. MacFarlane. 1972. *The Death of Hockey*. Toronto: New Press.

Lawrence, E. 1982. "Just Plain 'Common-Sense': The Roots of Racism." In *The Empire Strikes Back,* ed. CCCS. London: Hutchison.

Mackey, E. 1995. "Post-Modernism and Cultural Politics in a Multicultural Nation: Contests over Truth in the *Into the Heart of Africa* Controversy." *Public Culture* 7, no. 2: 403–31.

McCall, N. 1997. *What's Going On.* New York: Random House.

McFarlane, S. 1997. "The Haunt of Race: Canada's *Multiculturalism* Act, the Politics of Incorporation and Writing Thru' Race." *Fuse* 20, no. 2: 110–12.

Rose, T. 1994. "Rap Music and the Demonization of Young Black Males." In *The Black Male*, ed. T. Golden. New York: Whitney Museum of American Art.

Schindler, D., ed. 1995. *Basketball Rules Book*. Kansas City: National Federation of State High School Associations.

Thornton, A. 1997. "Driving the Lane against the Raptor." In *Sport in the City,* ed. R. Wilcox et al.

Toronto Star, 6 December 1995; 19 September 1997; 16 October 1997.

Walcott, R. 1995. " 'Voyage through the Multiverse': Contested Canadian Identities." *Border/Lines* 36: 49–52.

———. 1997. *Black Like Who? Writing Black Canada.* Toronto: Insomniac Press.

Wooden, J. 1988. *Practical Modern Basketball*. New York: Macmillan.

HOCKEY AND CULTURE

Gary Genosko

When I get close, it starts. Here, in my stomach. When I cross the blueline. The net pulls me. When I can't see it, I sense it. I can't sense it, I believe in it. Push me back, it pulls me more. Like a cord that tightens the more you stretch. Top of the circle. My stomach gets worse. It wants to get out. It has to get out. It's a taste in my mouth. Hack me. Pile on me like I'm a table in the bargain basement. "Groan." I like it. I gotta. I'm gonna.

Rick Salutin, Les Canadiens

From the mainstream to the avant-garde, hockey has served as an all-terrain vehicle for the aesthetic explorations of English and French Canadians. Whether it is Roch Carrier's famous short story "Une abominable feuille d'érable sur la glace" ("The Hockey Sweater") or Serge Morin and Serge Dufaux's 1983 film *De l'autre côté de la glace* (a still from this film featuring a whimsical goaltender appeared on the cover of the art magazine *Parallélogramme* [vol. 19, no. 4 (1994)], cultural and political allegiances have been registered through hockey's potent symbols. Indeed, for a poignant and sporting expression of Québécois nationalism, one need look no further than Rick Salutin's *Les Canadiens* (1977), in which the election of the Parti Québécois on November 15, 1976, lifts the burden of political expression from the backs of the players onto those of the Péquistes. Still, I want to break apart this Canadian binarism, without diminishing the importance of artistic accomplishments based upon it, and in so doing, let all the hockey being played across the country and beyond the rink, to be sure, engage a broader understanding of the subjectivities, cultures, and rituals of the game, with tolerance and respect. Discussions of hockey all too often suffer from normopathic tendencies that assume both standard or normative definitions of how to participate, in some measure, in its manifestations and a pathological attachment to such norms. Such assumptions crush plurality and all creative combinations and applications of the game in the expanded field of culture.

WHAT IS THE PLURAL OF HOCKEY?

When the New York weekly the *Village Voice* (March 9, 1993) ran excerpts from the libretto of Torontonian Brad Walton's hockey opera *The Loves of Wayne Gretzky*, in which the author stages an affair between the Great One and the Pittsburgh Penguin's star Mario Lemieux, the routine subjective formations (masculine, white, nationalistic) that have typified hockey culture were queered. Gay hockey opera may be a fleeting genre, but its implications for making the hockey subject aware of his/her homoerotic investments in the game are substantial. This fictional episode led to further coverage in the *Voice* (August 16, 1994) of Vancouver-based reporter Daniel Gawthrop's articles in *Xtra West* and the *Vancouver Sun* extolling the virtues of Vancouver Canuck star Pavel Bure: "androgynous, fawn-like features … lips like rose petals, bedroom eyes and fashionably coiffed hair." Coverage of hockey fans in Canadian gay communities, in the *Globe and Mail* and by CBC Television colour-commentator Don Cherry — whose televisual performances during intermission are tied to shifting constructions of hockey consumers, enabling him, out of one side of his mouth, to refer to foreign players as "sissies" and, out of the other side, to welcome gay fans into the fold — during a *Hockey Night in Canada* broadcast brought the issue of the diverse constituencies of hockey to the fore and further invested the game with a remarkable pluralism.

If one were to look for these kinds of openings to new, plural hockey subjectivities in recent books such as Richard Gruneau and David Whitson's *Hockey Night in Canada: Sport, Identities, and Cultural Politics* (1993), one would only be disappointed. The tired, singular, heterosexual hockey masculinity and, in certain important instances, the breakthroughs, and how they are not so subtly devalued, of young women such as goaltender Manon Rheaume at the professional level are rehearsed by social scientists Gruneau and Whitson. While the authors are better prepared, in methodological terms, to understand labour issues, they lack the expertise to speak convincingly of culture and identity. A few references to cultural theory appear here and there in the text, but these only enable Gruneau and Whitson to conclude that hockey is part of a global, post-modern, capitalist culture, even though it offers "new spaces for identity formation" to so-called new groups, about whom they have nothing to say.

HOCKEY NIGHT ON THE REZ

Thomson Highway understands well the strange effects a hockey game can have on a community. In his play *Dry Lips Oughta Move to Kapuskasing*, the fictional reserve of Wasaychigan Hill experiences a "revolution" when, in Zachary Jeremiah Keechigeesik's dream, the women of the reserve form a hockey team called the Wasy Wailerettes. The "particular puck" with which they eventually play circulates throughout the play, finding its way at one point into the bosom of Gazelle Nataways, only to be shaken loose later in the action, before the final game sequence (which is really a dream sequence) can unfold. The repetition of the question "Where's the puck?" heralds a nightmare sequence in the first game sequence in which Nanabush (in this instance as the spirit of Black Lady Halked — a parody of the pseudo-native emblem of the Chicago Black Hawks) sits upon a "giant luminescent puck." It needs to be recalled that in the opening sequence of the play it was Nanabush (as the spirit of Gazelle Nataways) who, with a bump of her hip, turned on the television to *Hockey Night in Canada*. Later, when Zachary wakens from his dream to return to the reality of his wife, Hera, and their new baby, he remarks how much the moon looked like a puck last night (harking back to the vision of Nanabush) and asks his wife whether she has ever thought of playing hockey, to which she replies: "Yea right. That's all I need is a flying puck right in the left tit, neee...." With the hockey game long over and the Smurfs on the television screen before him, all Zachary can do is point out that Smurfs don't play hockey! You won't find Thomson Highway in *Hockey Night in Canada*. And you won't hear about Maple Leaf great George Armstrong, whose mother was part Ojibway and French Canadian and who was subjected to the kind of racism that almost every hockey writer covering the "original six" — not nations, but NHL teams — considered inevitable: he was nicknamed "Chief." In hockey it is through all-too-common stereotypes, through nicknames, emblems, mascots, and marketing imagery of all kinds, that cultural differences and traditions are rendered benign and slightly ridiculous. Stereotypes of these sorts are the currency of the dominant hockey discourse, and they are also commodities, the exchange of which fosters belonging ("my team") but creates an impoverished cultural identity because it is defined by the marketplace.

Gruneau and Whitson confess that they grew up in the 1950s and 1960s in Toronto. They do not tell us if they remember Armstrong's nickname, nor what it meant to them to have the name of Tim Horton loosen itself from hockey and become just another doughnut shop (well, not just another shop, since Eddie Shack opened his doughnut shop in Caledon, northwest of Toronto, thereby moving the well-established cultural bond between doughnuts and cops into the hockey realm. A further, more general bond needs to be investigated, one that I call "fast ice, fast food." The investments of hockey players, both during their athletic careers and upon retirement, have pointed towards fast food outlets: does anyone remember Bobby Orr pizza? How about John Anderson burgers? I've already mentioned doughnuts. What do you think they serve at Gretzky's? And the food at Don Cherry's Grapevine was not much to write home about. Round, tepid, greasy food sitting in pools of fat, like pucks on melting ice. Anyway, Gruneau and Whitson meticulously avoid analyses of specific products (see my remarks below on Nike).

Remarkably, Gruneau and Whitson even avoid the important matter of collecting in hockey circles. They claim that "'communities' formed around acts of consumption ... are not political communities in any meaningful sense of the word." One can agree that capitalist subjectivity requires reductions and limitations and still understand that the pursuit of hockey through consumption needs to be freed from spectatorship and the caps-and-shirts analyses in order to move into areas of "social identification" that are less obvious but no less political. The very notions of "social" and "public" and "community" have rendered identification problematic. The paths of subject formation and identification are tangled up in doughnuts and memories and the fictional fact that Dry Lips oughta move to the Kap because she fell down, blocking the slap shot of her teammate Hera Keechigeesik and denying her a sure goal.

HEROES AT THE BAR

Labour conflict in sports inevitably leaves sportscasters and reporters in the difficult position of making the transition to the labour and even legal beats. This is an awkward situation at the best of times, as their airtime and word quotas prove to be difficult to fill with anything other than platitudes about the "history and future of the game," the "fans," the "nation," and themselves (the latter is more important than one might think, since the expression of indignation about labour strife is a subgenre unto itself in sports reporting that provides the occasion for the reporter to "sound off"). The issue is one of competence for the sportswriter. The boundaries of sports journalism are confused by labour and legal issues. The point is that labour issues are perceived by many covering sports to intrude upon the sporting domain like unwelcome visitors, interlopers, as it were, trespassing upon well-marked home turf. Perhaps this is why, after several recent labour disputes and the legal proceedings against influential hockey player agent Alan Eagleson, there has been such a deafening silence concerning the recent legal victory of retired hockey players with regard to a pension fund surplus to which they had been denied access. Long-retired stars who are still household names and many also-rans subsist on tiny pensions and in some cases operate small businesses, like the very visible Eddie Shack, graduating from selling Christmas trees to selling doughnuts.

The main issue concerns the judicial interpretation of a technical legal contract: specifically, a pension plan. A further issue involved the question of when a trustee could be removed from its position. Law has, of course, its own codes about which sports reporters are often not competent to comment.

Inflation in the early and mid-1980s gave rise to huge surpluses in the National Hockey League pension plan. This situation was not unique to hockey pensions. These surpluses arose for nurses, factory workers, and others, and had been unforeseen when such pension plans were established. Approximately $21 million of the league's pension surplus was directed by the board of the National Hockey League Pension Society towards the league to support collective-bargaining agreements and to provide a "holiday" from pension contributions. (In the pension/insurance industry "surpluses" arise from "experience rate credits" — which are like cash, as they can purchase holidays from contributions for employers and additional pension benefits for employees.) Some cash was also given to the six original clubs. Seven players challenged the allotment of funds, arguing that, according to the pension plan, any excess generated by the plan had to be applied *exclusively* for the benefit of player participants. They also challenged the ability of the Pension Society (owing to earlier agreements, there were no longer any player representatives on its board) to continue as trustee.

At trial, the judge found that the original language of the 1947 pension plan and its regulations, as well as agreements and memorandums between the league and the players throughout the 1960s and 1970s, required that "all monies" and "any benefits" be held "for the benefit of the Participant exclusively." The Pension Society was not free to assign the excesses to the benefit of the league. The trial judge did not remove the Pension Society as trustee, finding that its direction of funds was based on legal and actuarial advice that appeared sound.

The National Hockey League Pension Society appealed the part of the trial decision that required it to pay the surplus back into the pension fund. The players appealed the part of the decision that allowed the Pension Society to remain as trustee. The Ontario Court of Appeal upheld the decision of the trial judge on both the surplus issue and the trustee issue. Finally, on July 28, 1994, the Supreme Court of Canada refused to grant the Pension Society leave to appeal.

For lawyers, this case is about reading the language of pension agreements, and it will be used to support the claims of both employees and employers to pension surpluses. If sportscasters were able to comment on the legal matters influencing the business of gaming, hockey fans would be able to appreciate that this case produced a reward for retired players who worked for so little and that the league went all the way to the Supreme Court trying to do these players out of a decent pension.

The player participants are, then, owed their additional benefits, including costs and pre- and post-judgment interest on $21 million. Perhaps this scenario will make it to the stage like John P. Moore's *The Lindros Trial: Extracts from Regina v. Eric Bryan Lindros*, the text of which was culled from the transcripts of the trial concerning an alleged incident of spitting beer at a Whitby, Ontario, nightclub. But this time it won't be played for laughs.

MINOR HISTORY

The colour barrier was finally broken in the National Hockey League in 1958. This was rather late compared to major league baseball, for example, into which Jackie Robinson had broken 11 years earlier, in 1947. Hockey was, in fact, the last North American sport to have black athletes enter its ranks. On January 18, 1958, left winger William "Willie" O'Ree took to the ice for the Boston Bruins. A native of Fredericton, O'Ree had played semi-pro hockey for the Quebec Aces in 1956–57 before being called up by Boston general manager Lynn Patrick. He played only two games for the Bruins in 1958, scoring no points. He played again for the Bruins in the 1960–61 season, appearing in 43 games and earning 14 points.

During the 1959–60 season, O'Ree was sent to Kingston to play for the Frontenacs, the Bruins' farm team in the Eastern Professional Hockey League. At the beginning of the season, it was noted without any further comment in the local press that O'Ree, one of coach Cal Gardner's "veterans" on what was a not particularly successful team, "was the first Negro to play in the NHL." In 50 games O'Ree tallied a very respectable 46 points. Although Kingston's claim to being the birthplace of hockey is still hotly contested by Montreal, Kingston can claim for itself an important place in black hockey history, and not only in the case of the trail-blazing O'Ree. A smart hockey historian might stir the pot a little by arguing that the Quebec Senior Hockey League of the mid- to late 1940s was richer in black hockey talent, citing the all-black forward line (Manny McIntyre and the Carnegie brothers, Herb and Ossie) iced by Sherbrooke in 1947 as evidence. That the brilliant playmaker and triple-time MVP (most valuable player) of the Quebec league Herb Carnegie wasn't drafted is evidence, as sports reporter James Christie argued in the *Globe and Mail* (April 1997), of the NHL's — specifically Conn Smythe's — backwardness and conservatism. This is further evidence that the myth of the halcyon days of the original six needs to be finally debunked for the sake of a critical understanding of the game's history and politics.

O'Ree's career was mostly spent in the minors playing for Western Hockey League teams in Los Angeles and San Diego. Despite the obscurity that such a career path normally entails, he is widely known as "the Jackie Robinson of hockey" and has received civic honours from San Diego, honouring him as the first black in the NHL, and recognition of his historic role from the New Brunswick Sports Hall of Fame in his hometown of Fredericton. Additionally, the NHL's Diversity Task Force sponsored a Willie O'Ree All-Star Weekend in 1991, arranging for disadvantaged youths from the Chicago area to meet the players and develop their skills. In 1998 it was the fortieth anniversary of O'Ree's breakthrough. Despite the impetus of the fiftieth anniversary of Jackie Robinson's accomplishment, which was celebrated in 1997 and generated sufficient interest for sportswriters to turn their attention to the minor histories of the major professional leagues, it is unclear whether or not the same interest will be given to O'Ree's story.

Black hockey history has a further Kingston connection, since another left winger, Tony McKegney, arguably the most successful black forward in the NHL to date, played OHA Junior A hockey for several seasons with the Kingston Canadians, from 1974–75 through 1977–78, before he was drafted by the Buffalo Sabres. He was captain of the Canadians and scored prolifically as a junior.

McKegney was exposed to the virulent racism of the Old South when John Bassett drafted him in 1977 for the World Hockey Association's Birmingham Bulls. The threats by Bulls' season tickets holders to cancel their subscriptions if the team iced a black player convinced Bassett to release McKegney outright from his contract. McKegney's signing and release took place in less than a week's time. McKegney was not the first black player signed by a WHA team. Already in 1972 Alton White had played for the New York Raiders, making him the first black in the league, followed closely by Bill Riley and Mike Marson of the Washington Capitals, who played together in 1974. McKegney's experience in Kingston had certainly not prepared him for the racism he encountered in Birmingham. When he was captain of the Frontenacs, his picture was regularly in the press and his hockey exploits were followed with intense interest.

I have not mentioned all of the black NHLers (think about goaltenders for a moment and who comes to mind? — obviously, the first black goalie, Grant Fuhr, who broke in with Edmonton in 1981, and then, more obscurely, Eldon "Pokey" Reddick, who played for the Jets in Winnipeg for a season and a half in the late 1970s), but the list is short. The more general point is that the telling of hockey history through its minoritarian elements expands the cultural field of the game and the potential for new subjective formations that are not limited by the standard accounts — either of the history of the game or of the supposedly normal identities of those who play and watch it in the "Great White North."

ATHLETES AS PETS *in Gardens*

In *Landscapes of Modern Sport* (1994), John Bale advances the provocative idea that "the sportscape or athlete to which we show affection is the athletic analogue of the garden or the pet." Maple Leaf Gardens, he points out, doesn't contain any shrubs, but it nonetheless remains a garden, if only euphemistically, as a sportscape aestheticized through horticultural and architectural imagery. This garden is full of "pets" that are disciplined, functionalized, steroid-enhanced, and exhaustively trained to perform. These athletic pets are dominated so that they may best receive the affection of the spectators, their owners, and even, in extreme cases, their parents. Hockey netminders often adopt animal motifs when having their masks painted; Toronto Maple Leaf goaltender Felix Potvin is nicknamed "The Cat," for example. Just as animals are used in military contexts (in advertisements for weapons and equipment in professional magazines and the decoration of airplanes), a single attribute (stealth, strength, speed, agility) is abstracted from a given species, exaggerated, and reconnected with a new thing or activity. We should not, however, expect all animal motifs to be used positively. Distortions are commonplace — think of mascots whose imbecility is supposed to provide light entertainment between breaks in the action. But what is being played for its amusement value is the representation of an animal as a mentally and physically challenged child. This kind of mascot is in a direct genealogical line with cartoon characters whose flaws defined their characters.

The training thesis has been in circulation in less developed forms for some time now. In his discussion of the ambiguous healthiness of sports in "Sports Chatter," from *Travels in Hyperreality* (1986), Umberto Eco maintained that one of the "first degenerations of the contest" involves "the raising of human beings dedicated to competition. The athlete is already a being who has hypertrophied one organ, who turns his body into the seat of an exclusive source of continuous play. The athlete is a monster." The dedication to "total instrumentalization" makes the athlete a monster or, better, to follow Bales, a pet. But pets, while often distorted through selective breeding and the aesthetic determinations of what features are desirable for a given species on the show circuit, are also dearly loved, especially when they perform for their caretakers. While Eco recognizes that the athlete is dedicated to sports training regimes, however brutal and unhealthy they may be, Bales elides the matter of dedication. There has never been a greyhound, to use other words, that was dedicated to being trained to over-race and starve. Many people do, however, submit to exhaustive and repetitive training routines. Neither athletes nor pets submit to the kind of abuse that is common in such training.

By changing the register of the analogy ever so slightly, however, we are thrown back to the identification of black slaves and domesticated farm animals and slaveholders as wild predators, poignantly employed in the classic American slave narrative of Frederick Douglass, *Narrative of the Life of Frederick Douglass, An American Slave: Written By Himself* (orig. 1845; Franklin 1989). What this autobiographical narrative reveals is the prevailing nineteenth-century image of the black slave as a healthy animal who, if needs be, will be broken through labour, tortured and/or murdered, and selectively bred. It is not very far from the racism of the Old South to contemporary stereotyped representations of black athletes, that is, from animalization to the petishism of focusing the so-called naturally expressive black body. Indeed, consciousness, as we learned in the case of Canadian sprinter Ben Johnson after the debacle in Seoul, was denied to the black male insofar as he was figured as a "primitive," an animal-machine. Race and, indeed, gender oppression function through animalization, as does economic exploitation. As Patricia Hill Collins puts it in *Black Feminist Thought* (1990), "a race of 'animals' can be treated as such — as victims or pets."

DISCIPLINING ROAD HOCKEY

The town of Gananoque in eastern Ontario recently tightened up its By-law No. 83–32 concerning the regulation of traffic and parking. In addition to what you might expect to find in a traffic by-law, there is the following subsection on the matter of "Playing on Roadway Prohibited": "1. No person shall play or take part in any game or sport upon a roadway."

Sociologists of sport in Germany, such as Lüder Bach (1993), for instance, have shown a keen interest in the study of informal sports activities and facilities. The informality of such sports means the absence of a wide variety of prerequisites: institutional, individual, and organizational. The proliferation of informal sports occurs generally in the context of the absence of legal prohibition, which is only to say that the facilities being put to use allow for a secondary use above and beyond their primary uses. To put this more forcefully, primary uses are decoded for the sake of new practices that remake and remodel rules of participation. For generations of Canadian boys and girls, roadways have been places for playing road or "ball" hockey, skipping, playing hopscotch, or just throwing around any number of balls, Frisbees, and so on. Of course, quiet roads are preferred to busy routes, but no matter, since there is usually a safety protocol in effect: when a car appears, its presence is announced, the action stops, equipment is moved. The smallest, the weakest, and the least well equipped often get to play, although there is no denying the effects of neighbourhood pecking/picking orders.

Recently, I took up the matter of informal sporting activities in one of my sports columns for *Borderlines* magazine (Genosko 1996). Existing single-use leisure sites are being put to other uses — ski slopes are being invaded by snowboarders, bicycle paths and lanes are full of in-line skaters, and drained swimming pools are haunted by skateboarders. While the sportscape is changing, it is also being generalized. The sportscape is the city itself. Just as mountain bikers surmounted to some degree certain obstacles of the streetscape, culminating in the kamikaze subculture of the bike courier, skateboarders and in-line skaters are rediscovering these and other obstacles — curbs, stairs, hand and guard rails, gaps, edges, trash bins, parked cars, benches — and turning them into the found tools of street skating. Skateboarding is urban studies on wheels. Surrealists and situationists may have perfected urban drifting, but boarders and skaters are refinishing the cityscape with street-style high jinks by grinding on rails, pipes, and ledges of all sorts, riding walls, or flying over vehicles after being launched by jump ramps.

In effect, the Gananoque by-law makes road hockey a traffic offence, not to mention further eroding the rights of pedestrians. Moreover, it pushes informal street sports towards more formal frames, perhaps not all the way to the boarded iceless surface and the ball hockey association, but at least into parking lots and playgrounds, thereby displacing other activities. This legal re-territorialization of the roadway is designed to enable the cops actually to trap and deform the flows of unorganized sporting desire and its fuzzy, neighbourhood aggregates. The push is on towards organization and commercial interests: join the league, pay a fee, buy this equipment, consume! If you won't cooperate: pay a fine!

DOWN AND OUT IN THE NHL

Deprivation has reached a new low. Goaltenders are begging — in transit shelters and subway stations around Maple Leaf Gardens, as well as on TV spots broadcast during games, not to mention in Nike's promotional booklets distributed in the Gardens to launch an ad campaign.

But these are not just any goalies. These are humiliated, down-and-out goalies reduced to scratching together a living by panhandling, cab driving, break-dancing, cycle messengering, janitorial work, and hot dog vending.

Sure, they've kept their equipment, 30-odd pounds of rawhide, high-tech plastic, wire-enforced padding, clunky skates, and heavy sticks. But times are tough for these guys because, after all, have you ever tried to pedal a bike or break-dance or drive a cab in full goalie gear? These goalies haven't learned to translate their skills, let alone change their equipment.

We are far, far away from Ken Danby's iconic goalie as a study in concentration, as well as from the anthropological noodling of the Hockey Hall of Fame, with its wall of "ritually" decorated goalie masks.

Why goalies? The advertising campaign is in support of a line of hockey skates promoted by fast-skating and powerful-shooting forwards, all in a sponsorship deal with Nike. In the campaign's narrative, the formidable skills of these forwards have resulted in the dismissal of a series of goalies from their respective teams. The collective story told by these goalies is printed awkwardly on torn pieces of cardboard and held up for passersby to read: "I am a former NHL netminder. Please help. Read my story. Read my other goalie friends' stories. Read why you should never send either Mats Sundin, Jeremy Roenik, or Sergei Federov a birthday card."

Beaten goalies with dull skates and broken sticks have a hard time translating their netminding skills: "Will stop pucks for food," the sign of one reads; another offers private goaltending lessons and novel entertainment for parties. The insignias of their former teams represent an NHL merchandizing tie-in. Team logos are copyrighted property, after all. These goalies are licensed failures.

There are legions of homeless in New York and Toronto who are living evidence of the effects of Reaganomics and Ontario's current brand of economic and social Harrisment. There is supposed to be humour in the incongruity between the outfits and tasks performed by Nike's goalies. This humour is at the expense of the homeless and, especially, of the working poor. As manufacturing jobs leave the country, skills that once made a person employable become as useless as goalie equipment at a hot dog stand. The campaign implies that the fall from grace is a result of a personal shortcoming. No hint of structural matters here — neither a defenceman nor a right-wing ideologue in sight!

Tucked away in some of the images — on the hot dog wagon and the janitor's bucket — is the Nike logo. It isn't that the equipment of the working poor has a sponsor; rather, it is that no one can be independent, perhaps work at all, even panhandle, because everything is already owned by someone else, and hence, they must have their fee. Despite itself, Nike brings home the fact that we are living in the hell of a perpetual advertising event. Welcome to Nike Town, where even the soiled cardboard of the homeless bears a logo.

Nike's corporate luxury is to turn poverty and homelessness into an advertising icon, courtesy of its ad agencies, in the name of ice skates. No goalie I've ever seen could possibly stop a company like Nike when it is breaking full speed for the net. The market for hockey equipment is beginning to see some serious competition as footwear manufacturers get into the game.

This is the season of the goalie in advertising. Molson's, too, has its 12-armed goalie monster in the "I Am Canadian" print campaign. Molson's goalie is not exactly the Hindu deity Krishna in a Maple Leafs uniform, as we have come to expect since the film *Masala* (directed by Srinivas Krishna) rearranged hockey theology, but more like Kali having a bad day. Like Nike, however, Molson's thinks of hockey in terms of a showdown: a forward in alone on a goalie. "Showdown" was a gimmicky individual skills competition developed in the late 1970s to keep hockey fans glued to the screen during breaks between periods, the heaviest times of advertising during broadcasts. Despite Molson's ad copy about the pursuit of goals not involving any "corporate boxes, five dollar hot dogs or million dollar scoreboards" — just the sort of things that a beer company with a vested interest in hockey actually aspires to — it's still just "me versus the monster." No team, no help, and the only one cheering if you beat the goalie is yourself. "I Am Canadian" is, in the advertising life, another way of saying that not even you are your own, anymore.

THE TEMPLE OF HOCKEY

The floor plan of the Hockey Hall of Fame reveals a great deal about the metaphysics and ethics underwriting the current representations of the game. Essentially, the Hall sprawls along the east end of the concourse level of BCE Place, in the bowels of Toronto's financial district. It is an extension of the underground shopping concourse; in fact, the final stop on the official self-guided walk of the Hall (presented by John Armstrong in the Hockey Hall of Fame magazine) is a souvenir shop called the Spirit of Hockey. This shop cannot be avoided because it is also the Hall's exit. Commerce is the spirit of hockey, and its wares crystallize this spirit better, we are told, than "great memories" of the Hall and hockey itself.

The Hall presents one wave after another of history, internationalism, fragments of empire, family affairs, interactivity, and video-induced passivity in the name of sponsorships; someone unfamiliar with the game might be fooled into thinking that this is a temple devoted to the *Toronto Sun,* Ford, Esso, Blockbuster Video, Speedy Muffler, Molson's, TSN, Coca-Cola, and so forth. Commercial history is not only well provided for but intimately tied to the history of the game itself. Commercial ephemera originally tied to specific products — plastic buttons and instant desserts, coupons and gasoline, cards and bubble gum — become collectibles in heavily overcoded micro-markets but also serve as markers of historical phases (from the original six to expansion, the very idea representing the expansion of capital with the discovery of a wider American market and concomitant merchandising opportunities). Indeed, involvement in some aspect of the game can be demonstrated through souvenirs and, even better, through the ever-expanding universe of merchandise. The "family zone" figures the nuclear family as a consumption machine designed in the 1950s but built to last or at least accrue value as its own material history is translated into the obscure codes uttered by collectors in the throes of acquiring yet another piece of the puzzle. This vulgar capitalist ethics is but a warm-up to weightier justifications.

The hustle and bustle of the concourse gives way to the only part of the Hall at street level. The ascent to the Bell Great Hall is billed as the highlight of any visit. The Great Hall provides a direct line to the transcendental unity of hockey. It is the "core sanctuary of hockey's proud history" articulated by the presence of Lord Stanley's Cup, the focal point of the room, bathed in the kaleidoscopic light of the stained glass of the 45-foot-high dome. This rococo sanctuary was the head office of the Bank of Montreal until 1949, and a branch until 1982, later to be rescued from disuse when the Hall opened in 1993. The bank vault is still in use, housing the original silver cup donated by Lord Stanley in 1893. Hockey and banking history bleed together in a glorious vision of nation and culture building. The Great Hall is a trophy room commemorating great hockey men (inducted members of the Hockey Hall of Fame), a male preserve to be sure, of the Great White North. The architecture of banking still dominates the skyline of Toronto, just as it shaped the streetscape of the city in the nineteenth century. What would be more appropriate than an MBANX commercial featuring Stompin' Tom's "The Hockey Song"? This makes the symbolic economy of hockey obvious to everyone, even to so-called hockey purists sunk in their anti-labour meditations on the creation of the Lord. The Great Hall is described as a "quiet place in which to reflect on the richness of our past." Perhaps "the riches of the past" would have streamlined the message. It is a place of pilgrimage, with the cup itself playing the role of sacred relic. It is the sort of thing upon which one is compelled to lay hands. There are no annoying busy signals here. The connection is always clear as the cup soars towards the heavens, held aloft by the great heights of the city's towers of finance. Inspired by the French translation of Hockey Hall of Fame as "Le Temple de Renommée du Hockey," I said a silent prayer for the Maple Leafs, since only a god can save them now. "Oh Lordie," as Molson Canadian would have us utter.

REFERENCES

Bach, Lüder. "Sports without Facilities: The Use of Urban Spaces by Informal Sports." *International Review for Sociology of Sport* 28 (1993): 281–96.

Bale, John. *Landscapes of Modern Sport.* London: Leicester University Press, 1994.

Bathgate et al v. *National Hockey League Pension Society et al.* (1993) 11 *Ontario Reports* (3d): 449ff.

Collins, Patricia Hill. *Black Feminist Thought.* Boston: Unwin Hyman, 1990.

Eco, Umberto. *Travels in Hyperreality.* San Diego: Harcourt Brace Jovanovich, 1986.

Franklin, H. Bruce. *Prison Literature in America.* New York: Oxford University Press, 1989.

Gananoque, Town of. By-law No. 83-32: Being a by-law to regulate traffic and parking on highways, Subsection 64.

Gawthrop, Daniel. "Desperately Seeking Pavel." *Xtra West* 6 (5 November 1993).

Genosko, Gary. "What Is the Plural of Hockey?" *Fuse* 18, no. 4 (1995): 46–47.

———. "Hell on Wheels." *Borderlines* 41 (1996): 40–42.

———. "Kingston's Links to Black Hockey History." *Kingston Whig-Standard,* 23 April 1997.

Grierson, Bruce. "Hockey Nike in Canada." *Saturday Night,* April 1997: 64–73.

Gruneau, Richard, and David Whitson. *Hockey Night in Canada: Sport, Identities, and Cultural Politics.* Toronto: Garamond Press, 1993.

Highway, Thomson. *Dry Lips Oughta Move to Kapuskasing.* Saskatoon: Fifth House, 1989.

Salutin, Rick. *Les Canadiens.* Vancouver: Talon Books, 1977.

OF TIME AND SPACE AND HOCKEY

An Imaginary Conversation

Tom McSorley

Out there. Hockey players often use this term when interviewed about the game. *Out there* is a special, almost sacred space where wills are tested, careers are created and destroyed, and hockey is itself, like music, invented as it is performed. The presence of hockey in Canadian popular consciousness is deeply rooted and tenacious, in spite of the recent and rapid Americanization and corporatization of the professional game and the decrease in Canadian players populating NHL teams. There are songs by major Canadian groups invoking hockey themes; there are twenty-fifth anniversary coins, stamps, and deluxe video boxed sets commemorating the 1972 Canada–Soviet hockey series, which many interpret to be a watershed moment in Canadian cultural history; there is a proliferation of computer games and CD-ROM packages dedicated to hockey; and there is the annual publishing phenomenon of hockey books, which appear by the dozen and sell by the thousands in Canada and the United States. With all this rich and varied activity surrounding the sport, one is compelled to ask: just what is going on "out there" anyway?

More than winning and losing, certainly, as recent cultural studies of hockey and sport in popular culture have argued. Ideas of nation, individuality, community, politics, language, economics, and history collide and collaborate "out there," too, not just pucks and sticks and boards and nets. Indeed, given its historical roots and prominent presence in many forms of popular culture, it is clear that hockey is one of Canada's strongest, most insistent cultural "songlines," an icy repository of individual and collective memory played and replayed in endless variation, inscribed by generations on the frozen landscape of the very nation itself. Although we may dispute a current and rather hyberbolic T-shirt slogan, "Hockey Is Life," it is beyond question that the sport still occupies, in spite of profound demographic shifts in Canadian society and powerful encroachments of American popular culture, an extraordinary position in the Canadian imagination.

Literary critic Northrop Frye observed that Canadian culture is engaged in a search to formulate a response to a fundamental question unavoidable in the vast face of an alienating and

Canula

forbidding land: "Where is here?" Hockey offers a possible answer. Perhaps "here" can be located, in a paradoxical sense, "out there"; perhaps out there is actually in here. The exterior and interior encounter each other in Canadian terms in the hockey arena, that space where ice is brought inside, is transformed from a cold, dangerous natural world into a place of recreative play and competition. Beyond the nineteenth-century colonial Canadian image of "roughing it in the bush," the idea of out there becomes at once domesticated and transformed by the game itself in Canada's twentieth century. If the Canadian search for "Where is here?" is a negotiation between the conflictive and, given our climate, immediate notions of "in here" and "out there," then hockey is its most popular and durable cultural negotiator. As perennial as the Canadian winter that inspired it, the game of hockey is also as fluid, fragmented, improvisational, sublime, troubled, messy, and marvellous as the searching and uncertain nation that created it.

Trying to account for hockey in Canadian popular culture may be like trying to describe the colour of the air. Yet, like soccer to the British or baseball to Americans, the game speaks to us and of us. Hockey is arguably the greatest *pop* of all in our culture, and it demands attention. Who better, then, to reflect upon the nature and culture of the game than two of Canada's most original minds in the twentieth century? Imagine that economist and media theorist Harold Innis, one of the most consistently astonishing and influential thinkers in Canada in the twentieth century, meets Wayne Gretzky, the most creative player in the history of the game, as revolutionary in his approach to hockey as Pablo Picasso was to painting, James Joyce to literature, or Bela Bartok to music. Imagine that they meet at a Tim Horton's doughnut shop in Brantford, Ontario, for an assessment of their favourite sport at the end of the millennium. Both try to account for the shifts and changing contours of what's going on out there and in here. Fuelled by coffee, crullers, and Innis's favourite, Timbits, and like millions of Canadians before and after them, they go in search of hockey. Here is a possible transcript:

INNIS: Did you know that Don Cherry and Leonard Cohen were born the same year, 1934?

GRETZKY: Really? No, I didn't know that, but it is fascinating that these two men are linked in some way. To me they represent two different but not unrelated aspects of Canada and of hockey: the person of action and the dreamer. We invent the game of hockey, we dream of its possibilities, and we try to execute physically what these dreams show us. Cherry is pure will and determination, the sheer indomitable desire to overcome the odds, not unlike early Canadian settler society, in a sense; Cohen is grace, sophistication, hard-won fluidity, quiet inner power, and a deep, occasionally dark imagination — the opposite, complementary energies that gave the game Gordie Howe and Rocket Richard!

Because of the speed, intensity, and violence of hockey, the poetic side of the game has been overlooked. Recently though, that mythopoeic dimension is starting to infiltrate our understanding of this game we have dreamed and played. I am thinking of thoughtful, reflective books like Ken Dryden's *The Game* and David Adams Richards's *Hockey Dreams*, clever television advertising campaigns by equipment manufacturers like Bauer (featuring a brilliant, eminently appropriate metaphor of the ice surface as *tabula rasa*), popular songs like Stompin' Tom Connors's "The Hockey Song," Tom Cochrane's "Big League," and the Tragically Hip's "Fifty Mission Cap," not to mention the annual avalanche of coffee-table hockey books published at Christmas. It's always been there, this poetic dimension, but it takes time and attention to perceive and articulate it. Maybe it has something to do with the relative youth of Canada and of hockey in cultural and historical terms. You need a lot of history in order to develop a mythological groundwork for popular fictions, histories, and such. You know, if you do something enough times, it's inevitable that you'll start to think and talk about it differently. It's happened in baseball, cricket, and soccer, which are older games, and the same processes seem to have begun with the game of hockey.

INNIS: Exactly. I have always argued that time and history, and our cultural constructions of time, have a great influence on how we approach and interpret our popular cultural expressions, be they literary, musical, or sporting. Hockey does conform to this paradigm, as do all sports in one way or another. The processes of myth-making, the creation of theories of cultural expression, *do* take considerable time to percolate, to evolve in a relatively continuous yet ever-changing context that moves through time. Hey, what a great way to describe a hockey game — a continuous, changing context that moves through time! You see, I believe that theory emerges from practice, not the other way round: the empirical, trial-and-error philosophical disposition seems to be articulated in how we think about hockey, cinema, literature, and politics in Canada. Maybe this new renaissance in the metaphysical possibilities in hockey is indicative of Canada's groping its way out of the baldly empirical into the transcendental. We now think in a different way about what we have created and enacted for about a century.

GRETZKY: All this may be true, Mr. Innis, but this shift also has to do with the influence of American marketing techniques, big money, and American culture's insistent need for unifying, totalizing myths of individual power and triumph. Hockey is hard to fit into that mold, though, as it is largely a game of broken plays, reactions, and flow. The Russians used to say that the best hockey teams are the ones that adapt most quickly to contingency and chaos. I think they are right. You've got to be able to push here, hold back there, act here, react there. Hockey is full of accidents, random physical possibilities occurring at blinding speed; it lacks the more predictable tensions and premeditations of American sports like football and baseball. So, what I'm saying is that while the impulse to be transcendental about hockey may well be linked to the aging of Canadian culture, it may also be because Americans have raised the profile of the game and have demanded a commensurate mystique to pour into their marketing machine. Personally, I think it's very difficult to create a star system in hockey in the way that you can in baseball or basketball; hockey is a game of collaborations, accommodations, confrontations, and contingencies. It comes out of a different sensibility and must be mythologized or romanticized in a slightly different mode. There is a translation process that has to happen. Americans call this process "marketing," and NHL commissioner Gary Bettman is doing a lot of work to market this northern game to the United States. It takes time.

INNIS: Time is the answer, I agree, as evidenced by the still surprisingly low ranking of hockey in terms of popularity in the United States in comparison with the other professional sporting leagues. You have lived in the U.S.A. since your trade from Edmonton in August 1988. What is the difference in the resonances of the game in this American context?

GRETZKY: It varies. In northern states, hockey is more deeply rooted, obviously, but in the south it is sustained by technology (indoor arenas, television, radio), to invoke one of your favourite themes, Mr. Innis, and by a certain enthusiastic American curiosity. I've experienced how entranced people are when they first see a hockey game in person, even if they don't know any of the rules. They are awestruck by the sheer speed and seeming impetuousness of it all. The force of the game is immediate and extraordinary. Thanks to technology, we no longer need to play the game in cold climates. We can export the revolution, so to speak, to places that build arenas. The consequences of this change are not to be underestimated, Mr. Innis, and you know all about the notion of consequence. The responses to the game are undeniably different, though, but that can create a whole other series of ways to think about and imagine the game of hockey. Some of these ways are motivated by money and naivety and offend the traditional hockey fan (like that glowing puck that Fox has for its telecasts), but others, like the invention of roller blades, spread the game's appeal to places where snow is never seen yet the logic and passion of the game can be experienced physically.

INNIS: As you can imagine, I am pleased that you raised the topic of technology. I have argued in my writing that the history and development of Canada is intimately bound up with the creation and implementation of technologies of transportation (the east-west railroad linking sea to sea in the late nineteenth century) and communication (radio and later television as instruments of national coherence, an idea now under attack, unfortunately). Hockey, once a common Canadian passion that linked Canadians east to west, both through the players' regional origins and through the popularity of Foster Hewitt's radio broadcasts and, later, *Hockey Night in Canada* on CBC, now strikes me as being oriented, like Canada itself in many ways, on a north-south axis rather than on an east-west one. You yourself were playing in the north, in Edmonton, and then you went south to Los Angeles, St. Louis, and now New York. From the hinterland to the metropole, indeed, Mr. Gretzky. One of the consequences of the technology of communications is that the commercial imperative of television begins to dictate the present and future of hockey as a professional sport. Linked to this are the other technologies, as you mentioned, that make it possible to have ice in the southern parts of the continent so that the game can be played there without the attendant decades of indigenous development in a climatological sense. It is this combination of technologies that fascinates me, both because of the political economy of it, but also because of the question of sport and popular culture.

GRETZKY: In terms of political economy, it is increasingly difficult to keep the NHL game alive in smaller Canadian cities because of the distorted economics of the sport. Canada has always had to find a way to keep itself from being swallowed by the U.S.A., and professional hockey today is merely another expression of that. Remember, though, that even during the Original Six era, four of the teams, or 66 per cent of the league, were in American cities. [Today 20 of 26 teams are American based, representing 76 per cent of league franchises.] The technology has accelerated the process and the consequences of decisions made, so there are dangers. There are positive possibilities, too, like southern American boys and girls becoming interested in hockey. Just look at Cuba or the Dominican Republic and baseball, India and cricket, and Latin America and soccer; those hugely popular games are imports from distant former empires, but they have taken root and flourished. As your work has always argued, Mr. Innis, the world is a set of intersections taking place in a constant, changing way. Hockey is no exception, as you mentioned, both on and off the ice. The only difference is that Canada was never a world power, but we are quietly colonizing other countries with our game. [Laughs.]

INNIS: I would debate that last assertion, but I see your point. Some would argue that hockey is simply another natural resource that we are providing to make Americans rich. You yourself have been described as such in House of Commons debates after Oilers owner Peter Pocklington "sold" you to the Los Angeles Kings. Former prime minister Lester

Pearson described Canada as a "middle power," although we could argue it's more like "middle powerless" at the close of the twentieth century.

GRETZKY: I agree with your point, but this is the reality of our time, Mr. Innis. You cannot ignore that Canada is 30 million people next to a nation of close to 300 million. The twentieth century has belonged to the United States of America, not to Canada, as Wilfrid Laurier predicted, and that's that. So, maybe we can infiltrate them with hockey culture and perhaps we can even civilize them a little bit with our subtle northern combination of ferocity and finesse. [Gretzky laughs uproariously, and Innis soon joins him.]

INNIS: I once wrote about the consequences to the development of Canada caused by the fact that beavers don't migrate. Because they don't, those who trapped them and worked in the fur trade did not have to move around to follow the beaver. Because of this, permanent communities could be founded and social and political and economic organizations would develop in this physically stable context. This may be a rather self-serving illustrative contrast, but hockey players, of course, can and do migrate. This creates a whole series of consequences for the mobile labourer and for the evolution of hockey generally. Again, Mr. Gretzky, your impact on the popularity and growth of hockey after your move from northern Alberta to southern California is dramatic evidence of this process. Beyond your own case, what does this mobility of labour mean for the future of hockey in the Canadian consciousness?

GRETZKY: While the cultural impact can be exaggerated, it is true that the nature of professional hockey is, increasingly, one of the gun for hire, the itinerant worker. There is a long history of young Canadian hockey players leaving their home towns and moving away to the big leagues, usually in the U.S.A. Despite this and the technological advances, I still believe that climate is a critical component of cultural expression, and Canada's hockey dominance is forever linked to our lived experience of a cold, northern climate. That won't disappear, unless global warming makes water polo players of us all. In that sense, I'm not worried at all about the future of the game. Demographic patterns have changed in Canadian society, too. It's not just French and English and Aboriginal anymore. Hockey is beginning to reflect that change, as well as incorporating the exciting possibilities of women's hockey. To be sure, like every other sphere of Canadian cultural life, hockey is in danger of being swallowed up by the giant to the south. You know very well, Mr. Innis, about the hinterland and the metropole, so I don't have to tell you this. True, the north-south pull is greater than ever, and I myself represent one more domino falling, I suppose, but — not to sound too essentialist — the game of hockey emerged out of a set of geographical, climatological, demographic, and cultural circumstances, and although technologies can transcend climate to a degree, the game of hockey will remain Canadian. If a band like the Tragically Hip (from Kingston, Ontario, home town of Don Cherry!) can write a song about 1950s Toronto Maple Leaf overtime hero Bill Barilko and play to packed stadiums across Canada but only in small venues in the United States, I think that tells you something about cultural specificity. The need for nurturing and developing our own Canadian way has, in my opinion, not diminished significantly. Look, I've always been a passer: the more you give away, the more you get back. Canada invents the game of hockey, makes this amazing pass to the world, the world scores, and we all win.

INNIS: You are a decidedly Platonic thinker, Mr. Gretzky, but this image of the pass is an attractive segue. Let's move in our own way now from the empirical, if you like, to the transcendental. We have touched on the idea of time in hockey, but what about space? As you are one of the most gifted negotiators of hockey's spatial spheres of communication, the pass, what are your thoughts on the space of the game?

GRETZKY: All sports offer engagements with time and space, some emphasizing one over the other. Don't forget, hockey is also ruled by a clock, by time, unlike baseball or cricket. Aside from its three-period format where time stops and starts, though, hockey is for me primarily a way of inventing space. What I mean by that is that how you move through a game, how you move the puck by pass or by shot, creates, destroys, and recreates space. The game becomes like sculpture, with players in constant motion through space. Anticipating motion is a gift I have from somewhere, I guess, but I was also trained by my father to think about how hockey works spatially. He always told me to skate to where the puck is going to be, not to where it's been. That's what I try to do. Of course, there are pre-set patterns and systems at play in hockey, but they can be obliterated in an instant by a stray puck, a well-timed pass, an accidental collision, a random tumble, or whatever. It's been said before that hockey is like jazz: improvisational and open-ended in its form. It defeats the most concentrated attempts to control its forms and spaces. Maybe that's why, in pop-culture terms, the time seems ripe for hockey to emerge, because it is about creation, free-form adaptation, and not about premeditated strategy. The world out there on the ice is full of possibilities, like the accelerated contemporary chaotic world we live in with so much uncertainty. Maybe hockey is post-modern. I can't say. All I know is that the spatial metaphor of the ice as *tabula rasa* in that Bauer commercial is very appropriate: the game really is reinvented at the drop of every puck. Perhaps the collaborative open-endedness of hockey mirrors the Canadian culture that produced it. Canada is a very unusual place, historically and otherwise — a series of accommodations, really, and a federation caught up in an endless, passionate, restless search for reinvention. And it all takes place in a space we are simultaneously moving through and moving toward. It's that idea of being here while also being …

INNIS: Out there?

GRETZKY: Yes. Out there.

THE VISUAL AND ITS POPULAR MANIFESTATIONS

INTRODUCTION

On August 31, 1997, the world watched in horror as news of Princess Diana's violent and untimely death flashed across the airwaves. Indeed, this tragic event was to provide one of the most public spectacles ever witnessed. The princess's death prompted an unexpected and awe-inspiring response from admirers and detractors alike. People around the globe grieved for the English princess, and mourners in Canada were glued to their television sets. Many spent the week leading up to the princess's funeral watching every broadcast they could find. When the day of the funeral arrived, all of Canada's television networks reported live from London. Concomitantly, various services were held in Princess Diana's honour, and certain sites, such as the Princess of Wales Theatre in Toronto, the British High Commission in Ottawa, local cenotaphs nationwide in towns large and small, and British consulates in other cities, were unofficially designated as memorials to the woman whom the populace and the media dubbed "the People's Princess."

Throughout this text, there has been much discussion of Canada's relation to the United States, but the unspoken "other" connection that shadows Canadian popular culture is its colonial and post-colonial affiliation with the United Kingdom — a primary factor in the construction of Canadian identity as well as in its fragmentation (in such provinces as Quebec). Certainly, Canada's ties with the U.K. were apparent in Canadian responses to the loss of Princess Diana, an occasion that engendered a resurgence of strong colonial emotionality and nostalgia.

In this section, which focuses on various media events and the process of viewing, Ann Wilson traces the ways in which Princess Diana's life and death bear a marked resemblance to Canada's relations to and with empire. Charting Princess Diana's movement from a girl tagged "Shy Di" to a woman capable of challenging the monarchy, Wilson argues that this development parallels Canada's own affiliations with the "mother" country.

There have been no spectacles to date that can match the outpouring of grief over the death of Princess Diana, but this is not to suggest that a media spectacle need assume global status to be significant. In Anne-Marie Kinahan's essay, for example, the author discusses the trials and tribulations of visual artist Eli Langer, whose exhibition at the Mercer Union art gallery in Toronto raised disturbing questions about spectatorship and its legal ramifications. Several media critics believed that the artist's work bore an uncomfortably close resemblance to child pornography, and their protests led to criminal charges against Langer. Needless to say, as it raised serious issues of art and freedom of expression, the Langer trial was a controversial, contentious, and paradigmatic instance of the intersections of art and law, and Kinahan delineates the cultural ramifications of the exhibition and the ensuing hearings.

Sheryl Hamilton discusses the potentiality of the Internet in an essay that examines the possibilities the Net offers to women's groups. Using a case study on Studio XX, a women's "digital technology intervention group" situated in Montreal, Hamilton explores a number of different strategies through which women's groups can and are making their way into the public space of the World Wide Web, as well as into the broader public sphere of sociocultural debates, policies, and structures surrounding information technologies. Through a variety of activities, including feminist pedagogy, artistic performance, critical discussion, and online creative production, Hamilton examines how Studio XX seeks to alter the terrain of cyberspace, both on- and offline.

On another level, Bruce Gillespie addresses the process of viewing. In his chapter on "Gaydar," or, as he explains it, on gay men's ability to spot other gay men, Gillespie explores the ways in which people, and in particular gay people, read various visual signs as a means of assessing identity. Alerting readers to the complex process of visual characterization, Gillespie's article illustrates the fundamental role that the act of viewing plays in interpersonal relations.

This section, then, with its concentration on viewing, spectacles, and the interactions between the two, analyses areas like iconography, media, art, and personal interrelations. Emphasizing the importance of media events and their impact on constructions of self and identity, it also raises questions about citizenship, participation, and the possibilities open to the national public sphere in this electronic age.

THE DEATH OF PRINCESS DIANA

Mourning a "Very British Girl"

Ann Wilson

On August 31, 1997, few in Canada could have expected to hear the news that Diana, Princess of Wales, had been killed in a car crash that had also taken the life of Dodi Fayed, her companion, and the driver of the car, Henri Paul. Nor could anyone have predicted the collective swell of grief for Diana in England and other countries in the week between her death and funeral. In this essay, I want to explore the complex terms of English nationalism that are played out through the story of Diana's life, including the week leading up to her funeral. My argument is that Diana's life as a member of the House of Windsor serves as an analogue for the post-colonial experiences of Britain's settler colonies, including Canada. I want to suggest that Diana's life can be understood through a trope of inside/out, with the inside being a particular mode of Englishness represented by the not always compatible privileges of aristocracy and royalty, both of which Diana eschewed in ways that allowed her to be accepted as a populist princess. What interests me particularly are the ways in which the public image of Diana as both insider and outsider to these modes of privilege result in her becoming a celebrity, in her being accessible to the public as a celebrity, a status that is an expression of transnational capital. For all that Diana's life lends itself to a reading of her as someone striving to emerge from the House of Windsor, in effect, as a personal tale of emerging from being a colonized subject to an autonomous one, the pressures of celebrity complicate the story and suggest that autonomous subjectivity is a ruse. Finally, I want to suggest that this complication of transnational capital serves as a cautionary tale for the limits of a post-colonial inquiry that strives to assert a sense of national identity for settler colonies such as Canada.

A consideration of the story of Diana's entry into the House of Windsor, and of the commensurate fascination with her as a royal celebrity, might begin usefully with the photo-spread in *Time* magazine in the aftermath of her death. The spread, titled "The Saddest Fairy Tale," begins with the image of Diana as a toddler, huddled in a perambulator. She looks rather blankly at the camera. The photo takes up roughly two-thirds of the page; the rest of the page, together with the adjoining one, is filled with the famous shot of Diana and Prince Charles kissing after emerging onto the balcony of Buckingham Palace on their wedding day to greet the public. Before I consider that photo in some detail, I want to state the obvious: had Lady Spencer not married Prince Charles, she would be unknown. Her fame, her celebrity, and its accompanying power are effects of her marriage to the heir to the British throne.

What is fascinating in the photo is not the couple but those attending. The "fairy tale" couple kiss but neither party has contact with the other, beyond their lips: Diana's right arm is being clutched by a little girl — unidentified by *Time* but, given the scene, not an "ordinary" little girl — whose own right arm hides her face. Another of the flower girls, younger than the one clutching Diana's arm, looks at the couple. Offered as part of the visual telling of "The Saddest Fairy Tale," the two juxtaposed shots of Diana the toddler and Diana the bride offer more than suggested by *Time*'s caption: "Her childhood pram was transformed into the carriage that brought her to the palace in 1981 for a wedding kiss with Prince Charming." It would seem that *Time* means to convey that innocence led to the kiss of "Prince Charming," a world for which Diana was ill-equipped. But don't these images lend themselves to another reading?

The image of a toddler, someone who was presumably ambulatory and inquisitive, in a pram suggests the curiously cloistered life of the aristocratically privileged in England. And given that none of the party attending Diana and Charles were "ordinary" folk, doesn't the confident, yet bemused gaze of the little boys in the wedding party and the stance of the little girls — none of them looking towards the crowd, one hiding and clutching Diana's arm, one looking at the couple, and the third, the eldest of the three girls caught in the photo, casting her glance downwards — speak volumes about the intersection of class and gender within the world into which Diana was born? This scene of Diana and Charles kissing was offered by *Time* as the inaugural moment for a story that ends in the twisted wreckage of the Mercedes, the synecdoche of her death. But Diana, born into a family that inherited their title by rites of birth, could have been a little girl on that balcony had Prince Charles married earlier. And which of those girls might she have been?

Princess Diana was described by British Prime Minister Tony Blair as the "People's Princess," a populist title that speaks of her appeal to the public as a member of the royal family who had tremendous empathy for the suffering of others. Significantly, the force of this empathy, as Ludmilla Jordanova has suggested, is that it was so easily displayed and captured in the photographs that fed the public's increasing fascination with the princess. What receives emphasis in the representation of Diana as empathetic is gender: she was a woman who had known anguish and that anguish allowed her imaginatively to embrace the despair of children, of the sick, and latterly, of the socially disenfranchised who were marginalized by society, such as people with AIDS or those civilians maimed by landmines.

It doesn't take a great leap of imagination to understand how Diana, a child of divorce and a young woman seemingly cast out of the family into which she had married, might identify with those who were cast to the margins of society; her own life, after all, rehearsed certain experiences of marginalization. When Earl Spencer, in his eulogy, described Diana as "class-less" (presumably appealing to the public sentiment mobilized by Blair's calling her the "People's Princess"), class, as a category for understanding Diana, was elided. Had we heard her voice more often, presumably the class inflections would have registered strongly. As the scene on the balcony of Buckingham Palace on her wedding day suggests, Diana's story involves notions of class. Indeed, it depends on two competing notions of "class," both circulating around power and money: the royal family (and, indeed, aristocratic families like Diana's) stands as a sign of the inherited privilege of wealth and power; in contrast, celebrity involves the acquisition of wealth and commensurate fame and power within one's own life. Diana embodied both notions of class, while her husband embodied only the former, and Dodi Fayed, only the latter. The two modes of class represent differing articulations of power, the former rooted in a sense of class that circulates around nation; the latter, around power that is acquired through investments that are not bound to nation — the world is the marketplace. As Benedict Anderson (1983) suggests in his introduction to *Imagined Communities*, nation is often understood through tropes of family. But are there any widely accepted tropes for transnational capital? Or, is transnational capital a force without a narrative frame in the popular imagination? When Diana's casket, draped in the Royal Standard, was returned from Paris in the company of her former husband and her two sisters (Lady Jane Fellowes and Lady Sarah McCorquodale), a symbolic resumption of the "fairy-tale marriage" began. Diana was returned home, to the nation of her birth, in the company of family.

Notably, the resumption of the fairy tale depends upon particular figurations and oversights. Charles's love, Camilla Parker Bowles, does not register, and so there is a triangulated relationship between Charles (who had wronged his wife by loving someone else), Diana, and Dodi (her companion, perhaps lover, and indeed, perhaps betrothed). The return of Diana's casket to England in the company of her former husband and her sisters lends itself to a narrative of English nationalism articulated as romance. Diana is returned to her native land from foreign shores, returned to her families by birth and marriage, returned to her former husband from the company of her lover, a foreigner. Effectively, Diana was restored to a particular sense of England that, crucially, depends on two dead bodies who have no way of speaking for themselves.

Dodi al Fayed, as scion of a wealthy Egyptian family, occupies a particular place within the cultural imagary of England and its settler colonies, including Canada. He is the alien, the Other whose outsider status was rehearsed in the press that recounted tales of his father, Mohammed al Fayed, a man of immense wealth whose money had allowed him to buy a venerable English establishment of enterprise, Harrods. His acquisition of Harrods becomes a sign of the degree to which entrepreneurial Englishness has vanished in contemporary transnational economies where money, not national fidelity, rules. Significantly, Mohammed al Fayed — the manipulator of vast amounts of international capital — desperately wanted to be part of the English nation, repeatedly trying and failing to secure a British passport. "They could not accept that an Egyptian could own Harrods, so they threw mud at me," he told an interviewer (Ratnesar 1997).

The tense intersection of race and nation that was an element of the Fayed story in England became pronounced in the responses to Diana's and Dodi's relationship. As Barbara Cartland, mother of Diana's stepmother, commented at news of the liaison, "My only concern is that this Dodi is a foreigner" (Cohen 1997). No one was more skilled at displacing the anxiety of race and class than British Prime Minister Tony Blair, who, in dubbing Diana "the People's Princess," deployed an appellation of such sentimental and popular appeal that it seems a bit rude to ask, "Who are the people?" Diana's death and her new title suggest that her appeal was transcendent and that it unified a nation — indeed *nations,* if we allow that she was mourned by the English-speaking world — so that the tensions articulated through race, class, and nation are eased by femininity.

The media depictions of Diana's relationship with Dodi lend themselves to a post-colonial reading. Dodi figures, in the allegory of post-colonialism, as the outsider, the alien who was embraced (literally, in the photos of the couple on the yacht) by a woman eulogized by her brother as a "very British girl." It is as if Diana, reared with the cloistered codes of an aristocratic upbringing that led her to an unsuccessful marriage, flouted this social system that has limited relevance in the contemporary world. She sought to break out of old, restrictive notions of class and nation through a relationship with a moneyed foreigner. As alien, Dodi signifies a structure of inside/out, which seems key to understanding the popular appeal of Diana. The pictures of Diana with Dodi during the summer of 1997 signal the terms of that alliance, at least as it appeared for public consumption. Both are casually attired in the photos from the Fayed yacht, she in bathing suit revealing a body that is toned and healthy, suggesting that she had overcome the eating disorders to which her brother alluded in his eulogy. She seems to have a confident sense of her sexuality, giving her an agency that seems negated by her brother's description of her, in death, as a "girl." This apparent confidence and sense of independence helped spawn the sense of the tragedy of the crash, notions circulating that, with Dodi, Diana had found "true" love, a love that had ended before full realization.

For my argument, what is significant is the idea of Diana seeking solace with someone who was marked as outside the aristocratic privilege that she had known as a child and that had led to her marriage and made her a member — an insider — of a royal family that represents an imperial power now past. On a range of levels, Diana was also an outsider, to the worlds of the aristocracy, the royal family, and the "common" people. As Tina Brown notes in her commentary on Diana's death, Charles surrounds himself with "county friends" who are a "frightening lightweight crowd. They have a collective class unease about anything that smacks of intensity" (1997, 58). It bears reiterating that this is the "crowd" into which Diana was born, and thus, Brown's further comments assume some poignancy: "After Diana's public revelations of bulimia and self-mutilation, the country-house-party set permanently ceased to be part of her world. Televised confessions, talk of therapy, admissions of pain: it was all so emotionally aggressive, so unseemly — so un-English, in a word" (59).

But it was precisely these qualities, flying in the face of codes of aristocratic English privilege, that appealed to the public. It wasn't just that Diana had emotional anguish, to which she confessed, but her daring to speak of her pain with an often poignant lack of articulateness allowed her to appear to cross the borders of power, because the dispossessed, historically, have always been without a language that registers their agony within public discourse. Her personal pain, and her ability to use it as an empathetic entry to the pain of the dispossessed, made her appear as "the People's Princess"; but Diana, however much she didn't fit into the mold of aristocratic, and indeed royal, codes, was not an "ordinary" person. In the post-divorce phase of her life, Diana was a royal who was cast out of the House of Windsor with a large settlement and a sizeable inheritance from her father.

In providing a fairly protracted account of Diana as a young royal whose seeming fairy-tale marriage ended in divorce because she was both inside and outside the social codes of her husband and coterie, I want to suggest that part of the public's fascination with Diana was her hybridity, which was managed in such a way as to generate mystique. While some of the aspects of Diana's public presentation — her despair — allowed her to empathize with the suffering of the socially disenfranchised, she never lost her allure and became an "ordinary" person: she was "the People's Princess," a contradictory term that underlines the duality of Diana's popularity — she was both inside and outside royal and aristocratic privilege. While Diana may have been outside the royal family, she was still an aristocrat, even if she eschewed the codes of aristocracy. On that register of class, she may have been a qualified outsider, but that disenfranchisement from power gave her heightened access to another form of cultural currency, the power of celebrity.

For Canadians, some of the earlier aspects of Diana's life seem compatible with Canada's own sense of national identity as a young, vibrant country that — at least in English Canada — still follows the British traditions to which it is heir, traditions that are constantly being renegotiated and redefined, much as Diana tried to redefine her role within the royal family. And in the latter stages of her life, Diana's identity seems compatible with English Canada's more recent, post-colonial sense of itself as a nation that has emerged from the legacy of its inheritance from Britain and is now an autonomous player on the international stage, with a newly defined and wholly contemporary sense of national identity. Perhaps Canada's role in the landmines issue that Diana espoused serves culturally as a sign of the intersection of Diana's identity and Canada's.

In describing Diana's story as an allegory of post-colonialism, I have gestured to, but left largely unexplored, a crucial aspect of her life. Diana, in the course of her marriage and certainly in the phase of her life after her marriage ended, became a celebrity, that is, a person whose image had currency within the marketplace. The stories of her being pursued by hordes of paparazzi, eager to get pictures of her, indicate that the price of Diana's image was high. It is worth noting at this juncture that the value of those pictures depended on the notion of inside and outside: what the paparazzi sought were not pictures of Diana at sanctioned occasions, but pictures of her that would penetrate her mystique and reveal aspects of her personal life.[1] These photos have value on the international market, which is governed by transnational capital. While the narrative of Diana's marriage to Prince Charles challenges the codes of the royal family and, in the process, unsettles that very English institution of monarchy, the underpinnings of the story, as Diana becomes a celebrity, are the demands of capital for a marketable product. If Diana's story is an allegory of post-colonialism, then the story raises the vexing problem of the degree to which a settler colony like Canada insistently fashions its narrative of national identity as a struggle to gain independence from the domination of the colonizer. In the context of an allegory of post-colonialism, Diana's story, as she emerges as a celebrity, suggests that the notion of post-colonialism as overthrowing colonial domination may be problematic. If Diana's emergence as a celebrity independent of the royal family parallels Canada's emergence as an independent, autonomous nation, it is worth remembering that Diana's celebrity is within the terms of transnational capital. Is Canada's identity as an independent nation an effect of transnational capital?

I want to conclude this essay by suggesting that the inability of cultural commentators to address the impact of late capital on Diana's life led to her death being read as Diana being restored to the royal family and the archaic sense of the English nation with which it is associated. The question that I want to raise is this: If my reading of Diana's life as an allegory of post-colonialism is viable (a reading that allows for the currency of her celebrity to be read as a sign of autonomy), why have Canadian commentators so willingly accepted her restoration to the royal family? What is indicated by the success of Elton John's revised version of "Candle in the Wind," originally an homage to Marilyn Monroe and now a eulogy to Diana as "England's Rose"? In that song, celebrity, which is an effect of transnational capital, becomes domesticated into a particular Englishness that is fully compatible with restoring the old, if antagonistic, notion of English class privilege represented by royalty and aristocracy, two terms that intersect in their complicit project of British imperial prerogative. In short, the funeral of Diana, Princess of Wales, disables the post-colonial reading of her life.

As I suggested earlier, the return of Diana's body to England, her coffin draped in the Royal Standard and accompanied by her ex-husband and her two sisters, set the scene for the resumption of the fairy tale — this was because the bride, in death, was now acquiescent. As the first week of September unfolded and the royal family remained at Balmoral, the public, having witnessed the return of Diana to England, began to demand that the royal family demonstrate signs of grief commensurate with the public's sense of the loss of this woman, whom it had come to know largely in her self-fashioned, hybridized role as royal celebrity.

Perhaps recurring shots of Buckingham Palace, the site of that kiss that serves as the iconographic initiation of the fairy-tale marriage, conveyed the strongest image of the strain generated by the public's grief and the seeming lack of response by the royal family. While the palace, behind the gates, betrayed no sign of life, let alone mourning, outside the gates, the banks of flowers grew bigger with each passing day during the first week of September. Public demands that the royal family emerge from seclusion and display its grief led the Queen to return to Buckingham Palace to deliver a televised address. With the Royal Standard raised as the ancient sign that the monarch is in residence, the glare of television lights indicated to the crowds outside the gates that the monarch, to express the grief of the royal family over Diana's death, was using the technologies that had made Diana a celebrity. The image here is of the old regime acknowledging technology as an aspect of maintaining power within late capitalism.

On the Saturday morning of Diana's funeral, the horse-drawn carriage carrying her coffin left Kensington Palace and passed Buckingham Palace, where the members of the royal family waited outside the gates until the cortège had gone by, a sign of their joining their subjects in grief. Then, as the procession passed St. James's Palace, it was joined by the mourners (all male) who represented her family (by birth and by marriage) — Prince Charles, Prince William, Prince Henry, the Duke of Edinburgh, and Earl Spencer — their solemn, steady gait broken occasionally by Prince Henry. They were followed by mourners representing the various charities that Diana had supported, some of whom were unable to walk and so were in wheelchairs. The image had elements of inside and outside, the aristocratic and royal mourners followed by the ordinary people whose suffering Diana had recognized, whose lives she had touched if for no other reason than that her privilege and celebrity drew attention to their needs. In one sense, the image of the funeral procession suggests that Diana's death unified England in a collective mourning, but in another, the divisions between the privileged and the less privileged were visible as the mourners from the charities, the "ordinary people," walked behind the family, the royalty and aristocrats.

The events that began with the return of Diana's body to England and culminated with her burial signified the return of a princess to her home and thus her restoration to a "proper" Englishness, a state from which she seemingly had strayed in her liaison with Dodi Fayed, the Egyptian outsider to English society who had wooed Diana on the continent of Europe. In an age when England still harbours a view of itself as removed from the European community (evident in its reluctance to accept a common European currency), Diana's death seemed to justify xenophobia: she had died on foreign soil, in the company of foreigners. From the perspective of Canada, a country in which English Canada invests its sense of nation in its post-colonial relation to England, the management of Diana's death returns her to the "inside" and negates the "outside," except as a corrupting and, finally, deadly force.

That Canadian commentators have appeared to accept without question the recuperation of Diana to this particular Englishness seems astonishing if, indeed, part of her appeal for Canadians was her eschewing of some of the codes of this very Englishness. Her life lent itself to a reading as an allegory of post-colonialism, of the struggle to establish an autonomous identity while bearing the suffocating burden of being an "insider" in the patriarchal social order of aristocracy and royalty. Diana's life was a study in ambivalences — she was an aristocratic woman who wed into the royal family but who touched ordinary people with her humanity. Her struggle for an autonomous identity seemed a compromised undertaking because her means of distancing herself from the royal family was through her empathy, which, as an aspect of femininity, was a construct of the very patriarchal codes that she flouted.

Diana's "outsider" relationship to codes of Englishness was increasingly implicated in her celebrity. The unquestioning acceptance of her restoration to the royal family and to the nation and the minimalizing of her life outside these codes of Englishness are expressions of an unspoken anxiety over Diana's celebrity, which, as noted above, is an effect of transnational capital. Whereas nation (including the range of economies that comprise the nation) can be imagined through narratives that circulate around notions of the family, the sphere of the transnational has neither a narrative structure nor a constellation of images within which it can be understood. If Diana's life, from the moment of her marriage to Prince Charles, had an allegorical element where she and he came to represent the future of the monarchy and hence a perpetuation of an old sense of Englishness, and if her divorce allowed her life to be read as an allegory of post-colonialism, then her death is about her being restored to the familiar narrative structure of nation and family. But, as the image of mourners walking behind the coffin suggested, in the end Diana could not be the site upon which a cohesive image of Englishness might be produced. The image of the mourners is one of a nation divided and only temporarily united in grief.

The final image of Diana's life is her internment at her family's estate of Althrop. The burial itself was private, but pictures were released of her burial site on an island in an artificial lake on the estate. Some of the photographs showed Diana's brother, Charles, Earl Spencer, squatting amidst flowers, the bouquets that mourners had left, now opened and spread over the island. Again, the image is one of the public grief being incorporated into the family's private mourning; this might, from one vantage point, suggest that Diana's death unified commoners, aristocrats, and royalty, but the image has a nostalgic feel, as if this were a nineteenth-century portrayal of an Ophelia-like girl surrounded in death by water and flowers. Shakespeare's Ophelia, whose story takes place in an earlier age, disrupted the court of Elsinore, much as Diana disrupted the House of Windsor, and finally Ophelia's disruptive effect, like Diana's, was contained by her death. The burial of Diana on an island in an artificial lake may serve as the encapsulating image of her life. Buried on an island in a man-made lake, invoking images of Ophelia read by nineteenth-century painters, Diana was finally contained: through a week in September she was restored to an Englishness invested in nineteenth-century notions of nationalism and commensurate notions of patriarchy and masculine privilege, represented so strikingly by the family mourners who walked behind her casket. She was not a woman, but a "very British girl." That Canadian commentators have accepted this version of her life without question implies that our sense of ourselves as a post-colonial nation needs scrutiny. How "post" is our colonial identity? Until Canada, and other settler colonies, can find a narrative of identity that accommodates transnational capital, our recourse in forging a national identity will be to tales of family romance because the "imagined community" of nation is envisioned, thus far, as familial. Canada, like Australia, will always be a daughter of the empire.

ENDNOTE

1. The use of the word "penetrate" has obvious sexual connotations. In the instance of Diana, when the attentions of the paparazzi were unwelcome, the context of this penetration is analogous to "rape," a point made clearly by David Edgar in "The Floral Revolution" and Salman Rushdie in "Crash."

REFERENCES

Anderson, Benedict. 1983. *Imagined Communities: Reflections on the Origin and Spread of Nationalism.* London: Verso.

Black, Ian. 1997. "Conspiracy Scenarios Grow Wilder and Wilder." *Guardian/Observer,* 6 September. http.//194.205.156.69/Diana/coverage/19970907–10.html. 14 September 1997.

Brown, Tina. 1997. "Manhattan Chronicles: A Woman in Earnest." *The New Yorker,* 15 September: 58–61.

Cohen, Adam. 1997. "Diana's Unlikely Suitor." *Time,* 8 September: 35.

Edgar, David. 1997. "The Floral Revolution." *Guardian/Observer,* 10 September. http://194.205.156.69/Diana/coverage/19970910–03.html. 14 September 1997.

Jordanova, Ludmilla. 1997. Plenary address on the death of Diana, Princess of Wales. "Women and Literary History." University of Alberta, Edmonton, Alberta, 11 September.

Ratnesar, Romesh. 1997. "Outside Looking In: Like Diana, the Fayeds Have Long Struggled with the British Establishment." *Time,* 15 September: 46–48.

Rushdie, Salman. "Crash." *The New Yorker,* 15 September 1997: 68, 69.

"The Saddest Fairy Tale." 1997. *Time,* 8 September: 28–33.

Spencer, Earl Charles. 1997. "Sadness, anger and a brother's promise." Text of the tribute to Diana, Princess of Wales, at her funeral by her younger brother, Earl Spencer. *Toronto Star,* 7 September: D9.

A PORTRAIT OF THE ARTIST AS A SENSITIVE YOUNG MAN

The State, the Media, and

"The Ordeal of Eli Langer"

Anne-Marie Kinahan

CHRONOLOGY

May 13, 1993 — Child pornography legislation, Bill C-128, is introduced in the House of Commons and read for the first time.

June 15, 1993 — Bill C-128 is given royal assent in the House of Commons.

August 1, 1993 — Bill C-128 is enshrined in the Canadian Criminal Code as Section 163.1.

November 20, 1993 — Eli Langer's exhibit opens at the Mercer Union art gallery in Toronto.

December 14, 1993 — Kate Taylor's review of Langer's show appears in the *Globe and Mail*.

December 15, 1993 — Members of the Metropolitan Toronto Police "morality squad" visit Langer's exhibit after receiving complaints.

December 16, 1993 — Police return with a warrant and seize five of eight paintings and thirty-five of fifty drawings.

December 21, 1993 — Langer is charged with one count each of making, possessing, and displaying child pornography to public view.

December 23, 1993 — Mercer Union gallery director, Sharon Brooks, is charged with possessing child pornography and displaying child pornography to public view.

January 7, 1994 — Alan Borovoy, general council of the Canadian Civil Liberties Association, writes to Ontario Attorney-General Marion Boyd, urging her to drop the charges.

January 15, 1994 — PEN Canada joins the protest against the charges by writing to federal Justice Minister Allan Rock.

February 15, 1994 — Formal charges against Langer and Brooks are dropped; Crown attorney Paul Culver applies for forfeiture.

October 3, 1994 — Forfeiture hearing of Eli Langer's art begins in Ontario Provincial
  Court (general division); Mr. Justice David McCombs presides.

October 14, 1994 — Forfeiture hearing adjourns; McCombs reserves his decision.

April 20, 1995 — Judge McCombs renders his decision: Langer's art possesses merit and
  should be returned to him.

July 15, 1995 — Langer and his lawyer apply to the Supreme Court for permission to
  launch a Charter challenge against the child pornography law on the grounds that it vi-
  olates guarantees of freedom of expression.

October 14, 1995 — Supreme Court refuses to hear the constitutional challenge; child
  pornography law remains intact.

This article analyses media commentary on "The Ordeal of Eli Langer,"[1] a Toronto artist
whose work became the focal point of public debate over the presence of sexually explicit
material in a democratic society. The intention of this analysis is to demonstrate how the artwork of Eli Langer provided a public forum for the articulation of separate and diverse
moral constituencies. This analysis will show how the public response to Langer's work
and the discourses produced through subsequent media coverage were centre-stage in a
modern-day morality play in which various social actors engaged in the debate over art,
pornography, child abuse, freedom of expression, and protection from harm. The social actors that shaped the debate involving Langer were the state, the police, civil libertarians,
anti-pornography groups, and the media. Ostensibly, the issue at hand was the right of professional artists to exhibit their art in a recognized gallery. But also at stake was a conception of, and indeed a faith in, the benevolent state. Essentially, these groups aligned themselves
according to a belief in the powers of the liberal state. For the police and anti-pornography
groups, state intervention in order to protect the most vulnerable members of society is easily justified and falls within the power of the state. For civil libertarians and artists, however,
state intervention in matters personal, professional, or creative must be condemned, as it
jeopardizes the existence of the tolerant society. The discourses that these various groups produced provided the essential elements in the understanding of the "threat" posed by Eli
Langer and other artists like him who choose to visually investigate issues of sexuality.

   The print media occupied a privileged site in the analysis of "The Ordeal of Eli Langer"
for various reasons. First of all, they provided the primary interpretations of the issues at hand;
secondly, they provided a running commentary of events in Langer's legal ordeal; and
thirdly, a review of Langer's exhibit in the *Globe and Mail* brought his work to public attention. Hence, the media must be understood not as objective reporters of fact, but as an essential element of the news story under examination.

ARRESTING IMAGES: THE ART EXHIBITION/
THE PORNOGRAPHY CONTROVERSY

In an eerily prophetic article discussing the possible ramifications of Bill C-128, Peter
Wilson of the *Vancouver Sun* stated:

> Defending free speech in the arts should be easy … except that in Canada in fighting for free
> speech, you always have to defend yourself first. No, you have to say, I am not in favor of
> racism. No, I am not in favor of child pornography. No, I am not in favor of violence in our
> society. No, I am not advocating the moral destruction of our citizenry. (1993)

In the fallout of media commentary about Eli Langer, this defensiveness reached a fever pitch. Beginning with Kate Taylor's brief and hostile review of Langer's exhibit, published in the *Globe and Mail* on December 14, 1993, the primary definition of Langer was that of the child pornographer. While Taylor admitted that Langer was a talented painter, and never described him as a pedophile or child pornographer, her review provided the first public discussion of the two most questionable and oft-recited images from Langer's show:

> The paintings, gorgeously rendered in a duo-toned chiaroscuro of red and black, show children and adults in various forms of sexual play. A naked child sits on the lap of a naked man who might be her grandfather. A masked intruder climbs through a window into a bedroom where a naked girl straddles the neck of an adult and very erect man who lies on the bed. Langer's attitude toward these activities is ambivalent — they are depicted with both horror and fascination — but what is definitive about the paintings is that the children are not portrayed as victims but rather as willing participants. (1993a)

It was this discussion of the content of Langer's work that defined and foregrounded its explicit sexual element and became the primary means of identifying Langer in subsequent articles (Taylor 1993a, b, c, d; Lawton 1993a; Gooderham 1993; Drainie 1994; and articles carried through Canadian Press). While this may be explained as an attempt to refamiliarize readers with the particulars of Langer's art and the possible objections to it, it also reinforced the perception that the work was offensive and pornographic.

This review was followed, less than a week later, by an article announcing that the "Gallery may face porn charges" as a result of two complaints registered with the police. While only one of these two individuals had actually attended the exhibit, the police responded to these complaints by visiting the gallery on December 15th and returning a day later with a warrant for seizure. They seized thirty-five of fifty drawings and five of eight paintings (charges against one of the drawings were eventually withdrawn). On December 21, 1993, Eli Langer was charged with one count each of making child pornography, possessing child pornography, and displaying child pornography to public view. This was followed two days later by the arrest of Mercer Union gallery director Sharon Brooks for possessing child pornography and displaying child pornography to public view. While it would be disingenuous to argue that Taylor's review was solely responsible for the seizure of Langer's paintings and the resulting charges, it is imperative to note that her review reached a wider audience than Langer's show normally would have. In fact, this is one point that Taylor makes in her review: "Langer fits within the grand old tradition known as *épater les bourgeois* but the bourgeois who might be dumbfounded by these paintings will never venture into the Mercer Union. Instead, right-minded intellectuals, all determined not to be shocked and by extension ensuring they don't feel, stand around and ponder the works" (1993a). To argue that Taylor alone was responsible for the seizure of Langer's work ignores the fact that the decision to confiscate the objectionable paintings rested solely with the officers of the Metro Toronto Police "morality squad." However, the influence of Taylor's review should not be dismissed. Condemning his art as "a self-conscious, juvenile prodding of its own excrement" (1993a), Taylor's review was denounced by artists and critics for instigating Langer's arrest. This is not to argue that Taylor considered Langer a child pornographer, but rather that the influence and weight of the police seizure of his paintings, and Taylor's description of their subject matter, provided the primary definition of this issue.

In arguing that Langer was primarily defined as a child pornographer, I should not be seen as accusing the police and the state of a conspiratorial attempt to unjustly accuse Langer of crimes he did not commit. Rather, it is the effect of the child pornography legislation in the Criminal Code that successfully labels anyone who contravenes these provisions as a child pornographer or pedophile. As a starting point, one must realize that Langer's arrest under the child pornography provisions of the Criminal Code determined the content of the press coverage. Subsequent articles exist in contrast to the assumption that these charges were considered legitimate in light of the controversial nature of his art.

More than the description in Taylor's review, the police actions successfully labelled Langer as a child pornographer. Acting under newly enshrined child pornography legislation that criminalizes any visual representation of sexual activity involving individuals under 18 years of age, the police were able to seize the offending works with nothing more than a warrant and the belief that they were obscene. Surely the fact that the police confiscated Langer's paintings carried the rhetorical power that successfully labelled him as "threat." The unwritten assumption was that the police would not have confiscated the works if they were not pornographic. These actions, coupled with the disturbing images presented in Taylor's review, provided the moral force behind the urge to destroy the artwork.

Within the articles that discussed the charges against Langer and gallery director Sharon Brooks, there was some analysis of what was termed the "tough new anti-pornography legislation." In attempting to determine exactly what constitutes "artistic merit" and where the burden of proof rests, media and communications lawyer Brian Blugerman "stressed that the Crown will have to prove that the work does not have artistic merit, rather than the artist showing it does" (Taylor 1993d). However, this assertion was contradicted by Heritage Minister Michel Dupuy, who stated that "Langer will have to justify his art in court" (Lawton 1993a). Such diverse interpretations of the specifics of the law served to reinforce the perception that artists are considered guilty until proven otherwise, and that they will, in fact, shoulder the burden of proof.

The focus on the need for artists to prove the merit of their work was further enhanced by commentary offered by anti-pornography groups supporting the measures against Langer. Although most press coverage focused upon civil libertarian groups, many articles also included discussion of groups such as Canadians for Decency, Canadians Concerned About Violence in Entertainment (CCAVE), the Institute for the Prevention of Child Abuse, and their objections to sexually explicit material. In addition to providing the appearance of balanced coverage of all sides of this debate, the inclusion of these groups reinforced the central considerations of this issue. A central concern of the coverage of Langer's arrest was the attempt to determine if Langer was a child pornographer or a legitimate artist. In an editorial accompaniment to an article discussing the charges against Langer, the *Globe and Mail* stated that while artist and civil libertarian groups had denounced the provisions as interfering with artistic freedom, "Anti-pornography groups … hailed the legislation and said the artists' fears were exaggerated. Representatives of Canadians Concerned About Violence in Entertainment suggested that creativity should move in new directions that do not rely on the sexuality of children" (1993a). Questions over the right to decide what artists should represent were foregrounded in this discussion. That artists should find better subjects to occupy their time and creative energies was further articulated by representatives of Canadians for Decency. In a *Maclean's* article that appeared shortly after Langer was charged, Dolina Smith, president of Canadians for Decency, commented: "'This is sick stuff … I don't even like to talk about it. Can we let our children be destroyed for the sake of some artist's fantasy?'" (Jenish 1994, 68).

The belief that these images unquestioningly endorsed the behaviour depicted was characteristic of the rhetoric employed by the anti-pornography groups mentioned and this belief was best illustrated by a comment from Ross Dawson, managing director of the Institute for the Prevention of Child Abuse: "'I think if we're going to prevent the sexual abuse of children, then we have to have a clear statement in society that children are not to be used for the sexual gratification of adults'" (Fine 1994a). Dawson's comments also reinforced the belief expressed by Canadians for Decency and CCAVE, that Langer's art advocated such abuse or, more generally, that any sexually explicit art is *de facto* abuse and warrants strict controls. It was in response to such arguments that a large amount of mainstream press coverage denounced the charges against Langer and articulated a defence of the artist's work through a recourse to freedom of expression debates.

THE LIBERAL DEFENCE: LANGER AS SILENCED ARTIST

Although it has been my argument that the primary understanding of Langer was that of child pornographer, there existed a separate discourse that defended his freedom of expression and challenged the constitutionality of the law that enabled his arrest. It is imperative to note that these discourses existed simultaneously, often in the same articles, and while it may seem to obfuscate the issues, these discourses reflected the theoretical underpinnings of many debates over sexually explicit material.

In an article responding to the charges against Langer and Brooks, and to her own perceived role in those charges, Kate Taylor reasserted her right to negatively review Langer's show. At Langer's press conference on December 22, 1993, two artists had denounced Taylor's review. Andy Fabo had criticized her for not providing an historical analysis of sexual content in art and Elaine Carol had blamed her for instigating the charges. Responding to these criticisms, Taylor maintained that her review was widely misunderstood: "Artist and writer Elaine Carol went much further [than Fabo], lumping me in with the police morality squad as Langer's prosecutor. Misreading my review to have said the paintings were illegal — I had said the acts they showed were illegal — she denounced me as a 'self-appointed kangaroo court'" (1993e). Ostensibly justifying her review of Langer's art, Taylor in fact clarified her arguments regarding the content of Langer's show:

> I thought the work was more about the construction of sexual taboo than about the pain of abuse … but I also felt the artist was still working through his position…. I ended my review with a rhetorical flourish saying Langer was young and could paint well, and maybe when he grew up he'd be an artist. It was my way of stressing how ineffectively I felt he had dealt with his material, how immature and unformed his artistic position was.

Taylor's initial review concentrated on denouncing the gallery and the contemporary avant-garde rather than engaging with the content of Langer's art. Her subsequent article may be seen as an attempt to contextualize her criticism of Langer's show. While some critics and journalists dismissed Taylor's rebuttal as self-indulgent (Drainie 1994; Martin 1994), it is important to realize that her article served to distance the reviewer and, by extension, the newspaper from the charges against Langer and Brooks. This distance was further reinforced through the *Globe and Mail*'s editorials.

The editorial staff at the *Globe and Mail* wrote several articles discussing Langer's arrest, his right to freedom of expression, and the questionable motives behind the drafting of the child pornography legislation. In an article that provided background information on Bill C-128, the *Globe and Mail* took a firm stand against the far-reaching range of the new law. Characterizing it as a result of political strategizing, the article stated: "[L]ooking to send a tough message about crime in the final weeks of its mandate, the Progressive Conservative government quickly drafted amendments to the Criminal Code's obscenity provisions this spring. Bill C-128 … removed community standards as a test of obscenity and instead spelled out a definition of child pornography" (1993a).

The article further argued that the legislation's definition of pornography, and its hasty approval, had been the subject of much criticism from civil libertarians, legal organizations, and cultural groups. Presenting an image of the state as a potentially totalitarian structure with its own agenda, the article argued that this legislation was not necessarily constructed with the intention of protecting children, but rather to secure the party's political future.

The *Globe and Mail*'s position on Langer and his arrest was made even more explicit in the editorial "Art, or pornography?" Characterizing the legislation as a hastily drafted, ill-conceived effort to appear tough on crime in the dying days of the Conservative government's tenure, the article attacked the "timeless impulse" to censor that which may be disturbing. Criticizing the law for essentially providing the police with unchecked power to determine obscenity, the editorial questioned the impartiality of the police:

> [T]he decision on whether to lay charges in the first place is left with the police. Thus the gumshoes from the Metro Toronto Police morality squad were able to tramp into the Mercer Union, cart away a few armloads of pictures and, after consulting a crown prosecutor, lay charges against the artist, apparently without any reference to a higher legal (or artistic) authority.

While this description recounts the actions of the police in this case, it does so with a rhetorical flair that exploits the image of a totalitarian society, ruled by the police. It further elucidates the problems with obscenity provisions that disregard the concept of "community standards." Although many academics have questioned the legitimacy of such a concept, it does seem preferable to legislation that provides the police with such censorious powers. What is significant about this article is that it demonstrated the extent to which Langer became the focal point of an emergent public discourse that revolved around the existence of pornography in a free and democratic society. Furthermore, the editorial reinforced the perception that Langer's rights to freedom of expression were not only disregarded, but utterly annihilated.

The concept of individual rights within a liberal democracy became a paramount concern in Langer's case. This philosophical discourse was best characterized through the arguments presented by the director of the Canadian Civil Liberties Association (CCLA), Alan Borovoy. In an article carried by Canadian Press, Valerie Lawton of the *Toronto Star* quoted Borovoy asking: "'What public interest suffers when you show in a gallery, to adults who wish to go there, drawings that come from the imagination of an artist? It is just absurd for a democratic society to make that a criminal offence.… Genuine art has to be able to depict vice as well as virtue'" (1993a).

Borovoy's characterization of obscenity provisions as paternalistic is characteristic of liberal defences of pornography. That he invoked democratic values further reinforced the perception of censorship as an anti-democratic attempt to legislate morality, a claim that is given more credence through the aptly named Metro Toronto Police "morality squad." Borovoy's insistence that Langer's rights to freedom of expression had been trampled was further evidenced by subsequent articles that discussed the CCLA's petition urging then attorney-general Marion Boyd to drop formal charges against Langer and Brooks. In a letter originally sent to Boyd and subsequently made public, Borovoy argued:

> It is one thing to prohibit the creation of material that involves the deliberate commission of a crime against an actual child, but it is another thing entirely to criminalize material that emanates from an artist's imagination. To treat the latter material as criminal is to imply that exposure to it would be likely to influence someone to commit a criminal assault against a child. (Memon 1994)

Borovoy's arguments challenged scientific studies that attempt to prove a causal link between visual imagery and criminal behaviour. Through invoking such an argument, Borovoy engaged in a debate that has characterized pornography debates for years. What is even more significant about his argument is that he also engaged in a discourse that provided a separate perception of Langer, that of the silenced artist.

THE APPLICATION FOR FORFEITURE

That various organizations entered the public arena to denounce the charges against Langer illustrates the extent to which his arrest signified a touchstone in contemporary pornography debates. On February 25, 1994, Crown attorney Paul Culver announced that formal charges against Eli Langer and Sharon Brooks had been dropped and, instead, the Crown had applied for forfeiture of Langer's art. This action would result in the Crown demonstrating that the works, in and of themselves, were obscene, not that Langer himself was a child pornographer. Essentially, the art itself was put on trial, and if the Crown proved that the artworks were obscene, they could be destroyed. Defending the move to apply for forfeiture, Culver stated:

> This is new legislation, it hasn't been tested, it's novel. We will be seeing a judicial precedent. Everyone involved, the police, and the people who produce art, should have better perspectives after this process is completed.... We just thought that this (forfeiture) was the fairest way to proceed when you have a brand new law. (Zwolinski 1994)

Following the application for forfeiture, the consideration of artistic merit became a primary concern in the public discourse that revolved around Langer. While artists and journalists praised Langer's technical ability even before the charges were laid, the ability to prove the presence of artistic merit became both urgent and necessary. An essential element of the commentary on Langer hinged upon the problem of how to determine artistic merit in light of obscene and offensive imagery. From the outset, Langer's artistic ability was praised by the Mercer Union gallery, by critics who had reviewed the show, and by individuals who had attended the exhibit. Responding to the threat of pornography charges, the Mercer Union gallery released a statement defending Langer and his work:

> Mercer Union understands the origin of the work by Eli Langer to be imaginative, and to be in no way a measure of the acceptability of any implied activity in these works of art. We consider this work to be a serious exploration of the human psyche. Many contemporary artists have investigated sensitive issues and we see Langer contributing to these discussions. (Taylor 1993b)

That the gallery statement clearly placed Langer within an artistic tradition emphasized the belief that his art possessed merit and should be exempt from criminal prosecution. That Langer's technical accomplishments should be self-evident was reflected in a number of articles that compared him to other, more established yet equally controversial artists: "While his art is unusually explicit, Mr. Langer fits into a long tradition of portraying sexual subject matter in art. Critically acclaimed New York artist Eric Fischl has often drawn fire for his sexually charged paintings that have, on occasion, included scenes of masturbation" (Taylor 1993c). Discussing the blanket approach of the legislation in criminalizing the depiction of all types of sexual activity involving youths, Christopher Hume argued: "Under such provisions, Langer isn't the only artist whose work could be illegal. What about Paul Peel's famous painting of two children warming themselves in front of a fireplace after a bath? What about Eric Fischl's pictures of masturbating teens?" (1993). The placing of Eli Langer within an artistic context clearly established that for a large number of artists, journalists, and civil libertarians what was at stake in these debates was the preservation of artistic and aesthetic freedom.

For the editorial staff at the *Globe and Mail*, the protection of artistic expression, no matter how disturbing, is considered essential to the continuance of a rich, cultural heritage. Arguing that the motivations behind such depictions should be immaterial, the paper stated:

> Art, we should know by now, should not be judged by the motives of the artist. It should not matter whether Mr. Langer approves or disapproves of the scenes he depicts, whether or not he meant to condemn child abuse, whether he was making a social comment or an aesthetic one. What should matter is whether his work succeeds as a creative endeavour…. Art does not always uplift or edify. It may also disturb, shock or provoke. (1993c)

This argument was also reflected in the writings of many journalists who relied upon an artistic merit argument to defend Langer's art. Articles that discussed the credentials of the Mercer Union gallery engaged in this debate: "Certainly Langer's beautifully painted canvases could have fooled anyone into believing they were looking at art. So, too, could the venue — Mercer Union, one of Toronto's oldest and most respected artist-run galleries" (Hume 1993). While clearly establishing Langer's talent through the praise of his peers, this article also presumed that because the works appeared in a gallery, they were artistic and not pornographic. This line of reasoning was further reinforced by comments from Keith Kelly, national director of the Canadian Conference of the Arts. Arguing that artistic merit provisions were not considered before the police seized the work, Kelly stated: "If it's a professional artist working in a professional art institution, one can assume there is artistic merit. Why bother going through this lengthy and expensive legal process?" (Taylor 1993c).

Kelly's comments revealed an issue of concern that characterized many of the articles that condemned the police actions. This concern was elaborated upon by Elaine Carol: "The fact that we have to fight to get the work back, to deem it is art, is distressing … this work was shown in a recognized art gallery by a man who is recognized by his peers as an artist" (Zwolinski 1994).

What is surprising about these arguments is the belief that, after receiving complaints that an artist's paintings were child pornography, a truly horrific claim, the police were expected to consider the extent of artistic merit allowances before seizing the work. While this defence is provided within the child pornography legislation, the law itself is constructed in such a way as to render all depictions of youth sexuality illegal. It is imperative to realize that under this legislation, Langer did create child pornography through the depiction of children engaged in "explicit sexual activity." Furthermore, in the eyes of the police, art galleries should be subject to the same restrictions, and this belief was reinforced by Sgt. Robert Matthews who stated: "An art gallery cannot be used as a sanctuary for pornography"

(Jenish 1994, 69). A central concern articulated in these debates, then, is whether to permit the presumption of artistic merit in such cases.

These arguments demonstrate the conflicts over the determination of artistic merit in light of obscene imagery. Central to these conflicts is the prevailing uncertainty over how artistic merit is determined. Relying upon the assumption that artistic merit exists because the paintings and drawings were exhibited in a gallery does nothing to assist in the determination of obscenity. The journalists who actually discussed Langer's art (Kate Taylor and Christopher Hume) labelled it offensive and obscene, yet both foregrounded Langer's artistic ability. Certainly, the real issue in the determination of artistic merit has to be how to address the question of obscenity when a clear distinction between art and obscenity may no longer exist (Adler 1990).

THE FORFEITURE HEARING

The press coverage of Langer's forfeiture hearing enables an analysis of the ideological players that factored into this case. Reports explaining the reasons for the hearing established numerous aspects of the challenge posed to the state through the existence of sexually explicit art. The discussion of defence strategies, testimony presented for both sides, and statements issued by intervenors in the proceedings demonstrated the extent to which Langer's case became a touchstone in the determination of the boundaries of artistic expression.

What was significant about the press coverage of the forfeiture hearing that ran from October 3 to October 15, 1994, was that it allowed coverage of issues that had been ignored in earlier press coverage. It was revealed that a number of organizations had been "granted standing" by the court, which meant that they were permitted to address the court to offer different and diverse interpretations of the "threat" posed by the works under examination. The groups that were expressly involved in the hearing were Canadians for Decency, the Canadian Civil Liberties Association, the Canadian Conference of the Arts, and PEN Canada.

The media discussion of the theoretical arguments presented at the hearing established that the constitutional issues to be resolved involved the clash between the Charter of Rights and Freedom's guarantees of freedom of expression and the right to life, liberty, and the security of the person. Thus, the testimony of a forensic psychiatrist who argued that Langer's paintings were "a type of material that pedophiles use to fantasize and could lead to them acting out their fantasies" (Claridge 1994a) may be understood as arguing that the art poses the threat of real harm to children. Thus, the prosecution relied on the characterization of Langer as child pornographer, or as catering to pedophilic fantasy, in an attempt to demonstrate that sufficient harm existed to warrant the destruction of his paintings.

The arguments presented by the defence not only stressed the necessity to protect freedom of expression, but also challenged the legitimacy of the law in the first place. While the majority of the press coverage of the hearing detailed the testimony of Crown witnesses, the defence strategy was revealed in an article that appeared in the *Globe and Mail*.

> Addario intends to argue that the law violates Langer's constitutional rights in several ways. It authorizes "prior restraint" of free expression by allowing for police to seize materials, with a warrant, before a full hearing or trial is held; it does not give judges enough discretion to refuse such a warrant, if certain conditions are met by police; it violates free-expression protections in Section 2(b) of the Canadian Charter of Rights and Freedoms; and, in forfeiture provisions, it does not expressly provide artistic merit as a defence. (Fine 1994b)

Thus, through the coverage that delineated the arguments presented and strategies proposed, the eventual decision rendered by Judge McCombs would be understood as either championing the safety of children or championing the rights of freedom of expression.

THE JUDICIAL DECISION

The decision of Justice McCombs was the subject of several articles and editorials following the reading of his judgment. He had adjourned the forfeiture hearing declaring that his judgment would be reserved until further notice. Six months later, on April 20, 1995, he rendered his decision and once again sparked interest, debate, and concern over Langer's paintings. His ruling that Langer's art possessed merit and should be returned to him engendered public discussion over artistic freedom and justifiable restraints on freedom of expression.

Reprinting excerpts from Justice McCombs's decision, the *Globe and Mail* emphasized the judge's concern for the protection of children from harm, as well as the protection of freedom of expression:

> [F]or artistic expression to flourish, artists must be free to challenge and, of course, to fail. But, in the end, society's interest in protecting children is paramount, and where the safety of children is concerned, community standards of tolerance based on the risk of harm are more important than freedom of expression, no matter how fundamental that freedom may be to a free and democratic society. (1995b)

Thus, while McCombs essentially found that Langer's art possessed merit and should not be destroyed, his decision also foregrounded the reasonable limits that may be placed on artistic expression.

The *Globe and Mail* heralded McCombs's decision for his careful consideration of the presumption of artistic merit and its role in securing the existence of artistic freedom: "If we are going to pass laws cracking down on pornography, it is vital that artistic expression does not get trampled in the process. Judge McCombs's ruling on the defence of artistic merit does much to prevent such a trampling" (1995a).

The *Globe and Mail*'s proclamation of McCombs's decision as a victory for allowing "artists to take one more small step forward" illustrated the belief that these issues are best resolved in the courts. The analysis offered in the editorial relies on the assumption that judges are the ones most capable of rendering these decisions. Even the argument offered by Langer's lawyer supported the place of the law in the determination of artistic merit. For Addario, the importance of Langer's victory was that it successfully stripped the police of some powers: "'The police can no longer decide on their own that paintings in an art gallery ought to come down while their legality is tested in a courtroom.' Instead, the issue will be decided in court before the art is pulled off the wall" (Lawton 1995a, b).

These analyses are significant because they effectively support the role of the state, either through the police or through the legal system, in determining what images comprise legitimate artistic activity. That Judge McCombs's decision effectively changed nothing in the much hated law was noted by Christopher Hume, who stated: "There's nothing to stop the police from launching another action in the future, albeit with a judge's approval" (1995).

THE SIGNIFICANCE OF "THE ORDEAL OF ELI LANGER"

This analysis was an attempt to discuss the ideological players in the debate on pornography and freedom of expression and the extent to which these various groups provided a continuing commentary on the threat posed by Eli Langer's art. This analysis focused on Langer's art as the central site of various theoretical approaches to this issue. The public response to Langer's art was indicative of a debate concerned with the moral and political health of a nation. The public description of the subject matter of Langer's art crystallized theoretical concerns of the effects of sexually explicit imagery and the need to protect freedom of expression. Central to these debates was the consideration of the extent to which the state should determine the content of visual representations.

While groups such as Canadians for Decency articulated a moralistic opposition to sexually explicit material in general and to Langer's art specifically, civil libertarian groups argued the necessity of preserving freedom of expression at all costs. Central to both discourses was a consideration of the role of the police, the courts, and the state in arbitrating these matters. The media commentary engendered by Langer's legal ordeal represented the public airing of these separate ideologies, and while the coverage roundly denounced the restrictive measures against Langer, it also re-established the need for the state, through the legal system, to decide these issues.

The newspaper coverage of Langer's arrest, forfeiture hearing, and subsequent acquittal presented the image of the state as effectively resolving these issues. That the judgment was greeted with enthusiasm from artists and journalists alike reinforced the legal system as an appropriate site for the determination of issues such as artistic merit, obscenity, and the protection of expression. The media coverage of this case articulated a debate that is the cornerstone of democratic freedom: to what extent does the intervention of the state restrict and threaten the existence of the tolerant society?

Central to this analysis has been an understanding of the state and of print media as sites of ideological conflict in which various groups attempt to define what issues are relevant. The forfeiture hearing, and its resolution in Langer's favour, reinforced the logic behind the legal process. In the final analysis, it must be maintained that the system works: if Langer's art was truly bad, if it lacked sensitivity and merit, or posed an identifiable risk to children, surely it would have been destroyed. That his work endured the scrutiny of the law not only suggests that it deserved protection, but also that the state can and will make the distinction between art and pornography.

ENDNOTE

1. Originally coined by Robert Fulford in an article for *Canadian Art*, the phrase "The Ordeal of Eli Langer" is used in this essay to explain the construction of his case as a media event.

REFERENCES

Adler, Amy M. 1990. "Post-Modern Art and the Death of Obscenity Law." *Yale Law Journal* 99, no. 6 (April).

Bindman, Stephen. 1995a. "Kiddie porn law heads to top court." *Ottawa Citizen,* 17 July.

_____. 1995b. "Kiddie porn law faces challenge." *London Free Press,* 17 July.

Canadian Press. 1993a. "Toronto artist charged with pornography offences: Drawings of children seized after complaints." *Calgary Herald,* 22 December.

_____. 1993b. "Artist claims paintings not kiddie porn." *Calgary Herald*, 23 December.

_____. 1994. "Decision reserved in art hearing: Paintings depict children engaging in sex acts." *Montreal Gazette,* 15 October.

_____. 1995a. "Artists cheer pornography ruling." *Calgary Herald,* 21 April.

_____. 1995b. "Artists hail ruling seized paintings aren't porn." *Winnipeg Free Press,* 21 April.

_____. 1995c. "Ruling will impede police seizures, artists feel." *Vancouver Sun,* 21 April.

_____. 1995d. "Ruling affects police power to seize art from galleries: Judge orders confiscated works returned to artist." *Ottawa Citizen,* 21 April.

_____. 1995e. "High court won't hear challenge to child pornography laws." *London Free Press,* 14 October.

Claridge, Thomas. 1994a. "Langer works compared to materials used by pedophiles." *Globe and Mail,* 5 October.

_____. 1994b. "Judge urged to trash child porn law: Lawyer suggests public burning if Langer works ordered destroyed." *Globe and Mail,* 13 October.

Drainie, Bronwyn. 1994. "How can we tell if 'pornographic' drawings are art?" *Globe and Mail,* 8 January.

Fine, Sean. 1994a. "Porn charges dropped: Crown wants art forfeited." *Globe and Mail,* 25 February.

_____. 1994b. "Hearing first test of porn law's treatment of art: Crown seeks permission to destroy 40 works depicting children." *Globe and Mail,* 3 October.

Fulford, Robert. 1994. "The Ordeal of Eli Langer." *Canadian Art* 11, no. 2 (Summer).

Globe and Mail. 1993a. "New legislation hastily drafted." 22 December.

_____. 1993b. "Art, or pornography?" Editorial, 23 December.

_____. 1993c. "Art is its own defence." Editorial, 31 December.

_____. 1994. "PEN joins Langer protest." 15 January.

_____. 1995a. "What is art?" Editorial, 22 April.

_____. 1995b. "What does the Criminal Code mean by artistic merit?" Excerpts from Judge McCombs's decision, 24 April.

Gooderham, Mary. 1993. "Gallery director charged under child-porn law: Lawyer wonders whether Mercer Union, 13 members of board will be next." *Globe and Mail,* 24 December.

Hume, Christopher. 1993. "Offensive, and porn not always the same thing." *Toronto Star,* 26 December.

_____. 1995. "Art battle has been won, but the war continues." *Toronto Star*, 21 April.

Jenish, D'arcy. 1994. "Sensitive or Obscene?" *Maclean's* 107, no. 4 (24 January).

Lawton, Valerie. 1993a. "Child sex paintings not pornography, artist says." *Vancouver Sun,* 23 December.

_____. 1993b. "My work isn't porn, charged artist says." *Montreal Gazette,* 21 April.

_____. 1995a. "Child-sex-act paintings are art, not pornography: judge." *Montreal Gazette,* 21 April.

_____. 1995b. "Judge orders controversial paintings returned to artist." *Halifax Chronicle-Herald,* 21 April.

Martin, Sandra. 1994. "See No Evil." *Toronto Life* 28, no. 10 (July).

Memon, Farhan. 1994. "Boyd urged to drop child-porn charges: Artist's exhibit legitimate activity, Borovoy says in letter." *Globe and Mail,* 10 January.

Taylor, Kate. 1993a. "Show Breaks Sex Taboo." *Globe and Mail,* 14 December.

_____. 1993b. "Gallery may face porn charges: seized artworks show child sex acts." *Globe and Mail,* 21 December.

_____. 1993c. "Child-porn law used for the first time: Toronto artist charged after police seize five paintings, 35 drawings." *Globe and Mail,* 22 December.

_____. 1993d. "'I'm not a pornographer,' charged artist says: Tough new Criminal Code provisions denounced as being too broadly formed." *Globe and Mail,* 23 December.

_____. 1993e. "Don't shoot the messenger … or arrest the artist." *Globe and Mail,* 24 December.

Tyler, Tracy. 1994a. "Don't prosecute artist, rights group urges." *Toronto Star,* 10 January.

_____. 1994b. "Pedophile patients 'would love' paintings, court told." *Vancouver Sun,* 6 October.

_____. 1994c. "Artistic masterpieces 'threatened' by laws against pornography." *Vancouver Sun,* 13 October.

_____. 1995. "Artists sexual images ruled legal." *Toronto Star,* 21 April.

Valpy, Michael. 1995. "This time artistic freedom is upheld. Next time?" *Globe and Mail,* 21 April.

Wilson, Peter. 1993. "Kiddie porn laws make freedom of speech a tough sell." *Vancouver Sun,* 7 July.

Zwolinski, Mark. 1994. "Artist's porn charges dropped: But his artwork may be destroyed after hearing." *Toronto Star,* 25 February.

SUB-ALTERNET COUNTERPUBLICS

Feminist Interventions into

the Digital Public Sphere

Sheryl Hamilton

INTRODUCTION

In the introduction to their recent edited collection, *Cyberspace, Cyberbodies, Cyberpunk: Cultures of Technological Embodiment*, Mike Featherstone and Roger Burrows claim that the "literature on cyberspace is rapidly becoming a significant element in popular culture" (Featherstone and Burrows 1995, 5). Featherstone and Burrows are correct. This cultural obsession with "things-cyber" can be recognized in film studies and English departments in universities, in computer industry magazines like *Wired*, in popular business management writing (Davidow and Malone 1993), and in the popular media such as *Time*, *Newsweek*, or CBC television's *Undercurrents*. We are surrounded by what Stephen Pfohl describes as "the delirious cyberhyphenation of reality itself" (Pfohl 1997).

Many claims are made for information technologies in these various popular cultural sites, but one of the most prevalent is that concerning their impact upon "public life." For example, Michael Heim claims that

> [c]yberspace supplants physical space. We see this happening already in the familiar cyberspace of on-line communication. When on line, we break free from bodily existence. Telecommunication offers an unrestricted freedom of expression and personal contact, with far less hierarchy and formality than are found in the primary social world. The computer network appears as a godsend in providing forums for people to gather in surprisingly personal proximity without the physical limitations of geography, time zones, or conspicuous social status. (Heim 1993, 99)

Mark Dery suggests that "the upside of incorporeal interaction [is] a technologically enabled, post-multicultural vision of identity disengaged from gender, ethnicity, and other problematic constructions. On line, users can float free of biological and sociocultural determinants" (Dery 1994, 561). Yet another author labels cyberspace "the electronic commons" (Bettig 1997, 139). Cyberspace is discursively constructed as a virtual space where people of all types can gather, interact, converse, and debate, where the differences that mark them in "real life" do not hierarchize their communicative activity. Gunkel and Gunkel recognize that "[b]ecause of this proclaimed emancipation from the pitfalls of embodiment, cyberspace is now offered as the panacea for the perceived deficiencies of contemporary cultural and political organizations" (Gunkel and Gunkel 1997, 130). I agree and suggest more specifically that cyberspace is offered as a digital public sphere, reminiscent of Jurgen Habermas's formulation (1989). Cyberspace is an ideal and idealized space of communicative action. As one negotiates cyberspace, however, it quickly becomes apparent that while the technologies of cyberspace (the Internet, the World Wide Web, and so on) offer some interesting communicative opportunities, the model of a single, digital public sphere is problematic. This article problematizes the single public sphere model offered in popular culture discourses, suggesting that instead cyberspace as it exists in negotiation with various discursive formations — economic, social, political, cultural — generates a number of different spaces in which public communication and struggle take place. This "messiness" of a number of digital public spheres is illustrated by a case study of a women's digital technology intervention group, Studio XX. Through the experiences of this young feminist community group, I ask: What are the possibilities and pitfalls of the digital public sphere?

STUDIO XX

Studio XX (named for the female chromosome) was founded in Montreal in 1995 by a group of artists, activists, and academics for the purpose of addressing concerns around women's exclusion from, and marginalization within, the emerging "information highway," concerns not being adequately addressed in public discourse. The issues focused upon included the following: the continued numerical disparity between men's and women's use of cyberspace; the characterization by public policy makers of technology as "object" only, excluding its consideration as knowledge, practices, or discourses; problematic patterns of gendered online participation, such as flaming within feminist discussion groups or men's attempts to disrupt lesbian chat rooms; the dearth of feminist learning spaces; the lack of representation of women, and of issues of concern to them, in public debates around Internet technologies; and the focus by the public and commercial sectors on promoting these technologies as technologies of training and work, and rarely as technologies of pleasure, play, or politics.

These issues motivated and structured the multiple interventions of Studio XX at the level of art and popular culture, community activism, and feminist pedagogy. The Studio organized, and continues to operate, a number of different activities intended to disrupt existing, and produce alternative, public speech and practices around women and technology. The Studio produces a radio program on CKUT Radio McGill in Montreal called *The XX Files*. The show features a wide variety of interviews with women involved in technology and discussions of current issues; it also offers to the Studio's members the opportunity to broadcast their creative sound projects. The most popular activity hosted by the Studio is its monthly performance forum, *Les Femmes Branches*. Members and guests gather regularly for a two-hour "show and tell" arts salon. Scholars, activists, artists, writers, business women, and others present short creative works of any kind in an informal atmosphere that encourages discussion, exchange, and constructive critique. Presentations have included pirate radio, techno-erotica, cyber-sang (cyber-blood) Web sites, CD ROM demos, reviews of cyberfeminist books, National Film Board films, and more.

Studio XX hosts a fully bilingual Web site, including an online collection of Web art, women's travel adventure tales, essays, rants, book reviews, and links to other sites. Each year the Studio organizes a Web art festival, exploring the WWW as a site for artistic expression and distribution. Volunteer instructors offer affordable technology workshops for women; these range from introductions to specific software to more specific workshops such as "introduction to computers," "how to buy a computer," and "do-it-yourself computer maintenance." Members receive a fully bilingual newsletter updating them on all activities of the Studio as well as related activities of other groups. And finally, the Studio has begun a series of research and community activism projects with the Montreal women's community that explore their potential uses of information technologies.

Studio XX attempts simultaneously to intervene in the public sphere debates around digital technologies and to create alternative cultural sites for virtual and embodied public interaction. Nancy Fraser's still productive analysis, "Rethinking the Public Sphere: A Contribution to the Critique of Actually Existing Democracy" (1989), offers some interesting tools to help us analyse the activities of Studio XX, while also interrogating the single liberal public sphere model that grounds most popular culture representations of cyberspace.

THINKING ABOUT THE DIGITAL PUBLIC SPHERE(S)

At the heart of the notion of the liberal public sphere is a discourse of publicity where a space characterized by accessibility, rationality, and the suspension of hierarchies is produced by citizens. Fraser correctly recognizes that this discourse of publicity is, itself, "deployed as a strategy of distinction" (Fraser 1989, 57). This norm of publicity creates "a space of zero degree culture," or a space "so utterly bereft of any specific ethos as to accommodate with perfect neutrality and equal ease interventions expressive of any and every cultural ethos" (64).

This space of zero degree culture, produced by a norm of publicity, manifests in the discourses of cyberspace. For example, one writer comments, "All the things that separate people, all the supposedly immutable facts of gender and geography, don't matter quite so much when we're all in the machine together" (McRae 1996, 262). Another argues that others in cyberspace "judge you only through your postings, not by what you look like, your marital status, whether you have a disability, or any of the other things that are traditionally used for discrimination" (Anderson 1996, 138).

Fraser argues that there has never been, nor should there be, a single public sphere with the characteristics noted by Habermas and desired by proponents of democratic online culture. Recognizing that history has produced many different publics and that a number of competing publics may well produce more and better democracy, she calls for subaltern "counterpublics," or "parallel discursive arenas where members of subordinated social groups invent and circulate counter-discourses, which in turn permit them to formulate oppositional interpretations of their identities, interests, and needs" (Fraser 1989, 67). She suggests that "[i]n stratified societies, subaltern counterpublics have a dual character. On the one hand, they function as spaces of withdrawal and regroupment; on the other hand, they also function as bases and training grounds for agitational activities directed toward wider publics" (68). Their emancipatory power resides in that difficult dialectic.

I want to borrow this notion to consider Studio XX's attempts to intervene in, and to create, a number of digital public spheres. In considering the Studio as a subaltern counterpublic, I also explore some of the limits of Fraser's model. While Fraser very effectively problematizes the idealized Habermasian model, I suggest that she replaces it with an ideal of her own, a separate and autonomous discourse community not adequately considered in active engagement with other discursive formations. While Studio XX has been reasonably successful, as have been many women's groups, in producing a space of withdrawal and regroupment, it has faced, and continues to face, a number of very difficult challenges as it seeks to direct agitational activities towards the wider public sphere of the culture of information technologies. Studio XX's potential as a counterpublic sphere, a space to produce counter-discourse, is both limited by and produced within its engagements with other discursive formations particular to Canada and to information technology debates in the public sphere. I will examine four of these: information technology discourse, language formations, organizational technologies, and economic formations.

INFORMATION TECHNOLOGY DISCOURSE

One of the central functions of a subaltern counterpublic is the expansion of the discursive arena in response to exclusions within dominant publics. Fraser recognizes a practical limitation on the potential to expand discursive space in the private ownership of the primary means of communication, the mass media. This suggests interesting potential in a medium of communication like the Internet, whose ownership status remains uncertain.

Lack of private ownership alone does not, however, automatically resolve issues of access. For example, dominant public discourse continues to frame access as a material concern: namely, only once everyone has physical access to a modem and computer will democracy increase. Studio XX has found it necessary to define "access" as access not only to technologies, but also to the cultural capital, desire, interest, comfort, and knowledge necessary to participate meaningfully in these media. This expansion of discursive space does not necessarily, nor easily, translate into shifts in dominant public discourse, shifts in policy. Government policy is a social technology to manage the material and the measurable; governments are not equipped, nor do they see it as their role, to intervene in the gendered cultural domain of their citizenry.

Further, information technologies are located in a long-standing binary division between wildly pro- and virulently anti-technology discourses. Ironically, Studio XX has benefited from the positive framing of information technology in dominant public discourse because technologies like the Internet are assumed, a priori, to be economically viable and socially important. While producing instant relevance for the Studio's technology work, this framing also poses limitations to the potential ability to intervene critically. For example, in 1996, when a Studio XX member met with a representative of Industry Canada, she was asked, "Why do you focus on women and technology?" This lack of critically informed contextual knowledge about gender issues in the dominant public realm has to be redressed before a feminist counterpublic can even begin to make interventions in public debates.

The production of effective counter-discourse is further limited by Fraser's characterization of it as necessarily contestatory, in opposition to dominant publics, resulting in an unintended, but necessary, relationship between publicness and contestation. This does not recognize the possibility of a counter-discourse that is alternative, that makes a claim to publicness, but that not always is in response to dominant discourse. This framing as necessarily contestatory leads to a tendency for counter-discourses which are "anti," a risk particularly amplified in the discursive terrain of feminism and information technologies. Finally, Fraser's model also does not contemplate the possibility that dominant discourse is framed in response to existing or anticipated counter-discourses.

LANGUAGE FORMATIONS

The second discursive formation that affects Studio XX's success as a counterpublic (and a key factor in negotiating the Canadian public sphere) is language. Fraser suggests that counter-discourses "elaborat[e] ... alternative norms of public speech" (Fraser 1989, 61). I suggest, however, that Fraser does not adequately recognize that these alternative speech norms have normalizing effects of their own, that they are produced in language and are often politically charged.

Public speech is a complex and thorny issue for Studio XX. The Studio is materially situated within Montreal, which is a French-speaking city (with relatively large English and other language groups and many bi- and multilingual residents), in a French-speaking province, in a bureaucratically bilingual but essentially English-speaking country. Further, Studio XX is virtually situated on the WWW and the Internet, which remain overwhelmingly English-language-dominant media.

Members of subaltern counterpublics must be speaking members. Must they speak the same language? What happens when the language of speech is also a public or political issue? Studio XX has faced, and continues to face, challenges as it tries to negotiate the politics of public speech, both within its own organizational structure, dominated by allophones, and within the allophone colonization of the Internet. Fraser's model is premised on the assumption of the ability to speak, and on an equally valued notion of speech, within the subaltern counterpublic. While multiple languages in a counterpublic do not negate its oppositional potential, they do raise very real challenges. Further, this highlights the potential of dominant norms of public speech within, and not just outside of, counterpublic spheres.

ORGANIZATIONAL TECHNOLOGIES

Organizational technologies offer a third discursive formation relevant to a counterpublic project. Fraser recognizes that public sphere discourse takes place within institutions, which function "as culturally specific rhetorical lenses that filter and alter the utterances they frame; they can accommodate some expressive modes and not others" (Fraser 1989, 69). She further suggests that, in stratified societies, unequally empowered social groups tend to develop unequally valued cultural styles. The result is the development of powerful informal pressures that marginalize the contributions of members of subordinated groups both in everyday life contexts and in official public spheres (64). Thus, in order to have a meaningful impact upon dominant public sphere debates, a subaltern counterpublic must have the mainstream credibility to negotiate the institutional labyrinths of the public sphere and to produce sufficiently valued cultural strategies to have an impact on those official public spheres.

To produce counter-discourses effectively, Studio XX has found it necessary to become incorporated, maintain a physical space, and develop an organizational infrastructure. The discursive formations of organizational structures have a significant impact, however, on the Studio's oppositional potential. The Studio incorporated as a not-for-profit corporation, and to do so, it had to alter its collective structure and name an overt hierarchy (a president, treasurer, vice-president, and so on). While this structure is resisted in daily activities, there are numerous public, institutional contexts where the members so named are called to "perform" those roles. Thus, the members and the organization are disciplined into hierarchical, and indeed corporate, structures of governance.

There is also an increasing imperative within neo-liberal discourses of governance for civil society associations both to take on the responsibilities once shouldered by government and to justify their existence in the public domain through reference to a marketized discourse. Recently, when applying for discretionary funds from the municipal, provincial, and federal levels of government to conclude a research project with low-income women's groups, the Studio emphasized, not the deployment of feminist research strategies, nor the benefits accruing to women's groups, nor the production of feminist knowledge of information technologies, but rather how many jobs this particular project was producing in the relevant electoral district and the kinds of economic activity that could be directly traced from the intervention.

These organizational imperatives, these multiple ways of performing organizational self in different institutional settings, discipline the organization; projects begin to be conceived and framed, first and foremost for their economic, rather than their cultural, social, or political, value.

ECONOMIC FORMATIONS

Fourth and finally, as a subaltern counterpublic in the late 1990s, Studio XX is implicated in, and engaged with, economic formations that delimit and discipline its array of discursive strategies. Fraser defines associational civil society as non-governmental, non-economic, and non-administrative (Fraser 1989, 74–75). While economics may not be the primary function of civil associations, I suggest that Fraser's model does not account sufficiently for counterpublics' messy imbrication within market economies. This is particularly significant for an association like Studio XX, which attempts to intervene in the information technology economy. Notwithstanding a variety of quite creative coping strategies, the Studio, in order to make an intervention in the digital public sphere, must have training and equipment, which usually comes at some considerable cost.

For its first year, the Studio operated solely on self-generated funds. This imposed serious limitations on its ability to carry out its activities and posed hardship on individual members who "bankrolled" the Studio. Generating significant funds from within the membership runs counter to the feminist, low-cost ideology of the organization — members of subaltern counterpublics are usually, by definition, not members of the dominant economic public sphere.

Second, in the present economic climate, the effective generation of funds from the private sector implicates an organization within marketing discourses and practices, and requires considerable start-up resources, an acceptable public profile, and a well-defined market share.

For example, a government charity number would permit the Studio to issue tax receipts to private sector individuals and corporations for donations, reducing its dependence on public funds. However, in Canada, groups serving only women are not eligible for charitable status. To get around this, organizations must set up parallel corporate structures to serve as educational foundations; thus, state and corporate formations combine to normalize certain counterpublics over others.

Further, subaltern counterpublics in Canada, in particular, are in an odd relationship with the dominant public sphere. Fraser suggests a conflictual and implicitly autonomous relationship between dominant and subaltern publics. Unable to meet its original mandate to operate independently of public funds, however, Studio XX has joined the ranks of many Canadian counterpublics funded by the state. What are the implications of being a publicly funded body, specifically constituted to engage with the dominant structures of that public realm?

These tensions are particularly exacerbated in the neo-liberal context of the late 1990s. There has been a perceptible shift in the provision of grant funds towards organizations offering "training," "employment," and "job skills." Governments are also increasingly influenced by a discourse of public accountability. Feminist projects for change and popular cultural interventions do not secure the sympathies of public opinion, and so, again, projects become "for the economic development of women," to "create jobs in the information economy," as opposed to engaging critically with those very discourses. Finally, as a result of severe funding cutbacks in the cultural domain, competition between and among subaltern counterpublics is fierce, a tension that does not enter Fraser's idealistic vision. This pits counterpublics against each other in the struggle to survive, disrupting the potential for linkages and joint action, ultimately weakening the strength of their engagement with dominant public spheres.

CONCLUSION

Gunkel and Gunkel note that "the cyberspatial researchers who forecast and celebrate a utopian community that is 'raceless, genderless, and classless' do so at the expense of those others who are always already excluded from participating in this magnificent technocracy precisely because of their gender, race, and class" (Gunkel and Gunkel 1997, 131). While refreshingly critical of popular discourses of cyberspace, their analysis continues to be anchored in the assumption of the desirability of a singular public sphere, rather than of a model of multiple publics, albeit however differentially valued. Fraser's model of subaltern counterpublics complicates the terrain of negotiation and rejects an "all or nothing" perspective on social and cultural power. Notwithstanding some of the limitations of her model, she correctly identifies the emancipatory power of subaltern counterpublics as existing in the dialectic between their dual identity as a space of regroupment and a space of the production of agitational counter-discourses.

Given the cultural power and ubiquity of the discursive formation of cyberspace, the need for, and power of, counter-discursive interventions must never be undervalued. However, in a number of ways, Studio XX sits, to borrow a phrase from Donna Haraway (1985), in the belly of the monster, continually engaged within a mesh of dominant discourses, institutions, and formations — technological, linguistic, organizational, and economic. It is perhaps in this perpetual process of negotiation with those discursive formations that Studio XX functions most effectively as a digital subaltern counterpublic, working with other subaltern counterpublics for more and better democracy, digital and otherwise.

REFERENCES

Anderson, Judy ("yduJ"). 1996. "Not for the Faint of Heart: Contemplations on Usenet." In *wired_women: gender and new realities in cyberspace,* ed. Lynn Cherny and Elizabeth Reba Weise, 126–38. Seattle: Seal Press.

Bettig, Ronald V. 1997. "The Enclosure of Cyberspace." *Critical Studies in Mass Communication* 14: 138–57.

Davidow, William, and Michael Malone. 1993. *The Virtual Corporation: Structuring and Revitalizing the Corporation for the 21st Century.* New York: HarperBusiness.

Dery, Mark. 1993. "Flame Wars." In *Flame Wars: The Discourse of Cyberculture,* ed. M. Dery, 559–68. Durham: Duke University Press.

Featherstone, Mike, and Roger Burrows. 1995. "Cultures of Technological Embodiment: An Introduction." In *cyberspace, cyberbodies, cyberpunk: Cultures of Technological Embodiment,* 1–19. London: Sage.

Fraser, Nancy. 1989. "Rethinking the Public Sphere: A Contribution to the Critique of Actually Existing Democracy." *Socialist Review* 4: 56–80.

Gunkel, David J., and Ann Hetzel Gunkel. 1997. "Virtual Geographies: The New Worlds of Cyberspace." *Critical Studies in Mass Communications* 14: 123–37.

Habermas, Jurgen. 1989. *The Structural Transformation of the Public Sphere: An Inquiry into a Category of Bourgeois Society.* Cambridge, Mass.: MIT Press.

Haraway, Donna. 1985. "A Cyborg Manifesto: Science, Technology, and Socialist Feminism in the Late Twentieth Century." In *Simians, Cyborgs, and Women: The Reinvention of Nature,* 139–82. New York: Routledge.

Heim, Michael. 1993. *The Metaphysics of Virtual Reality.* New York: Oxford University Press.

McRae, Shannon. 1996. "Coming Apart at the Seams: Sex, Text, and the Virtual Body." In *Wired _Women, Gender and New Realities in Cyberspace,* ed. Lynn Cherny and Elizabeth Reba Weise, 242–63. Seattle, Seal Press.

Pfohl, Stephen. 1997. "The Cybernetic Delirium of Norbert Wiener." *CTHEORY: Theory, Technology and Culture* 20 (nos. 1–2).

C h a p t e r

23

GAYDAR

Bruce Gillespie

"So what do you think of the good father?" asks the bride in a low, conspiratorial tone. I glance over my shoulder at the priest walking towards our table at the rehearsal dinner, taking in his matching linen trousers and vest, ivory-coloured, Chinese collar shirt, and neatly coiffed silver hair.

"Oh yeah," I reply, nodding and taking a swig of my drink.

"Girrl, check out that linen suit!" squeals the emcee from across the table. "Who's he kidding?"

"Sssh! Not in front of my mother!" cries the bride, silencing us. The emcee and I exchange a knowing glance.

"Come on," I say incredulously. "She's *got* to know."

How could she not have known, I asked some straight friends a couple of weeks later, retelling the story. "The pressed linen suit, the rings, and he is a Catholic priest — it's not exactly unheard of! My gaydar was registering off the scale!"

"Your what?" asked one friend.

I was stunned. My friends, who are fairly current on queer issues and lingo, had never heard of gaydar. According to *The Gay Almanac,* it's "the uncanny and seemingly innate ability lesbians and gay men have to recognize and detect one another; drawn obviously from 'gay,' and 'radar.'"[1]

"Is it for real?" one asked.

Of course it's real, I assured her, feeling a bit rebuffed. She had seen me pick out fags at the mall, hadn't she? I, like so many other gay men, take great pride in my accuracy.

"Then how does it work?"

"Oh well, it's kind of ... well, it's something in the eyes, a certain sparkle ..." I found myself sputtering. Now that I was being forced to consider gaydar as a process for the first time, I realized I had no idea how it worked, only that it did and that I had used mine for a long time.

I began asking my friends how their gaydar worked to see if they could provide any insight, but to no avail. They were as perplexed as I was.

A column in the *Advocate,* a leading American queer magazine, only perplexed me more: "Not so many years ago," wrote Brendan Lemon, "deciding whether someone was gay took only a split second: a series of visual cues — his too-tight T-shirt, her razor-short haircut — served as an invariably reliable shorthand."[2] I have a hard time believing this is gaydar, cut and dried. If, in fact, gay men recognize each other using stereotypes, we're depending on the same methods as the high school hockey players to whom every boy with a swishy saunter was a faggot and every girl with an attitude and penchant for phys-ed was a dyke. "Changes in fashion and mannerism help produce radical changes in perception: Not everyone is gay, but everyone could be — at least among the 20-year-olds on the streets of New York." Lemon thinks this is a good thing, that this inscrutability indicates how gays are accepted today in mainstream Western culture.

But he never dismisses the idea that gaydar is the recognition of conventional stereotypes of gay men. Maybe that's what gaydar is for the older crowd, but I don't believe it. Not for the 20-something crowd, at least. Am I no better than so many puck-head tormentors in high school? I had to know.

I put a call through to the Gay, Lesbian, Bisexual, Transgendered Centre at Carleton University in Ottawa. I spoke to Doug Saunders, 26, one of the centre's two coordinators and a former drag queen extraordinaire. He said straight people often ask him to describe why he thinks someone might be gay.

"It's an extra sense that you feel about somebody, impressions about their sexuality, about who they're interested in, who they're attracted to sexually," he said. "It just sort of hits you — it's not something you actively use. It's almost like a vibe."

Saunders said he can determine a man's sexual orientation — 90 per cent accuracy, he boasts — after about 20 minutes of conversation, which gives him time to assess the man's attitudes and reactions. "It's the way they shake my hand, the way they look at certain people, as well," he said. These obvious signs, together with his feeling of a vibe, help him make a good guess. Saunders admitted that he himself could be part of the process.

"I'm very, very out [of the closet] and because I'm so out and so comfortable with my own sexuality, if someone is closeted, they might feel more comfortable around me because they would think, 'OK, he's gay and he's open, but he's still accepted by society.' So they might start exhibiting more signs of being gay and they might hint at it," he said.

Dean Ross agreed when I mentioned this idea to him. Ross, 39, works in the telecommunications industry in Ottawa and has been out of the closet for more than 25 years. He told me about a new staff member in his office and their first encounter. "He just kind of looked at me and then looked away, and I knew right off the bat that here was someone who was obviously gay and did not want to be exposed as being gay and recognizes me," he said. "It all came to me in quick flash."

Ross said mannerisms and attitudes are good tips in figuring out if a man is gay, but "eye contact is more of a confirmation. If you're not sure, then they look at you and there's a responsive recognition factor. I guess in its simplest terms, it takes one to know one," he said. "When you tell someone [a straight], they always say, 'It's the walk, right?' It's nothing like that, it's an aura more than anything."

Auras and vibes. It sounded hard to believe, so I sought out an expert. I tracked down Terry Goldie, an English professor at York University in Toronto, whose field of study is contextual meaning.

We met on a humid August evening as the after-work crowd was just starting to leave Pints, a popular neighbourhood pub in Toronto's gay village. A heavy breeze rolled in the window as I perused the crowd, making eye contact here and there. I gauged it to be a room of gays and lesbians — not a straight person in sight.

"My gaydar is non-existent down here," Goldie admitted, rolling his eyes. He's got a point — straight people are the minority along this stretch of Church Street. But that's not the problem in most situations when he uses his gaydar. "I must admit, I haven't made that many mistakes," he confessed with a wry smile. So what's behind his almost perfect gaydar?

"It's completely eye contact — absolutely." He said he experiences a moment of mutual recognition, the "I-know-that-you-know-that-I-know-that-you-know" moment. It didn't surprise him that some of the gay men I'd talked to chalked up their gaydar to vibes and auras. He said such feelings point to the idea of mutual self-awareness, that, in this case, one gay man is able to identify another because of their similar cultural experiences, and that recognition can be telegraphed through eye contact. Goldie admitted that this sounds hard to believe, but only because eye contact has never played the significant role in white, Western culture that it has in many other cultures.

"You know what it feels like to be in the shoes of a gay person in public," agreed Matt Guerin, 24, in a later interview. Until recently, Guerin worked at the video rental store at the corner of Church and Wellesley Streets in the heart of the village, one of the few places there that is frequented by gays and straights. "It's sometimes easy to recognize similar sensibilities in somebody else," he said.

Saunders said this shared background is definitely part of his process. "[My gaydar] works better with people my own age because I can relate to what they're going through at this stage in their life. I find it much harder to pick out an older gay man than a younger gay man." He can't remember feeling gay vibes from men before he came out of the closet, but "after being in the community for four years, being openly gay has taught me a lot about how to pick someone out."

Guerin said he had a much different experience. "I find my gaydar has really dulled in the last several years. Before I came out I was very good at spotting people I thought were gay. Maybe it's because I have less need to spot gay people in public because I have my own gay life [now]. I'm content in the sense that I know [about myself], with the life that I'm leading and the people in my social situations."

"It's gotten to the point," Guerin said, "where I take people at their word and don't explore. I'm not going to go out of my way to find out what someone is." Still, his gaydar does go off, usually when he spots an attractive man on the street. Guerin said sometimes he can spot fags by their dress — if they are, for example, wearing rainbow pride rings. Otherwise, he said, trying to identify gay men by their clothing or haircuts is shallow and he would not want to be judged that way. "I pride myself on not being stereotypical, and not because I'm internalizing homophobia; I'm just trying to be myself."

Saunders said he does not believe that appearances play much of a role in gaydar. "Oh no," he said with a deep, rumbling laugh. "I have a huge problem with that. I don't agree with that at all. I don't believe it has anything to do with clothing because there is such a wide variety of personalities in the gay community and different attitudes and different communities within the gay community. You've got your construction worker type, your boy next door, your drag queens, you've got your flaming queens …"

He sighed, sounding exasperated. "There's such a wide variety that I can't put it down to different dress or different appearances. I mean, that's ludicrous."

As for me, well, I always thought gaydar had something to do with eye contact. I still can't quite put my finger on what it is about The Look, but it's there. And even if I can't quantify the feeling any more than that, I'm damn sure it has little to do with a tight T-shirt or a short haircut. As Matt Guerin said, if it came down to that, those of us in the jeans and baggy T-shirt crowd might never get a date. For my part, I've decided to take Guerin's advice and take people at their word, like the priest at my friend's wedding. Did he set off my gaydar? Absolutely. Was he gay? Hard to say. But, for the record, I later found out he once dated a friend of mine. A male friend, that is.

ENDNOTES

1. *The Gay Almanac* (New York: Berkley Books, 1996), 88.
2. Brendan Lemon, "Scrambled Gaydar," *Advocate,* no. 739/740 (19 August 1997): 104.

Part

6

BORDER TRANSGRESSIONS AND INTERVENTIONS

INTRODUCTION

In 1994, a small Ontario city became the unlikely site of a series of brutal sex murders. St. Catharines, with a population of 100 000, located on the Niagara Peninsula between Niagara Falls and Toronto, watched with growing alarm as three young females were sadistically tortured and murdered. When the culprits, Paul Bernardo and Karla Homolka, were finally apprehended, the media dubbed them "Barbie and Ken," since their picture-perfect lifestyle gave them a certain resemblance to the famous Mattel dolls. Overall, the case shattered Canada's long-cherished belief that serial murders do not take place in the "peaceable kingdom" (despite the actions of such notorious sociopaths as Clifford Olson), but rather "elsewhere" and usually south of the border. Indeed, the Homolka-Bernardo cases raised crucial questions about nationalism, cross-border interactions, freedom of the press, and Canadian law and its relation to justice.

The reason for the prominence here of Homolka-Bernardo lies not in the criminals themselves, but in the points of debate generated by their ensuing hearings and trials. Banned from Homolka's hearing (the Canadian government had imposed a press blackout until Bernardo's trial), the Canadian public had to turn to U.S. and British coverage of the case to keep informed of what was happening. This media censorship, causing an enforced reliance upon foreign news sources, highlighted critical issues regarding the possibility of maintaining a nation-state in an electronic age. Moreover, the chapters in this section suggest, borders assume new meanings in an ever-shifting global landscape. Priscilla Walton and Michael Dorland examine a "true crime" book that appeared before Bernardo's trial (and thus during the press "blackout") as a means of challenging conventional constructions of "Canada."

193

Rejecting nationalist contentions that Canada is essentially "better" than the United States and arguing instead that it is different (and perhaps preferable), they, and the other authors in this section, reflect on the difficulties raised by boundaries and borders themselves — their meanings, their uses, their practical applications, and their transgressions. Consequently, while Walton and Dorland detail the repercussions of the Bernardo-Homolka murders on a Canadian community and the country in general, "Untangling *Karla's Web*" offers a springboard for explorations of borders and their implications.

Jody Berland, in "Weathering the North," for example, turns to a staple of Canadian identity — weather — and its fundamental relation to the concept of "Canadianness." Complicating the idea of "survival" as a staple of Canadian culture, Berland explores the changes that might ensue should global warming take effect: Will Americans travel to Canada every winter? How will Canadians cope in a climate that is not hostile six to eight months of the year? Such queries and others inform Berland's analysis of the fluctuating boundaries of the Canadian "climate," both physical and cultural.

On a different level, Kevin Dowler uses the 1992 World Series between the Toronto Blue Jays and the Atlanta Braves to dramatize Canada's relations with the United States. Since this was the first World Series to be held outside of the U.S. and because it was marked by such fiascoes as the unfurling of an upside-down Canadian flag at a game in Atlanta, Dowler moves from the baseball series to the larger issues posed by the Canada-U.S. Free Trade Agreement and its subsequent cross-border exchanges.

Appraising the border itself and its relationship to cultural and sexual boundaries, Lisa Pottie critiques the ways in which Canadian identity is predicated on its difference from American identity; at the same time, she analyses the opportunities that exist for Canada because it is a border culture. Crossing borders, Pottie examines the construction of Canadian "queer" identities and how they differ from their American counterparts.

As a whole, this section pushes at traditional conceptions of borders and boundaries, and it discusses the effects of popular interventions in the composition of "Canadianicity." Problematizing the very possibility of nationalism in a post-national age, the following essays investigate the changes apparent and those about to take place in Canadian law, citizenship, and public interactions with the nation-state. Shifts in the cultural landscape, whether through global warming, cross-border transgressions, or the borderless Internet, also create shifts in the way Canadians view themselves and their relations with others. Accordingly, this section confronts the importance of, and the constraints imposed by, national borders and boundaries, and investigates the possibility of their continued maintenance.

UNTANGLING KARLA'S WEB

Post-national Arguments,

Cross-Border Crimes, and

the Investigation of

Canadian Culture

Michael Dorland
Priscilla L. Walton

The abduction, rape, and murder of two Southern Ontario teenagers in 1991 and 1992 occasioned what some have called the most publicized legal case in Canadian history. Charged with the killings of fourteen-year-old Leslie Mahaffy and fifteen-year-old Kristen French were an attractive husband and wife couple, in their twenties, living in St. Catharines, ten miles from Niagara Falls and the Canada-U.S. border. With their conventional good looks and seemingly upscale yuppie lifestyle, Paul Bernardo and Karla Homolka rapidly became the centre of a complicated media and legal imbroglio. Because the police proved unable to gather sufficient evidence to prosecute the couple successfully, the Crown struck a deal with Homolka in return for her testimony against her husband. After a closed hearing, from which the press were either barred or forbidden to report the details at the time, Homolka received a twelve-year prison term in exchange for her agreement to act as the Crown's principal witness against Bernardo. One reason given for the publication blackout of the Homolka hearing was to guarantee Bernardo's right to a fair trial; even so, in a nonetheless electrifying trial, held in Toronto in the spring and summer of 1995, Bernardo was found guilty of the murders and sentenced to two concurrent life terms.

While these details may not appear to differ significantly from similar serial murders and their prosecution, the uproar generated by the Mahaffy-French killings was distinguished by a number of complexities. With American television broadcasting lurid details of a number of recent sensational trials, and television programs like the Fox network's *A Current Affair* impatient for particulars of similar cases, the American press's coverage of the Homolka hearing entailed, besides the details of these sad and sordid cases, their discovery of what appeared to them a particularly repressive judicial system which did not hesitate to violate what Americans understand as their First Amendment rights in the name of a greater public good. In other words, they discovered that Canada is different.

For its part, barred from Homolka's trial, the Canadian public was eager for information on the serial murders that had occurred in their own back yards, something of an anomaly

Originally published in *The American Review of Canadian Studies* (Spring 1996).

for them, accustomed as they were to expect such murders to occur south of the border. Unable to turn to the Canadian press for coverage, reports of which were delayed under the publication ban, the public looked to any available information source, and to whatever rumours were freely circulating. The police's reluctance to provide information on the case simply fuelled the fires of the rumour mill, which included unconfirmed reports of torture, cannibalism, and snuff films, all of which worked to undermine the provincial Attorney General's contention that the publication ban was meant to guarantee fairness for the accused. Instead, particularly in the face of Bernardo's own attorney's opposition to the ban, the public suspected the media censorship was a self-protective measure to conceal the Crown's plea bargain and collusion with Homolka.

With the publication ban still in effect, the Canadian public, or those members who could access alternative information sources, relied on contraband copies of American and British newspapers, illegal satellite reception of American tabloid news programs, and the designated internet news group "alt.fan.karla-homolka," for further information on the case. In December 1994, in a simultaneous convergence of the hunger for information and the season of good will's annual celebration of consumption, a new book appeared in shopping mall bookstores, courting Christmas shoppers. This first book on the case, rushed into print by Viking Canada, bore a purple and yellow cover prominently featuring Karla Homolka's brooding eyes, pouting lips, and enigmatic smile.

It was sealed with a black and yellow band sporting a warning label reading, "Special Blackout Edition," and offered to the public the lure of the forbidden fruit of evidence given at Homolka's manslaughter trial. The warning label pointed out: "A number of passages in this edition of *Karla's Web* have been blacked out to respect the publication ban," but purchasers of this "special edition" were informed that they were entitled to receive "a free copy of the blacked out passages when the ban is lifted"; each book included a postcard to be sent to the publishers for eventual receipt of the censored material.

The author and ban-breaker was not, as some might have assumed, the infamous "console cowboys" of the internet, like the electronic "Abdul," "Lt. Starbuck," or "Neal the Trial Ban Breaker," but rather, the noted Canadian literary critic and Carl F. Klinck Professor of Canadian Literature at the University of Western Ontario, Dr. Frank Davey.[1]

This was not Professor Davey's first venture into the public domain. In 1993, in the context of a federal election campaign, Davey had published *Reading "Kim" Right*, an analysis of the semiotic fields of meaning surrounding newly chosen Progressive Conservative Leader, Conservative British Columbia politician, and Prime Minister, Avril Phaedra "Kim" Campbell. Handpicked to succeed the unpopular Brian Mulroney as Prime Minister, Campbell's sudden emergence into the national spotlight as Canada's first female head of government contrasted sharply with the general public ignorance of the details of her biography and previous political history. Davey's book was a success, fusing as it does cultural analysis with political commentary, and Professor Davey seemed poised to undertake a larger scale analysis of the public events signified by the Bernardo-Homolka case. Thus *Karla's Web*, as its subtitle indicates, promised to be "a cultural investigation of the Mahaffy-French murders." The back cover blurb contends that this is "a uniquely intelligent look … at what the public, media and legal responses to these murders tell us about ourselves and about the future of Canada." Furthermore, *Karla's Web* claimed to raise "timely questions about justice, journalism, and the future of sovereignty in an ever more wired world."

Having paid $28.99 (Canadian), the purchase price of breaking the seal, readers discovered some three hundred pages divided into eight chapters, with such titles as "The

Martyrdom of Virgins," "Muzzled, Shackled, and Gagged," "The Fans of Ken and Barbie," and "At War with the U.S." By page twenty-one, they would learn that St. Catharines, a city that, "through historical accident bears the name of the tutelary saint of nuns and virgins," had become the site of "whispered rumours of betrayal, perversion, torture…." The rest of the sentence was blacked-out. Here and there, throughout subsequent pages, a sentence, part of a sentence, or a single word bore the black marks of censorship. Halfway through the book, the blacked-out passages became heavier, spreading to whole paragraphs and, at points, almost entire pages, including a number of the bibliographic references. Although the author could not reveal those specific details that fell under the publication ban, his book, nonetheless, lured consumers with the idea that it could and did. And with its cover promising information about "assaults, betrayals, [and] media manipulations," *Karla's Web*, in fact, reenacted the very media manipulation it condemned. Indeed, only after paying the purchase price of $28.99 did consumers learn that they had encountered nothing about the case that they did not already know; they also learned the pertinence of the old American adage: "when you pays your money, you takes your chances." Readerly disappointment at being "had" was not necessarily offset by the attendant discovery that what they had, in fact, purchased was a ticket to a High Tory sermon. Concomitantly, and perhaps more to the point, *Karla's Web* provides for an exemplification of the risks involved in using a popular culture form to critique the form of popular culture and the audiences to which it appeals.

The analysis presented in *Karla's Web* centres on the claim that the future of Canadian democratic politics had been seriously compromised, short-circuited by events beyond Canadian control. As a result, an unfortunate, if sordid, regional crime of little inherent significance soon spun out of control to become a site of contestation over the validity of the Canadian legal system and related institutions of legally constituted authority. If the Canadian legal, political, and institutional situation embodies a collective public project whose articulations are fundamentally different from their American equivalents, as encapsulated in the clause from the British North America Act, "peace, order, and good government," what is troubling to Davey is the recent proliferation of cultural actors whose actions can be seen as threatening to that conception of the public sphere. These actors include the Canadian press which, given its corporate structure as a private industry, reflects and reproduces the constant seepage of American norms and conceptions of the constitution of justice, a free press, civil actions, and culture. As a result of the seepage, not only had the Canadian press become Americanized, but the Canadian public as well now suffers from intrinsic misconceptions of what comprises the "public good" in the Canadian context. Thus, from this perspective, the necessity for interventions by public intellectuals is heightened by a sense of social responsibility to point out the "realities" of the Canadian situation and the repercussions that result from ignoring them.

As a student of Canadian history and literature, Davey wishes to remind his readers that the constitution of Canada (in W.P.M. Kennedy's use of the term) antedates the American revolution, to which it was in significant ways a reaction and an alternative conception of community. This meant that legally constituted authority rested upon an unwritten conception of law that was centuries old and embodied in established institutions, against which it was unnecessary to rebel, since they inherently represented the collective "good." In this view, change was a gradual and just process, as such a collectivity was nothing if not adaptable. As Davey puts it: "Rather than a doctrine of individual, gun-bearing liberty, guaranteed by a constitution, Canadians became accustomed to having collective common-law rights protected by centuries-old principles of legal and civil organization" (215).

The argument presented here, if founded on a plausible interpretation of history, is one often articulated by Canada's leading nationalists in the political as well as the scholarly domains. Preoccupation with the United States has been of consuming interest to Canadian scholars, at least since the 1930s. J.W. Dafoe's *Canada: An American Nation* (1935) reanimated latent fears first articulated by Goldwin Smith in the late-nineteenth century as to Canada's "inevitable" absorption by a monolithic North American civilization shaped by environment, culture, and technology. Given this premise, contemporary Canadian nationalism has developed largely within a debate over the degree of autonomy left to Canadian institutions, the influence of the U.S. notwithstanding, in maintaining a certain independence of movement, the location of which autonomy has varied since the 1930s from foreign relations, in interventions by the federal state in economics, in social policy, and in the regulation of Canadian culture. Paradoxically, it was in the 1960s, at a time when interpretative models of Canada-U.S. relations that left Canada with the *least* autonomy assumed almost hegemonic sway, that Canadian actions in the realm of culture (for example, literary criticism) seemed to assume a life of their own. (The literature here is considerable, but see Smith 1891, Dafoe, Underhill, Grant 1965 and 1969, Stewart, and Smith 1994.) In turn, without wanting to overemphasize the monolithic dimensions of Canadian nationalism, we wish to stress the extent to which it is a fundamentally *defensive* view of Canada that constantly puts Canadian institutions in a problematic relation to the development of the signifiers of modernity, such as the spread of a market-driven economy, the growth of consumer society, the development of information technologies, and their reorganization into the cultural industries of collective representation like the press, mass-market publishing, the movies, television, and the "information superhighway." Consequently, throughout much of the twentieth century, Canadian institutions and public intellectuals have reacted, often alarmingly, to contain what was perceived as the negative consequences of these various threats (economic, technological, and cultural) that were invariably attributed to the predations of the United States, and to the detriment of Canada.

In this light, the "cultural investigation" presented in *Karla's Web* highlights the ways in which the above concerns play out in the cultural implications and media constructions of the Mahaffy-French murders, which become indicators of the corrosive impact of creeping Americanization on Canadian institutions. Davey's argument, then, is only one instance of repeated attempts by Canadian nationalists to define Canadian culture, and then to contain it. Hence, Davey functions here as a representative of the predominant themes of Canadian nationalism and its discontents. Canadian nationalism, fixating upon what it perceives as the monolithic external threat to the Canadian economy, polity, or culture as embodied in the United States, has attempted to (re-)produce an equally monolithic system of defences. As a result, a particularly embattled construction of Canada, its politics and its culture, has established itself as the official defender of the orthodoxies that comprise "Canadian" life. It is with the embattled characteristics of these constructions that we take issue, particularly to the extent that they often entail a reduction of the Canadian public sphere to its equivalency to state ideological apparatuses and, in so doing, reduce the possibility of interventions to mere passive acquiescence. Within these reductions, it is scant exaggeration to conclude that one is faced with either loyalty or treason. And given these reductions, the space of Canadian public, institutional, and cultural existence becomes so confined to narrow and official definitions that the slightest dereliction is perceived not only as profoundly threatening to the established state of things but, even worse, as acting at the behest of the external enemy. Agency, in the Canadian context, then, is always perceived to be either governmental, and thus legitimate, or elsewhere, and hence illegitimate and threatening. For us — as a feminist cultural critic and former resident of St. Catharines, and as a communications scholar and former tabloid journalist — it is to the extent that *Karla's Web* so prominently brings these concerns to the fore, at the same time that it highlights the particular class, gender, and ideological assumptions often underlying the nationalist perspective that makes its analysis demanding of further detailed study.

In *Karla's Web*, the external overdetermination of agency is exemplified in the role of the American press in their coverage of the Mahaffy-French murders. Coming to the case with a different history of the spectacularization of crime and the glorification of criminals, in keeping with the image of gun-toting individualism deployed in Davey's account, the American press rapidly took control of the stereotypes by which Bernardo and Homolka would be represented. They functioned as the "picture-perfect couple next door," the incarnation of Ken and Barbie dolls (the products of the multinational — but American-based — Mattel corporation), and the unknown monsters that lurk in the midst of consumer normality. Deflected by the American press hijacking of representations of Homolka-Bernardo and their recycling in the Canadian press, these representations, in *Karla's Web*, become metonymic of American culture in its worst manifestations — with its romanticization of the heroic but self-destructive individual resonant in cultural icons from James Dean, Jim Morrison, and Janis Joplin to Charles Manson, Ted Bundy, and Jeffrey Dahmer. Hence, the main feature of these icons "is the constructed perception of them as simultaneously remarkable and transgressive, and often as remarkable because anti-social and transgressive" (114).

Particularly alarming, in this perspective, are the links forged between the political economy of mass culture, the manufacturing of images of transgression, and the damage to the psychological integrity of the citizen. Notably, here, the psychologically damaged are more often than not implicitly, and, at times, even explicitly, gendered female (112–16). Indeed, it is not accidental that there is a relationship between gender and the spread of consumption in the development of a mass culture, whose feminine composition lends itself to a range of psychological instabilities, most notably as represented by "fandom" (112). In *Karla's Web*, which builds on John Fiske's observations, "fandom is both a sign of powerlessness and a strategy for action and power creation. The fact that fans tend to be female reflects the fact that society does not encourage strong self-images in women, and at worst can create women unconsciously ashamed of their sex" (112). In turn, fandom is but a symptom of the more general cultural phenomenon of our times that Davey terms "the theatricalization of everyday life" (148), in which representations of "reality" are infinitely multiplied by the technologies of mass culture.

In this view, media technology "has this powerful theatrical ability to multiply realities, and in the process to alienate us from the experiential and moral contingencies of our own actions.... It is technology that has helped break down older communal structures of living, and helped create new structures of impersonal, 'fan club' affiliation" (148–50). While, in *Karla's Web*, the implications of the transformation of life into spectacle has widespread implications for understanding the irrationalities of twentieth-century culture, ranging from Nazi Germany to contemporary education, mass culture, and the breakdown of notions of personal identity, it is the consequences for Canada that particularly motivate this cultural investigation of the Homolka-Bernardo case. In media constructions of the couple, it was their seeming "normality" that was the cover for their criminal activities. On one level, Bernardo appeared to be a successful accountant; in "reality," he was an unemployed cigarette smuggler. The "picture-perfect couple" were, in fact, monsters of banality. Davey offers an explanation of this in the relationship between images of "normality" and consumerism:

> To be normal was to acquire a house and a car, to eat doughnuts and fried chicken, drink beer, buy aftershave, and absorb news reports about the weather, the economy, and a prosperous baseball team. In a sense, the "normal" person corresponded to the target readers and viewers of many of the media who were covering the murder story, and to the target audience of their advertisers. Moreover, the designated signs of normality were among the most bland and mass-produced possible: the subdivision house, the small sporty car, chain-store doughnuts and chicken. "Normal" consumerism was not viewed here as in any sense individualized. It did not include gourmet meals, architect-designed homes, or conversations on topics less commonplace than the weather. Instead, "normality" was to be understood as banality. (122)

Consequently, twentieth-century Canadian institutions had attempted, with limited degrees of success, to resist this largely American-defined banalization of "everyday life." As Davey recognizes, Canadian nationalism, if partially driven by a long history of anti-Americanism, has, more importantly, largely been a phenomenon of cultural resistance. It has been "not merely ... an unthinking hostility, but ... a recognition that Canada has represented an alternative way of being North American to that represented by the United States" (226). Thus, the differences and disputes between the two countries have simultaneously taken both economic and cultural forms. For Canadian governments, the overwhelmingly larger scale of the U.S. economy, with its greater capacity for the production of commodities, has made Canada extremely difficult to govern. Part of this difficulty translates into differential business costs, which make the price of Canadian goods and labour higher, to the extent that they include the cost of the social programs to which consumers' tax dollars contribute. Accordingly, individual acts of resistance to higher Canadian taxes and prices, which engender social phenomena, like cross-border shopping, have larger collective cultural ramifications. In a context of the widespread media dissemination of American ideologies of individual rights, Canadians who exercised their "'right' to lower prices" undermined Canada and its social programs when "during the 1989–93 cross-border shopping crisis — possibly in the company of Paul Bernardo — [they exercised those] individual 'rights' to buy and smuggle back from the United States cheaper clothing, cigarettes, food, liquor, and gasoline" (287). Hence, there is a slippery slope separating entrepreneurship from civil dissidence. In *Karla's Web*, the line between seemingly minor acts of civil disobedience and serial murder is a thin one indeed.

For a literary critic who has devoted himself to illuminating the ideological biases of other critics and, in particular, the limitations of their sociological interpretation of Canadian imaginative works, the argument in *Karla's Web* is sharply at odds with Davey's own critical methodology. In perhaps his best-known critical work, *Reading Canadian Reading*, Davey chastises other Canadian scholars for their "idealization of the present moment." As he then reminded his readers, referring to an earlier intervention on his part:

> I wanted to argue that [Canadian criticism] was a narrow and sociological view of literature, one which implied that literary texts were significant mainly as signifiers of pre-existent cultural "themes," which encouraged superficial readings of texts in terms of their explicit themes, and which assumed a unitary view of Canada in which Ontario became privileged as "normal" Canadian experience. I accused thematic criticism of concealing the ideological nature of its own positions (its consumerist concept of reading, its unitary view of the Canadian nation, its Ontariocentrism, its Tory privileging of tradition and continuity) beneath the guise of scholarly "objectivity." (*Reading,* 4)

Canadian critics, Davey contended, "have frequently been blind to the implications of their own approaches" (*Reading,* 5). The sudden myopia apparent in Davey's own argument in

Karla's Web, then, cannot simply be attributed to the critic's inability to analyse ideological positionings; rather, it can be read as symptomatic of the High Culture assumption that Low Culture so lacks sophistication it does not merit rigorous critique. Concomitantly, it exemplifies the inability of the nationalist argument to understand the complexities of the Canadian public sphere.

As a result, the dismissal, in *Karla's Web*, of media-constructed normality as banal because consumeristic elides the social class stratification evident in the privileging of "individualized" signifiers of gourmandizing and architect-designed homes (122) over a lifestyle of doughnuts and take-out chicken. This elision becomes even more apparent in the attack upon the lower classes for their laughable attempts to mimic the social rituals of their "upperclass" counterparts, as embodied in their desire for a "white wedding," wherein for the [lower-class] groom, "this may be the only occasion in his life that he dons a dinner jacket" (125). More tellingly, the discussion in *Karla's Web* of the internet ban-breaking attributes the outbreak of irresponsible and anarchistic acts on the computer network to a shift in the class basis of internet users. Where once, then, 'net users were all "efficient, 'can-do' people" with "advanced degrees, who led comfortable, middle-class lives" (269), the "democratization" (272) of the internet meant that "a co-operative and trusting approach to computer ethics" had now shifted "to many users unfamiliar with the utopian, academic understanding of individual freedom, self-reliance, and self-governance with which it was first associated" (272–73). The theatricalization of life that the media had brought about was now apparent in internet use "particularly among new users who experience the Internet primarily as entertainment" (273); new users could now theatricalize themselves through the invention of pseudonymous identities in "ways difficult in everyday interpersonal contact" (273). In much the same way as cross-border shopping slides into psychopathology, internet use increases the possibility for criminal behaviour ranging from investment fraud to child pornography.

Similarly, the gendered nature of the criticism of mass culture disguises an equivalent hierarchization of culture on gender lines. For example, particularly striking, in *Karla's Web*, is the relationship between the press narrators of the Mahaffy-French story who "almost all … told it as a Gothic story" (55), and the gendered origin of the Gothic genre: "The Gothic story emerged in late eighteenth-century England as a result of … an increase in the number of women novelists; and an increase in the number of educated middle-class women working as teachers, nurses, or governesses in upper-class homes" (55). Women's culture, here, becomes equated with mass culture and its Gothicizing tendency, and *Karla's Web* falls into the conventional trap of feminizing mass culture. The passive consumer of mass culture is the fan, and, significantly here, the fan, as we discussed above, is usually female, be she a member of the Bernardo fan club (110), an internet user of "alt.*fan*.karla-homolka," or the two women the author overhears spreading rumours or, from another perspective, narrativizing the Bernardo case:

> I was browsing in an uptown Toronto men's clothing store, when a woman friend of the sales clerk dropped in to visit. "What do you think of this Homolka stuff?" was among her first questions. For the other woman, the question came almost as a relief, as if she had been overfull of information. "Do you know what I heard that guy did to the French girl?" she responded at once. "He cut off her kneecaps — he just cut them off and left her there bleeding while going on with what he wanted to do to her. Can you imagine?" The woman evidently had done precisely that — she had *imagined*. I found the conversation fascinating at the very least in its demographics. (53–54, original emphasis)

To reiterate Andreas Huyssen's well-known observation, "What especially interests me here is the notion ... that mass culture is somehow associated with woman, while real, authentic culture remains the prerogative of men" (190). Moreover, and as Tania Modleski goes on to argue, "women find themselves at the centre of many historical accounts of mass culture, damned as 'mobs of scribbling women,' in Hawthorne's famous phrase, and held responsible for the debasement of taste and sentimentalisation of culture" (38). An extension of these arguments is apparent in the effort to situate the "origin" of the Homolka-Bernardo "Gothic" in English women writers and Canadian female sales clerks. Without embarking upon a critique of this genderization of mass culture and its devaluation, we would like to point out the connections between the passive consumer construction of the masses and the nationalist construction of Canada, which also resides in that feminine passive space and hence must be protected by cultural nationalists (see Walton and Jones). Their binarized construction of what differentiates "Canada" from "America" excludes alternative points of view and oversimplifies the dimensions of a larger problem (see Beale and Van Den Bosch).

Many other Canadian intellectuals, of which Davey's study is only a more recent version, have over the years attempted to provide an intellectual basis for distinguishing Canada from the United States (see Smith 1994). In attempting to develop a set of social or cultural values that would guarantee Canadian distinctiveness from the U.S., many Canadian nationalists have been convinced that state intervention, direction, and even ownership was fundamental to the entire process. As historian Ramsay Cook pointed out a number of years ago, it "is not merely that the state alone has the resources necessary to finance cultural survival ... it is also that a statist ... approach to culture would in itself be evidence that Canadian culture is different" (16). The limitation of this and similar arguments is that it places the entire burden of the business of distinguishing Canada upon the institutions and agencies of the Canadian state. It follows from this that it is only the state that can provide adequate solutions to public problems, and that the state is always acting in the best interests of the people. It follows as well that any objection to this division of labour emanating from public life is always wrong, and that there are no other possible interventions in the public sphere that are valid. Davey's plea, like that of other Canadian intellectuals before him, is for an ethical vision of social life (Shortt). Yet, this means that the sources of ethical judgment lie in the individual and not in society only.

This is not an option open to Davey, however, to the extent that his studies of Canadian imaginative works only uncover the profound alienation of the individual from the surrounding society. The advent of the post-national state Davey fears is "a state invisible to its own citizens, indistinguishable from its fellows, [and] maintained by invisible political forces" (*Post-National,* 266); this is not so much a new development, as Davey would argue, as it is an invariable condition of "the Canadian imagination" already identified in the Canadian thematic criticism which diagnosed a long-standing absence in the constitution of Canadian society (for example, McGregor). But, that absence has also been theorized as the historical weakness of the development of Canadian civil society (see Dorland). The theory of civil society, first developed by the intellectuals of the Scottish Enlightenment and currently undergoing a resurgence in contemporary political theory in the light of the antinomies of late modernity, postulates "not simply a 'neutral space' of market exchange where already-fully-constituted individuals meet to exchange property and develop commerce, manufacturing, or the arts. It is itself an ethical arena in which the individual is constituted in his individuality through the very act of exchange with others" (Seligman, 28).

In the cultural-nationalist model, predicated on the presumption of some absolute difference between Canada and the U.S., any form of civil objection is all-too-readily perceived as a threat to the government of Canada, to the notion of Canada itself, and hence, can only be American or of American origin. In this view, Canada's relationship to the U.S. reproduces the relations of fandom with its object of simultaneous fascination and repulsion. Significantly, in this Manichean dynamic, all of the agency resides on the American side, to which the Canadian state, outnumbered and besieged, can only react and Canadian society can only perform as a fan.

In this fundamentally passive construction, complicating matters further was the fact that as of the 1980s, abetted by the globalization of the international economy as represented by the Canada-U.S. Free Trade talks, the acceleration of technological innovation in commodity-trading, and the increasing spread of computerization, Canadian strains of populism and the state's ability to contain them were derailed by the importation, disseminated by the Canadian media, of a new individual-rights-based form of populism (in the form of the Reform Party) that not only had won parliamentary seats in the 1993 federal election but had also commanded nearly 35 percent of the popular vote in rural Ontario. The result was a general climate favouring the reduction of regulation over individuals as well as the lowering of regulations over business:

> Because of the high value populism places on the individual, and because of the mythological primacy of the individual and his or her "inalienable rights" in the United States, many of the populist arguments invoked United States examples, or even proposed directly that Canada should more closely resemble the United States. Canadian populism to a large extent widened the ongoing internal "war with the U.S." that has been a continuing part of Canadian politics. (Davey, *Karla* [1994], 285)

Significantly, the outbreaks of civil dispute, which are highlighted in *Karla's Web*, concentrate on those forms of right-wing (individualistic) populism that negate the legitimacy of the Canadian state. But notably absent from Davey's account are the Canadian social formations that have interceded in the public domain to open the construction of Canada for Canadians — the women's movement, Aboriginal rights activism, a social-democratic tradition that has no equivalent in American politics, and the constitutionalization of rights in the 1982 Constitution Act. All of these go unmentioned by Davey. As Robert Lecker has repeatedly argued, Davey's vision of the public role of the critic privatizes the public realm. In other words, the cultural nationalist position ignores those specific developments from within Canadian civil society that, precisely because they are indicators of agency, invalidate the grounds of the nationalist argument. A telling recent example of the difficulty of demarcating the realm of civil society from state actions was provided by the controversy over the so-called "Crusade for Canada," where members of the public converged on Montreal in a seemingly spontaneous appeal for an inclusive Canada that attempted to jump the discursive rails of the confining brinkspersonship of the official political positions on the 1995 Quebec Referendum. The difficulty of determining whether this was a spontaneous manifestation of grassroots populism or a sinister manipulation by federal forces illustrates the problem at hand.

In *Karla's Web*, it is thus striking, but not surprising, that the Canadian press, as a force in civil society, plays only an ignoble role in the construction of the Bernardo-Homolka case since it is seen as "subtly Americanized" and driven by the same commercial considerations and sensationalistic tactics of some of its American counterparts (*Karla* [1995], 349). Despite their erstwhile concern for a democratic politics in the Canadian context, cultural nationalists allow no possibility, except for their own voices, of there being any other actors. Hence, Davey's own work has been criticized because "the audience is given no means of asserting its commonality, particularly [since] the symbol around which this commonality organizes itself — cultural nationalism — is being undercut" (Lecker, 22). This is indeed the peaceable kingdom, since it is inhabited by no one but the cultural nationalists themselves.

With its exclusive preoccupation with the agency of the state, Canadian nationalism has made it virtually impossible for intervention into the public sphere by competing institutions that are not inherently suspect of covert Americanism. As it turned out, the suspicions that the publication ban on the Homolka trial concealed from the public improper actions by juridical bureaucrats were more founded than not. In fact, the discovery, late in 1994, that Bernardo had videotaped the rapes and degradation of his victims, thus making a partial record of his crimes, raised questions (albeit after the fact) as to the propriety of the deal struck with Homolka, since her testimony against him was superseded by the videotape evidence, which, in turn, problematized her version of the events. Similarly, the Canadian press's unsuccessful legal struggle to obtain access to the videotapes was not solely motivated by sensationalist voyeurism or a desire to run pornographic clips on the evening news, but by the belief they would have done their job responsibly, given the history of the press in the Canadian context. Arguably, in light of the proliferation of mass media and new information technologies, and their ramifications for law enforcement and criminal trials, the role of the press as a defender of the public interest and as a watchdog of government has become even more salient.

The ontological and epistemological implications of the ubiquity of amateur videotape as evidence in criminal trials, or as the source of news stories — in short, the "theatricalization of everyday life" — pose enormous problems for juridical procedures, for journalists, and for educators. These are problems that cannot easily be dismissed, but neither can they be left entirely to the discretion of government. To some extent, the full horror of the Homolka-Bernardo case only became apparent with the discovery of the videotapes that had preserved in all their immediacy the torture and degradation of the victims, and offered the possibility of an infinite reenactment of the crimes. In a sense, the videotapes turned everyone — from the immediate participants, to the reporting journalists, to the cultural critics, to the public at large — into audience members of a scene that remains obscene to the extent that all had become willing or unwilling participants in a *larger* notion of publicity. The case and its coverage, therefore, focuses issues regarding the dimensions and articulations of public-ness that remain greater than the specifics of the case itself.

In support of the argument proposed in *Karla's Web*, the development of Canadian institutions alongside those of their neighbour to the south constitutes a unique set of problems. However, Canada's population, rather than comprising some unified semiotic of Canadian nationalism, has never been more than a thin line stretched across the continent. In ways that cultural nationalists have been reluctant to recognize, Canada's is profoundly a border culture, across which interactions, patterns of influence, and exchange have always been more ambiguous and fluid than unmistakably one thing or another. It is no coincidence, here, that the major proponent of the global village thesis was Canadian media theorist Marshall McLuhan. This may mean that Canada, rather than always being the victim of belated modernity, is, in fact, a postnational society distinctly equipped to negotiate the uncertainties of postmodernity and the globalization of cultures and economies (as has also been argued by critics like Hutcheon).

To return to the banalization of everyday life, and the problematics of the doughnut and dinner-jacket culture that trouble *Karla's Web*, the doughnuts this text derides are also the doughnuts on which St. Catharines prides itself as "the capital of the world," and the doughnuts which serve as a signifier of the Canadianism of the hockey player, Tim Horton, for whom the premier (and now American-owned) chain is named. Is the doughnut then necessarily an American or Canadian doughnut? St. Catharines's placement at an intersection of U.S.-Canadian culture renders these questions problematic, since how can one separate the doughnut from its hole? The hole at the centre of the doughnut may be the absence of Canadian culture that the nationalists want to defend, or it may simply be the presence of the Canadian "Timbit." In other words, and to paraphrase W.B. Yeats, one cannot separate the Canadian dancer from the North American dance. Canadian nationalists, whether Robin Mathews, George Grant, or Frank Davey in *Karla's Web*, have attempted to do so, in ways that in the end say more about their own critical and ideological locus than they do about their object of study, which continues to elude their grasp. In this sense, it is perhaps an example of Canadian irony that the most comprehensive account of the Homolka-Bernardo case was that of the two tabloid journalists, Scott Burnside and Alan Cairns, of the *Toronto Sun*, who, contrary to every expectation aroused by their daily journalistic practice, produced a more even-handed explication of the events. It may be significant to recall here, given innumerable laments by Canadian nationalists as to the weakness of Canadian culture, that one of the leading North American supermarket tabloids, *The Globe*, was Canadian in origin and produced in Canada, from where it relentlessly bombarded American consumers with improbable and sensationalistic embellishments of American mass culture. But, like the Hardy Boys Series before it, *The Globe* may constitute the still unwritten story of Canada's little known cultural industries, unwritten because the official nationalistic discourse would never deem to grant it recognition. Quite the opposite of being mere fans, Canadians have not simply been acted upon but have been active participants in the construction of North American mass culture. Again, ironically, it is the margins of "culture," whether the writings of tabloid journalists or the imaginings of female sales clerks, that authorize and enact the very agency whose lack Canadian nationalists bemoan — at the same time that they deny it.

ENDNOTE

1. Since *Karla's Web* appeared, Nick Pron's *Lethal Marriage* (1995), Scott Burnside and Alan Cairns's *Deadly Innocence* (1995), and Stephen Williams's *Invisible Darkness* have been published. *Karla's Web* has also been reissued in paperback, with the blacked-out passages restored (1995).

REFERENCES

Beale, Alison, and Annette Van Den Bosch. *Ghosts in the Machine: Women and Cultural Policy in Canada and Australia*. Toronto: Garamond Press, 1996.

Burnside, Scott, and Alan Cairns. *Deadly Innocence: The True Story of Paul Bernardo, Karla Homolka, and the Schoolgirl Murders*. New York: Warner Books, 1995.

Cook, Ramsay. "Cultural Nationalism in Canada: An Historical Perspective." In *Canadian Cultural Nationalism,* ed. Janine L. Murray, 15–44. New York: New York University Press, 1977.

Dafoe, J.W. *Canada: An American Nation*. New York: Columbia University Press, 1935.

Davey, Frank. *Karla's Web: A Cultural Investigation of the Mahaffy-French Murders*. Toronto: Viking, 1994.

_____. *Karla's Web*. Toronto: Penguin, 1995.

_____. *Post-National Arguments: The Politics of the Anglo-Canadian Novel Since 1967*. Toronto: University of Toronto Press, 1993.

_____. *Reading Canadian Reading*. Winnipeg: Turnstone Press, 1988.

_____. *Reading "Kim" Right*. Vancouver: Talon Books, 1993.

Dorland, Michael. "Cultural Industries and the Canadian Experience: Reflections on the Emergence of a Field." In *The Cultural Industries in Canada: Policies, Problems, and Prospects*, ed. Michael Dorland. Toronto: James Lorimer, 1996.

Grant, George. *Lament for a Nation*. Toronto: McClelland and Stewart, 1965.

_____. *Technology and Empire*. Toronto: Anansi, 1969.

Hutcheon, Linda. *The Canadian Postmodern: A Study of Contemporary English-Canadian Fiction*. Toronto: Oxford University Press, 1988.

Huyssen, Andreas. "Mass Culture as Woman: Modernism's Other." In *Studies in Entertainment: Critical Approaches to Mass Culture*, ed. Tania Modleski, 188–208. Bloomington: Indiana University Press, 1986.

Kennedy, W.P.M. *The Constitution of Canada, 1534–1937*. New York, Russell and Russell, 1922.

Lecker, Robert. "Nobody Gets Hurt Bullfighting Canadian-Style: Rereading Frank Davey's 'Surviving the Paraphrase.'" *Studies in Canadian Literature* 18 (1993): 1–26.

McGregor, Gaile. *The Wacousta Syndrome: Explorations in the Canadian Langscape*. Toronto: University of Toronto Press, 1985.

Modleski, Tania. "Femininity as Mas[s]querade: A Feminist Approach to Mass Culture." In *High Theory/Low Culture: Analysing Popular Television and Film*, ed. Colin MacCabe, 37–52. Manchester: Manchester University Press, 1986.

Pron, Nick. *Lethal Marriage: The Unspeakable Crimes of Paul Bernardo and Karla Homolka*. Toronto: Seal Books, 1995.

Seligman, Adam B. *The Idea of Civil Society*. Princeton: Princeton University Press, 1992.

Shortt, S.E.D. *The Search for an Ideal: Six Canadian Intellectuals and Their Convictions in an Age of Transition, 1890–1930*. Toronto: University of Toronto Press, 1976.

Smith, Allan. *Canada: An American Nation?* Montreal and Kingston: McGill-Queen's University Press, 1994.

Smith, Goldwin. *Canada and the Canadian Question*. Toronto: Hunter Rose, 1891.

Stewart, Gordon T. *The American Response to Canada Since 1776*. East Lansing: Michigan State University Press, 1992.

Underhill, Frank. *In Search of Canadian Liberalism*. Toronto: Macmillan, 1960.

Walton, Priscilla, and Manina Jones. *Detective Agency: Women Re-Writing the Hard-Boiled Tradition*. Berkeley: University of California Press, 1997.

Williams, Stephen. *Invisible Darkness: The Strange Case of Paul Bernardo and Karla Homolka*. Toronto: Little, Brown and Co., 1996.

WEATHERING THE NORTH

Climate, Colonialism,

and the Mediated Body

Jody Berland

> A farmer one cold morning in winter went to his back door to holler for his pigs. It was so cold out that as he yelled his words froze in the air. His pigs didn't come home until his words thawed out in spring — then the pigs heard it.
>
> (Halpert 1976, 183)

> A body becomes a useful force only if it is both a productive body and a subjected body.
>
> (Horne 1986, 82)

WEATHER AND IMPERIALISM: THE NORTHERN DILEMMA

From a Canadian perspective, one can hardly say that the weather is getting worse. A worsening of weather would be constituted by a more intense polarization of seasonal extremes, the summers growing hotter, and the winters colder, which would very quickly become unbearable. But the greenhouse effect should provide us Canadians with singular relief, at least in winter, and at an experiential level, if not in terms of responsible political cognition. Scientists predict that the average annual temperature will rise nearly five degrees in the coming decades, which is almost as much as our present global average temperature has increased since the last Ice Age. The increase will be greater in the north, where our winters will grow shorter, and growing seasons longer. It is pleasant to think about warmer weather, but unpleasant to think about droughts: dry earth, dying animals, dwarfish plants, and other agricultural disasters. This imminent development obviously carries important implications for the collective experience of national culture north of the 49th Parallel.

Weather is the condition that mediates between ourselves, which is to say our bodies, and the vast landscape that (as it is so often claimed) enfolds and defines us as a distinctive

This essay was previously published in Ian Taylor, ed., *Relocating Cultural Studies*, by Routledge in 1993. An earlier version was published in *Provincial Essays*, No. 8: The Post-Colonial Gaze, 1989, Toronto. Thanks to Geoff Miles and Jennifer Oille-Sinclair, editors. It could not have been written without the helpful suggestions and resources offered by a number of people. Thanks to Chris Byford, Michael Dorland, Dennis Murphy, David Thomas, and many students in communications studies at Concordia University.

Canadian culture. In some weird and fundamental way, we *are* our weather. If we have nothing else very tangible in common, our reciprocal recognition as citizens "North of the 49th" is naturalized annually by our shared encounter with our weather. The prospect of radical change in the weather thus challenges the very foundation of our collective material histories: in farming, politics, culture, trade, temperament, and the continental balance of power, it is our geography and weather, or in other words "nature," which have been most often proffered as explanation for our plight. Of course this climatic mediation between us and nature is itself mediated; it is shaped by the everyday practices of our culture, by ritual, economy, technology, and systems of representation; and by the ways that these have been the subject of colonizing transformations by the economic and representational practices of European and American machineries of power. The consequently complex relationship which we have with the weather in turn modifies our daily interactions, our senses, our physiologies, as well as our meteorological conditions, and its cumulative history has produced a colonized morality of the body as well as a polluted sky.

Perhaps it goes without saying that this historical culturation, this shaping of uses and representations of the cold that is our indigenous condition, contains subtle but profound political consequences. Now that weather has been made the subject of overtly political international controversy, perhaps it is more evident that the inverted and repressed significance of Canada's weather presents a key to our past and future. Has weather not been transformed from privileged vehicle to privileged victim by "postindustrial" and "postnational" global imperialism? (In the southern hemisphere, where tropical heat invites more explicit connotation from the point of view of climatically moderate nations of middle Europe and middle America, the active term for this relationship has been "civilization.") Are we not, in Canada, in a privileged position (perhaps increasingly so, however ironic this may seem in the wake of global warming) to trace the history of intermeteorological colonization? For these reasons, coming to terms with the imperialized history and symptomology of our own weather may lead us towards better understanding of the fundamental topographical/meteorological irrationality of Canada's existence. From this reappraisal, a new post–free trade, anti-colonial, post-national collective self-consciousness, even patriotism, must surely derive.

But have the evening TV weather reports said anything about the problematic improvement of the nation's climate? Does our favourite weather person tell us: "Good forecast for you patriots. It will be cold today"? And would it make sense if the weather person did? Will the newspaper's "50 years ago today" column remind us of an earlier golden age of arctic cold, and nudge us into stoic protest against the colonizing intrusion of greater warmth, with its accompanying discourses of pleasure and profit? Or will our comprador bourgeoisie celebrate this climatic change on behalf of its potential fiscal benefits, renegotiating agricultural subsidy and trade agreements with the increasingly impoverished United States, while reiterating familiar platitudes about the manageable price of progress in regard to anticipated problems in more arid zones of the west, and once again ignoring altogether the extra-economic ethics of the nation's destiny? The ongoing construction of temperamental discourse is worth considering. Aside from exposing the foolishness of TV weather people across North America who uncritically celebrate sun in any season, it provides a rarely commented upon illustration of the structural double bind that constitutes Canadianicity, namely, that we are bound together by something constitutionally contradictory at its very core, not just the airwaves, but the air itself, something we love to hate, and nevertheless must hate to lose: our weather. Further, the epistemological and ethical contortions precipitated by the prospect of balmier clime raise specific issues about the social rhetoric and deployment of the body, which mediate and shape our experience of weather; these issues, in my view, uniquely illuminate the historical and contemporary dynamics of Canadian culture as a site of colonization, contradiction, resistance, and fortitude.

But it is not in response to this ecologically induced atmosphere of climatic change and confusion, I would suggest, that Canadians of my acquaintance complain so much more about the weather. Nor is this sensitivity due simply to the ageing process of this same population, which no longer cheers lustily at the invigorating prospect of after school hockey or leisure skating dating in the local park. At first glance, the explanation is simple. It is television. It is not only that TV weather reports offer a simple morality play each day following the news: sun is good, cloud is bad. When was the last time you saw a prairie blizzard on prime-time TV? Of course it never snows in California, people never freeze to death in Florida, and there is never nasty slush in those nameless Ohio or New Hampshire towns that provide the obligingly archetypical setting for soap operas.

Admittedly television is full of such apparently harmless deceptions. Is one idealization the same as any other? From the present vantage point, no. That is, it is not sufficient to critique this particular mediated landscape as *unrealistic*, or purely in pictorial or representational terms, especially since our own visual fictions tend to present an equally idealized pictorial landscape to signify the specificity of our regional horizons. No one believes in realism any more anyway, and the concept has nothing to do with television. Television's effects, in other words, work through and beyond the level of visual symbols; indeed we can see that television has come to represent (its coverage of the weather being exemplary in this respect) a major disciplinary apparatus whose main effect is to supervise the movement, location, ethos, and temperamental tolerance of our physical being while "naturalizing" this supervision as (in the context of the present subject) an act of nature. Thus we are forced to concede that our shivering intolerance of the cold reveals more than the epistemological effect of spectatorial fantasy, that this unpatriotic misery also exposes the explanatory limitations of thinking about televisual mediation in terms of representation at all, at least as representation is ordinarily conceived. For we really are colder, even if the winters are growing milder, and the result of our maladjusted bodies is an enormous, imperceptible, geological shift of our loyalties, our values, our morals, oh yes unto our very beings. That is the point I want to make about the weather.

UNDER COVER

> The foreman came out to give orders on the ranch — it was at the old Bar U. It was 75 degrees below zero. It was so cold, d'you see, that the words froze in his mouth — and so he broke them off and handed them around so the men could get their orders for the day.
>
> (Halpert 1976, 183)

If "everyone talks about the weather, and no one does anything about it," as Mark Twain observed a century ago (Ross 1987, 122), this infantalizing caricature of a quaint pre-industrial folk humour in the face of implacable destiny represents a paradox with particular poignancy in our case, for the relationship of Canadians to weather is very complicated and practically begs for "clinical" analysis. Weather is a privileged facet of indigenous experience, which is to say that Canada has never existed as a cultural or geopolitical entity without it, or independent of its effects. This weather forms the indifferent frame and cosmic limit of the society in which we live. Yet weather is also, at the same time, a site of continuous colonization of representational and technological practice, which is to say that weather has been the product of various cultural and disciplinary practices from the beginning. Thus the most brazenly unruled of all the cyclical processes of "Nature" turns out to be shaped differently by our different imaginations, and now haunts our material symbolic expressions through inversion, distortion, condensation, and absence.

Weather has contributed to the sedimentation of our culture in a dual sense: as a prominently featured part of shared experience in everyday life, and as part of a hierarchically mediated set of observational and scientific discourses woven through and across the everyday. At the intersection of these discourses, we find a web of complexly patterned descriptions of winter, summer, temperature, snow, rain, and drought, inside and outside, opportunity and nuisance, efficiency and disruption, tourism and money, agrarian logic and scenic beauty: ultimately, of the nature of human pleasure and achievement, and of Nature as an environment for pleasure and achievement. These discourses contain and repress the specificity of Canadian experience within the historical context of continuous colonization: in particular, the colonization of indigenous cultures by European settlers, and that of Canadian by American culture, especially since the United States expanded its technological prowess during the Cold War to signal its growing knowledge of weather as both a global and a manipulable phenomenon (Berland 1991; Ross 1987, 119). The result of this history is that our weather is constituted by a set of rituals with conflicting expressive and instrumental functions.

How can anyone appreciate cold, or the particular physical and social architecture of a culture shaped by cold, in a colonized public domain (pre)occupied with the programmatic valorization of business and pleasure? This pleasure, it is important to note, is dependent on the overt elimination of displeasure as its complement, which teaches us that displeasure (as dominantly defined) can never be pleasurable, and also the reverse, thus instructing us continuously in an apoliticizing, narcissistic, and xenophobic construct of pleasure itself. Living as we do in the shadow of the world's most powerful "technocracy of sensuality" (Haug 1986, 45), what could an affection for our natural habitus (outside well regulated episodes of Christmas snowmen, touristic landscapes, and winter skiing) reveal other than a pale, spineless toleration for inferior conditions? How can the indomitable, unpredictable, and anti-disciplinary excesses of winter precipitation be admitted into a public discourse that is so much ordered and enabled (as satellite views remind us daily) by the frame of technological mastery, without appearing to be caught in a pre-modern, pre-adult condition of perverse glee? Thus weather becomes the subject of constant, highly ritualized, usually humorous conversational exchanges in the face of looming discomfort and unjust catastrophe. Such exchanges signal a mature stance of complicit ideological hedonism and often ironic resignation (it is difficult, though not impossible, to be gracefully hedonistic — or ironic — when one is tying up one's boots or digging out one's car) and serve as uncontroversial boundary markers for most social encounters. And yet, on the other hand, how is the rising complaint against the heavens' injustices to be admitted into a public discourse of sociopolitical Otherness organized (as our pre–free trade government assured us) around an anti-hedonist and even stoic collectivist morality in conscious distinction from our southern neighbours? In this context a "realistic" depiction of wintry weather becomes a metonym for the political will for regional self-determination and social justice, as in historical films about prairie life or pre-war socialism, or the current CBC television drama *Street Legal*, whose urban contemporary leftist lawyers have been shown walking Toronto streets in falling snow. This quandary between the valorization of bodily pleasure and efficient consumerism, on the one hand, and anti-American-imperialism social democratic patriotism, on the other, is a tangible if covert contradiction in the ongoing construction of Canadianicity; as a result of the increasing dispersive advantages of the former discourse, and the virtual collapse of the second in the face of consumer commodities, free trade, and an increasingly sheltered personal visual and topological range (with cable and home video), it is becoming almost impossible to survive a winter free from ritual performances of betrayal. Can we detect a symptomology of sublimated guilt?

The pathology of Canada's relationship with weather is revealed at a glance. In the "case" of contemporary urban Canadians, we find that we are obsessed with weather. We talk about it continuously, especially when it is cold. And yet, aside from ritual grumbling, we have no evolved creative, poetic, iconographic, or epistemological language for it, few cherished myths (though many symbolic condensations, like the Mounties, whose endlessly recycled iconographic signification both references and counteracts the uncivilizing, lawless powers of northern winter hinted at so decorously in the inevitable snowy backdrop), no appropriate artifices or reconstructions with which to reclaim it. One of Canada's major painters, Patterson Ewen, did produce a large and beautiful corpus of work whose weather imagery oscillates between pre- and post-technological systems of representation. But the published critical and catalogue essays addressing this work do not mention the subject of the weather once. What can we make of such silences? Our weather occupies a zone of bad conscience, and in the gestures of our public appearances we would much prefer to keep quiet about it. (TV commercials for gas companies do not really count, and even if they did, an intemperate hysteria lurks behind the surface of dependable assurance which talks at you-the-driver through the snow-screened window.)

Only in comedy do we suddenly — almost as a "return of the repressed," you might say — recognize ourselves under the whiteout of a blizzard. Trudging, half-human figures bundled in wraps, obscured backdrops, a demolished and demonic landscape, the sound of spinning tyres, the "snow" on the screen — this is not grandeur, but uncontrollable absurdity. You probably know the enraptured, guilty, relieved laugh that erupts upon seeing it shown like this. Like in the SCTV mock-documentary production *Canadian Conspiracy*, for instance, where Canada is signalled repetitively — appearing suddenly and violently between palm tree'd pool side vistas of California and Florida — by the half invisible Ottawa capital region submerged under still falling snow. You know this is not entirely a friendly image, that this white grotesquery has nothing to do with the white magic that falls from the sky each November and turns us all into children, amenable and transgressive in equal measure, waiting for that supreme powerlessness when snow forces everything to stop and we can stay home without rebuke. You know that your laughter at this extreme depiction is also not entirely friendly, though it is not clear whether it is the snow or the sarcasm that invites your hostility. (Your attitude towards this, as towards the snow itself, depends on what month it arrives in; we have all been badly trained to apply concepts of justice to the sky.) This you prefer not to know, sensing that the issue is important, and revealing, and you do not have to know, because there is no other moment that brings the subject into thought.

Understanding the silence which otherwise occupies Canadian culture in the terrain of weather requires historical, psychoanalytic, semiotic, mythical, and political critique, and demands that these be deployed within a reflexive analytic mode prepared to recognize very complex strategies of repression, inversion, and displacement. Who could otherwise believe that in a mythic landscape dominated by "Nature" such capable forces of repression could have taken our weather (and thus our fortitude) from us? Under such circumstances it is only natural that the indigenous examination of weather (as a discourse, that is, not as a "natural" phenomenon) threatens to be snowed under by the heuristic arsenal.

The historical and analytic fragments that follow will help to clarify our current condition. We begin by returning briefly to the earliest relevant historical context, when the encounter of European colonialists with Canadian weather first found expression.

"AND THUS YOU SEE A STRANGE ABUNDANCE"

Journals of early explorers and missionaries who traversed the north reveal the difficulties of various aspects of their encounters with its strangeness. A Jesuit missionary named Paul le Jeune wrote of "the great trials that must be endured" by those who "cross over the seas, in order to seek and to instruct the Savages" (Thwaites 1959, vol. 7, 35). In a passage entitled "What one must suffer in wintering with the Savages," written in 1634, le Jeune describes the ordeal of navigating between the suffocating smoke and the pitiless cold, between famished dogs and disagreeable foods, compelled all the while to sleep, and drink, and walk plunged to the knees in the snow. This would not have been novel information for his correspondents, as French official circles (by this time thoroughly committed to the establishment of a New France) had already learned of both the severe cold of Canadian winters and the superiority of Amerindian housing in surviving it (Dickason 1984, 241) and maintained a film belief in its beneficial effects upon the health.

Perhaps in light of this, le Jeune averts the suspicion of petulance by writing of having given away the mantle off his shoulders, along with some other available comforts, under the evil and covetous gaze of "the Sorcerer." This powerful member of the community insisted on playing prophet, "amusing these people by a thousand absurdities, which he invented, in my opinion, every day. I did not lose any opportunity of convincing him of their nonsense and childishness, exposing the senselessness of his superstitions." (We do not learn what those superstitions were.) "Now this was like tearing his soul out of his body; for, as he could no longer hunt, he acted the prophet and magician more than ever before, in order to preserve his credit, and to get the dainty pieces" (Thwaites 1959, 571). Clearly this battle was connected with the just allotment of food, but it was conducted most vigorously, if we are to believe le Jeune's account, on the terrain of language, leaving both protagonists very much exasperated.

The language of the Savages was found "full of scarcity" on matters of piety, devotion, virtue; on theology, philosophy, mathematics, "all words which refer to the regulation and government of a city, Province or Empire"; on justice, flowers, punishment, kings, science, and wealth (21). Yet it was quite the reverse in other areas, where richness prevailed: in "the tongue of our Savages," adjectives changed in accord with the different kinds of substantives, thus, as le Jeune complained, yielding entirely different terms for *tabiscau assini*, "the stone is cold," *tacabisisiou nouspouagan*, "my tobacco pipe is cold," *takhisiou khichteman*, "this tobacco is cold" moving to larger objects *siicatchiou attimou*, "this dog is cold" and so on: "and thus you see a strange abundance" which both impressed and depressed the visitors in their attempts to penetrate and influence the Savages.

That Inuit have many words for snow is a commonplace among school children, having provided all of us with an index of that quaint and child-like adaptability to which we attribute their continuing willingness to inhabit its inhospitable terrain. Yet we understand their prolific descriptive resources in the terms of an objective, functional nominalism more or less parallel to our own, rather than in terms of any fundamentally different spirit of naming. Our terms for snow have a purely quantitative and instrumental purpose, which is to prepare us for how successfully we will be able to carry out the day's business, what the sports conditions are, how far its excesses might go in immobilizing us or relieving us from our duties, in extreme situations threatening to turn us into irresponsible citizens (fun-loving, not showing up for work, unable to drive, unless we are urban cowboys driving snowploughs, and mutually caring in the streets) in its own willful image. This instrumental and regulative approach emerged more emphatically with the appearance of broadcast weather reports, when high-tech meteorology was introduced on a mass scale as an indispensable resource for the predictive control of weather. As we will see, the weather forecaster's daily display of technical mastery was committed to the aim of protecting business from the effects of weather's more precipitous excesses. In like vein, our own public, essentially disciplinary discourse subjugates the weather by measuring its nuisance value. Therefore words like "flurry" (do not worry), or "storm" (cause for alarm). Our snow is either visual backdrop (welcomed only before the New Year) or functional condition; it has no independent life. Other ways of "naming" snow represent to our culture a childish inability or refusal to subjugate weather in this manner, as though a technology of everyday life without overt mastery of the elements, or a spirit-deity without central authority over them, is no technology, or deity, at all.

François le Mercier touches on this in 1666–67 in a "relation" entitled "Of the false gods and some superstitious customs of the savages of that country." Here we find one of many instances of that incomprehension with which the white colonizers gazed at their subject "savages." A Father Allouez cited at length by le Mercier asserts that

> [t]hese people are of gross nature, they recognize no purely spiritual divinity, believing that the Sun is a man, and the Moon his wife; that snow and ice are also a man, who goes away in the spring and comes back in the winter …

(Thwaites 1959, vol. 50, 289)

This is a snow without separate authorship, without explicated cause, attributed neither to a technologically displayed mass of cold fronts, as we see now in the northern margins of the south, nor to the vengeance of a god playing god, as Americans do in the south, especially after Easter. This "savage" snow is a snow that tells its own stories.

Our own contemporary narratives offer a conspicuous absence of comparable motifs. This can be attributed, at least in part, to a history of similar encounters between the native cultures and the European colonists, who could neither adopt the languages of the former nor adapt their own to the physical conditions which they encountered. Newly arrived European colonizers of the eighteenth and nineteenth centuries were for the most part unable to describe Canadian winter through the narratives within which they had already invented their presence in the wilderness: Wordsworthian romance, which offered benign landscape, natural beauty, and a luxuriously uncivilized passage of time; and cowboy frontierism, which offered heroic discovery and the occupation of uninhabited space. The encounter between this Romance and the Canadian landscape led to a condition of perceptual and representational repression, as Gaile McGregor (1985) has argued with respect to literature and painting, precipitated by the compelling urge to evoke the landscape, the space, the new natural and social milieu, without being able to confront or accept these in any indigenous terms. The new inhabitants struggled to accommodate their experiences in a language that was both inherited and imposed, a language that could neither articulate the brutality and detachment of this nature, nor celebrate the new ontology of isolation and collective dependency that shaped it-self around it. In response to this crisis, McGregor suggests, colonial culture soon elimi-nated "naturalistic" reference to nature altogether, and only permitted its return when the representational conventions had been properly tamed by American and European land-scape painting and romantic frontier literature.

Yet in other respects, the colonists adapted to the unexpected cold "with incredible ra-pidity, transforming the long four or five months of enforced semi-idleness into a season of indoor conviviality, highlighted by traditional religious and secular feasts" (Anderson 1976, 93). Like those aboriginal predecessors whose complexly structured winter/summer polar-izations of domestic and social life were noted by Mauss in *Seasonal Variations of the Eskimo* (1979 [orig. 1905]), colonial society quickly found its culture marked by radical seasonal difference, with winters providing a time for collective hibernation and ritual, and summers witnessing the physical dispersion of the community across the working land-scape. Among the Europeans, however, a dichotomy between preoccupation and represen-tation made itself evident; this split would achieve fully realized form with the entry of technology into the representational field, by which time, however, such rural rituals were being superseded by the aseasonal technologies of urban life.

SNOW REMOVAL

A tourist inquiring how cold the winter was in Banff, we told him it was so cold last winter that the ice froze in the Upper Hot Springs Swimming Pool. One boy's feet went through the ice, and he got his foot scalded. — Oh, we've lots of stories like that.

(Halpert 1976, 179–80)

The first film crew travelled across Canada on the Canadian Pacific Railway in 1902. Their purpose was to make films to send abroad to encourage emigration. The crew was instructed to show

the premium that western Canada offers for home-making and independence to the man of en-ergy, ambition and small capital; to picture the range cattle, fat and happy, roaming the foothills of the mighty Rockies; to tell the piscatorial enthusiast of cool retreats beside rush-ing streams where the salmon and trout lurk beneath the rock's over hanging shade …

(Berton 1975, 21)

The crew worked under a strict directive from the CPR "not to take any winter scenes under any conditions" (Morris 1978, 34). Canada was already, they felt, too much thought of as a land of ice and snow. The films were premiered in London in 1903, without any white stuff. This was the first, but not the last injunction to Canadian film makers regarding the pro-duction of winterless films.

This doesn't mean that there were no films about Canada with snow in them during the early years of movie history. Quite the opposite was the case! After 1920 Hollywood pro-duced "Northwoods" movies by the hundreds, and they all had snow in them. "In the eyes of the movie going public," Berton writes, "Canada seemed to be covered by a kind of per-petual blanket of white — an unbelievably vast drift that began almost at the border and through which the Big Snow People plodded about like the denizens of Lower Slobbovia" (1975, 25–26). This was obviously a childhood civilization: a landscape in need of con-quest, industry and law. Notwithstanding the thrilling and commercially successful adven-

↳ that's what killed the indicus and the dodo.

tures of Hollywood's top actors in this rural, log-cabin, woodsy, mythical north (the films, Berton notes, were rarely *made* in Canada, but they *connoted* Canada with pine trees, dishevelled French Canadian villains, Mounties, snow, and uninhabited virgin forests), it takes little imagination to understand why Canadian officials were anxious to counteract the uncivilized aura which had thereby attached itself to their winter, which was, we can safely surmise, uncivilized enough already.

Thus, of course, the Mounties, who fulfilled a crucial narrative function in the entry of this uncivilization into spectatorial drama. The battle for law and order can hardly be fought out in the wilderness without some appropriately iconographic representative of the law (and, conversely, of disorder). Hollywood's Mounties were as violently subjected to the symbolic as was the snow that was their inevitable backdrop, which without doubt has contributed to the humorous respect with which we retain them, in our more ironic modern iconography, in that frozen sphere.

Though Hollywood's love affair with the "Northlands" faded away, the anxiety about snow in Canadian film production did not. Restrictions on later film production derived not so much from the incentive to attract emigrants — though the infamous 1947 Canadian Co-operation Project resulted in the practice of inserting small, more or less arbitrary (and presumably snowless) references to Canadian locations in American films as a means to attract tourists, a trade-off for permission to continue Hollywood's suffocating economic control of film production and distribution within Canada — as from the pressure to produce exportable films. That is the only way to make sense of production processes signalled by headlines like "Shebib's Ordeal: Faking California in the snow" (*Globe and Mail,* 18 November 1972), for instance; Shebib put ice into his actors' mouths to eliminate the steam from their breath. Here, as in subsequent cases, the difficulty posed by winter was not so much how to survive the cold as how to disguise it. The pressure to export anti-indigenous images into an already overgrown California landscape is now fully visible in the film and funding policies of the federal government, which have become more depressingly familiar than a spring freeze.

The landscape of Canadian films, as a result, grows more and more picturesque in accord with the scenic conventions of North American pastoral spectatorship and abstractly regional urban nostalgia. Anglo films, including many contemporary feminist features, tend to forefront the local topography but forfeit its fearfulness. The camera pans across the local landscape with a rough affection (perhaps the wheels bounce, or the sound drifts, but the leaves are gloriously green) that is just this side of post-Wordsworthian pastoral convention, and the seasons are never later than a September blush. What remains of the natural milieu is a technicolour panorama fit for tourists, which we become in the momentary drift of sentimental and ostensibly patriotic pleasure. An exception is Bill Forsyth's *Housekeeping* (1987), filmed in British Columbia, in which a woman's unconventional and enormously endearing inability to distinguish between domestic and natural space is depicted in the always significant context of winter snow and spring floods. But its director is Scottish, and its story is "set" in the American northwest, so the related recalcitrance of weather and women can be depicted without evident trauma. Quebec film is a different matter, of course; often enough, as Barrowclough notes in the films of Lefebvre, landscape, seasons, and snow have "become characters in themselves and determining factors in either the depiction of character or event" (Barrowclough 1981, 17). Here snow provides a cinematic frame in a multiple sense: it appears as the content of opening and closing shots; as the central feature of a peculiarly stark, black and white pictorial aesthetic; as the unyielding framework within which space and time, character and action are both measured and obscured. Animating this narrative motif, in other words, once again, is the presence, the naming of snow, not as synecdoche, as referent for some external and sensually intangible physics, deity or power, but as an autonomous entity with its own movements and laws, its own effects in the sphere of character and collective history, its own singularly powerful poetics.

BODY POLITICS

> Only [in the seventeenth century] when [man] relinquished his concept of divine consciousness did he confront the choice of either developing his own and accepting all the moral responsibilities previously dispensated by divinity, or of merging with inconscient nature and enjoying the luxurious irresponsibility of being one of its more complex phenomena. He resolved this problem by the simple expediency of choosing both; the forms of our modern culture are an accurate manifestation of this ambivalence.
>
> (Deren 1980, 98)

We are still waiting for that miracle which, following those other miracles of science that brought us sound floating in space, electricity, two- or three-dimensional images, and flouride, will do something about the weather. This hope is not that dissimilar (first in inventiveness; second in structures of paradox, delusion, and vulnerability to conquest) from the hopes which once attached themselves to national cross-country broadcasting; even in light of the sabotage/betrayal of that enterprise, this desire has not yet confronted its own paradoxical or regressive character, other than through the sardonic humour that designs citywide domes and other devices too close to reality, too far from heaven for true salvation.

In the 1950s, in the climate of Cold War technological prowess previously alluded to, the new technologies of meteorological prediction were the subject of considerable journalistic enthusiasm. *Maclean's*, Canada's national news magazine, started with a gossipy article (Newman 1950) about the daily life of the weatherman. The emergent science of forecasts was headlined as a "crystal ball for profits" in *Saturday Night's* business column (Saltzman 1954); the writer, a popular CBC weather forecaster, points out that weather affects agriculture, logging, oil, employment, airplane travel, consumer sales, advertising, storage, pollution reduction, insurance claims and general litigation. "The point of all this," the writer concludes, "is that the business man, in casting about for help in the more profitable operation of his activities, should glance weatherwards ..." (Saltzman 1954, 29–30). A *Financial Post* report (vol. 51, 30 November 1957) on McGill's "stormy weather group" traces its scientific adventures in searching for appropriate instrumentation for radar photography and for photographing and transmitting "constant altitude" photographs of a 200-mile-radius circle. Broadcast, transport and military uses of such photographs are noted. "Weather," concludes the writer, "can cause great economic losses to many others who do not know before hand what to expect. It can be a source of great monetary gain to those who can understand and anticipate it." By this time, and in response to publicity like this, ex-government meteorologists were making a good living selling short-term weather modification and long-range weather forecasts to businessmen.

But as current climatology texts observe, this claim remains empirically questionable: we do not control weather's interventions in the circulation of commodities through prediction (unless we are farmers), but through architecture, as our enclosure in tunnels and malls — Canada has the largest and probably the most per capita in the world — demonstrates. In addition, despite the development of increasingly masterful satellite and aerial based observational technologies, meteorology (which provides the uncontroversial public-service rationale for such technologies) has encountered definite limits in the realistic temporal range of weather forecasts; what we can see from space is not necessarily commensurate with what we can know, or especially, predict, since weather "systems" still outwit computers. But on the basis of this predictive claim, meteorology joined medicine as "one of the first scientific disciplines ... to develop science-based services for the public" (Hare and Thomas 1974, 159). In this manner — via the ostensibly neutral, technologically beautified vehicle of science — weather entered the official landscape of Canadian culture. If, by the late 1950s, it was finally admissible to *show* the weather, this was because the technologies of satellite observation and weather "system" prediction enabled a rhetoric of management to dominate the subject. Only then could weather be depicted without bringing fear or embarrassment in its wake.

Weather enters official discourse; the children come indoors. Among the Inuit, this was the first change reported as a result of the introduction of television into their community. The children do not play outside any more, they say, and people stop visiting one another.

Or move from the topological to the ontological: like weather reports shielding us from unexpected storms, television shields us from that cognitive insistence on confronting necessity which constitutes the physiological fuel — and, arguably, foundations of an aesthetic — in much frontier or emergent culture. In the metalanguage of most television, credibility is dispersed by excess, and what counts, in an increasingly explicit contract between text and viewer, is the fabulosity of performance. In this domain the only currency is pleasure, and the only pleasant land is green.

This is not vision, not exactly language, something beyond temperament, something which approaches, more fundamentally, an *ethos* of the body. The components of this ethos are decipherable in our contemporary discourses on weather. If pleasure is increasingly the matrix against which experience is assessed, weather is the condition through which we negotiate such experience against the seasonal and cultural vocabulary of a place. Each region has its jokes and prohibitions, its seasonal festivities, its home remedies, its fears and forecasts that have become proverbs over time. These form the ambivalent pleasures of memory and place, of topophilia: the pleasure of the located body. This knowledge has different referents in the city, with television, and daily forecasts, and cars, and supermarkets, and salt in the streets, with time marked by weeks rather than seasons, and the visceral pleasures of beaches and sand at the end of a plane ride.

Beyond this, however, beyond the winter wraps, the clumsy boots at the door, the mess, the predictable aggravation and pointless suffering, and then the spring, and the unreasonable summer heat, there is something not resolvable, something that cannot be mastered or controlled by any individual male subject battling against the elements, something hinted at when we think of the winter deaths of the homeless, the stranded trains, disintegrating pavements, cancelled flights, cancelled classes, the familiar homilies with their certain knowledge that it rains on weekends and will freeze in February till forever.

In information theory, noise is anything which interferes with the intended communication; it is a rude interruption, a word in a foreign language, uninvited sound, crackle over the wires, dirt on the lens. White noise is noise without meaning, the physical fact which justifies the arbitrary categories through which sound enters culture. Good weather (like good children) is always silent. Like light, it forms the inaudible conduit for other information: the sound of birds through an open window, the sparkle of waves, the sun warming the skin, smooth morning traffic. Bad weather is weather that makes itself audible, that introduces noise to the body's interface with nature and the world, that threatens to demolish the discipline of everyday routine with no reason or need to explain. Bad weather is a transgression of silence and a threat to order. There is nothing in the world like the sound of rain. When you hear a cold wind, even on the radio, your spine tingles.

REFERENCES

Anderson, J.A. 1976. "The Early Development of French-Canadian Foodways." In *Folklore of Canada,* ed. E. Fowke. Toronto: McClelland and Stewart.

Barrowclough, S. 1981. "The Films of Jean-Pierre Lefebvre." In *Jean-Pierre Lefebvre: The Quebec Connection*. London: BFI.

Berland, J. 1991. "Reading 'Weather' as Culture." Unpublished manuscript.

Berton, P. 1975. *Hollywood's Canada: The Americanization of Our National Image*. Toronto: McClelland and Stewart.

Deren, M. 1980. "An Anagram of Ideas on Art, Form and Film." In *Cinematographic Apparatus: Selected Writings*, ed. Theresa Hak Kyung Cha. New York: Tanam Press.

Dickason, O.P. 1984. *The Myth of the Savage: And the Beginnings of French Colonialism in the Americas*. Edmonton: University of Alberta Press.

Halpert, H. 1976. "Tall Tales and Other Yarns from Calgary." In *Folklore of Canada*, ed. E. Fowke. Toronto: McClelland and Stewart.

Hare, F.K., and M.K. Thomas.1974. *Climate Canada*. Toronto: Wiley Publishers.

Haug, W.F. 1986. *Critique of Commodity Aesthetics: Appearance, Sexuality and Advertising in Capitalist Society*. Cambridge: Polity Press.

Horne, D. 1986. *The Public Culture: The Triumph of Industrialism*. London: Pluto Press.

McGregor, G. 1985. *The Wacousta Syndrome: Explorations in the Canadian Langscape*. Toronto: University of Toronto Press.

Mauss, M. 1979 [orig. 1905]. *Seasonal Variations of the Eskimo: A Study in Social Morphology*. In collaboration with H. Beauchat, English translation. London: Routledge and Kegan Paul.

Morris, P. 1978. *Embattled Shadows: A History of Canadian Cinema 1895–1939*. Montreal and Kingston: McGill-Queen's University Press.

Newman, P. 1950. "They're Selling Packaged Weather." *Maclean's* 69 (7 January): 33–36.

Ross, A. 1987. "The Work of Nature in the Age of Electronic Emission." *Social Text* 18.

Saltzman, P. 1954. "Crystal Ball for Profits: Ask the Weatherman." *Saturday Night* R. 70 (23 October): 29–30.

Thwaites, R.G., ed. 1959. *The Jesuit Relations and Allied Documents. Travels and Explorations of the Jesuit Missionaries in New France 1610–1791*. Vols. 5, 7, 8, 50, 51. New York: Pageant Book Company.

Chapter

CULTURES, BORDERS, AND FREE TRADE

Kevin Dowler

As Pat O'Brien of CBS exhorted at the beginning of game three of the 1992 World Series between the Toronto Blue Jays and the Atlanta Braves, "Mark this night down, folks; tonight we are all making history together. It's the first World Series game ever played outside the United States."

In a rather ironic twist — at least for Canadians — this was cause for American displeasure and resentment, manifested primarily in the small audiences and poor ratings garnered by the series. Indeed, O'Brien noted that it was "a whole new ball game, as *everything* in this first international World Series is turned upside down."

The allusion to inversion ostensibly referred to the incident that occurred before the beginning of game two, when the Marine honour guard paraded the Canadian flag upside down, an event that, as a result of the subsequent outcry, led to an apology to Canadians from then president George Bush. What this really represented, however, was American resentment over the literal turning upside down of the "normal" world: Americans found themselves having to cope with a moment when the inappropriately named "World Series" actually took on a transnational character, shattering their illusion of America's monopoly over their national sport and over their culture.

This resentment emerged fully in a segment aired during those moments when we were "all making history together." As O'Brien stated in his introduction, "As you might imagine, their [Canadian] customs are a bit different, and who better to chronicle these cultural nuances than our colleague Bill Geist of CBS News." In German, *Geist* means spirit, and it was the spirit of this piece that led to further controversy, as Canadians responded in turn with resentment towards the Americans' display of resentment. The opening shot of Geist's segment shows two children playing catch. As Geist walks into the frame, he states, "It is said that baseball is an American game, yet here on the playing fields of Toronto we see scenes like this, reminding us that baseball has become a sport that knows no boundaries." At this point there is a cut to a close-up of one of the children, which reveals that this game of catch is being played with a hockey puck instead of a ball. Geist then says, "On the other hand, maybe they just don't get it." This is followed by a grimace and a shrug that comes to characterize Geist's reaction to things Canadian encountered throughout the rest of the segment — these include a French-speaking border guard who attempts to seize Geist's foam-rubber Atlanta Braves tomahawk; funny-looking money; and the Queen of England, who is referred to with sarcasm.

After this display, it was a little harder, especially for Canadians, to tell who "didn't get it." Embarrassed by the Canadian reaction, CBS formally apologized during the next game for what it now called a "spoof." "We hope," said O'Brien, "that last night's essay by satirist Bill Geist was taken in a good-natured spirit in which it was intended; that is our hope at CBS." It was, however, precisely our "good-natured spirit" — as Canadians — that had been continually strained during this fall season, as American resentment spilled over into trade and politics with regard to cultural exemptions and NAFTA. After the series had been won by the Toronto Blue Jays, a commentator on PBS's *Inside Washington* — a political affairs program — commented that, though she might be called a xenophobe, she thought baseball was an American game and should only be played in America; she appeared quite upset that the World Series title was in foreign hands.

What is peculiar here is that we normally think of resentment as being reserved for Canadians. As Michael Dorland has written, while Canadians "possess such maturity as not to feel bitterness and resentment on economic questions, they are still capable of feeling particularly vexed on other accounts, such as being rebuffed by the *trade* partner with whom they want to share their future."[1] It is clear, however, as manifested in the American reaction to the World Series, that this vexation operates in *two* directions: both directed towards and coming from the United States. Canadians are continually upset by American insensitivity to difference, and Americans are vexed by the fact that others are not like them.

Confronting differences, of course, is an ordinary experience for Canadians, and it is therefore what sets us apart from Americans. For Americans, it is a special experience, since it challenges their assumptions regarding national culture. As Pierre Bourdieu suggests, "if the extraordinary question" were to arise regarding cultural values that are normally taken for granted, "a special experience would be required, one which would be quite exceptional for a cultured person, even though it would be, on the contrary, quite ordinary for all those who have not had the opportunity to acquire the dispositions which are objectively required" by the culture.[2] Americans, it seems, are accustomed to taking their own experience, to quote Bourdieu again, "as a transhistorical norm for every aesthetic perception."[3] A confrontation with another set of cultural or aesthetic practices — practices that may bring into question unspoken and unexamined universalist, or nationalist, assumptions — destabilizes the structures organized around a shared set of assumptions about what constitutes aesthetic practice or cultural practice. Nationalist and globalist pretensions, present in both popular and modernist aesthetic strategies, clearly exist in a state of tension with local and regional identities and practices, or with more recent turns in aesthetics in which the transnational aesthetic norms of avant-garde modernism have been challenged by so-called local practices. These confrontations are further implicated in the construction of nation. The tensions arising from such confrontations can be seen within Canada itself with regard to constitutional debates concerning the distinctness of Québécois, aboriginal peoples, and others. The various struggles are organized around the idea of culture as a spatial domain, with tensions occurring between region and nation, and between nationalism and internationalism.

Such struggles have, however, been as much a feature of American as of Canadian culture. The tension between regionalism, nationalism, and globalism is problematic for both nations and has by no means been restricted to the sphere of trade and economics, but exists as well in (and is preceded historically by) what can be called an aesthetic economy: the flow of aesthetic ideas and practices across borders. Such tension is also problematic for both levels (if I can put it in such a way) of aesthetic practice and production: that of popular cultural commodities and that of art itself. Art has perhaps had a much longer history of free trade than any other commodity.

The problem of regional identity versus national culture runs through both Canadian and American cultural history, and consists largely of anxiety over the production of a national indigenous culture and its relation to other national cultures, especially those of Europe. There is the sentiment that nationhood can best be legitimized through attempts to develop cultural contributions equivalent to those offered by other nations — a particularly vexing problem for North America, given the arbitrary nature of its spatial construction and the effects of ethnic mixing produced by immigration that militate against the establishment of a cohesive cultural regime. This particular problem emerged against the backdrop of the internationalization of cultural practices, which occurred much earlier than the current trend towards globalization on the economic front. Recent economic developments, however, further exacerbate the residual tension over cultural "parity."

The quest for international parity can be located historically in the attempts to establish indigenous cultural production at the level of the "best" (in a quasi-Arnoldian sense), however that might be defined. In Canada and the United States, cultural production has usually been indexed to, or — in terms of popular cultural practices — against, that of Western Europe. This was true of the United States, as nationalists in the early part of this century sought to legitimize the emergence of American forms of popular culture as America's contribution to world culture, primarily by rejecting European aristocratic standards of aesthetic production.[4] After the Second World War, however, American regionalism and nationalism were rejected as inherently jingoistic and provincial, to be replaced by international forms of modernist abstraction and their cosmopolitan pretensions.[5] The same sort of thing happened in Canada in the 1950s and 1960s with respect to the visual arts: Canada sought to identify itself as an international player in the art world by adopting modernist modes of aesthetic production and effacing regional differences. Similar shifts have occurred recently with regard to popular media and the cultural industries. In Canada, "place" is less and less frequently signified in explicit terms; instead there is the attempt to exhibit concordance with "international" standards of film and television production and to ensure a kind of placelessness as the guarantee of exportability and sales on the international image market.

A tension thus emerges in Canada from the apparent contradiction between the encouragement of a specifically Canadian cultural *industry* and the effacement of its very Canadianness. This is not only the prevailing policy with regard to the funding of popular culture commodities for export, but is also consistent with aesthetic practices as they seek to be identified with international trends in visual art. The idea of a Canadian "vision" in art has always been overshadowed by internationalist perspectives on aesthetic production. For instance, the development of local experimental film and video practices in parts of Canada in the 1970s should be seen within the context of experimental film and media practices that had already emerged in major centres in the United States and Western Europe.[6] This leads directly to the question of the relationship between local, regional, national, and international modes of aesthetic practice and to questions regarding the locus of formations of cultural identity.

A few years ago, Michele Mattelart, taking a slogan from a speech given by a French trade envoy — "Economy and culture, the same thing" — suggested that the "locus of the challenge" lay in recognizing the similarity between the terms economy and culture.[7] I am not sure, however, that these are the same thing. The nation, as Henri Lefebvre points out, is the entity directly concerned with the economy: to come into being, the nation requires both a market and the power to control the resources that enter that market.[8] On that basis, the issue is whether culture can be reduced in such a way as to imply the equation of culture with the state. A difficulty appears when culture is conflated with economy or with nation. For example, as Jody Berland has written, "the Free Trade Agreement ... establishes the legal power of transnational corporations to override policies seeking to defend various political and economic rights of national sovereignty, policies which until now were commonly justified in the name of culture."[9] As the latter part of this comment suggests, the "rights" of economic sovereignty are, and have already been (despite Mattelart), conflated with the notion of cultural determination. This conflation is, in effect, typical of what Ian Angus calls "English Canadian left-nationalism."[10] Berland, who employs Lefebvre in her own arguments, appears to have overlooked his point about the relationship between nation and economy; the idea of protecting national culture is a necessary fiction masking what is really the protection of markets. Those who are critical of the Free Trade Agreement thus appear to commit the same error as those who favour it — they equate culture with economic and political sovereignty. It is not clear, however, that these areas have been, or need be, yoked together in such a mutually determining way. Indeed, this is to overlook that there has been global free trade in aesthetics and cultural practices for a century or more, a trade that has not been implicated in the collapse of forms of national sovereignty.

Which brings us back to baseball. The resentment felt by Americans extends perhaps from the recognition that culture is not a national property and that its active export might result in its appropriation by others: witness, for example, Indian and Pakistani domination in international cricket, Britain's "national" sport. Here, with the international circulation of cultural practices, it becomes difficult to make the case for national ownership. As a nation, a country might be able to "own" an economy (although this is becoming increasingly difficult), but it is not at all clear that this is the case for culture, whether "popular" or otherwise.

I am reminded of a program I have seen on the multilingual television channel in Toronto. Developed by Asian Television Ltd., the show consists of teens dancing and singing to laser disc karaoke recordings of Indian stars performing disco and occasional Bhangra remixes of songs taken mostly from Indian films. The show represents a complex intersection of cultural and economic structures: laser video and television technologies developed in Western Europe, the United States, and Japan; a hybrid of traditional music and dance forms with contemporary American and European dance and music genres; and electronic musical instruments from the United States and Japan. The show represents another intersection as well, that between parents and adolescents on the issue of unsupervised gender mixing at high schools and at Bhangra discos that are organized by South Asian DJs and attended without parental permission.

This particular program cannot be understood merely in terms of nation and culture, especially that of Canada and its culture, since it stands at the intersection point of different nations and cultures, and indeed of generations as well. It brings into question the notions of localism and local practice, and at the same time problematizes further the notion of a relationship between nation-state and culture. The cross-border flow of ideas, practices, and technologies reorganizes the idea of authenticity and problematizes the identification of a genuine local practice. It indicates that a particular aesthetic or cultural formation is not organized around nation as a site, and we must be wary of conflating nation with culture and economic sovereignty, and resist the temptation to organize culture through the idea of nation.

ENDNOTES

1. Michael Dorland, "A Thoroughly Hidden Country: *Ressentiment*, Canadian Nationalism, Canadian Culture," *Canadian Journal of Political and Social Theory* 12, no. 2 (1988): 132.

2. Pierre Bourdieu, "The Historical Genesis of a Pure Aesthetic," *Journal of Aesthetics and Art Criticism* 46 (1987): 202–3.

3. Ibid., 202.

4. See, for example, Van Wyck Brooks, *America's Coming of Age* (New York: B.W. Heubsch, 1915); George Santayana, "The Genteel Tradition in American Philosophy," in *The Genteel Tradition*, ed. D.L. Wilson (Cambridge, Mass.: Harvard University Press, 1967); and Gilbert Seldes, *The Seven Lively Arts* (New York: Harper and Brothers, 1924).

5. See Erika Doss, *Benton, Pollock, and the Politics of Modernism: From Regionalism to Abstract Expressionism* (Chicago: University of Chicago Press, 1991).

6. See, for example, Stan Douglas, ed., *Vancouver Anthology: The Institutional Politics of Art* (Vancouver: Talon Books, 1991); Janine Marchessault, ed., *Mirror Machine: Video and Identity* (Toronto: YYZ, 1995); Peggy Gale and Lisa Steele, eds., *Video re/View: The (best) Source of Critical Writings on Canadian Artists' Video* (Toronto: Art Metropole, 1996).

7. Michele Mattelart, "Can Industrial Culture Be a Culture of Difference: A Reflection on France's Confrontation with the U.S. Model of Serialized Production," in *Marxism and the Interpretation of Culture*, ed. Cary Nelson and Lawrence Grossberg, trans. Stanley Gray and Nelly Mitchell (Urbana: University of Illinois, 1988), 431.

8. Henri Lefebvre, *The Production of Space*, trans. Donald Nicholson-Smith (Oxford: Blackwell, 1991), 112.

9. Jody Berland, "Angels Dancing: Cultural Technologies and the Production of Space," in *Cultural Studies*, ed. Lawrence Grossberg, Cary Nelson, and Paula Treichler (New York: Routledge, 1992), 49.

10. Ian Angus, *A Border Within: National Identity, Cultural Plurality, and Wilderness* (Montreal and Kingston: McGill-Queen's University Press, 1997), 3.

CANADIAN QUEER IDENTITIES

Cross-Border Shopping for

Politics and Fun

Lisa Pottie

On my return from the 1993 March on Washington, I observed to a colleague that the event had seemed to be trying to "normalize" gays and lesbians by focusing on our assumed eagerness to enter the military, since the hot issue that year in the United States media was "gays in the military." It all seemed so American to be obsessed with serving one's country; Canadians are far more suspicious of such patriotic devotion. That same year — 1993 — was also declared the "year of the lesbian" by American mainstream media. Lesbians appeared on the cover of *USA Today, New York, Vanity Fair, Newsweek,* and *Cosmopolitan.* Another normalizing trend was becoming apparent: the media presented us as good consumers, just another niche market to exploit.

As a cynical Canadian lesbian, I was prepared to criticize the American media's temporary and enthusiastic endorsement of lesbians. More generally, I am frequently bewildered and amused by the way Americans seem to yearn to make the news, either by recording it or being it — think how common it is to see Americans with camcorders documenting tragedies on the spot for the news at 11. Nevertheless, lesbians writing in American publications also criticized the coverage in 1993, but with a difference: they seemed to assume that the mainstream media would eventually get it right.

Military and lesbian chic in the media are connected by a phenomenon that has been observed by many lesbian and gay academics since the 1970s: the selling and consumption of lesbian and gay identities within Western market economies. It is, I think, relatively easy and somewhat problematic for me as a Canadian lesbian to criticize the commodification of identities as an American thing. While American ease of access to a huge internal and global market is, I would argue, part of the reason for the hot commodity status of queer theory, Canadian lesbian and gay academics have to sell their work in the same market. As a Canadian whose life is influenced by the omnipresence of exported American ideas and products, I have a vested interest in them; as a Canadian lesbian, I am necessarily an interested consumer of American images and theories of lesbian lives. But recognizing, connecting, and using the different elements of marginal identities in research is not simply for the purpose of selling them: one hopes that the process can also result in a critique that contributes to understanding how those identities are lived.

Leafing through my conference notes for Queer Sites, held at the University of Toronto in May 1993, and for the queer sessions of the Modern Language Association, also held in Toronto in December 1993, or browsing through the library shelves at the University of Toronto or at lesbian-and-gay friendly or -owned bookstores, I have been struck by how few texts refer specifically to Canadian experience. The only sources on lesbian and gay lives are the magazines produced by the community, occasional articles, and historical/sociological books like *Lesbians in Canada*. Moreover, as Steven Maynard points out, "while Canada hosted several of the first international lesbian/gay history conferences and *The Body Politic,* a Canadian lesbian/gay liberation magazine, played a key role in the early development of the lesbian/gay history movement, the international literature has remained largely unaware of work being done in Canada."[1] In American publications, Canadian experience is mentioned most frequently in reference to Canada Customs censorship of imported books and magazines, a worthy issue of course, but one that appeals to Americans as a freedom of speech concern. Canadian lesbian and gay experience is different from American, but how can we describe the texture of our lives? Lesbian chic didn't happen here. "Family values" hasn't arrived yet in a big way as a national obsession, although the Reform Party seems to be catching up. No Canadian government has attempted to enact laws prohibiting "special rights" to lesbians and gays, although in the summer of 1994 the Ontario government did fail to pass legislation protecting our fundamental rights. Lesbians and gays are not targeted quite so obviously as a consumer market — Canada as a whole is a very small market — and the "gays in the military" issue was hardly fussed over at all, as the military quietly amended its regulations. Canadians have been debating multiculturalism for nearly 25 years, ever since Pierre Trudeau got the government out of the bedroom and into our ethnicities, so the role of race and equity legislation is viewed quite differently in Canada. Here's where the Americans might in fact profit from Canadian legislative experience, if they cared to.

The above somewhat haphazard list of distinctions points to the ways that we Canadians have typically defined ourselves: we fall back on the old argument that was used to define the nature of God — by what "he" is not. We think of ourselves, then, as not American and not British, and are able to generalize only about English Canadians' tendency to say "eh." But if Canadians are defined by difference from another, then Canadian lesbians and gays are doubly so: not another nationality, not heterosexual. Such a process of negative definition, identity as deviation from a norm, as a division into subject and other, is precisely what Judith Butler seeks to undermine in her theoretical work on gender and sex.[2] But Canadians do more than define themselves negatively: in the assertion of what we are not lies some assertion of what we are. What usually provokes the Canadian "I am not" assertion is irritation at the perceived American or British assumption of their centrality, and an underlying belief that snobbishness about one's national identity is an indication of insecurity or a sign of immodesty.

The identification of the differences of Canadian lesbians and gays need not result in an assertion of a hegemonic, counterposed identity, but can result in a sense of how differences operate locally. Given the already present Canadian tendency to think of ourselves as Québécois, or Italian-Canadian, or Caribbean-Canadian, it might well be concluded that Canadian identities, including queer ones, are predicated upon the assumption of differences. But working against this argument's inference that Canadians, and Canadian lesbians and gays, are more ready to accept multiplicity and indeterminacy of identities are trends like the Molson Canadian "I am Canadian" advertising campaign, the rallying around the flag that occurred in English Canada during the Quebec referendum of 1995, and events like the Gay Games or Pride Week.[3] In the first two examples, Canadian identity is an aggressive or anxious assertion. In the second two examples, "lesbian and gay" is an international identity that transcends national boundaries. These contradictions coexist because identities are assertions of sameness and difference, and marginalized identities even more so.

Rather than attempt to catalogue an exhaustive list of the processes at work in the lives of Canadian lesbians and gays, I am going to offer examples from three different categories of contemporary experience that affect our lives, to try to convey something of the texture of living this identity. Naturally, there are limitations: while these broad categories may be identified as meaningful in the lives of many lesbians and gays, they may not be universally so, since other factors, such as urban vs. rural experience, age, sex, ethnicity, or identification with a lesbian and gay community, are also at work. The three categories are (1) political movements, (2) the popularization/normalization of marginal and stigmatized identities, and (3) the marketing and commercialization of lesbian and gay identities.

The history of lesbian and gay politics in Canada can be found documented in the Canadian Lesbian and Gay Archives, in films like *Forbidden Love,* and in books like Gary Kinsman's *The Regulation of Desire.* Since the bathhouse raids in Toronto in 1981, which galvanized lesbian and gay politics in that city, resistance and advocacy groups have grown up around the AIDS movement in the 1980s (organizations such as AIDS Action Now!), and there have been lobbying efforts from organizations such as Egale, based in Ottawa, and the Coalition for Lesbian and Gay Rights in Ontario (CLGRO), in Toronto; clearly, a broad-based, multifaceted political scene has developed.

American political movements have inevitably influenced the development of Canadian lesbian and gay politics. Stonewall is commemorated by Lesbian and Gay Pride as the beginning of the modern political movement, since it ushered in an era of activism.[4] That an American date commemorating resistance has been chosen for a Canadian event is one indication of what close ties there are between the political movements of both countries. A more dramatic form of AIDS activism also began in the United States, with ACT UP!, and to some extent its tactics were adopted in Canada, with die-ins and illegal demonstrations. However, the Canadian AIDS movement never did become quite as aggressive as its American counterpart; AIDS Action Now! in Canada pressured the pharmaceutical companies for compassionate release of new drugs and for ethical clinical trials, and lobbied the government for better funding, with success. Similarly, Queer Nation, another dramatic, aggressive political action group, staging events such as kiss-ins in suburban malls and the picketing of restaurants with homophobic employees, existed in Canada as well as in the United States, but was as short-lived in this country as it was in the U.S.[5]

While these examples of Canadian adoptions of American political movements might seem to suggest merely a sort of parallel with Canadian reticence thrown in, it is important to remember that the Canadian political landscape is very different and hence the context in which Canadian political movements occur is equally so. The case of Little Sisters, a bookstore in Vancouver that took Canada Customs to court over the seizure of imported lesbian and gay books and magazines, though of interest to Americans because of the issue of freedom of speech, occurred in a legislative context that is particularly Canadian. Janine Fuller, the bookstore manager, notes:

We have a real see-saw happening.... We have the government waiting for the Justice department to make their decision based on the money that we spend going to court trying to get
the fundamental rights that we as citizens tried to empower these people in government to
consider and put forward on our behalf. On the other hand you also have the Justice department saying it is a legislative matter and up to the government. It is a real grey area and sometimes we fall between the cracks and we certainly would be naïve to think that we don't.[6]

The failure of legislation in Ontario aimed at recognizing same-sex unions is another case
in point. In the United States, lesbians and gays have also lobbied for this recognition; there,
however, the rhetoric of family values and of the preservation of marriage has more impact. The majority of Ontarians were in favour of the legislation, but the bill failed over
the provision for permitting adoption by lesbians and gays. Blame was also assigned to the
ruling NDP for allowing a free vote rather than enforcing party discipline, which turned
the issue into a vote according to one's conscience, a moral issue rather than one of rights
and equality.[7] Since that time, the Ontario provincial court has approved the adoption of
children by the partners of lesbian mothers, and the federal government has been ordered by
the courts to amend all discriminatory legislation that prohibits lesbians and gays from enjoying full rights, particularly as members of couples, while allowing them to defer for a time
the question of sharing of pensions. In other words, while the see-saw between the government and the courts is continuing, change is happening in one forum or another at a speed
well beyond what has been occurring in the American system on the issue of same-sex
spousal benefits and rights. However, Canadian laws on pornography and the power of
Canada Customs have been less easy to undermine.[8]

The question of same-sex spousal benefits raises another issue, that of the popularization
and normalization of lesbian and gay identities. In the United States, lesbians and gays seem
to have colonized (and been colonized by) the mainstream media, from magazines to television. The same phenomenon is not evident in Canada, in part, no doubt, because of our more
limited market and the dominance of the American media. Nevertheless, the trend can be witnessed in other ways: victories over same-sex spousal benefits, suggesting that lesbians and
gays are just like everyone else; the protests from lesbians and gays as well as straights
about all the "weird"-looking people on Pride Day who give them a bad name; "Ellen" parties in Canada to celebrate her coming-out episode. The pressure to conform to an acceptable public image is apparently omnipresent. But normalization is also about limitation:
while lesbian and gay groups such as TCAN, a gay Toronto nudist group, may agree to
abide by the rules for the Pride Parade about public nudity, that does not mean that the
group will cease to exist or that the leather and s/m bars will disappear. Not everyone is interested in becoming "normal." Nor is cultivating a normal appearance any guarantee of
safety from attack on the street or in the workplace.

What distinguishes popularization and normalization in Canada from the United States
is how little attention is actually paid to the issue here. k.d. lang's coming out was accepted
with equanimity; the Alberta government embarrassed itself over its censure of her, not so
much for her being a lesbian, but for her being a vegetarian from a beef-producing province.
While pornography and public sex still command police attention, identity policing in the
Canadian lesbian and gay scene does not occur to the same extent as in the United States. This
last point is the hardest to prove, since it is a matter of lived experience. In lesbian and gay
communities in New York, Detroit, Washington, D.C., Washington State, Oregon, and
throughout California, I felt the pressure to appear normal in all these places, especially as

a lesbian, since long hair seems to be expected of women in all these cities. Nonetheless, my comments here are certainly particular to my own experience; because I live in the largest lesbian and gay community in Canada, I enjoy a freedom from conformity that is not experienced everywhere else.

Neither American, nor Canadian, nor British lesbians and gays are, however, likely to escape an even more encompassing and disturbing trend, commercialization. Commercialization goes hand in hand with normalization, since turning an identity into a lifestyle both normalizes it and makes it amenable to marketing. As Gregory Woods comments:

> Considering that one of capitalism's principal means of inveigling individuals into the cycle of production and consumption is the commercialisation of identity, one has to recognise that there is a seamless logic to the process by which, within a capitalist economy, identity politics likewise become commercialised and commodified. One key example of this must be the way in which London's annual Gay Pride march, a political demonstration, has turned into the Pride Parade, a leisurely walk from a tube station to an outdoor market.[9]

While manufacturers try to sell us cars and condos, we have created our own consumer culture as well: rainbow flags and ornaments, yellow triangles, queer slogan T-shirts, lesbian and gay holiday cruises, and gay-owned businesses of all kinds. Pride Day in Toronto has become one large consumption day, with straight vendors, too, seeing it as an opportunity to cash in. Marketers woo the lesbian and gay community with money to sponsor events, so that they can promote niche products like particular brands of beer or spring water. Even AIDS treatment advertising is subject to the same market forces. As Gregory Woods, again, describes it:

> Nor should it come as a surprise that the tendency of the HIV crisis to generate publicity for just about anything except health care and human rights has led, not only to such opportunistic advertising campaigns as Benetton's notorious use of a photograph of a man "dying of AIDS," but also the commodification of prophylaxis: condom shops, condom ads, condom pouches and pockets, and so on.[10]

A Canadian example depicted here is the Community AIDS Treatment Information Exchange (CATIE) recent promotion for information about new treatments. The ad was sponsored by a number of major pharmaceutical companies, and its images, obviously chosen to reflect diversity, project a dismaying sense of wholesomeness and healthiness given the real experiences of those living with HIV and AIDS.

Commercialization subsumes the first two categories, political movements and popularization, into itself. It is perhaps the most significant trend of contemporary Western lesbian and gay life. The international symbol of the rainbow offers a kind of transnational loyalty to an identity that is in fact experienced very differently in different cultures; however, at the same time, the consumption of explicitly lesbian and gay symbols allows us to project a particular image, to assert our existence as other, or at least as different.

I would argue that Canadian lesbians and gays occupy a space similar to the spaces marketers envision when they create "gay window" ads, that is, those ads "which avoid explicit references to heterosexuality by depicting only one individual or same-sexed individuals within the representational frame," and which then allows advertisers "to reach the homosexual market along with the heterosexual market without ever revealing their aim."[11] Canadian lesbians and gays are interested consumers of American images, products, and ideas. Nevertheless, like the lesbian or gay responding to the gay window ad, we see ourselves only partially or imperfectly reflected in what is offered for our consumption. There will continue to exist a home-grown lesbian and gay political and cultural scene, with political groups of every possible description, innumerable social clubs, from running groups to bowling and baseball leagues, a vital arts scene, with theatre, art, film, and writing, and a rich and lively bar culture. All these things form the texture of a kind of identity that, while still marginal and frequently despised by others, has created a vibrant and civil society, one that would be highly praised by sociologists searching for signs of a popular communal life in North America, if they could only see it. While the diversity of associations created by lesbians and gays may be a legacy of the failure of government and social institutions to support the community, it is also an indication that "lesbian and gay" does not constitute a homogeneous category any more than "heterosexual" does. Individual identities are informed by a multitude of factors, some chosen, some imposed. As Canadians and as Canadian lesbians and gays, we live both within and outside popular culture, shifting between majority and minority viewpoints, among international, national, local, and community levels of identity, assimilating, rejecting, and negotiating the images and commodities of contemporary culture.

ENDNOTES

1. Steven Maynard, "In Search of 'Sodom North,'" 118.
2. See, for example, Judith Butler, *Gender Trouble* and *Bodies That Matter.*
3. Lesbian and Gay Pride Day is an event celebrated by communities across North America and Europe, typically with a parade, a street fair, and entertainment. In Toronto, Pride Day attracts close to one million participants.
4. The Stonewall riot occurred on 28 June 1969, when the police raided a bar called the Stonewall in New York and the drag queens and lesbians resisted arrest. The riot spread throughout Greenwich Village as more and more lesbians and gays joined in, and it lasted for a number of nights.
5. For an interesting firsthand account of Queer Nation actions, see Frank Browning, *The Culture of Desire.*
6. "Queer Experts at the Little Sisters Trial: An Interview with Janine Fuller," 83.
7. The contrast between the highly publicized failure of the bill and the low-key overturning of the military bar in Canada is striking. It points to the differing degrees to which Americans and Canadians view military service as an indicator of citizenship. The two events, however, suggest that in Canada there is an "uneasy tolerance" of homosexuals similar to that in the United States.
8. According to the Supreme Court's Butler decision in 1992, pornography is self-evidently harmful to women. First prosecuted under the new law were an American lesbian sex magazine, *Bad Attitude,* and Little Sisters bookstore in Vancouver, for selling the *Advocate,* an American gay lifestyle magazine.
9. Gregory Woods, "We're Here, We're Queer," 160.
10. Ibid.
11. Danae Clark, "Commodity Lesbianism," 188.

REFERENCES

Browning, Frank. *The Culture of Desire: Paradox and Perversity in Gay Lives Today.* New York: Vintage, 1993.

Butler, Judith. *Bodies That Matter: On the Discursive Limits of "Sex."* New York: Routledge, 1993.

————. *Gender Trouble: Feminism and the Subversion of Identity.* New York: Routledge, 1990.

Clark, Danae. "Commodity Lesbianism." In *The Lesbian and Gay Studies Reader,* ed. Henry Abelove, Michele Aina Barale, and David M. Halperin. London: Routledge, 1993.

Maynard, Steven. "In Search of 'Sodom North': The Writing of Lesbian and Gay History in English Canada, 1970–1990." *Canadian Review of Comparative Literature,* March–June 1994: 117–32.

"Queer Experts at the Little Sisters Trial: An Interview with Janine Fuller." *Canadian Woman Studies* 16, no. 2 (Spring 1996): 80–83.

Woods, Gregory. "We're Here, We're Queer, We're Not Going Catalogue Shopping." In *A Queer Romance: Lesbians, Gay Men and Popular Culture,* ed. Paul Burston and Colin Richardson. London: Routledge, 1995.

Contributors

GAMAL ABDEL-SHEHID is currently completing his Ph.D. in sociology at York University. He works in the areas of sports, blackness, masculinity, and post-colonialism.

JODY BERLAND is associate professor of humanities, Atkinson College; and of social and political thought, music, and environmental studies, York University. She has written numerous articles on the relationships between media technology, popular culture, social space, and the environment. She is the co-editor of *Theory Rules: Art as Theory/Theory and Art* and the editor of *Topia: Canadian Journal of Cultural Studies.*

MICHAEL DORLAND is associate professor in the School of Journalism and Communication at Carleton University. He is the author of *So Close to the State/s: The Emergence of Canadian Feature Film Policy, 1952–1976* and the editor of *The Cultural Industries in Canada: Problems, Policies, and Prospects.*

KEVIN DOWLER teaches communications at York University. He is the author of "The Cultural Industries Policy Apparatus," which appeared in *The Cultural Industries in Canada: Problems, Policies, and Prospects.* He has also written on the development of American television criticism and researched the beginnings of Canadian video policy.

CANDACE FERTILE has a Ph.D. in English literature from the University of Alberta. She wrote her dissertation on the novels of Lawrence Durrell. She now teaches English at the University of Victoria and Camosun College and reviews books for several Canadian newspapers, mainly to support her addiction to reading. And yes, she loves to shop.

DEREK FOSTER is a doctoral candidate in the School of Journalism and Communication at Carleton University. His current research interests revolve around computer-mediated communication and the aesthetics of the interface. His recent writings focus on virtuality as a paradigm for social interactions, both online and off.

ROBERT FULFORD has been writing about the popular arts since the 1950s, when he was the Toronto correspondent for *Down Beat,* the international jazz magazine. He writes a weekly column on books for the *Globe and Mail* and a monthly column about media for *Toronto Life.* His most recent book is *Toronto Discovered.*

GARY GENOSKO writes about sports in the alternative Canadian press. A collection of his columns and articles, titled *Contest: Sports/Politics/Culture,* will be published by Arbeiter Ring (Winnipeg) in spring 1999.

BRUCE GILLESPIE is a former arts editor of the *Charlatan,* Carleton University's independent student newspaper. Now a freelance writer based in Toronto, he writes about the arts, culture, and politics.

SHERYL HAMILTON is a former practising lawyer who is now completing her doctoral studies in the Department of Communication Studies at Concordia University. She teaches in the areas of mass communications, media law, and media and gender. She has published in a number of journals and contributed to the forthcoming book *Wild Science: Feminist Readings in Science, Medicine and the Media*, edited by Kim Sawchuk and Janine Marchessault.

AJAY HEBLE is an associate professor in the School of Literatures and Performance Studies in English, University of Guelph. He has published widely on Canadian literature, post-colonial theory, and cultural theory; he is the author of *The Tumble of Reason: Alice Munro's Discourse of Absence* and a co-editor of *New Contexts of Canadian Criticism*. Heble is the founder and artistic director of the Guelph Jazz Festival.

MANINA JONES, an associate professor in the Department of English at the University of Western Ontario, specializes in Canadian literature. She is the author of *That Art of Difference: 'Documentary-Collage' and English-Canadian Writing* and co-author, with Priscilla L. Walton, of *Detective Agency: Women Re-Writing the Hard-Boiled Tradition*, as well as articles on detective fiction and Canadian poetry, fiction, and drama.

ANNE-MARIE KINAHAN is a doctoral candidate in the School of Journalism and Communication at Carleton University. Her research interests include pornography, the history of obscenity, the history of women's movements, and feminist cultural theory. Her contribution to this volume is an expanded version of a paper presented at the Canadian Communication Association.

ASPASIA KOTSOPOULOS has worked on a number of cultural publications as a writer, editor, and publisher. She is enrolled in the doctoral program in communications at Simon Fraser University.

MILES KRONBY is a writer and Web developer from Toronto who now lives in New York City. His articles have appeared in *Shift, Saturday Night,* and the *Globe and Mail.* He has developed Internet projects for Microsoft, the *New York Times,* and Conde Nast, and is the creator of SecretAdmirer.com.

TOM McSORLEY is executive director of the Canadian Film Institute in Ottawa. He is also a sessional lecturer in film studies at Carleton University, a freelance theatre and television critic for CBC Radio One, and a contributing editor for *Take One,* Canada's national film magazine. In his spare time, he plays a lot of hockey.

SHIRLEY ANNE OFF holds a master of arts degree from Carleton University's School of Journalism and Communication. There, she specialized in critical feminist cultural studies. In addition to working as a communications officer for Indian and Northern Affairs Canada in Ottawa, Off is the coordinator of Planned Parenthood's Insight Theatre, a popular theatre program designed by, for, and about youth.

LISA POTTIE has a Ph.D. in English literature from the University of Toronto. In addition to teaching at the universities of Guelph, Windsor, and Toronto, she has served as a development officer for the AIDS Committee of Toronto and worked in communications consulting. She is now a senior development officer at the University of Toronto. A long-time lesbian and gay community activist, she recently served on the Board of Directors of the Lesbian and Gay Community Appeal.

LESLIE SANDERS is associate professor in the humanities at Atkinson College, York University. She is the author of *The Development of Black Theatre in America* and has written numerous articles on African American and Canadian writers.

ELEANOR TY is associate professor of English at Wilfrid Laurier University. She is the author of *Empowering the Feminine: The Narratives of Mary Robinson, Jane West, and Amelia Opie, 1796–1812* and *Unsex'd Revolutionaries: Five Women Novelists of the 1790s.* She has edited two books by Mary Hays, *Memoirs of Emma Courtney* and *Victim of Prejudice,* and has written essays on contemporary ethnic writers.

LYNNE VAN LUVEN is a freelance journalist with a Ph.D. in Canadian literature. She has taught at universities in Alberta and Ontario and is currently director of professional writing at the University of Victoria. She is editing a book on creative non-fiction, for Coteau Books (Regina), which will appear in spring 1999.

ALICE VAN WART has a Ph.D. in Canadian literature and has taught at the University of Alberta and the University of Toronto. She has published two books of poetry and is the editor of Elizabeth Smart's journals.

RINALDO WALCOTT is assistant professor of humanities, York University. He is the author of *Black Like Who: Writing Black Canada.* His most recent project concentrates on the relationship between Canadian studies and black studies.

PRISCILLA L. WALTON is professor of English at Carleton University. She is the author of *The Disruption of the Feminine in Henry James* and *Patriarchal Desire and Victorian Discourse: A Lacanian Reading of Anthony Trollope's Palliser Novels*, and co- author, with Manina Jones, of *Detective Agency: Women Re-Writing the Hard-Boiled Tradition.* She is a co-editor of *The Canadian Review of American Studies* and a member of the Advisory Board for *PMLA.*

ANN WILSON teaches in the School of Literatures and Performance Studies in English at the University of Guelph. Her research interests circulate around issues of nation, performance, and performativity in popular culture.

ROBERT R. WILSON has taught at universities in Canada, the United States, and Australia. His publications include works of fiction, criticism, and theory. He authored *In Palamedes' Shadow: Explorations in Play, Game and Narrative Theory* and *Shakespearean Narrative,* and co-authored, with Shirley Neuman, *Labyrinths of Voice: Conversations with Robert Kroetsch.* His most recent book, *The Hydra's Breath: Imagining Disgust,* will be published in 1999.

MICHAEL ZEITLIN is an associate professor who teaches American literature, American studies, and psychoanalytic theory at the University of British Columbia. His publications appear in various journals and essay collections. At the University of Toronto, Zeitlin played quarterback for the Trinity College Black Pelicans, back-to-back Mulock Cup champions in 1983 and '84.

Index